Hans Martensen

Christian ethics

Special part. Second division: Social ethics

Hans Martensen

Christian ethics
Special part. Second division: Social ethics

ISBN/EAN: 9783337259587

Printed in Europe, USA, Canada, Australia, Japan

Cover: Foto ©Lupo / pixelio.de

More available books at **www.hansebooks.com**

CONCORDANCE TO THE GREEK TESTAMENT. MOULTON-GEDEN.

A Concordance to the Greek Testament: According to the Texts of Westcott and Hort, Tischendorf, and the English Revisers. Edited by W. F. MOULTON, D.D., and A. S. GEDEN, M.A. In crown 4to (pp. 1040). SECOND EDITION, *Revised throughout.* Price 26s. net; or in half-morocco, price 31s. 6d. net.

*** It will be generally allowed that a new Concordance to the Greek Testament is much needed in the interests of sacred scholarship. This work adopts a new principle, and aims at providing a full and complete Concordance to the text of the Greek Testament as it is set forth in the editions of Westcott and Hort, Tischendorf (8th), and the English Revisers. The first-named has throughout been taken as the standard, and the marginal readings have been included. Thus the student with any one of these three editions in his hands will find himself in possession of a complete Concordance to the actual text on which he is engaged. While the method employed, it may fairly be claimed, precludes the omission of any word or phrase which, by even a remote probability, might be regarded as forming part of the true text of the New Testament, on the other hand passages disappear as to the spuriousness of which there is practical unanimity among scholars.*

Professor W. SANDAY, D.D., LL.D., Oxford, writes: 'There can be no question as to the value of the new "Concordance." It is the only scientific Concordance to the Greek Testament, and the only one that can be safely used for scientific purposes.'

'It would be difficult to overpraise this invaluable addition to biblical study. . . . For all English students of the Greek Testament this great work is indispensable.'—BRITISH WEEKLY.

Prospectus, with Specimen Page, free on application.

The Historical New Testament: Being the Literature of the New Testament arranged in the order of its Literary Growth and according to the Dates of the Documents. A New Translation, Edited, with Prolegomena, Historical Tables, Critical Notes, and an Appendix, by JAMES MOFFATT, D.D. Second Edition. One large 8vo Volume, price 16s.

'The most important book on the credentials of Christianity that has appeared in this country for a long time. It is a work of extraordinary learning, labour, and ability.'—*British Weekly.*

The Christ of History and of Experience. Being the Third Series of 'Kerr Lectures.' By Rev. DAVID W. FORREST, D.D., Edinburgh. In post 8vo, New and Cheaper Edition, price 6s.

'An exceedingly able treatment of a great and important subject.'—The late Professor CALDERWOOD.

'An eminently stimulating and improving book.'—*Glasgow Herald.*

'Displays marked ability, and possesses unusual interest.'—*Manchester Guardian.*

'. . . It is scarcely necessary, however, to specify particular passages in a book which throughout exhibits literary and theological powers of a high order, and which abounds in observations and criticisms which could only have been penned by a masculine and fearless, but reverent, thinker.'—*Literature.*

The Miracles of Unbelief. By Rev. FRANK BALLARD, M.A., B.Sc., London. Fourth Edition, Revised throughout. Post 8vo, 6s.

** By special request, Messrs. Clark have issued Chapter VIII., entitled, 'Jesus Christ: His Origin and Character,' in separate form, with cover, price 6d. net.

'Written by an expert in science as well as theology, a fair-minded man who faces religious difficulties, not ignores them, and one who knows how to reason out his case like an accomplished advocate, without pressing it like an unscrupulous one. Mr. Ballard has rendered valuable service to the cause of Christian truth, and given us an excellent and useful book, deserving a large circulation.'—Professor W. T. DAVISON in the *Methodist Recorder.*

'It is a perfect mine of quotation for men with little time for study, who are called, as modern ministers are, to be not only visitors and workers but also preachers and teachers.'—*Guardian*

CLARK'S

FOREIGN

THEOLOGICAL LIBRARY.

NEW SERIES.

VOL. XI.

Martensen's Social Ethics.

EDINBURGH:
T. & T. CLARK, 38 GEORGE STREET.
1899.

PRINTED BY

MORRISON AND GIBB LIMITED,

FOR

T. & T. CLARK, EDINBURGH.

LONDON: SIMPKIN, MARSHALL, HAMILTON, KENT, AND CO. LIMITED.

NEW YORK: CHARLES SCRIBNER'S SONS.

CHRISTIAN ETHICS.

SPECIAL PART.

SECOND DIVISION: SOCIAL ETHICS.

BY

DR. H. MARTENSEN,

BISHOP OF SEELAND.

Translated from the Author's German Edition

BY

SOPHIA TAYLOR.

EDINBURGH:

T. & T. CLARK, 38 GEORGE STREET.

1899.

CONTENTS.

———

SOCIAL ETHICS.

THE MORAL LIFE OF SOCIETY AND THE KINGDOM OF GOD.

§ 1.

THE moral life of society is developed in the Family and the State; in the mid-regions or departments of Culture, Art, and Science; and, lastly, in the Church, whose inmost core is the Communion of saints. These several social organisms are to be regarded, on the one hand, as possessions, and hence as realized aims, in which man finds satisfaction, profit, pleasure; on the other, as moral individuals on a large scale, having each its special office to discharge. And I, the small individual, am to be a personal member of one and another of these social circles, to occupy with respect to them a relation at once of co-operation and appropriation, of toleration and devotion, while constantly aiming at my own perfection and the perfection of the whole.

One essential side of man's destination is displayed in each of the social circles, and the purpose of Christianity is to develope the " new man " within each. It is in proportion as the Christian *ideal of human nature* is realized in them, that the *kingdom of God* attains a social, and at the same time an individual, appearance on earth. The kingdom of God, however, neither does nor can attain its perfection in this world. These forms are only intended for this earthly and temporal existence, which circumstance, however, by no means excludes the fact that it is the eternal kingdom which is working out and fashioning itself under and by means of

A

these transitory forms. With relation to the perfection of the kingdom of God, they are to be regarded as the partial, which is to cease when that which is perfect is come, as mere interim incorporations of the kingdom of God, as shadows of future possessions to be manifested in the kingdom of glory. Although, like our whole life in this world, they have a certain relative value of their own, they are in their deepest import but preparatory and educational. It is by living in this forecourt that we are trained for the perfect kingdom of love, righteousness, liberty and blessedness, in which both the divine and the human, the community and the individual, together with man's many and various gifts and powers, will be exhibited in a *harmony* as yet inconceivable, and requiring a dispensation utterly different from the present.

THE FAMILY.

THE FAMILY AND THE MORAL WORLD.

§ 2.

The family, which is founded by marriage, is the work at once of nature and freedom, and is held together by both natural and moral ties, forms the *commencement* and *foundation* of the moral world. This world is ever beginning *anew*, and as it were over again, with the family. Philosophers like Rousseau, Kant, Fichte, etc., propose to found a theory of society, which takes the individual for its starting-point and consequently assumes him to be of mature age, or, in a general manner, a being endowed with reason. They derive the various circles of society from a relation of contract between atom-like individuals, entirely independent of each other, and have laid down a system of ethics and a science of law, which, notwithstanding certain advantages, have the defect of being contrary to nature. For the unit, from which a theory of society must start, unless an *a priori* miscalculation is to be made, must be not the individual, but the family. Such thinkers wholly forget, though the fact is daily before their eyes, that birth and education, generation and tradition, are inevitable conditions of the physical and intellectual life of the human individual. The individual human being does not come into the world without presuppositions; his very existence presupposes a father and mother, he is born either male or female, a *member* of a succession of generations, to be brought up from non-age to maturity. That marriage and the family form the commencement of the human race is also the view of revelation, which makes the whole race descend from one pair, who were necessarily indeed, in the strictest sense of the word, created, while their descendants, on the contrary, come into existence by generation and birth. But this also supposes the existence of an intellectual bond transmitted from generation to generation, and binding together the successive and ever alternating races of parents and children.

The family being, then, the beginning and foundation of the moral world, reflects within its particular limits the general type and order of the moral world, though this is individualized under very various forms upon the different stages of social life. This type, which is to be increasingly worked out, is that essential *equality* of differing personalities created in the image of God which exists in the midst of a system of *inequalities*. Even in the family it is evident that human beings are not appointed to a uniform equality, but to *social inequality*. The difference between the man and the woman, between the husband and the wife, a difference not merely physical but intellectual, and determined by their entire organization, manifests that inequality is a social law of nature. But this is by no means the only instance, for the family exhibits in all respects, by the relation between parents and children, whether male or female, between elder and younger brothers and sisters, between masters and servants, not a uniform equality, but a relation of superiority and subordination, a contrast between authority and dutifulness,—differences not to be obliterated, but harmonized and transfigured to a true religious and moral equality, to a relation of genuine reciprocity, by love and by the higher development of human nature.

And as the family thus sets before us the social type for the moral world with respect to the mutual relations of mankind, so does it also reflect that for the relation in which this world is to stand to nature, by bringing to our notice both *property* and *labour*. For a family can neither be founded nor maintained without property, without some material substance for human freedom to dispose of, such an amount of temporal possessions as is necessary to an existence compatible with the dignity of human nature, whether we speak of the mere necessaries of life or of its enjoyments also. Property must, however, be obtained, and that by labour; and it was to the first husband that the command was given, "In the sweat of thy brow shalt thou eat thy bread," including also, In the sweat of thy brow shalt thou provide for thine own. The foundation of property cannot be individualistic, that is to say, it cannot begin with the individual man alone, but must be founded on the idea of the moral and legal community. For the latter, property, whether private or common, is an indispensable condition. The importance attributed to property, in proportion to the extended body of the personality, will at all times correspond with the importance attributed to the personality itself, and, moreover, to the realm of personalities under these earthly circumstances. Certainly property cannot attain its full development before the appearance of the State. For who is to ensure me the possession of my property? Who is to decide the contentions concerning mine and thine, but the State? The existence of property is, however, assumed by that of the family, for proletariate families are abnormal phenomena. And even within the family it is evident that property has not merely an individual, but also a social importance; that it is a matter affecting not only an individual member, but the whole family, *i.e.* so far as a family property may be in question, and so far as the possessions of the father are transferred to the children in the person of the heirs. Without the law of inheritance, a sufficient motive to labour for the stability and future wellbeing of the family would be wanting, and work would be undertaken merely to provide for the moment ("from hand to mouth"). That children are the lawful heirs of their parents, is a principle which pervades the entire Scriptures (Gen. xv. 3; Luke xv. 12; Gal. iv. 1).

§ 3.

It was through Christianity, and through the liberty as well as the redemption bestowed upon the world by Christ, that the family first attained its true moral importance as a constituent member of the kingdom of personalities. In the ancient heathen world, where the highest object of human existence comes forth in the State, where, therefore, the destiny of man is but an external and earthly one, the family forms merely a point of departure for political life (Plato's books on the State). But Christianity, which recognises not only in the man, but in the woman, the immortal human being with his celestial destiny, which distinguishes between the outer and the inner man, and views the kingdom of saved personalities as the end of social life, has given to the family an importance of its own independent of the State, an internal aspect, by means of which it appears as a form under which the kingdom of God upon earth is manifested, as a seminary, not only for the State, but also for the *Church of Christ.* It is by means of the earliest and most primitive of human feelings, by childlike reverence and dutifulness, confidence and submission, love and fidelity, that the corresponding religious and moral elements of Christian faith and love, a life of communion with God, of willing submission to His holy law and gospel, are early developed in the soul. There is an action and reaction between the family and the other circles of society; and this applies in a quite special manner to the relation between the family and the Church. It is only when the family recognises its membership, not only in the State, but in the Church of Christ, that it can fulfil its vocation. And, on the other hand, it is only in proportion as it helps the gospel to strike root in the family, and thereby in those human feelings which are the earliest, the most primitive and natural, that the Church, whose office it is to penetrate all nations with Christianity, can extend, maintain, and assert itself among the people. It is upon the family that the stability of the Church rests. History also shows that, in times when faith has been weak and powerless, and almost extinct in public life, the sacred fire has been preserved for future days in those quiet domestic circles, where the Christian mother erects monuments which, unrecognised by the world, are nevertheless imperishable. It is by this, its inward connection with the family, that Christianity proves its unity with all that from the very beginning has been originally *human*. The family and the Church are in very truth the upholding and preserving circles within the moral world. It is by means of these alone, that authority and freedom, authority and obedience, authority and dutifulness, self-sacrificing love and fidelity, those main pillars of the moral world, are founded and erected in the human soul. To fight for one's native land was called of old to fight for hearth and altar (*pro aris et focis*). Every renovation of national vigour, every thorough reformation, must proceed chiefly from these two circles; and the cure of any diseases which may have penetrated them, must first of all be effected, unless the entire condition is to be regarded as incurable. For all renovation, whether of the community or of the individual, depends upon the fact of going back to the earliest, the primitive, to that which precedes all human arts and inventions. Now, the Church brings us the gospel, which leads us back from all idolatrous practices, all adulterations of the divine, to the primitive, the genuinely divine, to the only true God, and Him whom He has sent; to our heavenly Father's home, which we have forsaken, and walked instead in our own ways, in our own thoughts of God and things divine, in our own foolish wisdom, our false and supposed policy, our vain deification of art, our ascription of saving power to culture. It brings us back from all this to that eternal region of which we are natives, that we may be conscious of what we are in relation to God, and of what we ought to be. The family, too, of which indeed only a relative purity can be predicated, brings us back to what is primitive, to what is inherent in human nature, to what is fatherly and motherly, to love, dutifulness, devotion, fidelity, that here, too, we may know what we really are, by knowing the true human foundation for our life. Out of these, its first elements, has human society more than once been reconstructed. This is further confirmed; for, supposing the State and civil society to be in a state of dissolution, and public morality grievously corrupted, still, so long as the Church proclaims the pure gospel, and the people lend a willing ear thereto, so long as family life is on the whole pure, the possibility of rearing up again a ruined nationality still exists. Matters are in the most irretrievable condition when both Church and family have been infected by corruption, and have become incapable of reform.

Goethe, in his *Hermann and Dorothea*, had in view the importance of the family as the hearth of *patriotism*, and as in times of universal social revolution the " indestructible principle of the State," as Geijer, in his comparison of Goethe and Homer, well expresses it.[1] The poet here transports us into rustic, simple, and natural circumstances. But amid all the features of moral greatness which this incomparable poem exhibits, it is not the least that Hermann and Dorothea contract their alliance, as it were, upon a volcano, while storm-clouds darken and lightnings are flashing upon the horizon, while public life is visited with danger and distress — in the midst of the French Revolution, its wars, and all the troubles which these entailed, when the legal foundations of the State were dissolved, when all property had become insecure, and it seemed as if the world were about to sink into its original chaos. And yet they both contracted a marriage with hearts full of hope and comfort. Belief in life here appears in its fairest form. Love for the home fireside enlarges into love for native land, ready to make the greatest sacrifices, and to fight against the enemy "for God and law, for parents, wife, and children," combines with *heroism*, with the courageous resolution to meet the uncertain and dangerous future, and looks onward through the impending contests to the peaceful condition which is to follow them.

Monogamous Marriage.

§ 4.

The beginning of the family is marriage. Upon the natural basis of the distinction of the sexes, marriage is the uniting of man and woman into one personality. That partialness of individuality implied in the relation of the sexes is to be abolished in marriage, by the fact that each of these receives to itself its counterpart, the man thus first becoming a man,

[1] Geijer's Works (Swedish) First Div. vol. vii. p. 175.

and the woman a woman, in the full sense of the word. The man first finds himself in the woman, as in his other half, and *vice versa*. It is in this relation of reciprocity, this mutual help and assistance (*adjutorium mutuum*), this giving and taking, that each part first attains its true manhood or womanhood, and neither the physical nor the moral capabilities of either the male or the female nature can be developed without this relation. If indeed marriage is regarded only in its natural aspect, no other vocation is allotted to it but the satisfaction of natural instinct, and the propagation· of the race. But perverted and partial as such a view is, the opposite mode of regarding it, which considers marriage as exclusively a relation of heart and intellect, is no less partial. The so-called Platonic attachment between man and woman is of an entirely different character from the matrimonial, whose peculiarity is based upon the union of the heart and mind relation with the natural relation. " And they twain shall be one flesh" (Matt. xix. 5). The natural forms in this case the indispensable basis, but as certainly nothing more than the basis. The juridical definition of marriage as a junction of male and female (*conjunctio maris et feminae*, which points also to the sexual relation), a perfect fellowship of life (*consortium omnis vitae*), and lastly a community of right (*juris communicatio*), holds good also in an ethical point of view, if we lay due stress upon the *consortium omnis vitae*, which, however, first attained its full meaning through Christianity.[1]

It is implied in the very notion of marriage that it should be monogamous (" one man and one woman, whom only death can part "). Monogamous marriage was not indeed absent from the præ-Christian world, but was there only in a slight degree settled and assured. Heathendom exhibits in polygamy the profanation of marriage ; nor was its purity maintained even in Israel, as is evident from the history of the patriarchs. Christianity, however, restored the dignity of marriage as a divine institution, descending from paradisaic times (Matt. xix. 5), reauthorized monogamy, and recommended it to the moral consciousness, by asserting the lasting individuality of man, but especially by emancipating woman, raising her to the dignity of a free personality, and recognising

[1] Stahl, *Philosophie des Rechtes*, vol. ii. p. 337

her as a fellow-heir of the grace of life (1 Pet. iii. 7). Where polygamy prevails, the enduring importance of the individual is not as yet acknowledged, and marriage is degraded to a merely sexual relation. Woman is there regarded as a mere means of sensual enjoyment, or of propagating the race, but has no independent value. But an immortal being, belonging to a supersensuous and supernatural world, should by no means submit to so subordinate and unworthy a position, to a merely natural relation, and cannot be a mere medium of the race without maintaining within it a moral dignity acknowledged by others also. This is only possible where the marital relation is one of heart and intellect as well as of nature, and where conjugal love is inseparable from *fidelity*, which first impresses a moral character on affection, and absolutely excludes every other tie of the kind. Mutual and complete devotion, moreover, requires, that free choice should be the starting-point of conjugal intercourse.

The opposite extreme to the heathen debasement of woman is exhibited in the fanatical *worship of woman*, in that *adoration* and deification, combined with inviolable fidelity, of an individual woman, so often exhibited in the romantic love of the Middle Ages (especially in the *Minnesänger*). Islamism, on the other hand, most deeply degrades woman. It sanctions an insatiable voluptuousness, represents heaven as a harem, and thereby proves itself to be the religion of the false prophet, a view also confirmed by its injunction of unceasing cruelty to enemies.

§ 5.

Starting from the assumptions of Christianity, every satisfaction of natural instinct outside the limits of monogamous marriage must inevitably be pronounced immoral, a breach and an interruption of God's order; and this is equally applicable to an unnatural satisfaction of this instinct. In this respect we may recall the apostle's words, " Have no fellowship with the unfruitful works of darkness, but rather reprove them; for it is a shame even to speak of those things that are done of them in secret " (Eph. v. 11). Apparently the apostle is contemplating marriage from a low point of view, when, in his First Epistle to the Corinthians, he represents it as a preservative or remedy against unchasteness, when he advises those who have not the gift of continence to marry, because " it is better to marry than to burn " (1 Cor. vii. 9). It may not sound ideal when he thus openly speaks of matters about which others would prefer to be silent. But his counsel is based upon a thorough knowledge of human nature, as it actually exists since the entrance of sin, of the nature in which the flesh has become a power refusing to be silenced. He desires that where this instinct is strong, its satisfaction should be restrained by law and justice, and by a moral intercourse which should subordinate it to a higher power. The same apostle was also well acquainted with the highest ideal point of view from which marriage could be regarded, when he saw in the relation of a man to his wife "a mystery," namely, a type of the mystical union of Christ with the Church (Eph. v. 32). If the first-named point of view seems to many too low, the second will appear to them far too exalted and overdrawn. The comparison made by the apostle must not however be understood, as though marriage would be continued even in the future life. For "they who are accounted worthy to obtain that world, and the resurrection from the dead, neither marry nor are given in marriage; for they cannot die any more; they are equal to the angels" (Luke xx. 35). There is always a connection between death and the satisfaction of carnal instincts. Both, in their present kind and form, entered the world immediately after the fall, and both are to depart from it together. Marriage is only an earthly relation. But as such it is an image of the highest love, a preparation for the future and eternal kingdom of God.

Celibacy.

§ 6.

Though Christianity attributes so great a value to marriage, that, so far as its conditions exist, it must be regarded as a duty incumbent on each to enter into matrimony as a state appointed to him or her, yet there has existed in the Church from the very first an ascetic tendency, which has regarded celibacy as the higher and holier condition. Now, though much that is spurious and pernicious has been the practical effect of this ascetic view, yet, as involving a deeper element of truth, it must not be rejected without further ceremony. It also finds points of contact in the New Testament, and the same apostle who so emphatically extols the sacredness of marriage, and even says that they who "forbid to marry" give heed to seducing spirits and doctrines of devils (1 Tim. iv. 1–3), attributes a special holiness to celibacy. He recommends it not only " for the sake of the present distress " (1 Cor. vii. 26), *i.e.* the perils entailed upon Christians by persecution, which the unmarried might more easily endure than the married, who would be entangled with cares for wives and children. He unmistakeably regards a single life as in itself better and happier, if the individuals in question possess the same gift for it which the apostle had. "It is good for a man not to touch a woman," he says (1 Cor. vii. 1), and the context shows that St. Paul is, in this view of the matter, regarding marriage on the same, namely, its natural side, that asceticism does when it exalts celibacy. For though *chastity* within Christian marriage rests entirely upon the subjection of inclination to the sway of the moral principle, upon the suppression and government of selfish desire by the sympathetic relation of a mutual devotion of heart and mind, still conjugal intercourse—since man's nature has been interpenetrated by sin—has a side, which every morally sensitive man seeks to conceal under a sevenfold veil, at which he feels a sensation of shame, and over which divine grace itself must cast a veil. For the transaction is not absolutely a mere function of nature,—like other natural occurrences which none can avoid,—but a human *action*, during which the will is consumed and absorbed in the natural function. This is, however, the one main point to which asceticism directs its aim, perceiving therein an inevitable element of sinfulness, a partial absorption of the spirit in the lower animal life, a distraction and disturbance of the higher life, which is, so to speak, suspended thereby. St. Paul plainly gives us to understand that prayer is hindered thereby, by advising married persons to separate for a time that they may give themselves to fasting and prayer (1 Cor. vii. 5). Even the heathen, and that not only in the East, perceived in it a power disturbing and interrupting the higher life of the spirit, and transferring man to a state of bondage. To take an example from the Greeks, we may mention Sophocles, the great tragedian, who in his old age thought himself very fortunate at having at last escaped this "tyranny." The other main point which asceticism has in view is that state in the life to come in which they neither marry nor are given in marriage, but are equal to the angels. That this heavenly state is superior to our earthly condition, which is one of dependence upon carnal conditions and affections, can be denied by no one. And if it were possible during this life in every respect to anticipate this angelic state, the individuals to whom this was vouchsafed would indeed occupy a higher and more distinguished position, and be even here below nearer to heaven, at the same time serving the Lord with more *undivided* service.

And this is the point at which the true and false elements of the ascetic view may be separated one from the other. The truth is, that there are individuals, both male and female, but especially female, possessing a special gift for celibacy, which is in its deepest sense a natural endowment of angellike natures, whose desire for the kingdom of God so greatly preponderates over earthly desires, in whom the love of God and religious aspirations are so powerful, that earthly pleasure and affection are to them of slight importance, nay, though not experienced by themselves, are accounted from the very first as something passed by and behind them. In Oehlenschläger's tragedy of *Axel und Valborg*, the latter, amidst the sad circumstances by which her earthly love has been crossed, casts her eyes upon the white roses which have been handed to her in place of the bridal wreath of red roses, and breaks out into the words:

> " Erloschen ist die ird'sche, rothe Gluth—
> Wie Engelsflügel steh'n die weissen Blätter."[1]

But the individuals in question stand from the first at the point at which Valborg arrives only after bitter experience, and by means of painful renunciation. They begin with the

---

[1] " The earthly red glow is quenched,
The white leaves remain like angel-wings."

white roses, which recall the angels' wings; for them the red roses of earthly love neither have had, nor will have any existence. They feel exclusively the need of living in communion with God, in mystic intercourse, and in services of love for His kingdom, and anticipate in this sense the future state. While by reason of this anticipation we attribute to them a higher perfection, we cannot but, for the same reason, perceive in their life a certain amount of limitation and one-sidedness. It is just because they anticipate the heavenly life, that they are unable fully to live out the earthly life. They never experience the joys of married and family life, the great treasures therein involved; they never know its duties and its crosses, which together pertain to a complete earthly existence, destined to be absorbed, in due time, in a heavenly one. Such anticipations, however, if we are to bow before them, and acknowledge them as worthy in themselves and *given* by God, must be implanted in the nature of the individuals, and these individuals must *absolutely* be but *exceptions* in the totality of human nature. The false element of asceticism consists in the notion that it is possible to bring about such anticipations by practice, in its assumption that man can *make* his own nature angelic by "botching up the old Adam." It is on this account that the enforced celibacy of the Romish Church is so objectionable. For the great mass of its priests and monks, however many respectable individuals it may contain, and however many of these may have faithfully kept their vows of celibacy, is not composed of purely angelic and seraphic natures. A celibacy which has to be maintained by a continual struggle against unceasing incentive and inclination, by repeated efforts to stifle impure imagination, is far inferior to an ordinary marriage. Such a celibacy only justifies the saying, "It is *not good* for the man to be alone." It is among the imperishable services of the Reformation to have opposed this enforced celibacy, and justified the marriage state to the consciences of men, although it did not, like the Romish Church, make marriage a sacrament.

With respect to the celibacy of Christ, this is entirely unique, and must be regarded from its own point of view. It cannot, for instance, be explained by the fact that He was one among a multiple of the above-named angelic natures, which are nevertheless, in many other respects, included under sin. And as little does it find its explanation in the impossibility of His finding, as a falsely æsthetic notion supposes, any like-minded individual who was fitted for Him. He never could have sought such an individual, who must indeed, in a certain sense, have been His equal by birth; for as the Saviour of the world, the Son of God, and the second Adam, He was utterly incommensurable with any other human being, nay, with the totality of those lower earthly relations, into which He indeed brought a great blessing, but with which it was utterly impossible for Him to identify Himself. *His* bride could be none other than the Church. He was to be the ancestor of a new and higher manhood, and His coming forms a contrast to the condition in which children, who are only to continue the old Adamic race concluded under sin, are born. He came, on the contrary, to introduce into the old Adamic race an entirely new process of generation and birth, viz. *regeneration.* And if the old prophetic saying, "Here am I and the children whom Thou hast given me," has been applied to Him (Heb. ii. 13), those children are intended to whom He has given power to become children of God, who were born not of flesh and blood, nor of the will of the flesh, nor of the will of man, but *of God* (John i. 12). To conceive of the possibility of married life in His case, proves itself in proportion as such a thought is reasoned out, whether in the physical or moral and intellectual aspect, a profane thought, nearly akin with the view which denies His birth of a pure virgin. In one view, as in the other, the question is to degrade Him to the sphere of the old impure Adamic nature. In this connection it may be fitly remembered, that among all the temptations by which Christ was, according to Scripture testimony, tried, not one occurs in the most distant degree referring to the point in question.

§ 7.

All arbitrarily chosen celibacy is objectionable, and it is, moreover, an act contrary to duty to decline marriage for the sake of ease, or of maintaining a so-called independence. A celibacy determined on from duty and conviction must either have for its reason individual peculiarities, or special circumstances. We have already made mention of those angelic, those seraphic natures, in whose case the special appointments of *nature* must determine for their conscience the appointments of *duty*. And this applies also to those individuals in whom, though they have not this preponderating tendency to what is heavenly, inclination is utterly blunt and dead, and whose duty it therefore is to abstain from marriage. In some circumstances also it may be a duty to choose celibacy for the kingdom of God's sake, because the special activity to which an individual may be called for the cause of Christ, *e.g.* that of a missionary, would encounter in married or domestic life too many and too great hindrances to its full development. That even the office of reformer is nevertheless compatible with marriage is shown by the example of Luther and others, who also made their domestic life a model for the Church of Christ.

Many are compelled to live a single life, not from their own choice, but because circumstances have necessitated it. For such it is a duty to submit with resignation to the privation imposed upon them. This applies to those whose affection has not been returned, or who, for any cause, have failed to find the individual to whom they would wish to unite their own life. Such celibacy, resulting from an absence of reciprocity, occurs more frequently in the female than in the male sex, because it is not the woman's part to seek the man, but to be sought by him. Another reason for compulsory celibacy is found in the fact, that many men are without the necessary means of supporting a family or maintaining a home, a circumstance whose result is that many women must remain unmarried. This sort of celibacy, arising from a lack of the needful means of subsistence, which has in these days increased to an alarming extent, and induced immoralities of various kinds, is among the darker aspects of our present social condition. It is under the influence of these same circumstances, which have been the cause of so much compulsory celibacy, that the vast number of households without substance, and children without the means of maintenance or education, in short, the proletariate class, with all its misery, has grown up. And here we encounter the social question of the day. In this place we can only remark quite generally with respect to it, that no solution of the question can be found unless, through a reform of social relations, the possibility of a moral domestic life — which is inconceivable without daily bread—is open to a far greater number of individuals than is the case under the social conditions at present existing.

CONTRACTION OF MARRIAGE.

Choice of a Partner.——Marriage of Inclination and Marriage of Reason.——Mesalliance.

§ 8.

To all who do not belong to the above-named exceptions, there comes a time, which may be called the time of awakening love. As life and movement come to nature with spring, so does natural instinct unconsciously stir within the life of the young in the spring-time of life ; and a desire for affection, a seeking, a presentiment, a dreamy hope, which at last takes the form of inclination for some one individual woman, stirs more or less consciously in the soul. This propensity to love may often change its object, till at last the individual is found with whom is formed first the tie of betrothal, and afterwards that of marriage. To represent the mutual inclination of the man and woman, or love in its psychological aspect, its dreams, its dim twilight condition, its joys and sorrows, its development in many cases to passion, is essentially the province of the poet. To the true poet it also belongs to depict the ethical aspect of the matter. We here only direct attention to the fact, that love, with its moods and frames, that inexhaustible theme of the poet, is not in itself of ethic, but only of æsthetic value, having at best only the importance of a prelude, until it has developed to the point at which the mutual relation of those who love may be at the same time defined as a relation of duty, or as a relation of inviolable fidelity, extending through the entire life, and based upon the most hearty resolve of the will. So-called " free love," which would contract the marriage tie for only a certain period, viz. so long as inclination and fancy last, and would therefore æsthetically flutter from one enjoyment to another, is in its inmost nature immoral. Without the consciousness of duty, love can only be classed among the natural powers. Requited love first attains a moral value when it is regarded under a consciousness of duty, whereby inclination is restrained within those limits which develope its true strength. And unrequited love becomes only a consuming passion, unless a serious sense of duty teaches resignation and submission to the dispensations of Providence. In this respect we would call to notice Sibbern's Gabriel, who, in contrast with Goethe's Werther, who entirely succumbs when his attachment proves an unfortunate one, earnestly strives against his passion, and gradually re-attains to a healthy state of mind.

§ 9.

To choose a partner for life is nothing less than to choose one's future, a future decidedly influencing not only the external destiny, but also the development of character; therefore a future which one ought to be able to encounter with full trust and confidence. When we consider the levity with which this step is taken by so many, we can but wonder that there are so few unhappy marriages, and rejoice in the fact, that in no inconsiderable number of instances fortune has evidently more to do in the matter than judgment. But they who would not willingly make themselves the playthings of chance, have many and important considerations to ponder, before taking a step so decisive of the whole course of their lives. In this matter the main point is agreement of disposition, is that the individuals should suit, should be adapted to each other, should have such qualities as fit them to belong to, and to live always with, each other, not only in the greater events and vicissitudes of life, but also in all those daily recurring details, in which the peculiarities of the natural dispositions are brought forth, in which not merely its excellences, but also its faults, partialities, and deficiencies are exposed; in which, therefore, everything depends upon the existence of an agreement in religious and moral sentiments. Disagreement in the latter respect may have a disturbing influence upon the whole life. But whatever value we may attribute to accordance with respect to this higher and universal truth, it *alone* is not a sufficient foundation for a true and genuine marriage. In this matter we are always brought back to that which is purely personal, and therefore to the question, Do you feel so attracted to this very individual that you could love her, could devote yourself to her, even though beauty should disappear, and would she, on the other hand, reciprocate the feeling though you should be visited with want and sickness, in joy and sorrow, in prosperity and adversity, as God may send the one or the other, so that you both could patiently bear each other's faults, and continue to love and to labour for each other, and, in spite of everything, always to hope the best of each other? A Christian who is about to make such a choice, will always ask what may, in the particular case, be the will of God. And this will be recognised not only in the voice of his inmost heart, but also in the external circumstances of life. The question is to find out whether the internal voice coincides with the external circumstances and relations, which have brought the choice before him, as one naturally and suitably fitting into the whole course of the life. The greater the agreement existing between the internal and the external, the more the choice seems in both aspects advisable, the more confidently may we recognise therein the will of God, or the voice of duty, for the direction of our action. It is the greatest happiness to attain to a certainty, raised above all doubt, as to whether we have really chosen rightly. To choose with doubtful feelings is, under any circumstances, not only dangerous and mischievous, but also sinful. True certainty can only arise from the enthusiasm of love, from the heart's inmost impulse, combined with enlightened and quiet reflection. There is a certainty which is slowly attained, as well as one which suddenly springs into existence. Many individuals need a longer time for reflection before they can arrive at assurance or form a firm resolve, individuals in whom direct insight, inspiration, as the parent of resolution, is not so quickly found. Moreover, to guard against premature and imprudent decisions, reflection is in every case advisable.

There are, on the other hand, some in whom direct intuition, and that not only of the understanding, but of the heart, at once exists, and who feel quite certain from their first meeting. Still this quickly born certainty, if it is to be anything more than a fleeting vapour, must be able to stand the test of subsequent and sober reflection. We are here reminded of Goethe's poem, in which Hermann, having, through unexpected external circumstances utterly beyond his power to foresee, found Dorothea, and chosen her as his bride at the first meeting, says to his mother, to whom he is unburdening his heart:

> "Ja, sie ist's; und führ' ich sie nicht als Braut mit nach Hause,
> Heute noch ziehet sie fort und verschwindet vielleicht mir auf immer
> In der Verwirrung des Kriegs und im traurigen Hin- und Herzich'n."[1]

Before, however, the decisive step is taken, the choice already made by his heart should be confirmed by the consent of his parents, and the approval of experienced friends.

That marriage must not be entered upon without first seeking parental sanction, may be inferred even from the fifth commandment; and legal enactments as to age of discretion, which are matters of indifference to dutiful children, will not come into competition with this. An old proverb says, "*Der Eltern Segen bauet den Kindern Häuser.*"[2] We do not mean to say that parents have an absolute right and power to forbid a marriage, much less to force one upon their children against their own inclinations. It may, however, be asserted that if a marriage contrary to the will of parents is to be entered into with a good conscience, very serious *moral* reasons for it must exist, and all consideration demanded by the circumstances must be shown. Tragic collisions may indeed occur, and we need only refer to Romeo and Juliet, and the ancient enmity between their families, to the passionate love, utterly regardless of duty, of the youthful lovers, to the equally passionate and ruthless hatred of the parents on both sides, a hatred carried to the point of pronouncing a curse upon the love of their children,—a collision which may

---

[1] Yes, it is she; and if I do not lead her home with me as my bride, she will depart this very day, and perhaps vanish from me for ever in the confusion of war in this sad going and coming.

[2] The blessing of parents builds homes for their children.

occur elsewhere in various degrees, though under lower, less ideal, but still, in a moral aspect, very serious circumstances. In the history of Romeo and Juliet the results are tragic for all, for the children as well as for the parents, because there is sin on both sides, and right and wrong are intermingled in inextricable confusion. And every arbitrarily contracted marriage, in which the nearest relatives and the relation to them receive no consideration, nay, in which the tie between parents and children is broken, will sooner or later find its Nemesis. Even in the best cases, where moral right is on the side of the children, there will be in one way or other a bitter flavour, an element of unhappiness in the midst of happiness, of discord in the midst of harmony.

§ 10.

The contrast between a *marriage of inclination* and a *marriage of reason* seems reconciled in the true marriage, which is a union of the two. An inclination which does not include, though unconsciously, the element of reason, will soon prove to have been a delusion. What is called a marriage of reason is very often a marriage of convenience, or for the sake of money, or one contracted for the purpose of attaining a higher social position, rank and standing. All these are non-ethical, and while such a marriage may be called prudent, it is certainly not reasonable. On the other hand, there is such a thing as a really reasonable marriage, which, though differing indeed from one arising from affection, is still not really blameable, because duty is its motive. To mention a familiar example : a nobly-minded woman perceives it to be a duty, for the sake of filling the place of mother to the children of a deceased friend, to marry a widower who makes her the offer of his hand, although the feeling she has towards him is not love, but respect and confidence. No one would question the moral value of such a marriage.

By *mesalliances* are generally understood all those unions in which the definition of marriage, namely, that the two individuals should be one, cannot be fulfilled by reason of too great a discrepancy, whether of education or rank. It has been asserted, that only too great a difference of education can render a marriage a mesalliance, and that education can compensate for all differences of rank. We are far from depreciating the power of education, and willing also to grant that rank is no "caste," and that differences of rank must, especially in these days, be far more fluctuating than formerly, when the upper classes were separated from the lower by impassable barriers, and, so to speak, by a precipice. Still, we cannot help maintaining, that there are cases in which differences of rank must by all means be taken into consideration when the contraction of marriage is in question. For any one marrying a certain person marries into that person's whole family, and thus enters into circumstances and relations, which may come into collision with other interests of moral importance. This is particularly the reason why persons of princely rank, who occupy a peculiar position and owe special duties to the State, cannot marry persons of the citizen class without contracting a mesalliance. So far as the person in question could be entirely separated from family ties, could at once be isolated from father, mother, brothers, sisters, friends, so far would the chief difficulties be overcome. Since this, however, must be regarded as a moral impossibility, it is easy to imagine social conditions in which collisions of the gravest nature might occur.

Among mesalliances must also be included those so-called "monstrous marriages," by which, though no social relations suffer, yet nature itself is aggrieved,—cases in which there is an undue discrepancy of age between the parties, and an infirm and aged man marries a young wife, or *vice versa*. Cases in which an intellectual woman allies herself to a man of weak understanding—alliances which give an impression of being unnatural—belong also to these monstrous marriages. It is less monstrous, but still a mesalliance, when a gifted man takes a silly wife. The normal marriage requires that natural endowments and education should be of such a kind in both parties that a real reciprocity of giving and receiving may exist.

Church Solemnization of Marriage.—Civil Marriage.—
Impediments to Marriage.

§ 11.

Marriage is by no means only the affair of the married couple themselves, but, by reason of its far-reaching importance to the whole human race, the affair of the State and of the Church. Though a marriage is determined on neither by the State nor the Church, but only by the couple themselves, yet it can neither be contracted nor entered upon except by means of the State and the Church. Marriage needs recognition and *ratification* on the part of the State and the Church; it also requires the support and stay of the greater community to give it stability. The State must establish the conditions under which it will acknowledge a marriage to be valid, and children to be legitimate, and must consequently require also that a marriage should be contracted by means of a formal act, to render it known and manifest, and by means of which its actual contraction may be authenticated, a matter often of great importance. The Church, moreover, must, for the sake of its members, take care that no hindrance to the validity of a marriage, *e.g.* forbidden degrees of kinship or certain kinds of divorce, should exist. And it is by no means to be taken for granted, that the views of the Church and of the State coincide. By reason of the importance of marriage, not merely in a civil but also in a moral and religious point of view, the Church cannot but insist upon its being ratified by a religious act, by the persons who enter into such a contract sealing it as in the presence of God and of the Church, listening to the commands and promises of God, accepting the intercessions of the congregation, and receiving the divine blessing on a Christian carrying out of marriage. Undoubtedly no express command of our Lord or His apostles can be adduced for a religious solemnization of marriage. Still this came into use during the Church's development, by a necessity inherent in the nature of the ecclesiastical community. Hence no Christian would desire to avoid it, and arbitrarily to break with the ancient custom of the Church, an act which would imply that he was ashamed of avowing his proceeding before the Lord and His Church. On the contrary, he could not but be anxious that such a transaction should receive the Church's public ratification and consecration.

But marriage has its civil as well as its ecclesiastical side; and it must be regarded as a matter of great importance that Church and State should here harmoniously co-operate. For this reason the ecclesiastical and civil elements have, from remote ages, been so blended among Christian nations, that the Church's consecration has been the condition of the civil validity of marriage. If, then, the demand is in these days made that the civil should be severed from the ecclesiastical act, there can be no possible objection that the two aspects of marriage should come forth also in two different acts. But if this demand is to mean that civil marriage, an act in itself destitute of religion, is to make the ecclesiastical celebration superfluous, and that not exceptionally in the case of certain dissenters, but for the people in general, that the civil contract is to be absolutely necessary for all who enter upon matrimony, while it is to be left to the pleasure of individuals whether they choose also to participate in the religious ceremony, we can only see in such a proposal a grievous breaking up of Christian national customs. Respect for the sacredness of marriage must be undermined, if the State gives up the Christian view of the import of marriage, and degrades the nuptial ceremony into a merely individual affair, according to each man's notion or choice; if Government offers the people to release them from the consecration of marriage by the word of God and prayer, and requires nothing, so far as it is concerned, but that the legal contract should be executed. In spite of the subtlest distinctions and developments, the multitude will inevitably understand such an offer as a summons and invitation to omit the ecclesiastical ceremonial as a thing superfluous and non-essential, and in fact incompatible with the present times.

We must indeed concede that civil marriages *may*, under certain circumstances, be a necessary evil; when, *e.g.*, a general apostasy from Christianity has taken place among a people, and the majority of the nation consists of unbelievers. This would, however, be at the same time an evidence of great deterioration, and a sad state of affairs. As long as no such general apostasy takes place, it must be regarded as unjustifiable to invest civil marriage with universal validity and legality, and to require that a whole nation should accommodate itself to the notions of a minority of dissenters or unbelievers, for whom civil marriage must, forsooth, be instituted. By such an institution we undermine Christian sentiment and opinion and reverence for Christian tradition, and thus make ourselves responsible for hastening the religious and moral decay of a nation.

The defenders of civil marriage are wont to assert that marriage is older than Christianity, and hence that the Church's consecration cannot be absolutely necessary to marriage, nor a constituent of its idea. This is undoubtedly the case. We may remark, however, that the pre-Christian nations were by no means destitute of religion, but were, on the contrary, accustomed to combine religious observances with betrothal and the contraction of marriage. Also, that there is a difference in non-Christian marriages, which may be either pre-Christian or post-Christian, *i.e.* such as imply a declension from Christianity and a depreciation of its rites. It is marriages of the latter class which we should not like to see recommended to the people. In defence of civil marriage, Luther, who frequently makes use of the expression that marriage is a *secular* affair, is often appealed to. But in saying this he was opposing the Pope, who had presumed so far to encroach upon the office of the State as to determine points which lay within its province. It was the rights of the State which Luther was maintaining against the hierarchy, and nothing was further from his intention than to assert that Christianity and the Church had nothing to do with marriage.

It is also usually maintained that civil marriage, even supposing the religious element to be absent, is at all events a *moral* institution, and must be recognised as such. This is well. But it remains to be seen, as the practice of civil marriage becomes more usual, how seriously the State will consult the interests of morality after it has renounced its relations to religion. It will be seen not only in appointments concerning prohibited degrees of relationship, but especially in those concerning divorce and the re-marriage of the divorced. It will be seen whether the State will seriously care for morality by rendering divorces and re-marriages difficult, or whether civil marriage will serve only to increase the already too prevalent laxity of moral judgment, and still further to facilitate these transactions. It will be seen, moreover, whether it will be possible, when once the authority of Christianity is given up, to maintain monogamy any longer. We are fully persuaded that a monogamous marriage binding for life can in no other way be maintained in a nation than through the authority of religion, and that it can by no means be established upon the foundation of philosophical deductions. What is there to hinder civil marriages from being entered upon " for a time," without being binding for the whole life ? May not many advocates of " free thought " be cited as authorities for the saying, " Marriage for a time " ?

Christian custom and tradition is a power which, by its silent influence upon national life, still exercises a counteracting agency against civil marriage. This also encounters opposition from the female sex. We allude always to such civil marriage as would banish the Church solemnization as superfluous. For no woman of refined feeling will disdain humbly and hopefully to place her future under the guarantee of religion, nor be satisfied with a marriage ceremony deprived of all ideality, and which will condemn her to place her future exclusively under the guarantee of a merely legal contract.

§ 12.

Among *impediments to marriage* we would specially mention those arising from natural relationship (the forbidden degrees), that is, from the prohibition to those already united by the ties of blood to contract matrimony with each other. The general notion underlying this prohibition is, that they who are united by ties of blood already stand to each other in a relation of reverence, dutifulness and affection, which would be abolished by the matrimonial relation ; and that such marriages are an impure and unnatural mingling, a removal of boundaries placed by the Creator Himself. Even in Gen. ii. 24 it is said, " For this cause shall a man *leave* his father and his mother, and shall cleave unto his wife;" thus drawing a strict boundary between the already existing tie of blood-relationship and the new beginning which is implied by marriage. And when it is said that the man is to leave his father and mother, this does not forbid the marriage tie between parents and children only, but involves also the more comprehensive thought, that the man is not to seek a wife in his father's house, in his own family, but in another house, in another family. This must be regarded as an absolute prohibition of union not only between parents and children (Lot's daughters will always be held in abhorrence), but also between brothers and sisters. It has been observed that even among most heathen nations a natural horror (*horror naturalis*) of such unions has prevailed, a horror not found among the lower animals, and among men only in combination with moral abhorrence. This abhorrence also shows itself against marriages between step-parents and step-children, and between step-brothers and sisters, for in these cases there is a relation of dutifulness and affection, which must be maintained in its independence, and be neither suppressed nor profaned by the marriage tie. St. Paul condemned as a great scandal the case which occurred in the church of Corinth, of one who was living in connubial intercourse with his step-mother, and excluded the individual from the church (1 Cor. v. 1–5). Among poets, Sophocles has depicted the guilt of Œdipus, who, without knowing what he was doing, had married his own mother Jocasta, and could find no solace in the fact that he had done it ignorantly, but on the contrary conceived such a horror of himself, that, to cover himself in perpetual darkness, he deprived himself of eyesight. And Byron (in his *Manfred*) gives us, in Manfred's relation to his deceased sister Astarte, a notion of the unknown evil and horror attending the criminal attachment of brother and sister.

The absolute prohibition here mentioned extends by the force of analogy to the various ramifications of relationship (*respectus parentelae*), to the union between parents-in-law and children-in-law, between brothers and sisters-in-law, etc., to marriage with an uncle or aunt, with a brother's widow, with a deceased wife's sister, to marriage between the children of brothers and sisters, etc., though it is in such cases difficult to draw a line, which is differently defined by different legislatures.

Although, however, it may not be proved that the Mosaic laws concerning prohibited degrees (Lev. xviii.) are literally binding and indispensably incumbent upon Christians,— a notion refuted even by the Levirate marriage, with respect to which the law of Moses itself pronounces a dispensation (Deut. xxv. 5–10; cf. Matt. xxii. 23–32),—yet its profound view of these natural relations must always furnish us with a foundation for trying and deciding such questions, and should not be lost sight of in modern legislation. It must surely be confessed that there is at present too great laxity in this respect, and that the laws need revision in a stricter direction,[1] even if we should feel some hesitation at carrying out the prohibition to its extreme consequences. Dispensations are justifiable with respect to the more remote degrees of kinship, and cannot be entirely avoided. In such cases they are an expression of the fact that a concession may certainly be made in special individual instances, but that as a rule a husband or a wife must not be taken out of one's own family. With the ethical point of view is combined also a physical one. For experience, corroborated by numerous examples, shows that, when intermarriages are continued in the same family, without the introduction of fresh elements, the type of the family loses both in physical and intellectual power and energy. Children occur with all kinds of malformations, are born blind and deaf; nay, in England and France, many cases of mental derangement are traceable to this cause.[2]

There is one exception to what has been said above, viz. the children of the first human pair, who, though brothers and sisters, must needs have married. When they are referred to, however, we should do well to remember that this primitive family was directly identical with the whole human race. In this case the relation existing between children and

---

[1] W. Thiersch, *Das Verbot der Ehe innerhalb der nahen Verwandtschaft*, 1869.

[2] Compare the passage quoted by Thiersch : Dr. Prosper Lucas, *Traité philosophique et physiologique de l'hérédité naturelle*, where it is said : "Esquirol, Spurzheim, Ellis, etc., at least give this reason for the frequency of mental aberration and its transmission in the great families of France and England ; deaf-mutes among the humbler classes seem to proceed from the same cause."

parents was really one of contrast. With respect, on the other hand, to the mutual relation of the children, the contrast between the family and the race, and therefore also the relation to brother and sister, to one's fellow-men, to male and female "neighbours," was as yet concealed by an absence of distinction. It was not till after differences were developed, and the human race was divided into several families, which at the same time showed themselves to be affected with a certain partialness, and manifested their need of mutual completion, of supplying, as it were, each other's deficiencies, that the demand could be made, on the one hand, to maintain that relation of natural dutifulness and affection between the individual members of families, which alone could develope a brotherly and sisterly love properly so called, on the other, to propagate the human race by the union of different families among each other, and the formation of new families which this involved. The moral and natural horror mentioned above only appeared in the course of the actual development of the human race.

MARRIED LIFE.

§ 13.

In married life, husband and wife must fulfil the divine ordinance to which both have to submit. They are not to look at matrimony from the view-point of fortune, happiness, or enjoyment, but to regard it as a vocation, whose sacred duties they have to fulfil. The husband is, according to God's ordinance, to be the head of the wife (Gen. iii. 16 ; Eph. v. 23 ; 1 Cor. xi. 3), and also of the whole family, for which he has to provide ; while at the same time occupying his position in the national and civil community, in which he finds his sphere of action. The wife, on the other hand, is to be the ruling centre of the household, and though, by entering upon the marriage state, she is by no means obliged to separate herself from all other social or friendly intercourse, and is not thereby at all excluded from other interests, still the proper sphere of operation prescribed to her by nature itself is in her home. It is she who must make her husband's and children's home comfortable. When, then, we desire in a woman frugality, economy, method and neatness, such qualities are not to be despised as insignificant, mean, prosaic, but are, on the contrary, the indispensable conditions of that poetry of life which ought to flourish on the domestic hearth.[1] The wise king of Israel did not despise them in his description of the woman whose price is far above rubies (Prov. xxxi. 10). And when we say with Scripture, that the man is the head of the woman, and esteem it the woman's vocation to serve, though this may indeed be in conflict with modern theories of the emancipation of woman, it certainly means anything but that the husband is to be a despot, and the wife a slave. On the contrary, the contrast between the man and the woman is to be harmonized in the union and reciprocity of love. And it is just because she serves, because in her service of love she cares for husband and children, for the whole circle of those to whom her heart is bound, that she practically exercises authority, by impressing upon the whole life of the household the stamp of *her own* peculiarity. The right must also be conceded to her of executing this her domestic vocation in her own way, and according to her peculiar taste. Although the husband must in the last resort be master in his own house, yet there is also a sphere, and one whose limits must not be fixed in a purely external manner, in which the wife must rule, and in which her rights and authority must be respected, even by the husband. The philosophic Sibbern aptly remarks in his article, *Ueber die Liebe* (p. 107), "Every woman of sound sentiments desires this, viz. to be allowed the management of matters within her own sphere, as soon as she is conscious of her own ability. She can only do full and true service when her hands are left free to rule and order."

§ 14.

Married love is destined to *increase*, to develope. In many marriages this growth is checked, because the married couple, too secure in possession, neglect to be ever acquiring fresh mutual love and esteem. Their affection fades into indifference and merely external habit. This growth may be also im-

[1] Comp. L. von Stein, *Die Frau auf dem Gebiete der Nationalökonomie*, 1875.

peded and choked when love is too selfish, when those who love desire to belong to each other after a fashion altogether too partial and exclusive, when the one cannot bear that the other should in any sense exist for other pursuits, or for other individuals also, but regards all free emotion, all interest bestowed upon other persons or other matters, as a deprivation and an injury. This perverted desire for sole possession developes into the passion of jealousy, a malady fed by phantoms, by a mere nothing (as in the case of Othello), one in which a man makes himself sorrows, nay, inflicts upon himself the most grievous torments. When love is in a healthy state, married people have confidence in each other, mutually believe in each other's faithfulness, and know that love can only flourish and increase in that element of freedom which finds its natural boundary in the fidelity of one heart towards another. Within this self-drawn boundary, however, married life, if it is to be of the right sort, must be a living with and in one another, according to the whole nature. That love may attain its due maturity, married people must share everything with each other.

But this demand, that the husband and wife should share together both the joys and sorrows of life, should live with and for each other, and thus mutually promote the development of their personality, is an impossible one, so long as they are not in a condition to share also each other's interests. The husband must understand how to enter into the interests of the housekeeper, and thereby to educate not only his sense for details, but especially for the particular. And the wife must be in a condition to share the interests of her husband, and so to form, on her side, a sense for the general. She must take an interest in her husband's calling, and rejoice in and appreciate his pursuits; and even if there is much in them, and in a man's sphere of culture in general, which she does not understand, she will still increasingly attain a comprehension of his efforts and productions, of such of them, that is, as turn towards and exercise an influence upon practical matters. In many cases she may do good service to her husband, as his support and assistant in his business; and it may often be of importance to a man to listen to the advice of a sensible wife, whose more direct feeling and sound views may hit upon the right course with greater certainty than more intricate reasoning could. Generally speaking, there is not one of the interests that stir and engross a man, which has not an aspect into which a woman can enter, while, with respect to art and poetry, she is able to appropriate them entirely. Amidst this living for and in mutual interests, amidst the constantly resulting interchange of ideas, amidst joys and sorrows, and the whole variety of duties which daily life involves, amidst the continuous travelling of one and the same orbit, which, seen from without, may bear the impress of monotony, but must be ever new from within, amidst common experiences and a common participation in more absorbing events, amidst increasing intimacy, in which their hearts, their good qualities, their faults, are ever more fully manifest to each other; amidst all these, both must grow together, and love, too, must grow, be purified and matured.

§ 15.

It is in this harmonious intercourse, and in the constantly progressive growth of love, that the *happiness* of married life consists. Certain external conditions are indeed requisite to this happiness; but riches and superfluity are by no means to be reckoned among them. These considered in themselves are but an ambiguous happiness, and, especially at the commencement of married life, bring with them temptations, in which, unless they are earnestly resisted and overcome, the growth and prosperity of love are suppressed. We mean in this case the very same temptations which accompany poverty, namely, that the life of both husband and wife should be turned too much *outwards*, and absorbed in externals, at the expense of the inner life. It is not only the poor, but also the rich, who in many cases forfeit their inner life, and are inwardly ruined by the heathenish questions: What shall we eat, and what shall we drink, and wherewithal shall we be clothed? The poor do this because they suffer want; the rich, because they have a superfluity of everything, and know not *what* to choose. It must be regarded as a fortunate circumstance, and one likely to promote affection, for a man and wife to start from a more limited and needy beginning, and to rear the edifice of their home and family by their own labour and economy, to be able themselves to fashion a habitation and external surroundings for their love, exactly corresponding to its peculiarity, and which, just because they have themselves created and fashioned them, will afford them the same kind of delight as that which we take in trees which we have ourselves planted. Where everything is from the first bestowed or inherited, where, as far as the external condition is concerned, nothing is left to be desired or obtained, because there is a super-fluity of all things, there, with respect to externals, that joy of contentment which can only exist in narrow circumstances, the joy of finding that little can become much, is absent. The little, modest domestic festivities, with their homely senti-ment, the little surprises which affection prepares, and in which a gift, trifling in itself, acquires great inward im-portance, as involving the labour or the sacrifice of love, have, in more moderate circumstances, a special charm, not to be found where riches and abundance prevail, even supposing affection to be also present. The allotments of human happi-ness are distributed in various forms, and riches may certainly be a blessing; but they to whom it is appointed to begin their married life in riches and abundance, and who therefore miss the pleasure of building up their own home, must find their compensation for this deficiency by trying to prepare their joy and happiness in other aspects. But to the majority of those who enter upon the married state, we would wish neither riches nor poverty; but that condition of life which, lying midway between the two, comprises so great a variety of kinds and degrees.

<h3 align="center">§ 16.</h3>

No marriage is pure harmony and happiness. The experi-ence is soon made, that this paradise is at the same time a school replete with serious discipline and trial. It is now known by experience what is meant in the marriage service by " the cross " which is laid upon this state, and by the words that " the man shall eat bread in the sweat of his brow," a saying which, even when daily bread has not to be literally earned, finds its application in the work of every calling; that the woman shall "bring forth with sorrow," and that "her will," by nature arbitrary and inclined to despotism, "shall be subject to the man." The deep seriousness involved in marriage is also soon brought to light by this or that unexpected dispensation, by reverses, disappointments, cares for sustenance, loss of property, sickness, or bereavements, when father and mother must stand by the death-beds of beloved children, etc. Again, the seriousness of marriage is every day shown by the work which married people have with themselves and their own souls, by the conflict with sin, without which the growth of love above spoken of can by no means take place. In married life the former illusions of love cease, the qualities which each attributed to the other, when they saw each other in a beautifying light, disappear; and, on the other hand, many unsuspected faults, peculiarities, and deficiencies appear. Everything depends especially on resisting whatever militates against fidelity, as soon as it is perceived. Under this head we include also every temptation to mutual indifference, lukewarmness, reserve. The latter especially is a sign of retrogression in love, whose very nature it is to be communicative. It is the duty of each to strive against those faults in particular which give the most offence to the other, and render him unamiable in the eyes of one united to him in the bonds of affection. It is incumbent on both to bear each other's burdens, and this especially includes a patient bearing of each other's faults and weaknesses, a willingness to forgive them, and a readiness to lend all kindly help towards forsaking them. And no small portion of the burdens to be thus patiently borne consists of those occasioned by the individual temperament. In this respect a diversity of temperament is desirable in married people, for they will then be better able to help each other, than if they both had the same temperament, *e.g.* were both naturally inclined to melancholy or impetuosity. Against the warmth and vehemence of the one, the best sedative will be the gentleness and the silence, combined with kindliness, of the other.

Among the things which often trouble married life, must also be reckoned the ill humours and dissensions which may be caused by trifles. Thus it is an experience repeated under various forms, and one corroborated by many, that a woman who can show the greatest patience, resignation, and self control amidst serious domestic misfortunes,—times of sickness, for instance, in which she will for whole days and nights devote herself exclusively to the care of husband or children, and shun no sacrifice,—will in the ordinary course of things lose all patience and composure if, *e.g.*, a servant, with whom she is in other respects satisfied, should be guilty of some clumsiness, or if a bell should be pulled with more violence than necessary, or the table-cloth should get spotted, or some one should carelessly soil the clean carpet. Unimportant differences, little quarrels, disputes about trifles, may result in great disturbances. To avoid these, the rule may be laid down, that, on the one hand, trifles must not be neglected, for they have an importance of their own, and in many instances belong to the æsthetic side of the marriage state, the disregard of which may have the most pernicious consequences for its ethic side, a circumstance which husbands should more especially lay to heart; that, on the other, the trifling and the insignificant must be treated only *as such*, that is, as something neither great nor important, nor to be made a fuss about, that such things must not be causes of dejection or temper, which, as wives would do well to remember, is just as non-æsthetic. A certain element of. good-natured humour, a real superiority to such slight disturbances, a free bright feeling, which makes one disposed and able quickly to disperse the rising cloud, are in such cases of most beneficial effect.

§ 17.

But the true superiority to such temptations, the true power for bearing both the less and the greater trials of life, and at the same time strengthening the love which is well-pleasing both to God and man, is to be found in Christian faith. That work by which each seeks mutually to educate and help the other, must in its deepest reason be a work for mutual sanctification, for attaining through and with each other maturity for the kingdom of God. Christian faith teaches married people to regard each other not as beings destined for this earthly life alone, but as beings destined one day to rise from the dead, as fellow-heirs of the grace of life

(1 Pet. iii. 7). It imposes upon them a mutual responsibility for each other's souls, utterly unknown apart from Christianity. It is this faith alone which makes them skilful to bear the cross, whether we mean thereby the work of patience which they owe to one another by reason of their sin, or the outward lot which they have to bear together. Amidst the silent growth of faith and holiness must marriage approach that ideal which the apostle holds up, when he perceives in the intercourse of man and wife a type of the intercourse between Christ and the Church—an ideal so great and exalted, that we can only but gradually approach it amidst imperfections and weaknesses.

This Christian and religious character of marriage cannot be complete from the beginning. It would be an exaggeration to require its full, perfect impression, when a marriage is first concluded. Young married people cannot face one another in full Christian maturity; and so long as there is not open testimony to existing unbelief and decided denial of God, it will always be a dangerous matter, in choosing a partner, to require certain external signs of the state of heart towards the gospel in one's future partner.[1] Assuming a profession of Church membership, it would be far sounder, with trust in God, to have regard to what *may be* by God's blessing with respect to religion, than to what already exists. Just what the religious element in marriage needs is its history, and this under God's guidance is differently individualized in different marriages. It is only by means of actually living together, and of common endurance of actual trials, that either the religious or ethic maturity of marriage can be attained. And Christ's gospel will in married and family life become increasingly "the leaven" which penetrates invisibly and unnoticed the earthly and temporal relations. It will also increasingly become the "pearl," as will be manifested especially by the fact that marriage and the family will enter into more intimate connection with the Church and its means of grace, and an echo of Church life be perceived in domestic life. The desire to lay down certain firm rules binding on all for domestic devotion, would easily lead to pietistic and external formality.

[1] Comp. Harless, *Christliche Ethik*, p. 506, 2d ed.

MIXED MARRIAGES.

§ 18.

It is just because in the normal development of marriage the religious element is also developed as its fundamental support and blessing, that mixed marriages, or marriages between individuals of different Christian confessions, present very doubtful elements. Such couples will either go on living together in religious indifference, or, if a really vital development of religion takes place, and the discussions and disputes by which the one might seek to bring over the other to his confession are avoided, a deep and painful feeling of deficiency will be experienced. For such married people cannot participate together in what is highest and holiest; they cannot, *e.g.*, celebrate the Holy Communion together. Great difficulties will also arise with respect to the education of children. For, whatever engagements may be entered into, whether that all the children are to be brought up in the father's confession, or the sons in the father's and the daughters in the mother's, there is always a wall of partition erected between hearts. We by no means deny that there *may* be happy mixed marriages, when that Christian truth which is common to both is powerful enough in each to overcome the confessional difference. Still, there is always in such marriages a non-normal element; and though, in countries where various confessions prevail, the State is naturally disposed to favour mixed marriages, as contributing to the maintenance of more peaceable relations between the confessions, yet the Church will not be able to shut its eyes to the doubtful character of such unions, and that which makes them so undesirable. The Protestant Church can, however, herein exercise greater toleration than the Catholic, which regards membership in herself as indispensable to salvation.

Marriages between Jews and Christians are, from a religious point of view, monstrous, and were in former times forbidden as well by the Christian State as by the Christian Church, for to the Jew not only the cross of Christ, but also the acknowledgment of the Triune God, is an offence. Not till the present century did some legislatures declare such marriages allowable (though chiefly in the form of civil marriage), for the sake of producing greater union in civil society,—an experiment on which a celebrated ecclesiastical jurist remarks, that "its doubtful character is, from a Christian point of view, unmistakeable."[1]

Another kind of mixed marriage takes place when, though the parties both belong to the same Church, their state of heart towards the gospel is one fundamentally different,—the one believing, the other sceptical. It is in our days a frequent occurrence for believing wives to have unbelieving husbands: and "the Christian woman in the heathen household," whose picture is sketched by Bishop Münter (1761–1830) in one of his antiquarian treatises, is still met with under different circumstances in the midst of our so-called Christendom.

Passionate attempts at conversion will in such cases be of little avail. On the contrary, the words of the Apostle Peter must be remembered (1 Pet. iii. 1) concerning women, by whose holy behaviour unbelieving husbands, "who obeyed not the word," were "won without word." The quiet testimony borne in lowliness, patience, and gentleness to the truth, and the power of faith, the silent confession of the Lord in doing and suffering, will produce their effect, and smooth the way for the word when the "acceptable time" (2 Cor. vi. 2) is come. This applies also to the believing husband, who has the misfortune of being married to an unbelieving wife.

---

[1] Richter, *Kirchenrecht*, p. 609. Chancellor Müller, in his *Conversations with Goethe*, relates that he went one day to Goethe's, and had scarcely entered the room when the old gentleman poured forth his wrath at the new law (of June 20, 1823) concerning Jews in the duchy of Weimar, which permitted marriages between Jews and Christians. He foresaw the worst and most pernicious consequences therefrom, and declared that if the general superintendent were a man of any decision of character, he would rather lay down his office than bless a Jewess in church in the name of the Holy Trinity. All moral feelings which rest entirely upon religious feelings would, he said, be undermined in families by so scandalous a law (Müller's *Unterhaltungen mit Goethe*, p. 57). This trait is the more remarkable, as showing the instinctive power exercised by Christian tradition upon this great representative of Humanism.

SECOND MARRIAGE.—DIVORCE.

§ 19.

Marriage is dissolved by death. And there are marriages which have been carried out with such genuine feeling and mutual devotion, that a second marriage could scarcely take place. For though the marriage tie is appointed only for this world, and is not to be continued in the other, where they neither marry nor are given in marriage, yet the surviving partner will live in the spiritual communion of memory with the departed. But it is just because marriage is appointed only for this earthly existence, that to enter upon a second marriage appears always allowable, and in some cases and circumstances advisable. Thus the apostle advises the younger widows to marry again, and that for a reason which is stated (1 Tim. v. 11—15). Experience also teaches, that there are instances in which a second marriage is in truth *the first*, that is to say, that which most accords with the ideal, that in which the individual is first found who is in the true sense of the word a helpmate.

In the earlier ages of the Church, second marriage was not regarded with favour, a judgment which to this very day is the prevailing one in the Catholic Church. Another way of looking at the matter was brought about by the Reformation, in its contest against the over-estimation of celibacy, and in consequence of its more thorough occupation with Holy Scripture, which expressly declares the legality of second marriage (Rom. vii. 3 ; 1 Cor. vii. 15). Nor can we find in those passages where the apostle requires of the bishop, and of any man or woman taking a higher position in the Church, "that he should be the husband of one wife, or that she (the widow) should be the wife of one husband" (1 Tim. iii. 2, v. 9; Tit. i. 6), any disapprobation of re-marriage in the case of such persons. It is evident from the context (1 Tim. iii. 3), that the attribute of being the husband of *not* one wife, is placed on a level with drunkenness, covetousness, devotion to dishonourable occupation, etc., and therefore denotes conduct equally immoral and incompatible with individual worth. On the other hand, the condition of being the husband of one wife designates moral conduct in marriage, or *matrimonial fidelity;* and hence the apostle means to say that no stain of unfaithfulness with regard to marriage, no adultery of any kind, must affect the character of a bishop or of a widow who is chosen for the service of the Church.[1] The cases in question are those of fresh marriages contracted while divorced wives are still living. The facility of divorce and re-marriage among both Jews and pagans made such occurrences so common, that there can be scarcely any doubt that these were especially in the apostle's mind.

But while we maintain, upon the ground of Holy Scripture, the general permissibility of second marriage, we must still concede that in the Protestant Church it has been honoured in a non-critical manner, that sometimes it has been regarded as an advantage, as a thing almost meritorious in clergymen to marry several times, as though by such conduct they protested the more emphatically against celibacy and the Pope. We agree that it is not a very edifying spectacle to see clergymen entering, as men full of years, upon a second or third marriage, or—like that hot controversialist, Abraham Calovius, who had buried five wives and numbered thirteen children—contracting a sixth on the borders of the grave. When Thiersch brings forward this instance in particular, he is perfectly right in saying that it is an insipid, unpoetic view of marriage for a man directly after his wife's death to take a new one, just as he would put up a fresh candle when the former one is burnt out.[2]

§ 20.

Besides the separation which marriage sustains by death, there is another whose reason is found in sin, viz. when a married couple themselves dissolve their union. Such a separation cannot come to pass otherwise than by a violation of the divine ordinance, and can only be permitted out of consideration for an existing necessity, which, however, may always be referred to a transgression, a fault, at least of one

---

[1] Comp. Harless, *Christl. Ethik*, p. 501 sq.
[2] W. Thiersch, *Ueber christliches Familienleben*, p. 21.

or of both, though perhaps in different degrees; a fault which
has grown to such a height that, to prevent worse evil, nothing
is left but for the married couple to be rescued from it by
means of separation. There are marriages so unhappy, that
those who were destined to help now mutually hinder each
other's growth in goodness, nay, now are only helpers of each
other's moral ruin; marriages in which, in opposition to the
saying of God, that "it is not good for the man to be alone,"
it must be said that it is better for the man to be alone than
to continue in such a union—a union in which fidelity is
torn up by the roots, the inward personal tie cut through,
while only the external tie still chains man and wife together,
that they may mutually poison each other's existence. Such
an unhappy state of things, however, always points back to a
fault, to an inconsiderate frivolous entrance upon marriage,
which is now its own revenge. And as a rule, it points back
to neglects during married life, neglects in striving against
the first beginnings of discord. The pernicious consequences
of not opposing evil at its beginning are especially manifested,
when hearts are alienated from each other because an inclination to contract some other tie is awakened. Goethe's
Wahlverwandtschaften, whatever else may be thought of it,
contains a deeply psychologic, and in moral respects a warning, description of how an inclination germinates and increases,
and at last becomes an overpowering and irresistible passion,
because a false security has left its first movements un-
resisted, and allowed *Principiis obsta!* to be neglected. But
whatever may be the causes of discord, one thing is always
certain, viz. that in such a case "to be happy" has been
made too great a consideration, as though this were the only
aim of marriage, while the reflection has been lost sight of
that marriage does not exist only for the individuals, but that
they also exist for marriage, exist to fulfil *God's ordinance* in
self-denial and self-sacrifice, nay, in suffering, especially where
this is self-incurred. When we speak of this want of self-
denial, we have not chiefly in view those who as frivolously
proceed to divorce as they had before frivolously entered upon
matrimony. For it is needless to dwell with any detail upon
the fact that such behaviour is reprehensible, and that divorce
should not be permitted to such, even supposing civil legisla-

tion allows it. We have in mind those who are to be reckoned among the better sort, and who in other respects regulate their conduct by duty and conscience, nay, are in a certain measure influenced by Christianity. And how in such cases must their hearts have been gradually hardened before they could have resolved on this last and decisive step! How many a moment, how many an hour must have occurred in their daily life, when reapproximation, reconciliation, and mutual forgiveness were possible! And especially if they have children, what an urgent call are these to mutual patience and forbearance! We often speak of the innocent party and his unmerited sorrows; but has then the (comparatively) innocent party never neglected anything which might have warded off the last irreparable breach? Has he or she never shown a cold, hard spirit, when readiness to forgive should have been manifested? If Christianity is the ruling principle, it must lead both to the resolve that, even if the higher ideality of this marriage must be given up, they will nevertheless remain together for their home, their family, their children's sakes, but especially for the sake of God's ordinance, under which they have placed themselves. Nevertheless, if a breach, which is, humanly speaking, irreparable, has been made, if things have gone so far that the continuance of marriage would itself be a profanation of God's ordinance, and ruinous to the souls of those concerned, then there is in such cases an urgent *need*, though in many respects a self-incurred one, for which divorce is the only remedy; this, however, by no means implies that a second marriage should, without further ceremony, be permitted.

<h2 style="text-align:center">§ 21.</h2>

The Romish Church maintains the indissolubility of marriage, and appeals to certain passages of Scripture which are said to declare it so: "Whom God hath joined together, let not man put asunder" (Matt. xix. 6). It permits separation from bed and board (*separatio quoad thorum et mensam*), but not the contraction of a second marriage, because she does not regard the marriage tie as then dissolved, and so recognises no actual divorce. The Lutheran Church decrees the lawfulness of an actual divorce, and allows the innocent party to re-marry.[1] Holy Scripture names two cases in which divorce and re-marriage are allowable. It says, "Whosoever shall put away his wife, except it be for the cause of fornication (παρεκτὸς λόγου πορνείας), causes her to commit adultery; and whoso marrieth her that is put away committeth adultery" (Matt. v. 32). And again, xix. 9, "Whosoever shall put away his wife, *except it be for fornication,* and shall marry another, committeth adultery." The Apostle Paul adds another case, namely, that of malicious desertion (*desertio malitiosa*), when one leaves and of his own accord forsakes the other: "If the unbelieving depart, let him depart. A brother or a sister (*i.c.* the Christian partner) is not under bondage in such cases" (1 Cor. vii. 15). He here concedes to the forsaken, the suffering one, the privilege of re-marriage. The important question now arises, whether there may not also be other cases, besides those expressly named in Scripture; in other words, whether these sayings of our Lord and His apostle are to be regarded as literally laws, as ecclesiastical appointments delivered as such to the Church, or whether, on the contrary, we are to find in them *a principle* to be applied by the Church in such cases as should occur? The latter is our view of the passages quoted, and according to our conviction the only evangelical one. The principle, moreover, which they lay down is, that where the essential bond of marriage is broken, where matrimonial fidelity is destroyed in its roots, *but also there only,* divorce is lawful. It is so in the case mentioned by our Lord Himself. For here—viz. where πορνεία is understood not only of the merely external act, but extended to the corresponding degeneration of the heart and disposition—absolute unfaithfulness, the aversion of the entire personality from the husband and devotion to another, takes place. Nor is the personal tie of intercourse less broken, in the case brought forward by the apostle from the occurrences of his times. And we cannot but acknowledge, that Lutheran divines are fully justified in including among valid reasons for divorce, continued cruelty, personal ill - usage (*saevitiae*), and the plotting against one another's lives

---

[1] *Artic. Smalcald.* p. 355 (*Libri symbol. eccl. ev.* ed. C. Hase): "Injusta traditio est, quae prohibet conjugium personae innocenti post factum divortium."

(*insidiae*). So Melanchthon, and after him the Danish theologian N. Hemmingsen. To these reasons others were subsequently added, *e.g.* refusal of the *debitum conjugale*.[1] And to pass from these gross violations of matrimonial fidelity, there is also a mutual soul-poisoning, through which a complete inward breach at last takes place. "Incompatibility of temper" is indeed a reason for divorce, which has been and still is applied in the most superficial and irresponsible manner. Still it *may* also involve the saddest and most serious circumstances. There is an incompatibility of temper which, by constant exasperation and repeated annoyance, becomes of such a nature as to justify, if not divorce, still a temporary separation, which may at last become lifelong. It is, however, one of the very difficult points of the legislation in question, to observe the happy medium between unfair rigour and undue laxity. For we cannot but agree with what is said in an ancient order of divine service, that there are "unusual cases," which can hardly be met by definite rules.[2]

We are aware that *analogy* is in this matter a dangerous way, and one which has led to that so much discussed, and certainly lamentable laxity of legislation, which is, however, surpassed by the laxity with which authorities administer the law. But *abusus non tollit usum, i.e.* the right use is not obviated by abuse. The reaction, which has from time to time arisen in the Protestant Church against this pernicious laxity, cannot be declared unjustifiable. But when individual clergymen have either refused to marry the divorced in general, or have only consented to marry those to whom the reasons expressly stated in Scripture apply, we can only see in such conduct a non-evangelical partiality, which, besides, can never be carried out in a national church, and is opposed to the old consistorial practice of the Lutheran Church. If the saying of Christ is taken as a literal law, intended for direct and literal observance in the Church, the great difference existing between the social circumstances of His time, against which His words were

---

[1] Richter, *Lehrbuch des Kirchenrechts*, 5th ed. p. 635 sq.

[2] Richter, *Kirchenordnungen des 16 Jahrhunderts*, p. 455 ; *Braunschweig-Grubenhagensche Kirchenordnung.* Comp. Harless, *Die Ehescheidungsfrage* p. 129.

directed, and those which subsequently prevailed in Christian States, is utterly lost sight of. In the time of Christ, a divorce pronounced by the authorities was unknown; and it was left to any man to give his wife a writing of divorcement. It was of this that Christ said, " Moses, because of the hardness of your hearts, suffered you to put away your wives; but from the beginning it was not so " (Matt. xix. 8; Mark x. 5). It was against the frivolous and capricious use of this concession which prevailed in His days, that our Saviour's words were directed. If it had been His purpose to institute a law literally binding upon all, for His Church and for all times, we should have reason to complain that this law should have been communicated in so very incomplete a form. For the words in question, especially as reported by that evangelist who was at the same time an apostle (St. Matthew), speak exclusively of the right of a husband when his wife is guilty of a crime, but contain nothing at all concerning the rights of a wife—an omission which could not possibly occur in an actual law.[1] This circumstance, in particular, calls upon us to direct our attention to the principle involved in the occasional, and to a certain degree incompletely expressed, words of our Lord. When it is sometimes regarded as an excellence of the Catholic Church to allow of no divorce, and thus to exempt her clergy from the certainly painful office of re-marrying divorced persons, we are unable to agree with this admiration. The Catholic Church itself grants re-marriage to the divorced, though under a masked form ; for it has its so-called declarations of nullity, by which an existing marriage can be dissolved upon the ground of forbidden degrees of affinity, often discovered with the greatest sophistry, or of some irregularity or another, which is stated to have taken place with respect to formalities in the former marriage. Such declarations have often been made in favour of exalted personages. Thus the marriage of Napoleon I. with Josephine was declared null and void because the ceremony had not been performed by the lawful parish priest, and the emperor was free to contract another.

That the manner in which the matter of divorce is to this very day treated in Protestant States needs reform, must be

[1] Comp. H. N. Clausen, *De synoptiske Evangelier*, I. p. 237.

acknowledged by all who look upon marriage as a serious thing. That by an appeal to "that hardness of heart," which must be yielded and conceded to, the most inconsiderate concessions should be made to the frivolous and ungodly, and that, *e.g.*, a capricious mutual consent, or some unmerited misfortune, such as a repulsive and loathsome disease or madness, should be recognised as valid grounds for divorce, does not mend the matter. It is such lax marriage legislation which must take its share of the blame in many unhappy marriages, because it has to a certain degree exempted husband and wife from the duty of self-denial and self-control, and opened the barriers to caprice of all kinds. Only where a real moral *necessity* exists should divorce be permitted. Hence the question is not only to make *the laws* themselves stricter, but also *the administration of these laws;* for it is on this that so much depends, and for this that a more profound moral discernment is in so many instances required. It is indeed the Church's weighty duty to carry on, in all seriousness and affection, her attempts at reconciliation. But it is no less important that special judicial officials should be appointed (as a component of consistorial arrangements, where there are consistories) for the investigation of these matters, that thorough inquiry may be instituted as to whether, on the one hand, either separations or divorce should be granted, and, on the other, whether re-marriage should be allowed. It is specially with regard to this latter point that considerable restriction must take place, for permission to contract a fresh marriage is now accorded, without thorough examination of the case in question, without respect to guilt or comparative innocence. To this it will perhaps be answered, that in many cases the permission desired is granted for the purpose of thereby obviating immoral connexions. There are, however, connexions the sanction of which by the State or the Church is itself immoral. Such sanctions destroy the prevailing moral consciousness, which might be maintained and strengthened by a strict upholding of the moral point of view. It is true that, with respect to these matters, legislation can never be exhaustive, by reason of the individual character of the circumstances in question, and on account of the above-named "special cases," which cannot be brought under any definite rule, and which put in their claim, not only when divorce, but also when re-marriage is in question. Legislation must, however, strive, by all the means at its command, to maintain the sacredness of marriage in the spirit of Christ.

For those cases in which the Church is obliged to perform the transaction—sad in itself, and manifesting the imperfect condition of the Church—of marrying the divorced, it would be well that a special formulary, differing from that in ordinary use, should be employed. With respect, however, to purely civil marriages, the civil authorities, if they would not introduce therewith an immoral institution, and adulterate the moral ideas of the national consciousness, must turn their serious attention to the laws of divorce.

THE EMANCIPATION OF WOMAN.

§ 22.

It is in these days, when divorces are of constantly increasing occurrence, that the new doctrine of the emancipation of woman is also proclaimed, a doctrine including likewise the emancipation of man. It comes forth partly as the antinomian doctrine of "free love," which makes marriage an obsolete institution, and bases it only upon the free inclination of the heart, partly on the equally antinomian doctrine which insists on the elevation of woman from her former subordination to perfect equality with man. The former, by which this liberation is demanded in the name of "love," we designate as the *æsthetic*, the other, which demands it in the name of " the rights of human nature," as the *politico-civil* tendency of emancipation. Christianity, too, emancipated woman to an equality with man, by regarding her as a creature made in God's image, calling her to the grace of eternal life, making her a partaker of the same word of God, the same baptism, the same Lord's Supper as the man. But in this relation of equality, which unites man and woman in the closest and most loving association, Christianity maintains that mutual relation of superiority and subordination which is founded on the creation of the race. For the man is the head of the woman, even as Christ is the head of the

Church, and the Saviour of the Church. And as the Church is subject to Christ, so let the wives be subject to their own husbands in everything (Eph. v. 24; comp. 1 Pet. iii. 1).

It is this position of duty, and this relation of subordination, which the new doctrine by all means opposes, and from whose final abolition it deduces a series of far-reaching results.

On the part of the æsthetic tendency, "free love" is glorified in contrast with the constraint of marriage, and at the same time the woman of genius, superior to all prejudice, living in free love, in æsthetic and especially in artistic enjoyments, perhaps even in artistic productions, is exalted. This tendency already made its appearance in the romantic school in Germany, and found expression in Fr. Schlegel's notorious romance, *Lucinde*. It subsequently appeared in many forms both in Germany and France. Where the politico-civil tendency prevails, the general rights of man, which it is asserted have been withheld from woman, are exalted. To this tendency, which itself, again, presents many modifications, belongs, *e.g.*, Stuart Mill's article on the subjection of women. According to this, it is declared that the vocation of mother and of mistress of a family is one far too limited for a woman; that she is called by nature to the same public activity as man, but that the stronger sex have for years innumerable, by secret agreement, kept the weaker in a state of subjection, and hindered women both in the development and use of their capacities, through which they are born equal to men. It is added that even Christianity was unable in this respect to free itself from Eastern prejudices. Hence new laws are desired, in the name of "the rights of man," for the security of the rights of woman,—laws not only concerning property and inheritance, not only concerning divorce (*i.e.* for giving still greater facilities for divorce), not only permitting "marriages for a time," and leaving it to the pleasure of the parties for how long, but laws to place women in all respects upon an equality with men. These are the false revolutionary ideas of equality, which, having for a long time asserted themselves in political life, are now penetrating the family, and threatening to dissolve that tie which is the root of all human society. Each tendency is easily convertible into the other, and both may prevail in the same female individual. But

the æsthetic emancipation tendency, or that whose theme
with its manifold variations is love, is most akin to the
female nature, and is at the same time that which can first
be realized in actual life. The political tendency, on the
contrary, is more a theory, which may indeed be the subject
of much talking and writing, and is also well adapted to spread
unspeakable confusion of ideas in extensive circles, but can
never be realized, and is not so seriously intended on the part
of women as love. The utmost it can attain to is certain
attempts, or, so to speak, the making of certain starts. It
has done this in times of revolutionary excitement, as *e.g.* in
1848, when women met *en masse* with political petitions and
demonstrations, held political meetings, and even formed a
political club, whose fate, however, it was to be soon dissolved.
The women who are seen in casinos and coffeehouses in
masculine attire, with lighted cigars in their mouths, belong
rather to the political than to the æsthetic emancipation
tendency.

<h2 style="text-align:center">§ 23.</h2>

It may be asked, whether we do not admit that there is a
certain amount of truth at the bottom of these emancipation
tendencies? We certainly admit that, inasmuch as their
contention is against marriage being made binding by law, it
acquires a semblance of justification through the many unhappy
marriages in which wives are tyrannized over by their husbands
in the most undeserved manner. This condition has been
depicted in many novels, and accompanied by a cry of distress
for the liberation of woman from such unworthy slavery.
Nor can it by any means be denied that such pictures very
often correspond to a sad reality. But the idea that the evil
can be remedied by a gospel of the flesh, or in the way of
revolution and by revolutionary laws, is a radically false one.
Married people can cause each other thousands of annoyances
and torments which no civil law can prevent. Nothing but
Christianity can avail here, and such novel-writers, and
especially authoresses of this sort, are very far from reflecting
that all the calamities depicted just arise from the fact of
lives passed outside Christianity. They, on the contrary, reject
and despise the only remedy which could bring cure, or at

least alleviation. This applies also to speakers on the politico-civil emancipation. Christianity is rejected beforehand. And even if they assert that they by no means desire to do away with marriage, but, on the contrary, only to transform and ennoble it, they yet do in reality get rid of it. It is not possible to live harmoniously with an emancipated woman, who is not subject to her husband, who will not acknowledge that she can only exercise that rule which is her due in the family as his helper, and who on every difference of opinion, every passing ill-humour, offers him divorce. And if, in contradiction to the doctrine of the indissolubility of marriage, the greatest possible facility of divorce is stipulated for as its first condition, the marriage tie becomes anything but a moral institution.

§ 24.

When the reasons usually brought forward for the supposed right of woman to perfect equality with man are more closely considered, they are found to rest upon a view of the constitution, vocation, and natural talents of woman which is utterly at variance with reality. It is a thoroughly perverted tendency which would bring her out of her home and family into public life, in which the more she devotes herself thereto—though only by means of her imagination—the more she will necessarily miss her vocation. Woman possesses capacities and gifts not granted to man, and with respect to which man is not and cannot be her equal. But her capacities, as we had occasion to show in another connection, are pre-eminently of a pneumatic-psychic, therefore not of a purely pneumatic nature; and it is just upon this particular, this predominance of feeling, which fits woman to be the helpmate, comforter, housekeeper, mother, sister, and friend of man, and to exhibit the general human, and at the same time Christian element, that the excellence, the special glory awarded to woman depends. Her capacities and talents are not fitted for public life. Womanliness is refinement, modesty, a wise reserve with respect to surroundings, and a fear to overstep the boundaries prescribed by nature. The veil is the attribute of womanliness. Womanliness means a deep receptivity for what is most exalted; it does not, however, make a show of what is received and appropriated, but keeps it in the heart, to be imparted only in that narrower circle in which it is rooted and at home.

In saying this, we would by no means have women excluded from a share in scientific and artistic culture. Nor do we dispute, that, especially with respect to art, female talent is found capable of producing meritorious work, worthy of publicity. Generally speaking, the boundaries between the male and female nature—and this applies to every living being—are not drawn with a line, nor in an exclusive manner, as though the one could possess nothing that belongs also to the other. Still we maintain, that only exceptionally should such literary and artistic activity on the part of women be given to the public. The present time, on the contrary, presents us with a fearful exuberance of feminine productions in the literary market. We also affirm, that the artistic and literary activity of a woman ought to be subordinated to her chief vocation, which directs her to her home and family. And finally, we are persuaded that it is not given to women to develope a really creative talent, or to break up new ground in either art or science, to produce anything of real importance in the *history* of art or science, anything of importance to *progress;* and that therefore the history of art, as well as the history of science, would be entirely the same in their form and development, whether the works of female dilettanteism had ever seen the light or not. The advocates of emancipation, *e.g.* Stuart Mill, are of opinion that epoch-making female works of art and literary *chef-d'œuvres* will make their appearance, so soon as women are released from that tyranny of men which has paralyzed their talents and restrained their development; that now a Homer, now an Aristotle, now a Beethoven, will come forth from the ranks of the female sex. We will, however, delay no longer over an assertion which is a mere airy nothing, but keep for the present to experience, to "the inductive method," and refer thereto whatever else the future may in this respect bring to light. The art in which female talent can attain to real independence may perhaps be the histrionic, just because this is in so special a sense an imitative art, a second-hand poetic production; an

art which, however, in another aspect, has its doubtful feature
for women.

§ 25.

An attempt has been made in these days to meet the
demands of the spirit of the age by creating female students,
with full academic rights, and also with claims to government
examinations to give them access to government offices; for
there is a special difficulty about ecclesiastical ones, because
it is written, "Let the women keep silence in the church"
(1 Cor. xiv. 34 sq.). In all this we can, however, see only
caricatures and airy forms, which must of necessity dissolve
into their own nothingness. The sole faculty in which
perhaps there might be room for female pupils seems to be
the medical. For in itself it is by no means objectionable
that women should be acquainted with certain branches of
the healing art, for the purpose of affording assistance to
persons of their own sex. But we question whether it is just
and right that they should afterwards be placed on a level
with male physicians as equally authorized, and whether they
should not, on the contrary, be restricted within certain
limits in the practice of their art, and indeed only allowed
to exercise it under the supervision of such men as have the
opportunity of a more extended scientific survey. When the
advocates of emancipation further demand that legal appointments, *e.g.* those of advocates and judges, should be accessible
to females, and also that they should not only be capable of
voting for, but also of being themselves chosen, members of
parliaments and diets, they are allowing their imagination to
depict a female nature quite different from the actual one,
and are especially overlooking the unjuridical nature of
woman, which is more inclined to be determined by feeling
than by objective reasons and their calm consideration. Nor
do they state how business is to go on before and after the
confinement of these female advocates, judges, members of
parliament, etc. One cannot really act as if such natural
occurrences either did not exist at all, or were to be just
slightly touched upon and passed over as with a feather
broom. Such things assert themselves with a reality which
plainly shows that a woman's sphere is her *home,* and not

public life. It is just because the State must not set itself
in opposition to its own fundamental element, the family, but
must, on the contrary, guard and protect this institution, to
which it belongs, that the woman should bear and rear children for her native land, that it cannot commit itself to
appointing women to offices through which family life, that
important foundation of all society, is destroyed.

To show the political talents of women, the examples of
certain princesses, who have exhibited on the throne great and
statesmanlike genius, have been adduced, and the inference
has been drawn, that it might be desirable to appoint also
female ministers, especially presidents of councils (so Stuart
Mill). 'It is undeniable that women of great political genius
have reigned, *e.g.* in England, Russia, and Austria. It may
perhaps be conceded that Queen Elizabeth of England possessed
so firm a political spirit as never to allow her female weaknesses to influence affairs of State, and that her private
inclinations never induced her to dispense with the respect
due to the ruler of the country. Such specially endowed
individuals, however, can only be regarded as exceptions to
their sex, who by a certain *lusus naturae* have received the
qualities of men. When the poet Oehlenschläger makes his
Queen Margaret say : " Yes, ' woman,' which means the same
as wife, bride, daughter or sister, hanging on man like the
weak ivy supported by the oak, which it embraces. But a
princess whom a nation obeys is herself the oak," this very
comparison of a *woman* and an *oak* proves that a special
exception from the female sex is here depicted, without our
denying on that account that woman may also be represented
under other images than just the ivy. It must, besides, be
recognised as true tact on the part of the above-named
princesses, that none of them, so far as is known, have chosen
female ministers or even a female president of the council, but
have always appointed men to these positions, and listened to
their counsels. But a rule cannot be founded on exceptions ;
and in general it must be regarded as a " strange abnormalism,"
that a woman should undertake a vocation which is the most
manly of all, viz. that of king. Certainly Riehl makes a
perfectly just remark when he says : " Female succession to
the throne manifestly belongs to the mediæval view, which

regards the whole country as the private property of the reigning house, and hence, when a male heir fails, the female has to undertake the government; but the purer the idea of the family and the State becomes, the more certainly will female succession to the throne be done away with."[1]

§ 26.

When the heralds of unlimited emancipation deny, in their fanatic zeal for equality, the *intellectual* inequality of man and woman, they also deny, in the most irresponsible manner, their *physical* inequality. A glance at the bodily organization of woman unmistakeably shows, not only that she is not intended for the work which requires the physical strength of man, but also that she is not called to the same intellectual work and efforts. This point of view must be observed even in education and school instruction; and where it is lost sight of, such a proceeding is its own infallible punishment. From the standpoint of emancipation and absolute equality, it must certainly be required that girls should receive exactly the same instruction as boys; that they should not only be instructed in the same subjects, but that the same claims should be made on them with respect to school attendance and school work. This experiment has been made in more than one place, especially in North America, but it has always entailed most pernicious consequences. Here, too, all regard to nature, to its needs and demands, has been lost sight of. Where schools have continued to require the same intellectual labours from girls as from boys, the consequences have been that an ever increasing number of girls have during the fulfilment of their school duties languished, grown pale and faded, and become at the same time unfit for their future callings. Indeed, the conviction has been arrived at, that nature and its laws and hints must be submitted to, and this requires that, at certain regularly recurring times, the female constitution should have repose, or at least be spared making great exertions.[2]

---

[1] W. H. Riehl, *Die Familie*, p. 31.

[2] Comp. Hornemann's *Hygienische Mittheilungen*, vol. viii., " Ueber die Bedeut-ung des Geschlechtes in der Erziehung" (Dänisch).

§ 27.

The design of the preceding discussions has been to bring to light the false assumptions from which the doctrine of emancipation proceeds; we now proceed to take a view of the emancipated woman herself. And what, we ask, does even the most highly gifted gain, by giving herself up to the ideas and doctrines of emancipation propounded by men who have invented the new gospel of lawlessness (of antinomianism) for the State and for the family? For women did not of themselves think of the *theory* of emancipation, but learned it from men. And even granting that they possess the talent of propagating this theory in novels and romances, they still received the first impulse from the men of " free thought," and are, in an intellectual sense, in this matter the misled. And what do they gain by giving themselves up to dreams and fancies of the greatness and importance to which they are called in public life, and to complaints at the restricted position in which they have hitherto been kept by the injustice of civil society? And what do they gain—for we cannot keep back this question—by surrendering themselves to *free love?* In this connection we are always brought back to love as the fundamental theme, which, though often imperceptibly and unconsciously, resounds through the whole, and to which, though often by bypaths, the whole movement returns. They gain nothing else than the fulfilment in themselves of the saying, " Whoso exalteth himself shall be abased." For every creature who would in its self-exaltation soar above the limits prescribed by its Creator, plunges into deep humiliation, not only failing to attain the forbidden height it struggled after, but also sinking far beneath the dignity to which it was destined.

Such a woman dedicates her life and efforts to being in every respect equal to men. She despises the more restricted position of the ordinary woman; she dreams of open public life, and directs thereto all her efforts and aspirations. But all that she thus gains is to become less and less a woman. And yet, however zealously she may bungle in that which is only enjoined upon the man, she will never become a man. And since she can never wholly get rid of her feminine nature, she becomes a sort of hermaphrodite, half man and half woman, and neither of the two entirely. She takes up a hostile position to the Christian doctrines of marriage, and of the subjection of woman to man. She despises Christian marriage as an obsolete institution, and endeavours to place herself in a position of absolute independence with respect to the male sex. But hereby she is unconsciously betrayed into a false dependence upon men. For while she is emancipating herself in her relation to men, she forgets that they are doing the same in relation to her; that however much they may flatter her, and praise her beauty, genius, and superiority of mind, her free and unprejudiced opinions, etc., they yet very well know that she is not their superior, but their inferior, and that she cannot free herself from certain female weaknesses; that she has cast away her best shield and defence against the latter, viz. Christianity, and the modesty bestowed upon her by nature; that she has herself torn off the veil of womanly reserve and shame, and may therefore the more easily become the prey of attacks which lie quite beyond her calculations. What right has she to complain if perchance her heart— without her even knowing how—should be seized with *real* love to a man, to whom she has given all she has to give, and who now in base faithlessness leaves her to the loneliness of her deeply wounded heart? *True love, that sign of her true womanliness, becomes her punishment.* Then she appeals to fidelity, laments and complains of broken faith, and thereby really appeals to marriage. But has she not—differing herein from her sisters, who have come to this pass through weakness —expressly acknowledged the doctrine of the false prophet, which derides fidelity in love as an obsolete conventionality, because love depends alone upon the free inclinations of the heart, and has lost all claim when this voice is silent? She had indeed thought and firmly trusted—showing herself in this respect a woman—that in *this* case love was so strong on both sides, that fidelity would endure, that faithlessness would here be an utter impossibility. It was just a womanly illusion.

But even when a case like that described does not occur, —and there may be emancipated women so self-centred and proud, that they never let matters come to real love,—the saying, " Whosoever exalteth himself shall be abased," will still be fulfilled. She has torn the veil. There will come hours and seasons in her life when she will experience a deep inward wretchedness, a state of homelessness, and feel herself like a plant torn from its native soil, which can be planted and strike root nowhere; when, from her supposed elevation and fancied freedom, she will long in vain for a quiet unnoticed life, restrained by duty and conscience, within the home and the bosom of the family.

§ 28.

We close these remarks on emancipation with the proposition, that the woman who in marriage places herself under God's ordinance, is by no means excluded from all influence upon public life. She exercises a real influence in Church and State, upon literature and art. But it is an *indirect*, not a direct, influence. She is the helper of the man ; she stands at his side, and on his level, and can, in many respects and in many ways, assist him in his efforts and operations. She can also co-operate with him in her own sphere by silently contributing to the formation of a general opinion, a prevailing tone with respect to public affairs, so far as these present a side which may interest and be accessible to her. The influence of women upon public opinion, both in a good and a bad sense, has often proved itself far-reaching and important. But she has one special means of operating upon public life, upon the Church and the State, — a means of operation which man does not exercise, a power among the greatest in human society. For is not the whole future generation, in the first stage of its development, entirely in the hands of the woman ? As a mother she exercises the greatest influence, viz. the influence of the future upon public life. What the Church owes to Christian mothers, what great teachers of the Church have testified of the religious impressions they have received in childhood from their mothers,—impressions which have proved themselves fruitful germs in their lives,—what their native land owes to mothers who have inspired their young children with patriotism, need not be further discussed. And it is just because women exercise so great an influence upon the rising generaticn, that the religious and national element should form the groundwork of her *education.* Her mother-tongue, the poetic literature of her native land, and its history, are of far greater importance to the future vocation of the growing girl than a barren fluency in foreign languages.

To guard against possible misunderstanding, we add one more remark. We are by no means opposed to all and everything that aims at affording women wider scope for the full exercise of their real capacities, or of the rights which are involved in their vocation. If, in consequence, certain subordinate employments, which originally belonged to men, should be performed by women,—in saying which we do not contemplate only work in factories, and also occupation in printing, telegraphy, etc.,—this may perhaps be regarded as pertaining to the civil side of female emancipation. We should, however, be misunderstood if taken for opponents of these and similar arrangements. With regard to such work as women are just *as capable* of executing as men, the right of engaging therein ought to be granted them. Still, such female man's work seems to us undesirable. This kind of competition with men has in it an element alien to the feminine nature. It is done, however, for the sake of a maintenance, and finds its justification in the necessities of the times, that is to say, partly in the circumstance that there are in our days so many unmarried women, and partly in the fact that many marriages are contracted in which the labour of the husband does not suffice for the maintenance of the family, on which account the wife must seek employment, in many cases, alas! away from home. It is connected with the distress which has produced the social problem of the day (the labour question), and is a portion of the "struggle for existence."

FAMILY LIFE AND FAMILY AFFECTION.

§ 29.

When a marriage expands into a family, and a home arises, a family life and a family feeling, animating and uniting individuals as members of this little whole, of this home community are also formed, and find their expression in family affection, as well as in the position which the family takes up and maintains towards other social circles. By family affection we understand not only the mutual affection of the individuals for each other, of parents for children and of children for parents, of brothers and sisters for each other, etc., but also the *common affection* of the individual members of a family for the whole, viz. for this family, this house, in which in its wider sense those more nearly and more distantly related must be included. It means the common affection for that *home*, with all its features of intimacy and comfort, for that particular mode of life and domestic arrangement, for those home manners and customs, for those daily family gatherings, for the appointed hours, the little family festivities, which in Christian families find their yearly returning climax in Christmas, the festival of children and no less the festival of the aged, who love it the more the older they grow, which in every home has its own peculiarities, and whose image lives in memory long after its lights are extinguished.

True family life and genuine family affection can only obtain a *form* by means of a due proportion between authority and dutifulness. Where there is no authority, no will to govern the whole, no appointed order in the house, but only a spurious individualistic liberty, where each member of a family does what he pleases, goes his own way, and seeks his own enjoyment; or where false notions of equality have entered, where children and servants are emancipating themselves, and placing themselves on an equal footing with parents and masters; there family life is, in fact, destroyed. The opposite extreme is when the authority of the father or mother rules in such a manner that a spirit of fear is diffused, weighing down the family by its pressure, and making its order a constraint. The normal state of affairs prevails where authority rules in indissoluble union with affection, and exercises thereby a beneficent enfranchising influence, because each individual feels that allowance is made for his own peculiarity, and has full liberty to develope within its limits, where obedience to the will of parents or masters is one with dutifulness, with a devotion founded on reverence, or, in other words, where a just relation between superiority and subordination is maintained between the members of the family in an indissoluble union of duty and love, and indeed as a thing self-evident.

But true family life and genuine family affection depend not only on a just balance between authority and dutifulness within the family properly so called, but also upon the maintenance of a due relation of subordination and dutifulness between this family spirit and other spirits, viz. those social powers which fill a higher position than the family. To be sure, the family forms the beginning and starting-point for the whole moral world, the postulate of the other social formations. But the family must not isolate itself; it must readily accept not only the protective and sheltering, but also the fostering and fertilizing operations of the universal social circles. Nothing which is of common human interest must be alien to it. Without an active sympathy for the general, family consciousness degenerates into spiritless prosiness, or, where this is less the case, into narrow-hearted injustice and selfishness. Family isolation and family selfishness are a manifestation of sin, which plays a pernicious part in human life. History tells of kings and rulers who have sacrificed even the interests of the State to those of their family, have plunged their people into misery, and involved them in tedious and disastrous wars for the sake of their family quarrels, as Shakespeare has described in his historical plays. It tells also of the family selfishness of the nobles, which has brought States to ruin, of the nepotism of popes and other ecclesiastical rulers. And not only the history of the world, but also the history of daily life, exhibits not a little of the selfishness of the family. We speak not only of manifest violations of law and justice, as, *e.g.*, when a family seeks to appropriate by unjust lawsuits what belongs to another, thus evidently transgressing the commandment, " Thou shalt not covet thy neighbour's house," but would adduce especially that kind of injustice which is evidenced when family affection isolates itself from the interests of public life, and so makes itself guilty of a great neglect. There are those who lead what is called a beautiful and model family-life, but who are so absorbed in it that an interest in the affairs of their native land and of civil society is to a great degree lacking in them, a fact which undeniably makes such family life less exemplary. An official who is indeed praised as a good and well-meaning father of a family, but who neglects his office for it, or performs it without lively interest, and in only a half-hearted manner, shows hereby—and the more so the more important the office entrusted to him—a very defective morality. Nor is he, in truth, even a good father of a family, since by negligence of this kind, by his lack of higher aspiration and effort, he sets his family a bad example. It may, however, be said on the other side, that there are some so entirely absorbed in public life as to neglect their families for its sake. Our great task is to make it our aim "to fulfil all righteousness" in every sphere of life.

But family affection must be above all things subordinated to the kingdom of God, which is the ultimate and highest aim of human life, and the family must become the chief means of promoting its diffusion and spiritual supremacy. Christianity, at its entrance into the world, destroyed the family peace of many homes; and it still produces the same effect when, in families which are either quite unaffected by the gospel, or in which an external conventional Christianity is domiciled, individual members are aroused to faith, and the new life and new testimony to Christ bring disturbance and discord into the home. In such cases the saying of our Lord is fulfilled: "I am not come to send peace on earth, but a sword. For I am come to set a man at variance against his father, and the daughter against her mother, and the daughter-in-law against her mother-in-law. And a man's foes shall be they of his own household. He that loveth father or mother more than me, is not worthy of me; and he that loveth son or daughter more than me, is not worthy of me" (Matt. x. 34–37). Whatever doubtful and difficult circumstances may hereby arise, and however mistakenly those members of a family may act, who are awake to Christian truth, but whose Christianity is often made an unseemly display of, and whose whole behaviour is one fret and ferment, still the fact itself, that *ordinary* and *worldly* family life is disturbed by the gospel, is one quite in order, and in conformity with the divine economy. An entirely untenable position is, on the other hand, taken up when, as too often happens, the attempt is made to banish or keep away from the home Christianity and the peace of God, out of regard to family peace and domestic concord, as though these formed the highest good. Such disturbances of peace are a *crisis*, which the Lord Himself calls forth in a household, that hearts may be penetrated by the great questions, "What is truth? What must I do to be saved?" and that its members, young and old, may be brought to reflect on that which really brings peace, both to individuals and to the whole family.

Parents and Children.

§ 30.

It is the *duty of parents* to educate their children, and the *right of children* to be educated. The new-born child comes into the world not only as a member of a family, but also as a future member of the State and of the Church, of the kingdom of man and of the kingdom of God. Hence its education must, within certain limits, be subjected to oversight on the part of both the State and the Church, and neither may nor must be in all respects left to the mere will of parents. Children are not the serfs of parents. It is, however, the right as well as the duty of parents, as guardians of the wards entrusted to their charge, to provide for them in this most important respect. Christian education must proceed on the foundation of Christian baptism, and its sole duty is to perform the will of Christ with respect to the child, to lead it to lay hold on eternal life, to which it is called in baptism. This, however, by no means excludes, but rather includes, that the child shall be also educated for life, in its true sense, in this temporal state. Christian education specially aims at educating *the will* of the child, at laying a foundation for character, and this is an aim diametrically opposed to the views of many parents, who regard the development of their children's intellectual powers, or that of their talents, as the main concern. Children must be educated to reverence and obedience, to filial piety and love, to faith in their God and Saviour, and to this task must the cultivation of their physical and intellectual endowments be subordinated. Good education will seek equally to guard against excessive strictness, and that tenderness and gentleness which are but weakness. History and experience furnish us with examples of both extremes. A distinction has accordingly been made between generations who have been educated amidst blows, and others who have been brought up amidst caresses and flattery; and it might be shown that the flogged and chastised, who lived in their youth under the stern discipline of law, have borne better fruits than the flattered and caressed, who grew up in an atmosphere of lawlessness, self-will, and tenderness. The more, however, education is carried on in the spirit of Christ, the more will it show, in mutual interpenetration, both firmness and love, authority and liberty, law and gospel.

§ 31.

The apostle commands that children should be " brought up in the nurture and admonition of the Lord" (Eph. vi. 4), but combines with this precept, a warning " not to provoke children to wrath." Without discipline, indeed, there can be no education, for self-will must be broken, if a will for what is profitable, a will for what is good, is to be cultivated. One chief means is the early cultivation of habits of diligence and order, of punctuality and regularity in the whole mode of life. Punishment cannot be omitted, but it must be love which punishes; and all temper, caprice and injustice must be avoided, lest children be irritated and exasperated. For children have by nature an acute power of discrimination, which enables them to distinguish between a just and an unjust arbitrary treatment. The higher aim of all discipline and punishment must be that a spirit not of fear, but of genuine dutifulness and love, should prevail; that what is right should be done for the pleasure felt in doing right, and that abhorrence of evil, and especially abhorrence of all *falsehood*, and of all *impurity* or defilement, should become natural. Not only should obedience to parents be inculcated, but also reverence for all that is worthy of honour, so far as it comes within the circle of consciousness. We sometimes hear the complaint that the young have so little reverence, but this greatly arises from the fact that parents, and grown people in general of the present generation, feel too little reverence for whatever is worthy of honour, and are, on the contrary, ruled by a spirit which is supereminently critical and destructive. Example exercises, in this respect, a powerful influence. Would you bring up your children to revere and admire all that is great and noble, have reverence and admiration yourselves, and do not give them the daily example of a carping and haughty disapprobation, which finds nothing right, and has no ideal to look up to. The infection is communicated to children far more quickly than we are inclined to think, and the tender plants get covered with a blight which checks their growth.

The education of a child to faith, the development of the religious organ, is, as far as the first stage of life is concerned, the task of the *mother*. As the mother gives the child its first bodily nourishment from her own breast, so is she called upon to give it its first spiritual nourishment, and this she must derive from her own heart. It is always a thing to be lamented when a mother is unable to nurse her own child, and it is far more lamentable when she cannot spiritually tend and nourish it, but must either take a kind of wet-nurse for the purpose, or leave it entirely without nourishment. It is the mother who must teach her child to pray, and lead him to the Saviour, must tell him the first elements of that gospel history which is so attractive to the mind of a child. At a subsequent stage, instruction, whether imparted by the father or at school, must assume a more didactic character. Still, as a rule, care must be taken not to introduce too much moral instruction into everyday life, not to preach too much, not to talk too much of religion and Christianity, a proceeding which may so easily be ineffective, if not pernicious. Far more effective than this much speaking is it for children to see the *power* of faith in their father and mother, to see that the gospel alone, in the daily labours and vicissitudes of life, is their stay and refuge, their only consolation in life and in death. More effective and powerful than long instructions and exhortations is a single opportunely spoken testimony to the Lord, spoken perhaps in words, but brought forth by an inward necessity, by the circumstances of life, and expressed with real living energy. It is very desirable that the young should be accustomed to regular attendance at church, if only care is taken that no hated constraint is used.

Hand in hand with this care for the higher life and the disposition of children, must go a care for their physical well-being. A healthy body is a good foundation and support for a healthy development of the mental life, and a one-sided, spiritualistic education makes not only weak bodies, but also weak and sickly minds. Whatever one-sidedness may affect Rousseau's and other schemes of education, they have at least the great merit of having directed attention to the care and consideration which must in education be devoted to the physical part of man, to healthy and nourishing food, bodily exercises, bathing, the cultivation of the bodily senses, etc.

§ 32.

" We plant and water, but it is God who gives the increase " (1 Cor. iii. 7), is a saying which finds its application in the matter of education. Experience shows that we must not expect too much from education, since children of the same parents, and sharers of the same advantages, often turn out so differently, an experience made already by the first human pair in the case of Cain and Abel. One of the children may turn out well and be religious, while the other turns out ill and is wicked. We here encounter the mystery of freedom, and are brought to the recognition of the fact that every individual *makes* himself what he is. On the other hand, we neither can nor must deny its value to the truth, that the development of character is conditioned by influences from without, and that many children have been ruined in consequence of bad education, though they have themselves also been guilty of their fate. It is the sacred duty of parents to do what is in their power, as those who are responsible and will have to give account in this respect. The great difficulty is, that in education all does not depend upon teaching and instruction, though these form part of it, but upon the kind of life exhibited by parents, upon that *power of personality* which they may exercise upon their children. The reason why parents in so many instances feel humbled by the consciousness that they are not equal to their task, is because they are themselves such imperfect individuals. How often do we feel deeply humbled by seeing our own faults plainly brought before us in our children! Hence it is the duty of all, who are called to the task of education, to be constantly educating themselves, and letting themselves be educated by the Lord, by means of His word and providence, His chastisements and consolations.

§ 33.

Education is designed to lead children from non-age to maturity; and when this maturity is attained, when the children themselves begin to lay the foundations of new families, the relation of obedience in which they stand to their parents ceases. But if the relation of obedience ceases, that of filial piety never ceases, but lasts through the whole life. And though the authoritative position of command on the part of the parents ceases, the love which the aged bear their children need not cease. But here, too, we often see in life the sad opposite of what ought to be, irreverence and ingratitude towards aged parents, on the part of grown-up children who have a home of their own. The fate of King Lear is repeated even in tradesmen's and peasants' families, in which the aged parents have sacrificed their property and made themselves responsible for their children, and are then treated by them as incumbrances, who are only a burden. At all times and in all classes of society we meet with aged people, who see themselves and their fate mirrored in King Lear upon the heath. On the other hand, life also shows us examples of parents who stretch their authority beyond due bounds. There are mothers who will by no means let their children be free from their control, although they have attained the age of majority. They regard with jealousy the marriage of their sons, because they can then no longer be to the former extent themselves the objects of their confidence. There are also mothers-in-law who treat their daughters-in-law as though still in their minority, by their constant remonstrances and criticism. Here, too, the question is to keep within just limits, and to reflect that love seeketh not

her own, and that the older generation has, with respect to
the younger, frequent occasion to lay to heart the Baptist's
words: "He must increase, but I must decrease" (John
iii. 30; comp. Ruth i. 13).

§ 34.

In discussing the relation between parents and children, we
do not forget there are also *childless marriages*. Among the
Israelites it was regarded as a grievous misfortune and a
reproach, for a married woman to have no children. Hence
Elizabeth, when she had conceived in her old age, said: "The
Lord hath looked upon me to take away my reproach among
men" (Luke i. 25). The chief end of marriage is here placed
outside itself, and made to be the increase of the chosen
people, to which each individual married couple was to
contribute, while they at the same time continued their own
existence on earth in their children. Abraham, the father of
the faithful, by Sarah's connivance, nay, by her request, took
a secondary wife to obtain descendants. In Christianity, on
the contrary, the eternal value of personality is acknowledged,
and marriage, together with the whole course of married life,
has a worth of its own, even without regard to children. It
cannot however be denied, that this may be felt to be a sad
privation, which must be submitted to as a dispensation of
Providence. There is lacking the visible fruit, the living
confirmation of marriage, the pledge of affection, which is
beheld in children, the reflection, the duplicate of the life of
the parents, in the new life growing up under their own eyes.
There is lacking the continuation of their own life upon earth.
Hence childless couples often seek a compensation by adopt-
ing orphan or forsaken children, and regarding them as their
own.

With the consideration of childless marriages is combined
the question, whether it is absolutely a blessing to have children. Many answer this question in the affirmative, nay, even
add, that the more children there are in a family the greater
the blessing; and this notion may certainly be supported by
the Old Testament view. But then it is lost sight of, that the
circumstances which apply to Israel and to the preparatory

dispensation cannot, without further ceremony, be transferred to other nations. If an unlimited number of children is to be esteemed a blessing, proletariate marriages would unquestionably be the most greatly blest. But when we look at these marriages, with their troops of weakly, hungry children, whose parents are not in a condition either to feed or educate them, and by means of whom over-population is ever attaining larger dimensions, we feel called upon to question the unconditional nature of the blessing. The blessing is only one upon the condition of there being, at any rate, a home in which such children may find food and clothing, and be brought up in the nurture and admonition of the Lord. It is difficult to recognise a marriage blessing in a troop of homeless, starving children. But even where the condition of a home exists, and whether we think of many children or of one, a blessing, in the full sense of the word, is realized only where *education* succeeds, where children turn out well, and are pleasing to God and man. The notion, that it must be an absolute blessing to have children, is founded upon a confusion of possibility and reality, of beginning and development. In every incipient human life is involved a possibility of blessing. But for this possibility to be a blessing, for this beginning to lead to a right development, and not to become a curse and a grievous complication, many conditions are required, conditions not consisting in external circumstances only, but depending upon the acts of the *free will*. Christ says (John xvi. 21): "A woman, when she is in travail, hath sorrow because her hour is come; but as soon as she is delivered of the child, she remembereth no more the anguish, for joy that a man is born into the world." The joy of which our Lord speaks at a man being born into the world means joy in the new life now beginning, and the possibilities therein involved. It is the nobleness "of *human nature*" which the maternal eye sees in her child, a nobleness to which he is called, but of which he has not yet taken possession. Hence this joy is one as yet unconfirmed, one which stands on very shaky foundations, and may sooner or later be changed into a great sorrow. When Cain was born, Eve rejoiced, for she thought she had in him the child of blessing and of promise; and he grew to be only her grief and sorrow. When Absalom was born to David, there was joy in the house; but this joy was turned to sorrow when Absalom rebelled against his father, and filled David's family with confusion. When Judas Iscariot was born, there was joy that a man was born into the world; and yet he became the son of perdition, and the Saviour said of him those grievous words: " It were good for that man if he had not been born " (Matt. xxvi. 24). True and well-founded joy that a man is born into the world, can only be joy for the whole life, for the whole history of a man, is in fact only justified when this life has truly participated in the glory to which man is destined; and this, even if there is no declension from baptismal grace, can only happen after a successful endurance of great dangers and temptations. Upon this depends the conditional, the hypothetical nature of the blessing involved in the birth of a child, when the joy must always be combined with fear and trembling. The more the children, the greater the responsibility.

Children are a gift, which does not fall directly from heaven, but which their father and mother must get from the fount of creation; and children born out of marriage are not a gift but a theft from this fount, whereby the image of God is brought into this world against His will,—a fact which, however, does not exclude the possibility of God's acknowledging His image, in this as in other cases. When, however, we regard children as a gift, we must not forget that this gift is directly and forthwith changed into a great and difficult task, and that with each fresh child a fresh task arises. This deserves further and deeper consideration, as well by those who already have children and may possibly have more, but who do not sufficiently reflect that they may impose upon themselves tasks too many and beyond their power, as also by those who are grieved that their marriage has remained childless. A married woman has a deep and thoroughly natural desire for children. But if her wish, her earnest prayer is not granted, she would do well to ask herself, whether she is sure that the gift she so heartily desires would be a real blessing, whether she is certain that it would not, if granted, bring with it a task whose unsuccessful accomplishment might plunge her into still deeper sorrow.

MASTERS AND SERVANTS.

§ 35.

To the family in its wider sense belong the domestics, the servants, who must be treated as members of the household, and share in the weal or woe of the family. Such at least was the aspect in which they were formerly regarded, though now in most places such a notion is quite out of vogue. A false individualism has in this respect also diffused its pernicious effects. It is indeed esteemed as one of the advantages of the day, that domestic servants enjoy full individual liberty, and it must be acknowledged that they are freed from the oppressive dependence in which they were formerly placed. But this individual liberty is combined with the dissolution of many ties which otherwise bind men together in salutary mutual dependence, with opinions and a turn of mind which would get rid of every relation of superiority and subordination in the social system, and places men in positions of mutual indifference as independent atomistic personalities, each of whom pursues exclusively his own selfish interests. Domestic servants in our days are not only full of absurd notions of liberty, but also of as absurd claims of equality. The latter,. however, do not so much aim at reducing all to an equally low and mean position, as at raising all to an equally high one; one man having, according to these ideas, the same claim to gentility as another. On the other hand, this individual feeling for liberty, and its selfish interest, is also manifested by masters. The domestics are excluded from the family, and instead of an inward and moral relation between authority and dutifulness, one of merely external contract is introduced between masters and servants, a relation which can be abolished after a short period, and which in many instances lasts but a week or even a day. The power of money has also taken the place of the moral forces, and a servant, not feeling in the least degree constrained by either affection or devotion, will be easily induced by the prospect of higher wages to change masters even after a very short period. The whole relation turns upon work and wages, and is entirely a non-personal one.

This applies also to the position occupied by many masters, who regard their servants only from a utilitarian point of view, and hence come to terms with them chiefly by means of wages, apart from any personal interest. For servants regard not their board and lodging, but just the wages as the chief matter. But notwithstanding all their liberty, the condition of domestics is not an enviable one. The means and possibilities of obtaining the independent and advantageous position aspired after, are not always at the command of this liberty. It is obliged to bow to circumstances, and social *necessity* may very frequently bring servants into positions of oppressive dependence, very inconsistent with their notions of liberty and equality. To name only one frequently occurring example, it ill accords not only with false ideas of emancipation, but even with true ideas and feelings of humanity, when masters show so little consideration for their servants, as to allow them no proper sleeping-rooms, but to let them sleep sometimes in the kitchen, sometimes under the staircase, or in other holes—a want of consideration found also in the construction of modern domestic offices, in which no care is taken to provide suitable quarters for the servants.

It would be unjust to make such statements without limitation. There are honourable exceptions in all classes of society, from the highest to the lowest. Still such is the direction in which the current sets in our days. Hence it must be dwelt upon as a moral demand of the times, to give serious attention to whatever may serve to draw domestic servants into closer connection with the family, to make them members of the household, and to restore, in place of the merely legal relation now existing, a moral relation of mutual fidelity and trustful devotion. But if, in place of the mere contract and the mere power of money, which lead only to an external, temporary and mercenary service, the moral forces are to predominate, the spirit of Christ must rule in the house. The apostle's exhortation must be obeyed, that servants (those who serve, generally speaking) should be obedient to their own masters, not with eye-service only, but as the servants of Christ, as those who do the *will of God* from the heart ; and that masters should know and consider that they have themselves a Master in heaven, with whom is no respect of persons (Eph. vi. 5–9).

Where this spirit prevails, servants will be contented with
their position, and glory in fulfilling with all fidelity the
vocation to which they are called.   There masters will lay to
heart the physical as well as the spiritual wellbeing of their
servants, and we shall not hear the complaint, that masters do
not treat their servants in a manner worthy of human beings,
that they rob them of their day of rest, and hinder them from
reading or hearing the word of God thereon.   There, too, will
care be taken—a care in which the State must co-operate and
assist—to provide that the old age of faithful servants should,
after service of many years, be free from anxiety.

HOSPITALITY.—FRIENDSHIP.—SOCIABILITY.

§ 36.

By the mutual relations both of families and individuals,
wider circles of social intercourse are formed, among which
may first be named that of *hospitality*.   In its widest signification, hospitality is a form of sympathetic relation to other
men, by which we open to them our house, our family circle,
and let outsiders share the advantages of our own family life.
Guests are not members of the family, but are, as visitors,
admitted to the enjoyment of all the house affords.   The
proper and original meaning of the word hospitality ($\phi\iota\lambda o\xi\epsilon\nu\iota\alpha$),
is the virtue thereby denoted as exercised towards strangers.
In ancient and mediæval times this virtue was practised to a
wider extent than at present, because the state of the law was
then imperfect, and the roads insecure, because culture and
civilisation had not yet called into existence the many public
houses of entertainment, where a stranger may find shelter
and refreshment for money.   Hence it was a duty, that a man
should freely open up his house to, and provide for, the stranger.
A certain character of sacredness and inviolability was attributed to a stranger thus received, and this feeling has been
maintained among all nations.   And however past and present
circumstances may differ, hospitality, both in its broader and
narrower meaning, may and should be continually exercised,
partly by entertaining strangers (Rom. xii. 13), partly by

affording access to our domestic circle to the stranger who has inspired us with confidence; now by collecting about us those who are deprived of the advantages of family life, now by uniting friends, who have families of their own, in exhilarating social meetings. It is by such means that the virtue of hospitality, which may become one of reciprocity on the part of different families, is cultivated.

Hospitality is expressly inculcated in the New Testament. " Forget not to be hospitable, for thereby some have entertained angels unawares " (Heb. xiii. 2). The apostle is alluding to those patriarchal times, when angels visited Abraham under the oak at Mamre. We might also refer to the heathen myth of Philemon and Baucis, who received gods under their roof without knowing it. And the saying of the apostle still finds its application. For by exercising hospitality, by treating with sympathy and hearty interest those who are still in many respects strangers to us, by showing ourselves kindly, and opening our house to them, as circumstances permit and opportunities offer, it may also happen to us to entertain angels, *i.e.* men in whom we must recognise *messengers* sent to us by God, or from the world of mind and ideas, and whose sojourn in our house, whose conversation, whose influence upon our souls, may bring us a blessing far outweighing all we can do for them. In commending hospitality, we cannot fail to refer to that profound utterance of our Lord: " I was a stranger, and ye took me in " (Matt. xxv. 35).

<h2 style="text-align:center">§ 37.</h2>

The exercise of hospitality is exclusively connected with the home, with the family. *Friendship*, however, considered in itself, is not necessarily connected therewith, but may also be independent of it. Friendship is a union between individuals for mutual help and strength, a union not founded on respect alone, but chiefly on sympathy. It is not, however, limited, like the love of the husband for the wife, to a single individual. A man may fitly have several friends. But genuine friendship is always a mutual personal appreciation, a mutual relation of trust and faithfulness, in which one depends upon another, and is fully certain of his devotion and attachment of his interest and readiness to afford personal assistance. Hence, though it is possible to have more than one friend, one cannot, even though we have many acquaintances and are on friendly terms with them, have many friends. For, as Baggesen (in his *Gjengangare*, or the *Revenant*) says:

> " Zu trauter Freundschaft ist es nicht genug,
> Dass man auf Du und Du ein Glas geleert,
> Auf Einer Schulbank bei einander sass
> In Einem Café oft zusammentraf,
> Sich auf der Strasse höflich unterhielt,
> Im selben Club dieselben Lieder sang,
> Als Publicisten Eine Farbe trug,
> Auch in der Presse sich einander pries," etc.[1]

But even in friendship itself there are different degrees. We may feel attracted to a mutual giving and receiving with respect to a person, by one side of his nature, without such a feeling growing into a complete friendship. A genuine friendship, ruling the whole personality, is by no means an ordinary possession. It is always conditioned by a common view of life, a common conviction with respect to what is supreme and most sacred, but not to the exclusion of differences in details, which may, on the contrary, contribute to promote both intellectual activity and development, as well as mutual interest. As a rule, friendships are formed in youth, in the period of transition from family to public life, in those years of transition when the youthful gaze is fixed on ideals, when common love for the ideal draws kindred souls together, and unites them in a faith in one and the same future, in common purposes and resolutions. In more mature age the forming of new friendships has its difficulties, for we live in the midst of our families, and are engrossed in the duties which the realities of life have called forth. It is to be regarded as a special happiness, when the friendship formed in youth is maintained and continued through after years. It more frequently happens, that an altered view of life alienates friends from

---

[1] For true friendship, it is not enough to have emptied a brotherly glass to each other, to have sat on the same form at school, to have met frequently at the same café, to have conversed courteously in the street, to have sung the same songs at the same club, to have worn the same colours as politicians, to have extolled one another in the press.

each other in the course of years, that the hope of a lifelong friendship was an illusion, because natures were so different, a fact but gradually perceived, or because characters developed in an entirely opposite direction, and interests and duties were entirely changed. Those who, in the enthusiasm of youth, have walked together, often perceive that their paths must separate, nay, discover that, without being aware of it, they have for a long time been going different ways, while they thought they were advancing side by side. In such a case, friendship, properly so called, has ceased, and even where an exactly hostile feeling, or evident indifference, has not ensued, we find a merely external relation of mutual goodwill, without any inward communion of heart and mind. Who is there but could bring forward examples from his own experience? Or, to cite a famous one, take Goethe's youthful friendship with Stollberg, Jacobi and Lavater, and the changes which took place therein in the course of years.

That which is true of male is equally so of female friendships. As a rule, a woman makes friends in her early years, before she becomes a wife and a mother. If she can still retain them after having been, by means of her husband, of her domestic affairs, transferred to other and quite different interests and views, she may regard her lot as a favoured one. A relation of heartfelt friendship, differing from love, which may be so beneficial in maturer age, is in all cases objectionable between young men and women, because it is in their case so difficult to keep within the boundary line between friendship and love.

When we regard youth as the special season for forming friendships, we by no means deny that they may also be brought about by providential circumstances in maturer years. Nevertheless, the older we grow, the more difficult does this become. And even supposing we do acquire, at an advanced age, new friends, whose value we acknowledge with all our heart, still those common memories by which an old friendship is consecrated are lacking. It is one element of friendship to have passed through events together, and the older we grow, the less prospect there is of a fresh course of events. But the rarer a hearty and well-founded friendship, in which our inner man can find true support, is, and the higher the value we must attribute to it,—for the intermediate forms of friendship, that is, such as hover between perfect friendship and mere acquaintanceship, are not difficult to be obtained,— the more important it is to employ every means in our power to maintain it when it is found. One chief condition is, not to flatter each other, and not to cherish illusions. We must bear to see each other as we really are, must tell each other the truth in love, and be able to endure it when told. We must be capable of having patience with each other, of forgiving and loving each other, even in spite of clearly perceived faults, of whose removal there is often very little hope. We must be able to make sacrifices and to acknowledge each other under all circumstances. In a word, *fidelity* must be maintained, if friendship is to be maintained. Unfaithfulness does not consist with genuine friendship. "Trust no friend unless you have proved him in the time of trouble" (comp. Ecclus. vi. 7). It is, for instance, inconsistent with friendship if a man is attacked, and public opinion is against him, that his friends, who indeed share his convictions, but from cowardice do not venture to appear as defenders of the good cause, should renounce him, and by silence, if not by words, say with Peter: "I do not know the man." Unfaithfulness between friends may, however, be of very different kinds. There is a wide distance between Peter and Judas. Not every violation of fidelity should cause an irreparable breach. And, on the other hand, fidelity in friendship must not be confounded with party spirit, as though we were obliged to follow our friends, and to defend them, even when their cause is at variance with truth and justice. In this respect we say with Holberg: "Friendship must not be confounded with factious association. When any one feels bound to defend another in all his proceedings, whether good or bad, this is not friendship, but a culpable fraternization. I am of opinion, says Cicero, that no friendship can exist except in good things (*hoc sentio, nisi in bonis amicitiam esse non posse*)."[1]

Among the ancient Greeks and Romans, friendship was accounted one of the noblest of possessions. They saw in the relation of friendship, an ideal of that individuality and moral freedom which were repressed in other departments of life,

---

[1] L. Holberg, *Moralhke Tanker* (Rode's edit.), p. 486.

personality being in the ancient world restricted by the law of the State, by the general interest. Antiquity offers us touching examples of true friendship, and its thinkers (Aristotle, Cicero) have made it a subject of observation and investigation. The Christian revelation has been reproached for giving no precepts concerning friendship. But if the New Testament contains no express precepts on the relation, this is something very different from saying that Christianity leaves no room for it. Nor are typical instances wanting in the New Testament. We do not here confine ourselves to the relation in which Christ stood to His disciples, because this was of so unique a kind; although we have from His own mouth the expression: " Ye are my friends; I have not called you servants " (John xv. 12). We refer to the disciples in their mutual relation, to Andrew, Peter, Philip and Nathanael, who in their early years were united to each other by their common love for an ideal, which they saw realized in Christ, concerning whom they joined in the confession: "We have found the Messiah" (John i. 41 sq.). That the relation of friendship, thus appearing in the Gospel of St. John, is not expressly spoken of, is doubtless owing to the fact that it is received into the common relation of discipleship, the tie of Christian brotherhood. But innumerable examples in the history of the Church show, that the Spirit of Christ by no means designed to banish the relation of friendship from our earthly life, but rather to purify and glorify it. The friendship of Luther and Melanchthon is universally known. Christian friendship is rooted in Christian faith, in the confession: "We have found the Messiah." It subordinates its own ideals to the ideal of the kingdom of God and of Christ. In Christian faith, friendship has a foundation which is more solid than any other, and the Christian love which individualizes itself in friendship, adorns it with fidelity, truth and sincerity, which is akin to humility, with self-denying and patient devotion in a far deeper sense than any heathen sentiment is capable of doing.[1] In the Old Testament dispensation, the friendship of David and Jonathan is typical; compare Ecclus. vi. 16: " A faithful friend is the medicine of life, and they that fear the Lord shall find him."

[1] Fr. Delitzsch, *Philemon, or Christian Friendship.*

In the numerous correspondences which have in our times been made public, examples are given of the different kinds of friendship which have been here touched upon. There are correspondences which exclusively concern the scientific, the political, or the æsthetic interest, without entering into the deepest human interests. In Schiller and Goethe's famous correspondence, we see these two friends co-operating for those great aims of culture which both had in view. We see how these highly-gifted men spared neither time nor diligence in their works, how they mutually assisted and exercised a plastic influence on each other by a vigorous interchange of thought on problems of art. But we find here nothing at all on what concerns the deepest of human interests. What is shown us in these letters, important as they are with respect to mental cultivation and its history, is rather the friendship of great artists than of great men. In a moral aspect, those correspondences will be the most instructive, in which friends treat of the deepest of human affairs. As an example we would name the letters given in the *Life of Fr. Perthes.* Here are found not only mutual expressions of opinion on the great events of the times, and the great works of art and literature, but also mutual personal utterances and confessions of a moral and religious nature. The whole book deserves more than one reading, not for information alone, but also for the moral strength and religious stability it is calculated to promote.

§ 38.

Though friendship, as being a purely personal relation, may be developed independently of family life, it yet combines in an unconstrained and natural manner with hospitality: friends are accustomed to meet in *social intercourse.* What is sought in society is mental refreshment and recreation, by means of mutual communication and conversation. And just because refreshment and amusement are here the main point, social intercourse, so far as it pursues no aim external to itself, nor seeks to originate or effect anything special, must be regarded under an æsthetic point of view. Its yield is to be only the pleasure enjoyed during the hours of personal companionship. Hence it follows that this pleasure is an essential purpose of conversation, a purpose which will, however, assume a special character differing in different circles. On the one hand, conversation must not be empty and void of matter, which would render it tedious; still less must it involve what the apostle calls "foolish talking and jesting, which are not convenient," *i.e.* frivolous jokes; but neither, on the other hand, is it to be pedantic and didactic, as though the question were to work up the whole contents of our thoughts, or to exhaust a subject in a learned lecture, a proceeding which would involve labour and effort, when the intention is to rest from work, and even from mental exertion, not to confine the attention to one subject, but, on the contrary, to set it at liberty and ease. Hence conversation must be characterized by unconstrained ease, as well as by a certain generality, so that all may take part in it. Every member of the social circle should contribute to the animation and ennoblement of conversation. To remain silent in society is a neglect of social duty, and may give offence; on the other hand, it is a transgression of social duty, and no less offensive, for any one to monopolize conversation, and transform other guests into mere auditors. When a family and its narrower circle of friends meet, conversation must assume that more kindly and intimate tone which it cannot take among strangers.

What value is to be attributed to social amusements, such as dancing, card-playing and other so-called social games, must be determined according to what was said on " Things Indifferent," in the General Part (§ 133 sqq.). We have first of all to inquire whether they have æsthetic value; and if this is not denied, they must then be found to be consistent with the rules of morality. They differ from art by the circumstance that they are carried on only for one's own immediate gratification, but not for the purpose of producing a work of art. That *dancing* has its æsthetic value cannot certainly be doubted, and occasionally it may be raised to an art. It proceeds from that lively pleasure which is expressed by easy and graceful movements of the body, in meetings of both sexes. In an ethic aspect, we remark that there are indeed dances and balls where virtue is danced away, but that, assuming purity and modesty to be maintained, dancing in itself must be considered morally allowable. It serves to exhilarate the feelings of the young, and in its combination with music, with its measure and time, belongs to the poetry of youthful life, on which account dancing is becoming only for the young. On the other hand, children's balls are highly objectionable. The amusement sought in *card-playing* may probably consist in the fact that a voluntary and not too laborious mental activity is here combined with chance, with what is not seriously but playfully called good or bad fortune. Mere *games of chance,* in which all depends upon accident, are in themselves insipid, but may become of very serious interest in a bad sense, and must powerfully excite the passions if money is played for, and comparatively large sums are staked; they are then absolutely immoral. As for ordinary games of cards, in which a mixture of chance and skill takes place, and only trifles are played for, just to give the game a certain appearance of earnestness, Schleiermacher thinks that the individual mental activity is in them so subordinate, that it must be possible in social meetings to do something better, to impart to each other something more profitable, and that card-playing is always a sign of an imperfect and low grade of social life.[1] We do not feel called upon to contradict this; but as card-playing cannot be regarded as in itself immoral, we adhere to the view, that the question whether this or that person may seek or find amusement in it must be decided on purely individual grounds. In larger parties, cards must often be offered as an assistance, a resource, a kind of refuge for escaping from a conversation in which, for various reasons, we may not desire to join. The best use, perhaps, which can be made of this diversion may be the rest it gives from much talking, or from more serious mental labour. The authority of great scholars and great statesmen might be adduced in this respect. *Chess,* in which chance is entirely excluded, is a game exercising the judgment, in which the pleasure sought is purely intellectual.

Among all nations we find social gatherings combined with the pleasures of the table. A common meal serves as a symbolical mark of mutual communion. The apostle lays down the rule of all such intercourse, when he says, " Whether you eat or drink, or whatever you do, do all to the glory of God " (1 Cor. x. 31). " To the glory of God " does not mean

---

[1] Schleiermacher, *Die christliche Sitte*, p. 696.

only: with thanks to God for His gifts, but also that the gifts are used according to His will, and therefore that the bodily is subordinated to the spiritual. Hence it is open to objection that food and drink should, as though they were the chief aim and object, obtain an undue independence, that families should, as we see with such increasing frequency, desire to shine by outvying each other in the luxury and superfluity of their entertainments. When this is made the main concern, the right point of view for social intercourse is lost sight of. The invitation of an unduly large number of guests at the same time, without considering whether these guests suit each other, can only be explained from such a misunderstanding. All that is cared for is, that they should all partake of the many dishes and various wines, and their intellectual entertainment is regarded as a matter of indifference. It is generally supposed that due social justice has been fulfilled when the respective guests are seated at the board, no matter what mental *rapport* may exist among them. Such society, while destitute of any intellectual stamp, entirely forfeits also any family character, which, even where prosperity and wealth prevail, requires a certain restriction and limitation. It is, to our mind, anything but refreshing to have the impression of being at a splendid *table d'hôte* in an hotel, rather than in a private house, among a family or friendly circle.

Distinct from domestic sociability is that which is found in the *salon*. Here the home and the family retire to the background. This kind of social intercourse is cultivated by persons of high position, who are in one way or another called upon to be representative, who stand in relation to a great number of persons, all of whom they could not possibly receive into their family or friendly circles, but whom they nevertheless desire to assemble now and then about them, and to whom they wish at the same time to afford an opportunity of meeting each other. Such society may be designated as formal; for the peculiarity of this social circle is form and show, the external appearance, and that which strikes the eye. Individuals here enter into an entirely external relation, and touch one another only on the surface. The same may be said of conversation, which here moves only on the surface of matters, and soon leaves one subject to take up another; and these subjects are themselves but the latest outward occurrences, and those which are forgotten by next time, because already put in the background by others. Still this formal society is not entirely without its value, not quite devoid of importance. In certain positions of life and grades of society, such *reunions* are indispensable. That contact between persons who would otherwise find no opportunity of meeting, though in the first place merely external, may be a starting-point for something better than itself. And the formal culture, assurance and ease needful for moving in such circles, which demand talents by no means bestowed on every one, have, like all other formal culture, a value of their own. Only we must maintain, that the society of the salon is in intrinsic value infinitely beneath the society of the home, because, notwithstanding all the respect paid to persons, or at least to their surfaces, it is by its very nature impersonal. For in a salon each is estimated by what *he represents*, not according to what he is himself. All the guests move among each other as the mere representatives of an external position in life, a rank, an office, a property; but none is there as himself. An individual who should enter into no other social engagements, but exclusively frequent salons, that world of mere representations, of mere semblances and phenomena, would soon become inwardly hollow and empty, be himself changed into a mere phenomenon. Experience also shows that royal personages, who are unable to withdraw from this kind of social intercourse, nay, who have to reckon it among their duties, take care to find opportunities for enjoying the rest and refreshment of the quiet domestic circle, where, in contrast to society of so purely representative a nature, the simple and genuine is done justice to. A better form of salon-life, exhibiting at one time a pre-eminently political, at another a literary and æsthetic character, has during certain periods prevailed in France. Intellectual women (*e.g.* Madame Recamier, born 1780, died 1849) have been the centres of a salon-life, of a *bureau d'esprit*, in which the aristocracy of genius and education have assembled around them. Intellect, wit, originality have been the characteristics of these circles. It was rather minds than persons that met and encountered each other in the rapid play of conversation.

Their personal nature must be sought in the homage, nay, the adoration, offered to the queen of such a society.

In all the social engagements considered in the preceding pages, it is a duty to cultivate a feeling for that which is the special characteristic of each kind of association, to recognise each, even the most individual, within its appointed limits. They call for the development of the qualities called good taste, tact, discretion, — qualities which must be as much observed in the most intimate friendships as in the external relations of politeness. All social culture must in its inmost nature be genuine human culture. Society points beyond itself to those social circles which are broader and higher than the family and merely personal associations. These higher circles will form the subject of our consideration in the paragraphs which follow.

THE STATE.

THE STATE AND JUSTICE.

§ 39.

The family enlarges into the people, and when a people is organized into a community subject to common legal institutions determining the relation between authorities and subjects, a *State* has come into existence. While the family shows us a kingdom of love and dutifulness, the State, on the contrary, exhibits a kingdom of right and justice, where the individual sympathies which prevail in the family retire, and individuals only count as persons whose freedom stands in prescribed relation to the general law of the State. *Right* is the rule imposed by law upon the human will. *Justice* is the regulating and dispensing power which maintains and defends its enforcement in presence of human arbitrariness. Hence it is not only legislative, but also judicial and re-tributive. But the State is only the kingdom of *external* justice. Its commands are not directly moral. It says not only: you ought, but: you *must;* and is able to effect the fulfilment of its decrees by *force.* And though the neglect and transgression of its laws cannot be prevented, yet the magistrate beareth not the sword in vain (Rom. xiii. 4), but punishes the transgression. The State is not a human invention, but a divine *ordinance* (there is no magistracy [*Obrigkeit*] but of God, Rom. xiii. 1). This does not, however, exclude the fact that it is also a human ordinance ($\kappa\tau\iota\sigma\iota\varsigma$ $\dot{\alpha}\nu\theta\rho\omega\pi\iota\nu\eta$, 1 Pet. ii. 13); for its administration and execution have, by means of a long historical development, been entrusted to the hands of sinful men.

The State further proves itself a human ordinance by the fact that it is not, like the Christian Church, of divine *institution*. No State—except the Church-State of Israel, which was intended exclusively for that nation—can be referred to a special divine act, to which it owes its commencement. The origin of the earliest States is for the most part hidden in the obscurity of the past, and what we can ascertain concerning them shows us that, in contrast to the Christian Church, which had a perfect and sacred beginning, they all arose from imperfect beginnings. There is much in favour of the view, that the formation of the State arose from the family, from patriarchal conditions,—in other words, that some single individual who represented the highest authority in the family, some head of a family who had by his personal qualities attracted the admiration and confidence of many, extended his authority over the whole tribe, then over several tribes, who afterwards grew together into a nation. But history teaches us that States have also been formed, not by an authority originating in an individual, but through a union of several heads of families, of free, independent, prominent men, who formed a mutual offensive and defensive *alliance.* The Middle Ages offer us an evident example in the Norwegian colonization of Iceland, an example which at the same time brings to light the amount of truth contained in the otherwise untenable view which makes a social contract the foundation of the State. In investigating the origin of the State, we encounter both the monarchical and the republican principle. The monarchical is, however, the primitive and the most ancient; the republican, the derived, appearing in history as the contrast of the earlier.[1]

History, moreover, shows us that States have arisen not merely from imperfect, but also from criminal beginnings. We learn from Scripture that the first empire arose from usurpation (Gen. x. 8–10). Nimrod began to be a mighty one in the earth; he was a mighty hunter before the Lord, and the beginning of his kingdom was Babel. Nimrod signifies: Let us rebel! (*i.e.* against the Lord by founding a dominion for ourselves), and the name may have been given him by those who abhorred his violence. When he is called a mighty hunter, this may perhaps in the first place be under-stood of hunting properly so called, but it is not a far-fetched notion to see in this name, as Herder expressed it, an allusion to his being a mighty hunter of men, whom, both by force and stratagem, he may have allured, caught and enslaved. The idea that the origin of States was to be referred only to mighty men, conquerors, " rebels," who raised themselves into despots, was the prevailing one with the theologians of the Middle Ages, and has in modern times been advocated by papists, who hence infer, that the Pope has continually to intervene in protecting nations against tyrants, who desire to make might right. But though many constitutions bear the marks of Nimrod, viz. revolution and despotism, still history bears satisfactory testimony to the fact that conquest and violence have by no means been the sole road that has led to the foundation of States.

Although the State cannot be directly referred to divine institution, it is yet in its inmost nature a divine ordinance. It is founded upon an inward necessity—an idea which, however, could exercise no authority over the wills of men, unless a determination of the divine will were recognised in it. This was a truth which even the heathen felt more or less clearly, inasmuch as their obedience to the law of the State was, so to speak, overgrown with their faith in protecting and guiding deities. And the State being a divine ordinance, its origin as well as its continuance rests, in spite of human sinfulness, upon divine providence. For a multitude of very

---

[1] On the whole question, comp. Geijer's interesting and instructive treatise, *Der Feudalismus und der Republicanismus* (Saml. Schr. Div. 1, Vol. I.).

various forces and circumstances, not depending upon the will of man alone, must co-operate, if a State is to be formed and to endure for ages.

§ 40.

The State, as an ordinance of God upon earth, reminds us chiefly of the sin, arbitrariness, violence and crime, against which it is designed to provide a protective barrier and a restraint. Hence in the book of beginnings (Genesis) we read, that when God, after the deluge, established His covenant with Noah, He at the same time gave him the command, " Whoso sheddeth man's blood, by man shall his blood be shed ; for in the image of God made He man " (Gen. ix. 6). In this legal appointment, the oldest known to us, and pronounced as a divine command, we have an essential element of the State under patriarchal circumstances. It certainly does but state generally that *man* is to punish the murderer ; but the fact that no private vengeance on the part of the relatives of the murdered is spoken of, decidedly shows that *the magistracy* is referred to as the organ by which justice is to be administered. As God, immediately after the deluge, confirmed the natural ordinance of seed-time and harvest, cold and heat, day and night, and thus gave a promise that it should be maintained so long as the world endured, so did He at the same time lay down a legal ordinance for the maintenance of the human race. Older theologians, and Luther among them, have rightly found in this passage, if not the institution of the State, yet still the appointment of a magistracy. For if God bestows on man a power over life and death, He undoubtedly bestows upon him at the same time power over that which is less, and it is His will that human affairs should be subjected to the power of certain personal organs authorized to punish the guilty. Still we cannot stop at this definition, important as it is, and emphatically as it needs to be dwelt on at the present day, when a lax and irreligious humanity is only too much inclined to overlook or forget it, and to start from the demand that the State should only exist for the convenience of individuals, provide for their supposed benefit, and therefore release as many as possible from all kinds of restrictions. For the definition of the State is far more com-

prehensive than this, which would make it a mere barrier
to defend society against those criminal acts into which sin
breaks out, and which render social life impossible, unless they
are encountered not merely by the reaction of reason, but of
reason equipped with physical force. The duty of the State
is not confined to prevention and punishment, but includes also
that arranging and distributing justice which carries out
impartially the *suum cuique* in every relation of civil society.
The State comprehends the entire life of the nation, with all
the aims and efforts which have their foundation in the God-
given destiny of man, hence the family, trade, art, science, nay,
the Church itself. For it not only extends its protection,
within the boundaries of law, to all these circles and departments in their mutual relations to each other, but also, by its
wise care, cherishes and promotes these manifold possessions,
so far as this can be done by means of external arrangements.
It is true that in these days a one-sided individualistic theory,
deficient of any religious foundation, would limit the duty of the
State to securing the personal liberty of individuals, and providing for that mutual transaction of business which is inseparable therefrom. In so doing, this theory specifies, and that in an
insufficient manner, only what is barely necessary and indispensable in an orderly commonwealth. For it is perfectly
correct to say that property and personal freedom assume each
other as the first elements of common legislation. Without
property there is certainly no personal liberty. But as the
individual is not his own sole aim, but is also a *member*
of a greater whole, so property must not be regarded as
only private property. For even private property has also
a social side on which it must be regarded as pertaining also,
under certain limitations, to the property of the community.
This is shown, *e.g.*, in time of war, when *a country* is defended
against a foe, and when it is by no means certain personal
possessors or estates that are defended, but the territory
belonging to the whole nation, and inherited from its fore-
fathers.

The principle of law is fully developed only when the State,
not satisfied with taking under its protection the rights of
the individual, guards also the rights of the community and
its common employments, and consequently the circles and

institutions interwoven with them. These it not only protects, but also supports and promotes, thus showing itself to be the guardian justice of *the whole*. The State is not indeed itself to realize these duties and aims, for this would be to step beyond its boundaries. It must not, *e.g.*, interpose in the internal affairs of art, or science, or the Church, but must let these several powers follow their own nature and obey their own laws. It should, however, furnish those external conditions by which they may attain their own development, and co-operate in the task of the whole. This task is to exhibit, so far as possible, the manifold attributes of human nature in the individual form of a nation.

The State, as the region of external justice upon earth, has by this very character both an ethic and a physical side. Its physical side is power. A State without power is a non-entity; and States have from all times exhibited a tendency to increase their power. But the State only approximates to its ideal in proportion as the use of its power is determined by justice and law, and it is upon these that all real authority in the State depends. This is the ethic side of the State, for external justice is a form under which the ethic is manifested. External presupposes internal justice, and external acts, so far as they do not proceed from an inward disposition, are devoid of an animating principle.[1] Every relation between a government and its subjects must be founded upon mutual confidence and loyalty, and compulsory enactments at variance with the prevailing opinions of the majority will never take root. Without that moral foundation whose ultimate support is found in religion, power will inevitably be abused and get into impure hands.

---

[1] Trendelenburg, *Naturrecht auf dem Grunde der Ethik*, p. 20: "The spurious independence of the juridical, which was regarded as a scientific advance, not only distorted the theory of law, but also deprived it of its dignity, favoured mechanical views, and robbed the notion of law of all vitality."

THE NATIONAL STATE.

§ 41.

The State presupposes a nation and a country, and in union
with the nation and the country forms a realm in the political
meaning of the word.   A nation is an individual social
organism defined by nature, a joint body, which again is an
individual member of the great body of the human race, and
exhibits human nature on a small scale.   A perfect national
life cannot be led while a people is in a nomadic state, as in
the times of the migration of the nations, or of the wanderings of Israel in the wilderness.   Such a life must be passed
in the land in which the nation has its strictly defined abode,
its altar and domestic hearth.   Between the people and the
country there exists and developes during the course of ages
a relation of reciprocity, in consequence of which the country
receives in many respects, by means of culture, an impression
of the *national peculiarity;* while, on the other hand, the
national peculiarity and civilisation receive from their natural
surroundings a stamp which is reflected most especially in
popular legends and in the moods and images of all national
poetry.   National peculiarities are shown not only in the
physiognomy of a people,—as in the case of the Jews,—but
especially in their language and dialect.   Where we meet
with men of a strange tongue, there we also encounter other
nationalities.

As nationality is the natural basis of the State, so is it also
the condition of all human, all moral and mental development.   It is only in society that man, generally speaking,
can attain his appointed development; and those only who
belong to the same nation can have direct association with
and mutually understand each other.   And this not merely
by reason of their common wants and interests, but more
especially by means of their one common language, their
mother tongue—that indispensable condition of perfect mutual
communication and comprehension, whether in lower and
temporal or in higher and spiritual matters.   It is only by
means of speech that mutual intercourse can take place

between man and man ; only by means of speech can spirit communicate with spirit ; and even the Spirit of God—as Pentecost testifies, when men of every nation heard themselves addressed each in his own language—would, when establishing a communion between God and man, address men of every nation in their own mother tongue. Hence his nationality is an indispensable possession for each individual in the nation, and one which it is his duty to maintain, improve, and perfect.

§ 42.

But great as is the importance which we attribute to nationality, an individual nation cannot be sufficient to itself, and can only attain its destined development in co-operation with other races. Though nations at first repel each other, and national selfishness, arrogance and vanity, national hatred and wars are somewhat old in the history of the world, they nevertheless exercise an irresistible power of attraction upon each other. Not only do their physical, their so-called material wants, and those things which pertain to the ennoblement and embellishment of external existence, make nations, in the progress of culture and civilisation, increasingly dependent on each other, and bring them into relations of reciprocity, but their higher interests, art, science, religion, the Church, also create between them a relation of solidarity. Trade and navigation, the art of printing, the discoveries of science, which have given us, *e.g.*, railroads, steamships, and telegraphs, have powerfully contributed to promote *international* intercourse both in physical and intellectual respects. They have all contributed to the diffusion and establishment of a cosmopolitan sentiment, embracing the whole earth and the entire human race. This in its turn has caused the different nations to learn each other's languages, and thereby to be capable of mutually transposing themselves into each other's peculiarity, and has also led to the cultivation of *international* relations. The cosmopolitan sentiment, which an increasing international intercourse demands, though it must not indeed either obliterate or deaden patriotism, should yet appoint it its rightful boundaries. Certainly the individual nation must perform the fundamental duty of *self-assertion*, must maintain and stand up for its own God-given peculiarity, and never cast itself away by slavish imitation of foreigners. It should, however, be at the same time conscious that this alone is not the fulfilment of its duty as a nation. Of this it is capable only when, in conscious devotion to the general tasks of history, to the great common aims of the human race, it perceives itself to be an individual member of the great family of nations. The task of history does not devolve upon one or other single nation, but is the joint task of the whole human race, and can only be realized by the co-operation of all the nations who are qualified to participate in the historical development, that is, are possessed of constructive political talent. Each separate nation, even the most highly gifted, is affected by some limitation, some deficiency. Hence the different nations should, with respect to both their intellectual and material gifts, occupy towards each other a relation of mutual giving and taking. A nation which desires to learn nothing, to receive nothing from others, but in its self-glorification falls back upon and retires within itself, in time alienates itself more and more from what is of general human interest. And when it is sometimes asserted by certain fanatics for nationality, that a nation should not submit itself to the influence of other nations, lest it should thereby forfeit its own peculiarity, the question might be suitably asked, whether the kind of independence which is afraid of being lost by that contact with others also independent, which is according to the will of God, is of any special value? and whether a *genuine* independence is not attained by just this very reciprocity? For we cannot but esteem it an abnormal circumstance that any nation should, in its relation with others, be solely receptive, and in no respect also communicative.

We have already remarked that nationality is the natural basis of the State. The result of such a fact would seem to be that the people and the State, the national and the political elements, are co-extensive. This is, however, an inference not justified either by the actual state of affairs or by history, and one which must also be limited from a higher standpoint. In reality, we not infrequently find different nationalities included in one and the same State; and, again, different States possessing one and the same nationality. Such a relation may indeed be considered as somewhat unnatural, and the attempt may be made to sever the heterogeneous and combine the homogeneous. It will not, however, be possible entirely to obviate this mixed relation, because no single nation must regard itself as solely its own proper object, nor lose sight of the fact that it is at the same time a member of the great commonwealth of nations. Political conditions and relations are not founded upon nationality alone, they depend also upon the relative amount of power, and upon a combination of various interests. Each single nation gets involved in the movement of the whole and in the course of the world's history, which is not always a process of justice, and often demands national sacrifices. Different nationalities find themselves in different states in consequence of political complications. Nor can such a mixed condition be regarded as exclusively, and in all cases, an evil or a fatal necessity. There are certain countries which are naturally transition-lands, in which different nationalities meet and combine with each other with respect both to language and customs. And though the diverseness of the nationalities united in a single State may occasion much friction and contest, leading possibly to severance and separation, yet such nationalities may also, after having been during the course of a long common history more and more blended together by joint experiences and common adversity and prosperity, contribute to each other's strength and culture. They may consequently represent, in a special manner, the economy of the whole, the idea of *internationality*, and thereby contribute to the general development of the human race, in opposition to a one-sided, self-contained nationalistic tendency. A one-sided policy, which would determine the boundaries of States exclusively according to nationality, has found favour in these days. But this is to be explained by the character of the preceding period, in which nationality was looked on as a matter of indifference, and possessors of political power regarded nations as mere aggregates, to be considered from the view-point of "square miles, capability of taxation and military strength;" and which might, from considerations of expediency, be fitly combined, by piecing and patching, into new political conglomerates.

This one-sided national policy also finds its explanation in the first Napoleon's treatment of nationalities, and in his design of making "the great nation" the principle of civilisation for others, whose peculiarities he despised, mortified and ill-used, thereby revolting and exciting the popular mind against himself, and provoking the reaction of the nations themselves. It was the rising of Germany and its war of liberation—at the same time that Fichte and Schleiermacher were delivering their ever memorable discourses—which introduced a revival of nationality as an essential factor in the policy of States, a factor which the great emperor had utterly ignored. The natural consequence was, that to some this development served as an impulse to a new kind of one-sidedness. Nationality, which had hitherto been taken no account of in politics, was now to be everything. A policy, however, which calculates exclusively with the factor of nationality, and raises it to the foremost place, cannot be carried out, because a number of other factors, which limit and modify the national tendency, must inevitably be allowed for. A nation may, for example, be so small that the maintenance of its position as a State in a system of States is absolutely impossible, unless it is combined with a population of another nationality. In such a case the plan of reckoning according to square miles number of population, military strength, etc., has its advantage

§ 43.

If we next inquire as to the relation in which Christianity stands to nationality, we find it, in the first place, one of contrast; nay, at the first glance it might appear as though Christianity denied instead of acquiesced in national feelings and decisions. For Christianity insists rather on the universal than the national, breaks through national limitations, abolishes the separation between Jews and Samaritans, Jews and Gentiles, Greeks and Barbarians, and seeks in all the inner, the immortal man, whose vocation is in that kingdom which is not of this world. The apostles, the first confessors of Christ, forsook their native land and their own race to spread His kingdom in all the world, and lived as men who had no earthly home. What Christ had predicted of

Jerusalem was fulfilled. They had to behold their country and people, with the whole Jewish State, destroyed, to be everywhere but pilgrims and strangers, and to have their citizenship in heaven alone (though St. Paul on one special occasion appealed to his Roman citizenship to escape ill-treatment) (Acts xxii. 25). But this position, alien to nationality, this circumstance of living as a citizen of heaven, without a native land or home on earth, was by no means intended to be permanent. The kingdom of God was to be the leaven which should leaven the life of the world. Christ commanded His disciples to evangelize all nations, and bring them into the relation of discipleship (Matt. xxviii. 20), and declared that He would gather all nations to His judgment-seat (Matt. xxv. 32). The apostle says: "God has made of one blood all nations of men for to dwell on all the face of the earth, and hath determined the times before appointed, and the bounds of their habitation (arranged the periods of their historical development and the boundaries of their places of abode, prescribed to all the land which should be their home, and which their children should call the land of their fathers), that they should seek the Lord, if haply they might feel after Him and find Him" (Acts xvii. 26 sq.). This implies that nationalities also were as such to play their part in the economy of the kingdom of God. For a nation to become Christian, means that its heathen'sm and national selfishness are ended, and that it is to submit itself to the guidance and purification of the Spirit of Christ. It means that the nation is to partake, by Christian faith, of the blessings of the gospel, and under all dispensations, whether of weal or woe, to find in it a refuge and support. It means that the nation is to cultivate, under the fertilizing influences of the Spirit of Christ, the gifts God has bestowed upon it, the pound with which it has been entrusted, and thus to occupy its God-ordained position in the entirety of the human race, when all nations shall be comprised under Christ in one Christendom. Hence the relation of Christianity to nationality is not only a purifying, but a cultivating or perfecting one.

It is the task of every nation which has placed itself under the educational influence of Christianity, to know its own peculiarity, to cultivate and perfect it so far as it is good and imparted by God, and to resist it so far as it is sinful. This is a knowledge as difficult to nations as to individuals, for it is by no means an uncommon occurrence for a nation to be under the illusion that it has a vocation for something for which it has absolutely no vocation, and that it possesses powers of which it is devoid, while neglecting to cultivate those really bestowed upon it,—an illusion with which a misconception of its historical situation is generally combined. Hence it is one special duty of those who are the leaders and teachers of the people, to help to cultivate a feeling and perception of their national peculiarity, whether in its good or its evil aspect. In all ages it has been the characteristic of false prophets to flatter the people, and represent their faults in an ideal light, while true prophets have ever sharply criticized their sins. On this account they have—though posterity may have garnished their sepulchres—always been unpopular with their contemporaries, nay, have suffered the lot of Cassandra. When, *e.g.*, the true prophets of Israel, in those dangerous times when the State was on the brink of ruin, warned the nation, in virtue of the enlightened view of the position of the kingdoms of the world accorded to them, not to enter into a conflict with the superior power of the enemy, and exhorted them to humble themselves before God, and to bow patiently beneath His dispensations, who had for a time given dominion to the hand of the heathen world-ruler, declaring at the same time that their day and hour would also come; when they preached : " In returning and rest shall ye be saved" (Isa. xxx. 15), the multitude hearkened far more willingly to the words of the false prophets, who flattered their national pride, confirmed them in their vanity and independence, dazzled them with vain hopes, and invited them to rash enterprises and delusive alliances.

§ 44.

It is only by means of Christianity that nationalities can attain the development to which they are really appointed. Without Christianity, " the principle of nationality," so constantly in men's mouths, nay, so idolized in these days, is both insecure and ambiguous, and in itself utterly insufficient for political culture, and for culture in general. The ambiguity of this principle, which designates both those gifts of God, which must be maintained and defended, and the merely human, nay, the ungodly characteristics, which must be resisted, is specially apparent when we go back to the origin of nationalities. We cannot, indeed, avoid entertaining the notion, that the national individualities, which were, according to God's plan, originally comprised in the unity of the one human race, should have developed themselves, after a duly organized fashion, from that unity. But the sacred tradition deposited in the Book of Genesis (ch. xi.) informs us, that the nations by no means came forth from this unity in an organized manner, but by a violent dispersion. We are told that, in the beginning, there was but one race and one language, which leads to the assumption that there was also but one consciousness of God; for only the same consciousness of God, only the One God present in the consciousness, could keep all together as a unity. But that a change in this their relation to the One God had occurred, is plainly shown in this ancient record. For it is said that men came to the resolution of building a city and a tower, and this for the purpose of not being scattered abroad on the face of the earth. They desired by the building of the tower, whose top should reach unto heaven, at Babel, to make themselves a *name;* to erect an enduring monument upon earth. And the ancient document evidently regards this as a sinful proceeding, as Titanic arrogance and rebellion against the One God. Their dread of dispersion shows that, in the inmost consciousness of their spirits, a shock had taken place, a declension from the One God (and therefore from monotheism) had already set in, that polytheistic notions were already excited, that many gods, *i.e.* the world-powers, had found entrance into their hearts, and were banishing therefrom the One God. In the midst, however, of this *internal* commotion and dispersion, when new powers, new rulers, were taking possession of their souls, which were increasingly surrendered to them, they were made uneasy by their severance and separation from the one Being, and defiantly sought an *external* tie to keep them together. Thus it came to pass that the Lord came down and confounded the languages of men, and, by an external act of sovereignty, caused an external separation and dispersion. Tongues and speeches were coufounded, as a testimony to the inward confusion of minds. And now arose "the nations," the different fragments of the unity, which forthwith departed one from another in all directions, every people with its language, which was severed from the central, the divine word, which had formerly united, but now departed from them. The mythological process now produced polytheism, in other words, national religions made their appearance, each nation becoming possessed of gods of its own. We cannot, however, conceive of the matter otherwise than by assuming, that though the occurrence itself was a sudden one, its effects extended over a longer period. The nations were dispersed in the different countries, each as its prevailing desires and inclinations prompted it to seek one or another region. The variety which should have been developed in an organized and harmonious manner from unity, assumed more and more the appearance of an unnatural rupture. The nations became increasingly alien and incomprehensible to each other, and in their selfish isolation, their mutual attitude became increasingly hostile. One people only, viz. the descendants of Abraham, was separated by God's special call and election from this split and confused mass, and educated to maintain communion with the one true God, in opposition to the polytheistic heathen ($\check{\epsilon}\theta\nu\eta$), with their confused dialects, separated from the divine word. It would lead us too far to consider in more detail the old tradition preserved to us in Genesis. We refer all who would more thoroughly investigate this subject to Schelling's introduction to his *Philosophie der Mythologie*, which is allowed to contain whatever has been most profoundly thought and said on the subject, and has, at all events, taken a deeper view of the problem than any previous work. We would here only mention the fact, that the notion of the nation and the national, regarded from the view-point in question, includes not only the idea of what is given and ordered by God, but also that of apostasy from God, of the *heathen* element, which places the creature above the Creator, nature above God, of severance and departure in selfish isolation, of mutual inaccessibility. and unintelligibility. According to revelation, " the nations," the confusion of tongues and polytheism, are inseparable ideas. It is part of the vocation of Christianity to redeem the nations from this disruption, to transform a relation of disunion into one of organization, to combine and unite the nations, to make each accessible and intelligible to the rest. This it is to effect by awakening in them the true consciousness of God, by re-uniting the various languages with the one divine word, by assembling and comprising the nations under the new Adam, who, as the head of the human race, restores their internal unity. This vocation of Christianity was plainly announced by the Pentecostal miracle, the contrast to the confusion of Babel. Each nation was here addressed in its own tongue; and it was the new language of Christianity which spoke in the various tongues, and united the various nations, by collecting all in the one holy Catholic Church of Christ.

The condition, then, of this redemption of the nations being their thorough purification, both morally and religiously, in the intellectual purgatory of a sharp and really effective criticism, it might be thought that it must be evident to every one how impracticable it is, without further ceremony, without the application of criticism, to combine and revive nationality and Christianity, mythology, *e.g.* northern mythology, and Christianity, and thus to introduce an obscure non-critical confusion, tending only to adulterate the peculiarities of both nationality and mythology, and not less so of Christianity itself. It may be of importance to the development of the national self-consciousness for a people to look back with appreciation and fondness at its mythology, inasmuch as it may therein recognise the ideals of its infancy and youth; but it is these very ideals which must be *judged* by Christianity before we can determine how far they have any other or greater significance for us than that of prehistoric and poetic memorials.

THE CHRISTIAN STATE.

§ 45.

Humanity is above nationality, indeed the latter is only a natural form in which the former is realized. And the national State which would not withdraw in heathen isolation —which would also involve its having a religion of its own differing from that of all other nations—must withal recognise and manifest itself as a *state of humanity* (*Humanitätsstaat*). This signifies more than a *state of culture* (*Culturstaat*), since the inmost and deepest interest of humanity is not culture, but morality and religion. Humanity can neither be delivered from its limitations, nor come to a true knowledge of itself, without Christianity; and it is only under its influence that it can reach its full and true development. Moreover, every notion of humanity which is not the Christian one, is more or less affected with falsehood. Hence the truly humanistic State is one and the same with the Christian State.

The Christian State is a notion which excites much opposition in these days, and many avoid, nay, are ashamed of admitting its validity or acknowledging that they hold it. The revolting impression given by the many abuses formerly connected with it, and the influence of the ruling spirit of the age, have caused the whole idea to be regarded as a great mistake, and the question to be asked, Since the kingdom of Christ is not of this world, what has Christianity to do with the State or with politics? But it might with equal reason be asked, What has Christianity to do with nations? And one answer is, that it is designed not only to redeem and bless individual souls, but also to make nations Christian, to bring them in their entirety into the relation of discipleship, to place them under the influence of its educational operations. And this is to admit that its design is also to evangelize and influence States, legislative bodies and institutions, by means of which popular life can alone attain its form and fulness. Generally speaking, nothing is more unreasonable than the view that the State, the most comprehensive of all earthly institutions, and one which so decidedly plays a chief part in the world's history, should be withdrawn from the influences of Christianity, and thus excluded from that transformation of things temporal which Christianity is designed to effect. The necessity for the Christian character of States is mainly founded on the fact that the State does not exist for the sake of this or that subordinate aim, but for the sake of human nature itself, that its vocation is to furnish and work out all those external conditions which are indispensable to the general development of human culture and prosperity. It is for this very reason that there can be no constitution or government worthy the name which is not pervaded by a thorough understanding of the nature and destination of man, of the history of the race and the ultimate object of human history. This ultimate object is above the State, nay, reaches beyond the sphere of the State; but the State must nevertheless regard itself as a means subservient thereto, and should in all its institutions keep it in view as a last resort. The object of the State will ever be erroneously viewed, so long as it is not consciously placed in relation with the object and aim of the human race. This, however, brings us back to the world of moral and religious ideas, the world of *revelation*, for it is this which shows us the principles which are fundamentally determinative for all human existence, and also in very deed *norm - giving* for States and politics, as teaching how rightly to estimate the goods of this life, the various tasks of human existence, tasks in whose fulfilment the State must also bear its part, and for whose due estimation it needs a supreme and trustworthy standard. It is, for instance, undeniable that a very different estimation is accorded to marriage and the family when the State starts from the Christian view, according to which the kingdom of God is the one supreme aim of mankind, to that which it obtains from the heathen view, in which the State itself is the supreme good, the highest aim of mankind and everything else (as in the Platonic Republic), the mere instrument of the State. Again, the necessity for the Christianization of States rests upon the circumstance that the State is the realm of external justice. But external justice cannot be carried out or administered without internal justice; in other words, without a religious and moral disposition, by which alone it can come to pass that the laws are obeyed not from fear of punishment, but for conscience' sake. Such a disposition, too, will alone make men capable of self-denial and self-sacrifice for the good of the community, and this again brings us back to Christianity, which, with its heavenly citizenship, makes us truly fit for citizenship in this world.

The importance, then, of Christianity to State and polity by no means consists merely in the direct utterances of the gospel on the subject. These are chiefly limited to its certainly weighty and fundamental characterization of the State as a divine ordinance, and to the demand of obedience and justice therewith combined : " to render unto Cæsar the things that are Cæsar's, and to God the things that are God's " (Matt. xxii. 21).   Its far-reaching importance lies not so much in its directly political assertions, as in that *supra*-political or meta-political element which it introduced into the world, by which we mean that which precedes the political as its pre-supposition, that which lies outside and beyond it as its aim and object, and by which the political element is to be pervaded as by its soul, its intellectually vivifying principle. The metapolitical consists in the duly proportioned view of *man*, of human nature and of the ultimate object of human life ; and the true metapolitic is, in our opinion, that Christian view of the world and of life which throws an entirely new light upon the State, by placing it in relation with a kingdom which is not of this world, and thus forcing it to recognise its own position as a mere *medium*, as destined to subserve this more exalted kingdom.   It was indeed a misconception of Bossuet to write a polity ,to be extracted from the Bible (*Politique tirée de la Sainte Ecriture*), obliging him, as it did, to have recourse chiefly to the Old Testament, whose theocratic polity was adapted only to the Jewish people and their peculiar position.   We must, however, by no means overlook the fact that the history of Israel has a *typical* significance, and exhibts to us, under many varying aspects, the truth, that a nation enjoys peace and prosperity as long as it cleaves to God, but falls into trouble and ruin, and becomes the prey of foreigners, when it departs from Him, and hence that nationality cannot be self-sufficing, that it is not capable of independently going its own way.   In any case, however, we are almost challenged, by the proposals from time to time renewed, to set up a meta-politic science of the suprapolitical, of the nature and destiny of man, and of the aim of history especially with relation to the State.   And for the fundamental ideas of such a science the Scriptures would certainly be the first and special source. Many chief points of the Book of Genesis, and especially the 11th chapter, which treats of the origin of nations,[1] must be

---

[1] Constant. Franz, *Die Naturlehre des Staates als Grundlage aller Staats-wissenschaft*, 1870, p. 145.

included in the sphere of its considerations. As there can be no physics without metaphysics, so neither can there be political without metapolitical science, consciously or unconsciously making itself an inevitable necessity; and if the true is not adopted, the false must be. Machiavelli and Napoleon both adopted a fatalistic metapolitic. In our days there are politicians whose metapolitic embraces the view that man is only an intelligent animal, and that the object of human life is bounded by this world, and is mainly to be found in the satisfaction of the material interests. What results will accrue to the State when politicians with such a metapolitic debate and vote on school and Church questions, or on marriage legislation, cannot be doubtfuL

<h2 align="center">§ 46.</h2>

Proceeding from the assumption that no State can exist without moral ideas, which in their turn rest upon religious ideas, whether true or false, we define the Christian State as that whose fundamental moral ideas are determined by Christianity, as that which finds its most determining, and therefore its suprapolitical impulses and ideas in the Christian view of life and of the world. In this view the kingdom of God among men is the centre and aim of history, and the State is a mere instrument for the development and promotion of the kingdom of God and mankind on earth. Or the Christian State may be defined as that which knows no better or more trustworthy postulate for civil virtue than the disposition which has its roots in Christianity, and which it therefore strives to cherish and propagate by all the means at its disposaL It must indeed be admitted that the manner in which the Christian view of life and of the world, as well as the use to be made of it, has at different times and under different circumstances been understood and practised, exhibits no small variety. In this respect we need only mention how much the Christian State of the Middle Ages differs from that of the Reformation, and how far Calvin's ideas of the Christian State and those of the Puritans deviate from those of Luther. Nevertheless the Christian State remains under all its forms essentially unlike any other, by reason of the *suprapolitical* principle on which it is founded. This principle, however much it may be modified in different confessions, maintains a unique character, which cannot be mistaken even in those political formations which present us with only caricatures of the Christian State.

The Protestant State, so far as it still maintains its Christian character, and has not sunk to the level of a liberalistic and rationalistic state of humanity (*Humanitätsstaat*), generally exhibits its specific character in protecting and supporting the national Church of its own confession, and in promoting the Christianity of the people by the maintenance of Christian customs and usages (*e.g.* by the institution of Sundays and Holy Week). It manifests it also by care for the education of the people in Christian schools, by guarding the sacredness of marriage, and by impressing on its laws and institutions the general ideas and principles of Christianity. But if it is the duty of the Christian State to promote, as far as it can by external arrangements, the kingdom of God, as the kingdom of redemption, it is also bound to pay due regard to the just claims of emancipation (comp. General Part, § 159–162 : " Redemption and Emancipation "), and to organize a system of religious liberty and freedom of speech in harmony with existing circumstances. *Religious liberty*, as vindicating the rights of personality, of free self-determination in matters of conscience and salvation, is demanded by Christianity itself. It must, however, be granted only in such proportion as it has become a real necessity, and must especially find expression in *laws concerning Dissenters* corresponding to actual circumstances. An unlimited and entirely unregulated religious liberty, inviting, so to speak, sects of every possible variety to settle in the land, and to act as they please, is an evidence rather of religious indifference than of true toleration.

§ 47.

How far the Christian State can be a fact, depends chiefly on whether the " Christian nation " is a fact. By this it is not meant that vital personal Christianity must be possessed by all, but that the nation should on the whole bow to the authority of Christian tradition, and occupy towards it a position of discipleship, though but an elementary and incipient one. In these our days, however, an emancipation has taken place within Christian nations, not merely from illegal restraints, but from Christianity itself, whose authority it is desired to throw off. Among many not only of the higher, but also of the lower classes of society, faith is undermined, and souls are being endangered by doubt and indifference. In place of the gospel of Jesus Christ, the modern gospels of humanism and happiness, with their rationalistic, naturalistic and materialistic doctrines, have found acceptance in extensive circles.

In declaring unbelief and the religionless humanism combined therewith to be the chief powers engaged in that process of dissolution now evidently going on to no small extent in the Christian State and Christian nationality, we are constrained to bring forward with still stronger emphasis one essential characteristic of the times, viz. that *spurious, irreligious,* and *immoral (non-ethic) individualism,* which at the same time appears as a doctrine, a form of antinomianism. This element of the ruling tendency of the age depicts to us the peculiar fashion in which the process of dissolution is taking place. There exists not only a one-sided religious individualism, which is undermining the Christian State, and exercising a solvent effect upon national unity, by splitting it up into a variety of sects and small church parties; there is also an irreligious and non-moral individualism, which is by its very nature selfishness, a system of opinion and practice which consciously and formally lays down the doctrine, that the earthly prosperity of the individual is the highest reality. This modern repetition of heathen Eudæmonism, of the heathen search after enjoyment, which has in our days attained terrible extent and diffusion, and fearfully increased in strength, has become a power as pernicious in operation upon the Church as upon the State, a power destructive of all that presents an appearance of organization. In the intellectual world this egoism acknowledges nothing to which it should be subject, but takes up a negative or sceptical position towards everything, regards all persuasions concerning things divine as mere " views," " standpoints " and " private opinions," of equal value and equally legitimate, because it considers nothing universally binding, and recognises nothing as possessing an authority to which all must bow. In *political* respects, this individualism would have the State confine itself to being an institution whose only object it should be to protect the interests of individuals, an institution concerning itself indeed with all that pertains to personal security and material prosperity, but not venturing to . use its authority for enforcing general moral aims and duties. Hence it desires to relegate religion, art and science to the sphere of private life. In *social* respects, in all that concerns the relations between man and man, it manifests itself in an infinite number of ramifications, in the circumstance that individuals, instead of acknowledging their solidarity as members of one body, instead of appropriating to themselves that apostolic saying, that if "one member suffers, all the members suffer with it " (1 Cor. xii. 26), confront each other as " self-reliant, independent " personalities. It shows itself in the maxim, " Every one his own neighbour," in the fact that humanity and sympathy are only shown by mere abstention from opposing others in their care for their material interests. It is seen in arrangements tending as far as possible to a release from *mutual obligations*, in the *laisser faire* and *laisser aller* maintained on all sides, though with the indispensable limitation naturally arising from the fact that this principle applies to all, that each may therefore profit by it, unobstructed by others. That we should, on the contrary, interest ourselves by loving help in the affairs of others, that we should disinterestedly assist each other, nay, make sacrifices for this purpose, and especially that we should be capable of self-sacrifice for some great common moral aim, to whose realization each should hold himself subservient, all this is, from this standpoint, out of the question. Social selfishness has, under the ægis of liberalism, attained in our days special development, and been greatly increased both by the progress of natural science and the rule over nature therewith combined, and by the ever-increasing development of industry and capital. The opinions in question, which set up *the earthly mammon and earthly enjoyment as the supreme object,* and are consequently destructive to all the higher interests of life, are being more and more widely diffused. For this object it is that men are competing, to this goal that their untiring and passionate pursuit is directed. They desire to be rich, and fall thereby "into temptation and a snare, and many foolish and hurtful lusts" (1 Tim. vi. 9). They require not only sensual, but in a certain sense also intellectual satisfaction for their selfishness, and are wont to bestow an ideal designation on the objects of their restless aspirations, and call them "the blessings of culture and civilisation." The characteristic, however, of these blessings is always, that they are but temporal and earthly, and are only prized as such. For from this standpoint art and science are not valued for their own sakes, but merely as an additional adornment, a decoration of this earthly life of sense. The aim striven for is to have circumstances as pleasant, easy and secure as possible in this world. As for heaven, and the kingdom which is not of this world, such persons desire to have nothing to do with it. They wish to breathe only the air of earth and things temporal, and to have it perfumed with the fragrance of culture; the atmosphere of eternity is too keen for them. Such opinions and dispositions being incompatible with Christianity, we find them assuming towards it in many respects a polemical attitude. Especially is this the case with respect to the Christian State, because therein Christianity asserts its authority in public life and its institutions. Many as are the other destructive forces actively engaged in the dissolution and dechristianization of the Christian State, these opinions are among the most important. They have found acceptance not only among the possessors of property, who have the means of procuring enjoyments, but also among the classes who are destitute of such means, and who, full of malevolence towards those more highly favoured, are longing for the gratifications they enjoy. This tendency numbers many followers among the baptized, among those who, calling themselves Christians, are labouring through this *their heathenism* at the work of destruction. It has also at its command a powerful representation in *modern Judaism,* which has in these days begun to play so great a part in Christian countries, and which must be reckoned among the decided and irreconcilable opponents of the Christian State.

§ 48.

Our reason for bringing forward modern Judaism among the forces at work for the dissolution of the Christian State and of Christian nationality, and for expatiating upon it at some length, is, that in any case a new power has in it appeared upon the stage, on which it was formerly unable to play any part. For the position of the Jews in Christendom was formerly one of oppression ; nor can it be denied that they suffered at the hand of Christians, especially during the Middle Ages, much hardship and ill-treatment, to which, however, they gave but too much occasion by their usury and extortion. In the succeeding period they were *tolerated*, and obtained civil rights. Then came the prevalence of the principles of the French Revolution, and of a liberalism based thereon, when political rights were granted to all without distinction and without regard to religion, when so many of the bonds of society were dissolved, and all relations pervaded by individualism. In this state of affairs the Jews received a degree in civil society, and entered upon a course in which they could act aggressively against Christendom. We are not here speaking of orthodox Talmudistic Jews, but of the preponderating majority of modern Jews, who have entirely alienated themselves from the religion of their fathers, without, however, having on that account given up their national pretensions. The religion of these modern Jews consists essentially in the cosmopolitan principles of the French Revolution respecting the universal rights of men, and the ideals of culture and civilisation therewith combined. Having completely imbibed these, they now declare them to be the true contents or spirit of Judaism, as the genuine religion of humanity, from the realization of which they expect an earthly Messianic kingdom, a kingdom of earthly prosperity, in which the children of Israel will, both by the power of capital and that of speech, intellect and culture, give the keynote, be the leading influence, and exercise supremacy over all other nations. among whom Christianity is becoming

more and more an effete matter, which they have long
outlived. For, that the people of Israel are to exercise
dominion over all other nations, that their nationality
represents, as it were, the royal nationality, to which all
others stand in a relation of vassalage, is a view which they
have by no means discarded with the other traditions of their
nation. On the contrary, they have in these days made a very
effective beginning for the exercise of this supremacy, by
possessing themselves of three instruments of power, which
exercise a decided influence on the entire social and political
condition. These are capital, admission into legislative
assemblies, and finally the press. By capital they bring their
influence to bear on political matters, even with respect to
peace or war. In legislatures they even combine with
liberalism, and vote for the entire separation of Church and
State, for the refusal of money contributions to Church
purposes, for civil marriage, and other liberal proposals. And
the newspaper press is in several of the chief countries of
Europe mainly in the hands of Jews, who, by talented and
brilliantly written articles, manufacture public opinion on all
the questions of the times, nay, determine it even when
disputes between Christian confessions, between Ultramontanism and Protestantism, pope and emperor, are the order of
the day—of course deciding all from a Jewish standpoint.
A modern Jewish literature has already been developed and
propagated in extensive circles, which diffuses in all possible
manners, as a thing which only the uneducated, or those who
have remained at an obsolete standpoint, can either deny or
dispute,—the view that the climax of literature and its noblest
blossoms are not to be found in *Schiller* and *Goethe* and the other
heroes of modern humanism, but in Heine, Börne, and similar
Jewish authors, who vindicate the rights of free thought
against that narrowness of Christianity from which those
heroes cannot be wholly absolved. Lessing is, in their
estimation, the most illustrious man of the earlier period of
humanity, because he was the author of *Nathan der Weise*.
The supreme object of all these efforts is the before-mentioned
Judæo-Messianic kingdom of humanity. And one main condition upon which its attainment depends is none other than
that Christianity should be thrust out of public life. For this

object, the entire banishment of Christianity from public life, from legislation and from public institutions, and the snapping of all the ties by which nations are united to Christ, they labour consistently night and day. And this they do because the Messiah, in whom Christians believe, but whom the Jews rejected and crucified, is always an insufferable stumbling-stone in the way of their efforts, because the confession of Him by the nations, because laws and institutions bearing any kind of testimony to His sway and His kingdom, are an offence to them, and give them an impression of reproof and censure. That this Messiah is a false Messiah, His kingdom illusory, is the delusion under which they have lived from the times of their fathers, the dream whose realization they are concerned to promote. In this dream they are powerfully supported by the declension which has appeared in Christendom itself, and by all that folly and baseness so plentifully found among Christians, to which they delight to appeal. For the purpose of realizing their ideal, they combine, as we have said, with liberalism, and preach in every key the gospel of *toleration*, by which they mean that all religious confessions are to be matters of *indifference* in political and social life. Under the name of toleration they labour to do away with all religious and ecclesiastical distinctions, and especially with the various privileges depending thereon, seek to relegate Christianity entirely to private life, and to reduce its importance to that of a merely individual matter, and desire, especially, that access to all offices of the State without exception, *e.g.* the judicial, should be open to all, and subject to no religious conditions. They wish to have Christian instruction banished from public schools, and will at most allow the teaching of a deistic religion and general moral notions, without the addition of anything of a positively dogmatic nature. They desire that the name of Jesus should be named in public schools only as that of an historical personage, but not as the only name whereby men can be saved, inasmuch as this would involve annoyance to Jews, a concession which has, by the help of liberalism, been already made in Holland. The Jews have also concluded an alliance with national liberalism, nay, have on certain occasions even supported the efforts of nationality. This, however, they evidently do, not for the sake of nationality itself, but only in the name of individualistic liberty, which they hope thereby to promote. For their efforts in and of themselves are of as purely a cosmopolitan character as were the "rights of men" in the French Revolution. For nationalities themselves, viz. those of Gentiles and Gentile-Christians, with their historical memories, and for their institutions, which bear the impress of their historical origin, they feel no kind of interest. They are not really at home, that is, not in heart and mind, in any nation, although they appropriate with great facility the language and the prevailing manners and customs of daily life in each and all. They can wander from nation to nation, and can in an every-day external sense get on and feel at home anywhere, provided they find *individual liberty and free competition.* It is for these that their heart beats most warmly, while the weal or woe of other nations touches them but externally. They feel themselves a nation in contrast to "the nations" (Goiim) of heathen origin, and maintain the feeling of their superiority, even if it be acknowledged by none but themselves. And if they sometimes also manifest both civil and unalloyed human virtues, still it has been repeatedly noticed, that in periods of great historical crises, which have been decisive of a nation's destiny for life or death, when the hearts of all have been hovering between hope and fear, the Jew has composedly gone on with "business matters," and, "cool to the very heart," has been able to calculate with wonderful judiciousness the rise and fall of the stocks, and to devote himself heart and soul to the speculations connected with them. We can therefore only regard it as a mistake to have granted to Jews, without restriction, the same rights as to the children of the soil. They live among every people only as guests, and should as such be treated with all humanity. But however cordial the welcome given to a guest, no one thinks of making him co-ruler of his house. The Jews have now become, in virtue of the principles of liberalism, nay, of national liberalism, as well as by their enormous wealth, the ruling class in society, and are evidently aiming at a still further extension of their power.[1] In this matter, however, the motto, *Respice*

<hr>

[1] Comp. J. de la Roi, Stephan Schultz, *Ein Beitrag zum Verständniss der Juden und ihrer Bedeutung für das Leben der Völker (Die Judenfrage in der*

finem, finds its application.   All excess meets with its counter-action.   The secular adversary of the Jews is the same which liberalism has to encounter, viz. socialism.   And they may not be in the wrong, who think that when the dreadful day arrives in which socialism and communism will for a short time be in power, it will be seen how little their spurious emancipation has profited the Jews, and that when the great persecution of the opulent breaks out, the Jews will, in all probability, be the first sacrifices.

§ 49.

But the *respice finem* must be understood in a deeper and farther-reaching sense.   We know from the prophetic word that God has not cast away His people, and that His gifts and callings are without repentance (Rom. xi. 29); that after a long period of obduracy there will be at the end of the days, at the close of the world's history, a regeneration of the people of Israel, which, in its effects upon the rest of the world, will be as life from the dead (Rom. xi. 15).   In a certain sense, then, a superiority does belong to this people in history, not only because at their first beginning theirs was the adoption and the glory, the covenant and the promise, and because Christ descended from them after the flesh (Rom. ix. 4), but also because they are the people who, when their obduracy of more than a thousand years' duration is at last softened in the furnace of tribulation, are to give to the world a last great testimony, to make a last powerful pro-clamation of the Saviour whom they crucified, and whom, while the veil was on their eyes, they so long mistook and persecuted.   They will then, to the disgrace of the unbelieving

Gegenwart, p. 168 sqq.).   Const. Franz, *Der Nationalliberalismus und die Judenschaft.*   Even an esteemed author of the Liberal party, R. Mohl, considers the bestowal of political rights upon the Jews premature.   He supports this opinion mainly by "the double nationality of the Jews."   A Jew may be a German, an Englishman, etc., but he is above all a Jew.   There are, however, functions in the State which demand an undivided patriotism, the whole, not merely the half of a man.   Of course, he does not think that under the present state of affairs the rights already conceded to them can be resumed.   "The wine is drawn," he writes, "and must be drunk" (Mohl's *Politik,* II., *Die Judenemancipation,* p. 673 sqq., in the interesting section, "Uebereiltes, Unbedachtes und Unfertiges in der Tagespolitik").

and apostatized Gentile Christians, like the converted Paul, confess Him as the Son of the Living God, and openly preach Him with demonstration of the Spirit and of power. Then will be fulfilled the words spoken by the Lord on His departure from the temple at Jerusalem: "I say unto you, Ye shall not see me henceforth till ye say, Blessed be He that cometh in the name of the Lord" (Matt. xxiii. 39). As yet, however, a blindness and obduracy, still on the increase, endure; and if we ask how we are to conceive of the manner in which the change one day to take place can be possible, we certainly have nothing but a presentiment to appeal to. Still we believe that they are not far from right, who think that the persecutions which will in the latter days set in against this people, as reactions against their sway over the other nations, will furnish the impetus thereto.

§ 50.

We have entered with somewhat of detail into the position of the nation of Israel, because it is not possible to attain to a correct understanding of other nations so long as we lose sight of that one which from the first has formed a contrast to them, and especially because a full appreciation of the process of dissolution now evidently taking place among Christian States is quite impossible if this essential factor is not taken into account. When we, however, direct our attention to *all* the forces which combine to bring about this result, to the various forms of unbelief, of spurious humanitarianism and individualism, and consider the influence which these forces have already exercised upon the constitution, legislation, and institutions of States, we cannot fail to be persuaded that it is only in a very limited sense that our present States can still be called Christian. While their traditions, laws and institutions, their manners and customs, show themselves to have been in many respects influenced and determined by the principles of Christianity, it is at the same time evident that other more recently accepted principles, hostile to, or at least widely divergent from, Christianity, have exercised a determining influence upon them. Thus, then, have modern constitutional governments emancipated them-

selves, by means of universal suffrage, by non-religious legislatures, and equally non-religious and creedless ministers,
from the authority of Christianity, as of a thing which may
properly be dispensed with when the government of realms
and kingdoms, or the enaction of laws for the regulation of
national life, is in question. On the other hand, the necessity
and authority of Christianity are acknowledged by the appointment that the king must profess the Christian religion. The
attitude of most governments with relation to the idea of the
Christian State is one of hesitation ; they neither dare to give
it emphatic authority nor to dismiss it altogether. Their
principles and themselves being eminently on the side of
liberalism and individualism, it is individual freedom which
in religious respects they assist and favour. One restraint
after another is loosened and dissolved, and the maxim of
laissez faire and *laissez aller* is applied also in the province of
religion. On the other hand, there is a consciousness, or at
least an obscure feeling, that the State cannot dispense with
the Church, which prevents men from venturing to carry out
the separation of Church and State. Hence the old traditions
and institutions continue to be upheld, while the process of
dissolution is at the same time quietly allowed to go on.
The assertion that such States are Christian might with equal
justice be either affirmed or denied.

If it is asked, then, what are the future prospects of the
Christian State ? a twofold possibility, as so often happens in
history, presents itself in this case also. Either a revolution
in thought and feeling, produced by a nearer and clearer view
of the abyss which has been arrived at, will take place in the
Christian people, among whom a large amount of vigorous
conservatism still exists and operates,—and then, as a result
of this revolution, a revival, a renewal of Christian political
institutions, whereby the destructive forces will be so arrested,
restricted and confined within due bounds, that a just limitation will be set to individualism by the whole, and by a
regard to the welfare of the whole. Or, on the other hand,
the dissolution now in process will hold on its course ; governments, nay, monarchy itself, will be more and more involved
therein ; Christianity will increasingly retire from public life,
the nations will be to a greater and greater extent unchris-

tianized, and their national peculiarities will be from day to day obliterated and exterminated by abstract humanitarian notions and a Jewish power at once material and mental. Then, sooner or later, a socialist revolution, in which the Jews will play a chief part, will break out in consequence of the strife between possessors and non-possessors of property; and, after the waters of the deluge have abated, a new social formation will appear. Amid all these eventualities we cannot, for our part, cease to regard " the Christian people " and " the Christian State " as normal, or as that which ought to be and must be, and for whose preservation and development it is a duty to labour. That a different state of things actually exists cannot shake our persuasion. Christian ethics cannot, without further ceremony, regard the actual as the reasonable, even at the risk of seeing its demands regarded as Utopian.

THE STATE AND THE CIVIL COMMUNITY.

The Classes.

§ 51.

Within the province of the State, and under its control as the all-directing power, is developed the civil community. At the first view this seems to be a mere association, an external combination of individuals among a people for the mutual supply of their common wants. But this association, when considered according to its true nature, is a communion, —in other words, it is not a merely external, but an *organic* combination, arising not from choice alone, but also from a natural necessity, from an organizing power independent of the several individuals. On the one hand, the individuals acknowledge the family union, and bear also the same national stamp,—unless, as in the case of America, the civil association consists for the most part of immigrants belonging to widely differing nations; on the other, a " division of labour," for the supply of the manifold material and intellectual requirements, is an essential necessity, and hence arises a multiplicity of activities for the attainment of the various moral aims which work together for the all-embracing aim of humanity. According to these various activities, mankind is divided into different *classes*. They who belong to the same class have the same vocation, and consequently similar interests, opinions, culture and mode of living, *i.e.* are, generally speaking, of a common type. Classes are not castes, that is to say, unchangeable appointments of nature, to which men are bound from age to age, and from one of which there can be no transition to another. But as little can they be regarded as the work of mere human caprice. On the contrary, together with the development of the national life itself, they were formed by a union of liberty and necessity. Without different classes, a people would remain an indiscriminate gelatinous kind of mass, and the civil community be degraded into an association of atomistic individuals. The civil community, then, is not a mere combination of individuals, families, communes, but a union of the different classes in their interaction and co-operation. It is only by the means of his class that the individual stands in relation with the State.[1]

To whatever extent the French Revolution, with its abstract principles of liberty and equality, aimed at annihilating classes when, in its opposition to the ancient abuses and prejudices therewith connected, it uprooted the wheat with the tares; and much as our modern constitutions, with their universal suffrage,—a voting by merely indiscriminate masses,—have entrenched themselves against the class principle, these cannot vanish from the world, but assert themselves now as ever by an ineradicable natural necessity. The consciousness is now increasingly working its way, that every constitution which is to be stable must be based upon the distinction of the classes.

§ 52.

The classes are rightly divided into those which labour for purposes of a material and corporeal nature, and those whose efforts are devoted to more exalted objects,—a distinction which of course must not be regarded in an abstract manner. Consistent and important, however, as this division is, it is not

---

[1] Comp. F. Walter, *Naturrecht und Politik im Lichte der Gegenwart*, p. 115 : "The word people is but an abstraction, the classes are the reality."

sufficiently definite for the relation which the different classes occupy to society and the State. This requirement is only satisfied by their division into *private* and *public* (Stahl). The public classes are those whose activity is of direct service to society, and is, so to speak, carried out in the name and for the sake of the community. The private, or as we might as rightly call them, the individualistic classes (understanding the expression *sensu medio* without any *arrière pensée*), are those which work in the first place for individuals, those whose activity arises from individual interest, and is only *indirectly* serviceable to the community as such. The public consist of the nobility, the military class, and the class of civil and ecclesiastical officials. The private classes, on the other hand, are the agricultural or peasant, the industrial and the commercial classes. Physicians, lawyers, teachers and artists must, inasmuch as their labour is in the first place for individual interests, be also included in the latter category.

The nobility, as being in a special manner connected with the monarchy and the State, must on this account be reckoned with the public classes; while the great proprietors as such belong to the private classes. Large landed property is not the only attribute of the nobility,—though without it an essential condition of their existence is lacking,—but in addition to this certain hereditary rights and privileges, accompanied by a higher position in society. In ancient times there were noble races, from which the king proceeded, and the nobility in the course of time developed more and more into the dominant class, in imitative similarity to kingship. It is well known, on the one hand, what oppression of the other classes was induced by this assumption of authority; and, on the other, how the nobles have in our days been deprived of the greater part of their *political* privileges. It can, however, by no means be asserted that they have therefore been in every sense done away with as a class. They possess a specific class-consciousness in those historic remembrances through which they are in a special manner interwoven with the national history. It is their vocation, in their nearer access to the person of the sovereign, to protect and defend the throne, and in their more exalted and independent position, to represent in every aspect the interests of their native land, to support and promote them, and to be ready, as the foremost in the country, to make when needed sacrifices for the cause of their fatherland. And although they have forfeited those political privileges which they formerly exercised to the prejudice of the other classes, there still ever exists a connection between an hereditary nobility and an hereditary monarchy, which, without the support of the former, would occupy too isolated a position. In States where the representation is based upon the class principle, and where a nobility of really historical· importance remains, there is also good reason for the determination that the nobility must be represented as a class. Generally speaking, it would be well not to make too absolute and inconsiderate an attack upon the hereditary privileges of the nobles. For, suppose I were born not an inheritor of noble blood, but of a millionaire's riches, is this my hereditary right to be attacked, and am I to be deprived of it? Or will any man proceed in so illogical a manner as to make a difference in favour of capital alone?

As the public classes, however, receive their importance from the institutions with which they are connected, we shall not at present enter further into them, but devote our attention more particularly to the private classes, inasmuch as they play a more prominent part in modern society than the others. For individual liberty has in them attained a degree of development, which it must on the one hand be confessed is justifiable, profitable and productive of good results, while on the other it has also borne bitter and pernicious fruit, and has involved society in perplexing and perilous circumstances, out of which the egress is difficult to find. This applies especially to the industrial classes.

§ 53.

Among the tasks of culture is that of the *agricultural* or *peasant* class to produce, by the cultivation of the land, the raw material which is to be worked up for the supply of the manifold wants of man. In ancient times a kind of sanctity was attributed to agriculture, not only on account of the mystery hidden in the seed, and the marvel manifested in seed-time and harvest, in the growth of the corn, the fruits and the flowers, but also because the cultivation of the soil is a main condition of all higher culture, of the civil community and of the State. The field labourer has in his daily labour a direct call to piety and patient submission to the divine guidance of human affairs, for it depends entirely upon the gifts of nature, and is conditioned by rain and fruitful seasons from heaven. "Behold, the husbandman waiteth for the precious fruit of the earth, and hath long patience for it, until he receive the early and the latter rain" (Jas. v. 7). Nature in this case does much, human labour comparatively little. We may plant and water, but it is God who gives the increase. In his fellowship with nature, which repeats from year to year its uniform circle in the succession of the seasons, the life of the agriculturist obtains a stamp of uniformity, and he acquires a liking for settled habits, a partiality for the accustomed and the traditional. With this uniformity is connected a certain regularity and simplicity of life, a plainness and moderation in food, clothing and habitation. And it is certainly a well-founded assertion, that it well becomes the agricultural class to have its special dress, independent of the ceaseless freaks and changes of fashion. This class is, by its natural position and tendency, more addicted to conservatism than to progress. Its conservatism as such is not indeed political. The peasant feels but a slight interest in politics, in affairs of state properly so called, although he may appear to do so in times of excitement, in *states of political intoxication*. At all events, his real interest in politics is but a very *indirect* one. His conservatism is based on the fact that he is bound to the land, to the soil, that he desires not merely to increase his possession of land, but above all things to preserve his land, farm and husbandry for himself and his descendants. If the farmer has but got his own affairs in good order, he finds it, in his natural and not yet super-refined way of thinking, quite proper that the authorities or the king should take care for the rest. In saying this, however, we are not imputing to him mere common selfishness, nor even indifference to the affairs of his country, but only pointing out what it is that forms with the agriculturist the starting-point for his view of politics, what is his normal point of contact with interests of a general kind.   It is by reason of this natural conservatism, which thus binds him to the soil of his native land, and imparts to his mode of life, his labours, his customs, a stamp of stability, that the peasant class is justly regarded as " the reliable class in unreliable times," as the class best adapted for the defence of the country.

During the last generations, important progress has been made in the development of the peasant class, and indeed in the direction of a greater extension of individual freedom, in which respect liberalism has rendered great and unmistakeable service.   The peasant class already, in former times, released from the unworthy vassalage of serfdom and of subjection to the owners of the land, have lately been freed from other bonds, and it was a great advance in personal independence when free possession took the place of compact tenancy.   Still various dangers and inconveniences are connected with this emancipation.   We will here confine ourselves to pointing out a moral danger, namely, that the peasant class, when in prosperity, may fall into the temptation of being henceforth discontented with the mode of life best adapted to it, and enter upon a new one connected with an undue amount of luxury.   The dissolution of the peasant class has begun when it is itself zealous in doing away with the boundaries which separate it from the other classes, and within which it possesses a power and strength of its own, when the rustic is ashamed of his plain garments and his wife desires to dress like a lady, when the luxurious claims of hospitality become common customs, and a spurious æsthetic tendency at the same time prevails.   This is also the case when the peasant, with his semi-education obtained from the newspapers or the speeches of unenlightened demagogues, and backed up by the right of universal suffrage, lifts himself out of his own level, and becomes a would-be politician, argues about things beyond his own horizon, *e.g.* is zealous against " Latin " in schools and scholarship, and sets up rural education as the model.   For all these things and such as these are the unwholesome results of emancipation, and may, especially when political agitation and spouting are carried too far, at last lead to the agricultural ceasing to be the reliable class.

It must also be reckoned among the unwholesome results

when an aristocratic arrogance is developed within the agricultural class, namely, in the relations between owners of farms and day-labourers, when the former do not accord to the latter a personal independence proportioned to that which they themselves enjoy in full measure ; or, to speak more correctly, do not provide them with its *conditions,* a fact which at the same time shows that the work of emancipation is not yet fully carried out, and that an essential portion yet remains to be accomplished. As long as democratically-minded owners and their liberal leaders have no inclination to effect an improvement in the condition of their house and farm servants, their notions of equality are not to be depended on, and they would do well to cease from asserting that they are exerting themselves for general social interests.

Together with the peasant class, we would mention the great landowners. It is of great importance that this class of society, which practises agriculture on a larger scale, and at the same time occupies a higher grade both as to property and education, should live in the midst of the rural population. It forms not only a powerful conservative element for the support of the State, but can also assist the peasantry both by counsel and action ; it can, by dwelling in their midst, essentially contribute to the diffusion of culture and of more enlightened views, among which are included the acquaintance with new discoveries and inventions in the department of husbandry attained by the peasant class through its means. Where this class of society is chiefly penetrated by Christian opinions and interests, it will not only strengthen the Christian and church life of the population by its example, which is of so great importance, but also powerfully co-operate in obtaining for the Church and for education their due position.

§ 54.

While the class of husbandmen fulfils its task in the cultivation of natural products and raw material, that of the *industrial class* is performed in the working up of these products for the supply of human wants. It includes the artisan and the manufacturer; the artisan labouring for the special wants of the individual, the manufacturer for any abstract general want

(Hegel). This class is specially referred to diligence and the inventive faculty. In it, especially in the artisan class, is developed an incipient feeling for art, an endeavour not only to produce work which is solid and adapted to its purpose, but also to impart to it a feature of elegance and beauty. The great artists of the Middle Ages began, as must always be the case, as simple artisans; as handicraft is the parent of plastic art, so does art react upon handicraft, a great example of which is furnished in Denmark by the influence which Thorwaldsen's works of art have exercised upon the taste of the artisans.

Nothing but the raw material is provided for the artisan and manufacturer; labour must do everything in producing the desired objects. This is in direct contrast with the position and task of the husbandman, whose produce nature does the most in bringing forth and maturing. The artisan and manufacturer must manage and economize *time* in a very different and far stricter sense than the husbandman. The seed grows in the ground while men sleep and human labour ceases, which by no means applies to the productions of industry, when the hammer and the needle rest or the machinery is still. Hence the industrial class must strictly number and use up the hours of labour, nay, under certain circumstances, must work day and night to finish by the right time the work that is begun. *The clock*, that ingenious contrivance by which the human understanding has compelled a piece of mechanism to measure time, and which introduces *punctuality* into our daily life, is made by this class, and has its main significance precisely with respect to it.

The contrast between this and the agricultural class is further exhibited in the greater favour shown by it to progress than to conservatism. It is ever aiming at surpassing by new inventions what it has hitherto accomplished. It is by them always producing new wants in human society, and thus begetting not only a luxury which is justifiable, an employment of things pertaining to the enjoyments and elegancies of life, a use of comforts beyond what is actually necessary, but also at times an unjustifiable luxury, a preposterous refinement of life, by which the general prosperity suffers, and men are rendered effeminate. The industrial class being in close connection with the commercial, which unites different countries and nations, it is rather cosmopolitan than national. Its relation to the rural class is like that of the moveable power of money to the settled landed proprietor. The great impulse which industry has in our times received, and through which capital has become a first-rate power in society, arises partly from the greater division of labour introduced by new machines and the ingenious application of steam power, partly from the extension of individual freedom, which, resulting from the French Revolution, found its expression in *free competition* (Adam Smith). This has done good service, by loosening the oppressive and restrictive fetters connected with the ancient *guilds* and *corporations.* But not only unjustifiable, but all restrictions were abolished; corporations, instead of being reformed to suit the times, were at last entirely done away with, individual liberty was in every respect placed on its own footing, and free competition brought forth the right of the stronger, and excited a struggle of all against all. Hence a great calamity, to be more closely investigated in the following pages, also burst upon the human race as the result of free competition.

§ 55.

The task of the *commercial class* is to *sell* the productions of both nature and art, and to make them into *wares.* It forms the medium between producers and consumers. In its connection with navigation, it brings the different quarters of the world into mutual intercourse, and is consequently a powerful promoter of culture. " Commerce, by its command of material traffic, carries intellectual intercourse upon its shoulders " (Stahl). Commerce cannot be carried on without money, but cannot always be transacted with ready money. Hence it depends upon *credit*, upon confidence and mercantile solidity; and hence a punctual and inviolable fulfilment of obligations entered into is a main point in the morals of the commercial class. As business cannot be carried on without credit, neither can it without speculation, without a survey of the possibilities of advantage or profit. Hence it is the part of the commercial class to be watchful, to give heed to opportunities, while its upper members are also obliged to take account of the circumstances of the world in general. Resolute conduct is also indispensable for seizing with rapidity the favourable opportunity and instant, for in mercantile affairs the saying holds good that time is money! Speculation for profit's sake is indeed of doubtful moral worth, a fact which in ancient times found expression in the belief that Mercury, the patron of trade, was also the patron of thieves and eloquent deceivers; in the myth that he, though only born in the morning, stole fifty oxen from Apollo in the evening, two of which he immediately sacrificed in his own honour, and that when at last the theft was discovered, and he was obliged to restore the stolen property, he bought back the eight and forty oxen on the most profitable terms, persuading Apollo, by plausible speeches, to exchange them for a lyre, which he had ingeniously formed of a tortoise shell strung with cords.

The regard which the trading class must certainly have to its own profit must be made a moral action, by being placed in duly proportioned relation to the condition of surrounding society, and by not converting it—as in the case of many Jews—into a calculated extortion. And though the merchant carries on his trade in the first place as a private business, he must still be at the same time penetrated by the consciousness that he has to serve the community, and to labour for its welfare.

This class also is by its very nature rather cosmopolitan than national ; nevertheless its national feeling comes forth in its divisions between the protective (which is properly the national) and the free trade (the cosmopolitan) system—a contrast whose solution is not possible *in abstracto*, but only approximately, by a regard to the circumstances, both national and international, occurring at the time. Absolute freedom of trade was advocated by Adam Smith (1723–1790). He spoke apparently in behalf of cosmopolitanism, but really in behalf of national self-interest, of the prosperity of the English nation ; for with free trade and free competition, the advantage is always on the side of the most powerful, and free trade is quite in the interest of England. In opposition to Adam Smith may be mentioned Fr. List (1789–1846), who by no means denies the cosmopolitan ideal, but demands also that each nation should first of all fully develope its own productive powers, and maintains that for every nation there comes a time when a restriction of international commerce must take place, when the prohibitive and protective system becomes a necessity, if it would not lose its economic, which is connected with its moral, independence.[1]

§ 56.

To the private or individualistic classes discussed above, may be added the so-called " fourth class," that is, the labouring class, including all those who possess nothing but their power of labouring, are without property, and work for a certain amount of wages in factories, workshops, fields and docks, live from hand to mouth, and even if they marry and have a troop of children, are scarcely in a condition to lead a real family life. These day-labourers, who claim in our days to be a recognised class, with guaranteed rights in the civil community, are generally, though not quite correctly, designated the *proletariate*. For this is a more comprehensive notion. It includes, indeed, all who are without property, but is often made to comprise also the accessory notion of the rabble, of that element of society which *ought* *not* to exist, and which

[1] Friedrich List, *Gesammelte Schriften*, 3d part, *Das nationale System der politischen Oekonomie.* — The close (or protective) commerce (*Geschlossener Handelsstaat*) of the elder Fichte forms the sharpest contrast to Adam Smith. Fichte requires that commerce should be as independent as possible of foreign countries, and that all rivalry between mutually outbidding competitions should, as an incalculable element, be excluded ; the State must seek to supply the wants of its citizens from its own resources, and no one except *the government*, which must only do so in the public interest, may carry on trade with foreign countries. Often as scorn has been cast upon this work of the philosopher,—a work based, it must be confessed, upon very idealistic constructions, and inculcating a new kind of communism,—and frequently as it has been designated a philosophical chimera, its fundamental notion has nevertheless been realized in another form, viz. in Napoleon the First's continental system, which was an attempt to combine the entire continent of Europe in a close or protective commerce against the former supremacy of England. The reason why this attempt found no sympathy was, that the continental nations had every reason to fear that, even supposing them freed from the supremacy of England, they should but fall under that of Napoleon I. To say this, however, is not to renounce every continental system without further ceremony, and an advocate for such a system has just appeared in Fr. List (comp. Fichte's *Werke*, III., preface by the younger Fichte, p. 38 sqq. List's above-named work, 389 sqq., *Die Continentalpolitik*).

implies a combination of poverty and demoralization—an accessory idea not necessarily contained in the word proletariate. This may be found in all classes of society. We may speak (with Riehl) of an aristocratic proletariate, an impoverished nobility, whose incomes are far below what is befitting their rank ; an official proletariate, inasmuch as certain subordinate positions scarcely supply the barest necessaries of life. In the proletariate must also be included very many literates and journalists, who being not only without material support, but also devoid of intellectual capital, live upon the credit which the great ignorant or half-educated public accord them ; theatrical critics, who levy a tax, in proportion to their incomes, upon actors and opera-singers for favourable criticisms, strolling players, circus-riders, and musicians, from the virtuosos who appear in concert-rooms down to the male and female singers in public places of entertainment, who live on the pence which the guests are pleased to throw into the cap that is sent round, organ-grinders, etc. All such, in short, the refuse and dregs of the other classes, are by Riehl comprised in the fourth class.[1] We think, however, that the true boundary of its contents is found when they are restricted to the above-mentioned class of workmen, who have given rise to the so-called labour question of the day. The rest of the proletariate cannot form an actual class, because it comprehends only the refuse of the other classes,—an assertion utterly inapplicable to the workmen in question ; for however great may be the faults manifested by the latter, they must nevertheless be regarded as an element agreeable to the nature of things already introduced into the development of human society, and needing and desiring to be liberated from the state of restraint in which it finds itself.

§ 57.

Notwithstanding those features and interests which are common to all, each class, whether private or public, views life from its own special view-point, and the estimation in which it holds the varied tasks of life is in many respects conditioned by its particular interests and degree of culture.

[1] Riehl, *Die bürgerliche Gesellschaft*, p. 272 sqq.

Leibnitz says that every monad views existence *suivant son point de vue.* And it is true not only of individuals, but also of the greater individualities which we call classes, that each regards and judges of life *suivant son point de vue.* Not only existence in general, but also the social life of man, presents one image to the consciousness of the official, and another to that of the artisan and manufacturer, and again another to the mind of the nobleman, and another to that of the artist, etc.; and it would be a singularly attractive spectacle to be able all at once to behold these differing reflections of the world and of life! We are here, however, speaking of the *social* view of life. The view and the estimation which each class forms of the objects and tasks of civil society, is more or less particularistic and limited. But over the several classes, over the civil community, with its many particular intersecting aims, stands the State, as the ruling and directing power of the whole, the legal ordinance, which assigns its place to the individual and the special. Viewed even in this aspect, we see the importance of a strong monarchy. For the monarch is over the classes, belongs to no class, even though he may have originally proceeded from the nobility, and is raised by his position above all particularistic interest.

The State and the civil community thus form a unity in which two systems, the political and the social, are continually acting upon each other. The State is the system of government, *of law* and *of justice,* encompassing and pervading the whole civil community. The latter is the system of *life interests,* which is developed within the province of the State and governed by its laws. Without the civil community, the State would be an empty form; without the State, the community remains a multiplicity, a varied substance, without the governing and directing unit. That the State and the civil community are two different things, will be evident to every one who will ask himself the question: What, then, remains when the State is dissolved, *i.e.* when the government and legislature are transferred to another State? The nation and its language have not therefore ceased to exist. Family life goes on as before, and though individual classes, especially the military and official, are suspended or inoperative, the rest continue their former life. Thus social life to a certain degree goes on uninterruptedly, even 'after political life has essentially lost its independence.   We say essentially, for certain elements of political life, individual legal enactments, communal regulations, will remain and assert themselves. The normal state of things, however, is the union of the political and the social—the *ordre politique* and the *ordre social*—co-operating in the same spirit, and corresponding with each other.

Thus there remains always the same great whole, which we call the State, whether we regard it from the view-point of the political, civil community, or on its social side.

THE COMMON WEAL.

Division of Property.—Riches and Poverty.[1]

§ 58.

The duty of the State in its union with civil society is to promote by the means at its disposal the *common weal.*   The common weal is a notion which even ordinary consciousness has viewed in a manner more or less ethical (*i.e.* in connection with moral requirements).   Taken in its full meaning, it signifies nothing less than the highest earthly good, a state of general prosperity, through an harmonious union of ethical and material possessions ; a condition, therefore, in which labour and profit are intimately blended.   This is, indeed, an ideal which points to the golden age.   But though, as earthly things are now constituted, it may never be fully attained, it should still be ever kept in view by those who direct the State as an end to be striven for.   It will be realized only in the same proportion as those social evils, poverty, sickness and sin, together with unbelief and immorality, are opposed and overcome.   To attain approximately the aim in question, the State government must keep in view the welfare, both of the whole community and of individuals, in other words, must allow its due influence to the truth both of socialism and of individualism.   The State must, in all its acts, certainly have a care for the individual,

---

[1] The following §§ 58–69, which have already been published as a separate article, under the title of *Socialismus und Christenthum, Ein Bruchstück aus der speciellen Ethik,* are here given in the connection to which they originally belonged, slightly altered in some passages, and enlarged by some additions.

and make it its duty, that the greatest possible number of persons should enjoy the largest possible portion of earthly prosperity. The common weal is not yet duly cared for as long as care for the whole makes the individual only a means for the whole, and not his own proper end, nay, crushes him under the great wheel of the State machine. But as little is the common weal properly and justly provided for where the State promotes individual interests in such wise that the rights of the whole suffer. This is a state of things which gives rise to all kinds of confusion, and, as must soon be evident, to the violation of those very individual rights which it was the object to maintain.

Although the common weal is anything but limited to material prosperity, still a certain measure of *affluence* is one of the conditions of an existence compatible with the dignity of human nature. Hence it appertains to the common weal, that there should be in human society a due distribution of those material possessions, which are comprised under the notion of *property*, a distribution in proportion to the social position which an individual occupies, to his vocation and labour, and therefore, in the right sense of the expression, a distribution " in conformity with class." National prosperity does not exist where we meet with a sharp contrast between affluence and superfluity on the one hand, and poverty, want and misery on the other, and where an abyss yawns, so to speak, between the two conditions. National prosperity does not depend only upon the quantity of property existing in a nation, but is rather determined by the way and manner in which it is distributed. It is only present where the far larger majority form a well-supplied middle class, with a moderate proportion of personal property. Hence political economy, whose object is national prosperity and its conditions, has every reason for taking to heart Agur's prayer, " Give me neither riches nor poverty; feed me with food convenient for me" (Prov. xxx.). The same sentiment is expressed in the words of a Danish poet, which may be rendered as follows:—

' Where superfluity is rare,
And want is rarer still,
Does daily bread, a portion fair,
The land with blessings fill."

The prosperity attainable by a nation depends not only on the industry and inventive genius of its people, but also on certain natural advantages, which we must refer to a higher and to us unfathomable counsel. Prosperity depends on the combination of both factors. Even a glance at the form and composition of the soil shows us a very varying distribution of the gifts of nature. How niggardly is nature to the Greenlander, dwelling in the frozen regions of the North Pole, and how liberal to the inhabitants of the south, with its luxurious fruitful lands, which so invite man to enjoyment, that he has only to receive from the hands of nature the fruits which are offered him, without labour on his part! This unequal distribution we must accept as an existing circumstance, concerning which we neither can nor ought to dispute with the Creator of all things. Everywhere something is placed before man as a *task*, towards which his labour, his powers of invention, his improving hand, must be turned. What is true of the contrast between abundance and want of material possessions, applies also to that distribution of mental gifts among men, which shows the same striking inequality between rich and poor. Want and poverty will always occur in human society, and that not only through men's own faults, but also as the result of providential dispensations; and grinding poverty, that large ingredient of human misery, is often indeed connected in its ultimate reason with sin, whose effects have penetrated our race to such an extent, that an individual often has to suffer for that which is the fault of the whole. Poverty is just as inseparable from the present dispensation as sickness. But as the efforts of human society must at all times aim at limiting the prevalence of sickness, so must they also at diminishing and alleviating poverty, at bridging over and levelling the immoderately widened gulf between rich and poor. And not more strenuously must the eccentric notion, that man is capable, by his own prudence and exertions, of absolutely banishing from the world the contrast between rich and poor, be rejected, than the fatalistic notion, that nothing can be contributed on the part of man to remedy it, that an unalterable divine decree has, once for all, so settled the sharply contrasted lots of men, that the poor have only to resign themselves in a quietistic manner to their fate. This is a view which entirely overlooks the fact, that the divine decree concerning man and his lot is not an absolute one, but is, on the contrary, conditioned by human freedom. The *Christian* view of the world and of life, which asserts the validity of both providence and freedom, is opposed not only to that enthusiastic and arrogant view of human freedom, which would endow it with an innate power of transforming the world, but also to that fatalistic and quietistic view of human circumstances, which would make them utterly unchangeable and insusceptible of modification,—a view which makes them, like the Indian caste-system, mere appointments of nature.

§ 59.

Christianity, at its entrance into the heathen world, found society divided not only into rich and poor, but also into *bond* and *free*. To this relation between free men and slaves our attention must now be more particularly directed, on the one hand, because a certain internal relation exists between the working class of our days and the slavery of the ancient world; on the other, and especially, because we shall thus perceive the view-point from which *labour*, that main source of national prosperity, was contemplated in Grecian and Roman heathendom. All the heavier manual labour, by which the satisfaction of man's bodily needs was supplied, was committed exclusively to slaves; for it was regarded as a thing unworthy of a free citizen, who, living only for the exhibition of what was beautiful in human nature, for affairs of State, and for his own mental development, needed for these purposes much free time or leisure (*otium*). The higher the degree of culture, the greater was the depreciation of, the repugnance against, all merely bodily labour. The notion that in the midst of such labour, even of such as aimed at the supply of man's lower wants, a moral and religious development of personality can and is to take place, was alien and unattainable to the deepest thinkers, even to a Plato and an Aristotle. There were but two classes of men, only one of which, viz. the minority of the free and rich, passed an existence worthy of human beings. The other, the large majority, consisted, according to the prevailing notions, only of lower natures, made for work, not for enjoyment, and, generally speaking, only in the world for the purpose of forming the requisite foundations, and bringing about the conditions, by means of which the minority of "kingly souls" might lead a becoming, dignified and reasonable life, and enjoy the leisure necessary for so doing. That each individual in this exceedingly large majority of slaves possessed an immortal soul, a soul destined to an undying life, was entirely beyond the sphere of vision and conception then prevailing. The slave was accounted only an "animated instrument," and the instrument was in its turn regarded as a mindless, soulless slave. It was without further question assumed, that the soul of a slave was entirely incapable of virtue, and of all and everything noble and elevated, that it was only set upon what was evil, and must therefore be continually kept under the rod. Even Plato declared it advisable that slaves should be diligently chastised. For a slave differed but little from domestic animals, which in like manner exist merely for the use and profit of mankind. A slave was indeed capable of understanding the voice of reason, when it became outwardly audible to him through his master; but in and of himself he possessed no reason, could set himself no reasonable task, nor invent the means for its accomplishment. And if even certain individuals among these slaves did find a better lot, and if many were employed in the practice of the arts and in literary work,—for there were certainly men among them who manifested not merely reason and knowledge, but even genius,—the majority, at all events, led a sad existence, and were ever increasingly demoralized, partly by the example of their own masters. To these dark shadows should we direct our attention whenever we hear those oft-repeated eulogies of the noble " humanity," the free political life, the refined culture, with its art, its poetry, its drama, which are said to have existed in Greece and Rome, and when even their religion is extolled as far more humane than Christianity. When we contemplate this night side of antiquity, there is a bitter irony in the hymn which Schiller, in his æsthetic intoxication, sings to the gods of Greece, and thus praises those happy times:

"Als ihr noch die Welt regiertet,
An der Freude leichtem Gängelband
Glücklichere Menschenalter führtet,
Schöne Wesen aus dem Fabelland!"

For these beauteous beings were utterly indifferent and un-pitying towards human want and misery. Neither the Grecian nor the Roman religion contained the slightest element fitted to act as a corrective thereto, and to lead to deliverance from such a state of bondage, from such a degradation and abuse of human nature in countless multitudes, who were simply re-garded as destined by fate—to furnish the manure of culture. Even philosophy looked upon the relation between bond and free as founded in a fixed law of nature. Aristotle referred slavery to that order of nature whose commandment says: the lower must serve the higher.

Such a state of things, however, could not but have a dis-turbing and restrictive effect upon national prosperity. Where the free man does not choose to work himself, and the slave works only because he is obliged, and does only just as much as is indispensably necessary to escape the threatened lash, the production of material possessions can never take place in such abundance as would be possible under better conditions. The French historian, Tocqueville, makes the same remark with regard to the present state of America, when he says that in those States where labour has hitherto been performed by slaves, there has been a striking stand-still, nay, a barren-ness of production in comparison with the States in which slavery was being abolished, and labour performed by free men, for in these agriculture, trade and industry had received an impulse and were flourishing. Tocqueville is of opinion that the abolition of slavery is as much the interest of the whites as of the blacks.

Together with the emancipation of slaves, Christianity, by its proclamation of true liberty and equality, introduced their deliverance from that unhappy and unworthy condition in which millions were once deprived of their human rights. Christianity proclaims that all men are essentially equal, because all are created in the image of God,—equal, because all are sinners in bondage to the law, and exposed to judgment; equal, because all are called to the liberty of the children of God in Christ. It by no means desires to abolish necessary distinctions in human society, but aims at harmonizing them in the union of love. It interests itself in the despised of this world, in the weak and oppressed, in the woman, the slave, the poor. It found its earliest confessors chiefly among the poor, whose want of the good things of this world made them peculiarly receptive of the gospel of the kingdom which is not of this world. It warns the rich in forcible language of the dangers and temptations of riches, as graphically exemplified in the parable of the rich man and Lazarus. Riches are called an idol, Mammon, whom men serve, but whose service is incompatible with that of God. And the rich are exhorted not to put their trust in uncertain riches, but in the living God. It is indeed a misconception to think that Christianity desires to convert human society into a community of mere ascetics, living in constant and voluntary poverty. But Christianity certainly values riches only so far as they are placed at the disposal of the moral and religious spirit, and the rich regard themselves as the stewards of God, as administrators of property entrusted to their care, for the use and due application of which they will one day have to give account at the judgment-seat of God. Now, where riches are thus regarded as a trust, of which an account will have to be rendered, they will certainly be employed in alleviating the necessities of the poor and helpless. And this was quickly seen in the multitude of hospitals and benevolent institutions which, as a thing utterly new and unknown in heathendom, suddenly sprang up wherever Christianity was propagated in the Roman empire. For not so much as a single individual among either the rich, the wise, or the highly cultivated heathen had ever thought of such continuous assistance to their suffering brethren, but, on the contrary, had one and all left them to their fate. But riches will be also employed in the interest of the whole community, and for the promotion of the comprehensive aims of culture, for Christianity has by no means abolished or declared invalid the old command: "Subject the earth to yourselves." To the execution of this behest, riches are on the one hand a specially useful means, while on the other the poor are to do their work, not like those slaves of ancient heathen days, but as free men, as those who get not merely wages for their labour, but are also esteemed and respected for its sake.

Christianity is far from desiring to put an end to slavery by political agitation of any kind. It is contented with announcing a new view to the world, and arousing in it a new sentiment, which must of necessity involve the abolition of slavery and the recognition of the true equality of all men with each other. In this respect we may here mention the Epistle of St. Paul to Philemon. A slave named Onesimus had escaped from his master Philemon at Colosse, had come to Rome, and been converted to Christ by the apostle, who was there in prison. St. Paul sent him back to his lawful master, with this letter of recommendation, in which it is said, among other things, vers. 10–12: "I beseech thee for my son Onesimus, whom I have begotten in my bonds, which in times past was to thee unprofitable, but now profitable (*i.e.* a true Onesimus) to thee and to me, whom I have sent again: thou therefore receive him that is mine own bowels." Also vers. 15, 16: "Perhaps he therefore departed for a season, that thou shouldest receive him for ever; not now as a slave, but more than a slave, a brother beloved, specially to me, but how much more unto thee, both in the flesh (*i.e.* the civil and earthly relation) and in the Lord." A glimpse of apostolical authority is first seen in ver. 21: "Having confidence in thy obedience, I wrote unto thee, knowing that thou wilt also do more than I say." When we consider how much the slaves of antiquity were despised, and how a runaway slave, when once he fell into his master's hands, was usually treated, we shall soon be convinced that an entirely new view and feeling, which were to be the foundation of a thorough transformation of social relations, were here asserting themselves. We commend to every one a careful perusal of this short epistle in its whole context. It is one of the most refined and charming that has ever been written.

§ 60.

It is just this estimation of bodily labour which plainly shows how Christianity, which everywhere honours corporeity, introduced an entirely new element into social relations. While agriculture was held in honour among the Greeks and Romans, and a Cincinnatus was not ashamed to follow the plough, handicraft was, on the contrary, thought very meanly of. "The business of the artisan," says Cicero, "is sordid work; nothing noble is compatible with the workshop." For these reasons handicraft was left to slaves or the half free. Christianity, on the contrary, ennobled it, and gave its sanction to the totally different view, already prevalent among the Israelites, by whom manual labour was highly esteemed, and who required even the scribes to be acquainted with some kind of trade. Joseph, the foster-father of Jesus, was a carpenter, and, according to tradition, the Saviour of the world Himself worked at his foster-father's trade. The Apostle Paul, in addition to his great labours for the kingdom of God, practised the craft of a tent and cloth maker. In his letters to the Church at Thessalonica, whose members appear to have consisted for the most part of artisans, he exhorts them to work with their own hands, adding the significant saying, that " if any one will not work, neither let him eat " (2 Thess. iii. 10). As a motive to labour he also brings forward this purpose: " That he may have to give to him that needeth " (Eph. iv. 28). The importance attained first in the Christian world by labour, may be perceived by the trade guilds of the Middle Ages, which were combinations not merely for common work, but also for the promotion of all and every interest of life. Workmen and apprentices lived under one roof with their master and mistress; and the guilds or corporations, held together by the bond of the same Christian faith, took upon themselves the care of providing for the sick. The individual was, with respect to his moral conduct, constantly under the control of the whole. Great ability was developed by their corporate agency, and the great artists who built Cologue Cathedral and Strasburg Minster were produced from their midst. A sharp contrast was here manifested to that depreciation which the slave and his work had to endure in the ancient world.

Christianity — though chiefly and above all intent on gaining individual souls for the heavenly citizenship—also exercises, by means of its evangelical principle of liberty and equality, its peculiar view of riches and poverty, and its ennoblement of bodily labour, a refining and reforming influence upon civil society, even with respect to the questions of the right distribution of property and the prosperity of nations. In proportion as nations suffer themselves to be pervaded by the principles of Christianity, and therefore in proportion as the material interests of life are subordinated to its higher and spiritual interests, and are regulated thereby, in other words, by the aims of humanity and of the kingdom of God, will a path be opened for a juster and more consistent distribution of property, and the extremes of riches and poverty, of superfluity and want, be equalized. Where these extremes prevail, it is always a sign that a nation is not yet penetrated by Christian principles, or that a declension from Christianity has taken place, and heathen principles have regained influence and authority. The assertion that Christianity has nothing to do with the nation and national prosperity, cannot but lead to the assertion that morality has nothing to do with political economy, that only a material, and not by any means an ethical, importance is to be attributed to the notions of riches and poverty, labour and wages, and that political economy, when seeking to discover the best means and lever for national prosperity, must confine itself to investigating the natural laws of society (the laws of production, of the relation between production and consumption, of the rise and fall of values and prices, of population, etc.), without at the same time bringing these laws into relation with those of the moral government of the world. On the contrary, the very problem which this science has to solve, is how to place human profiting by natural laws under obedience to moral laws. It will then be seen that "godliness has the promise not only of the future, but also of the present life " (1 Tim. iv. 8), and that both a partial individualism and a partial socialism, so far as each asserts itself in political economy, first find their corrective and their higher truth in the ethic socialism of Christianity.

POLITICO-ECONOMIC INDIVIDUALISM.

The Labour Question.

§ 61.

, Partial individualism in political economy came to light and was vindicated with special emphasis in Adam Smith's celebrated work, *On the Wealth of Nations, its Nature and Causes* (1776), which has since become the main foundation of the political economy of modern liberalism. Smith gained by it the world-wide renown of raising political economy to the rank of a science, and opened an abundance of hitherto unanticipated views into the natural laws of human society. But with all the greatness of his genius, and notwithstanding the acknowledgment which must be paid to his real merits, it must be confessed that the system itself is a purely naturalistic one, and treats moral requirements with utter indifference. The ideas of the man were really developed under the influence of the French Encyclopædists, by personal intercourse with Helvetius and D'Alembert, and the financiers Turgot and Quesnai. The opinions prevailing in those circles were thoroughly naturalistic, and exclusively directed to the possessions of this world, while heaven and the Christian representation of the supermundane destiny of man were more and more lost sight of and transformed into shadows. Self-interest was accounted the ruling principle in the morality of this circle, and it was supposed that its own immediate interest must also be the ruling principle in the morality of the nation.

That the ethical element is entirely absent in the views of Adam Smith, at least as they are laid down in this epoch-making work, is evident from the fact that he always makes the greatest possible quantity of material possessions the sole aim to be pursued, without in any way considering its relation to the higher tasks of human life. The division of labour and free competition are regarded by him as the means by which this aim is to be attained. By labour, however, he means only physical, which in his eyes is alone " productive," labour. Artists, scholars, physicians, preachers, statesmen and officials are unproductive and barren, because only nourished and supported by the labour of others,—an assertion founded on the idea that *bodily* nourishment and *sensuous* enjoyment are the chief and most important interests of the nation. Labour itself is viewed as only the necessary means for the attainment of riches and the enjoyments of sense, and not as at the same time a duty resulting from the destination of man, and in the performance of which he is to find pleasure and satisfaction

Labour is thus deprived of its dignity. The labourer is regarded not, properly speaking, as a man, but only as impersonal labour-power, as an instrument which, as soon as it is used up and worn out, is replaced by a new one. From this point of view this system also desires that the wages paid to day-labourers, and to servants of every kind, should suffice to transpose all into a condition in which they may *propagate* the race of day-labourers and workmen, because society is ever needing fresh instruments.

The object in question is promoted by the division of labour, by means of which production may be much increased. For the skill of the individual workman is materially enhanced if he devotes himself exclusively to the preparation of one and the same object, while the time is also spared which would be lost by going from one kind of work to another. This division of labour takes place chiefly by the employment of *machinery*. To use an example quoted by Adam Smith, take the work of the pinmakers. By means of machinery, such a division of labour takes place that one draws out the wire, another straightens it, a third cuts it up, a fourth points it, and a fifth prepares it to receive a head. Two different manipulations are required for the preparation of this pin's head; the fastening it on is again an independent business, and polishing the pin is another. And, finally, it is a separate kind of work to stick the pins in papers. Thus the one trade of pinmaking is divided into about eighteen different kinds of work, each of which is, in some factories, executed by different hands; while in others, one person perhaps undertakes two or three. Adam Smith says that he saw ten persons, some of whom executed two or three different offices one after the other, finish twelve pounds of pins in one day. There are 4000 pins of medium size in a pound, so that these ten persons made together 48,000 pins in a day. But if they had all worked apart and independently, without any of them having been specially taught one of the above-named knacks, not one would certainly have produced twenty, perhaps not even a single pin a day.[1] Excellent, however, as this may be, the moral question will arise, whether it is an employment worthy of a man, to devote his time, nay,

---

[1] Smith, *Wealth of Nations*, I. 7 sqq. (4th ed. London 1876). Comp. Roscher, *die Grundlage der Nationalökonomie*, 9 Aufl., Stuttgart 1871, p. 121.

the greater part of his life, to putting on pins' heads.   In this too greatly extended division of labour the doubtful moral element consists in the circumstance, that this enormous production of *things* takes place at the cost of *men.*   For how must it be with the mind of a man who has during a long series of years passed the hours of the day, and perhaps many of the night, in an absolutely unintellectual employment, in which the mental part of his being is utterly idle, nay, in which he himself at last becomes a piece of machinery!   When we contemplate the division and subdivision of labour which is ever going on, and whose sole aim it is to produce the greatest possible amount of material commodities for the embellishment of this or that great industrial exhibition, we are involuntarily reminded of the saying of Christ: "What shall it profit a man, if he gain the whole world, and lose his own soul?"

It was in direct opposition to the system prevailing in his time, when the State carried beyond all bounds the guardianship of its subjects, and when guilds and corporations, with oppressive privileges restrictive of all free development, were the order of the day, that Adam Smith brought forward his demand for free competition in all departments.   He taught that the State must keep aloof, must not interfere, must follow the principle of *laissez faire, laissez aller;* that if a statesman should give directions to private individuals how to dispose of their capital, he not only gave himself useless trouble, but was arrogating to himself an authority which ought not to be conceded to any individual, or assembly, or town council; that the sole duty of the State was to remove the old restrictions, which had too much repressed individual liberty, and made free movement and life impossible.   For Adam Smith regards it as a law of nature, that every one best knows how to manage his own affairs, and that the economical activity of the individual, though put in motion by the spring of self-interest, by care for his own advantage, must nevertheless lead to what is most beneficial to the common prosperity; that each, while labouring for himself, is at the same time labouring for the whole.[1]   Thus common prosperity is the natural result of general selfishness.   But it is just at

[1] Smith, *Wealth of Nations,* II. 42 sqq.

this point that the moral element of the system in question is doubtful. For free competition, when not restrained by higher considerations, is only a naturalistic, a physical principle. And what is thus indirectly introduced is the right of the stronger, a kind of club-law, a war of all against all, such as is presented to us in the animal kingdom, in which free competition for all the goods of life takes place on the largest scale, and the weaker creatures are constantly being destroyed by the stronger. The ethic element called forth by free competition is said indeed to consist in the arousing and strengthening of personal moral power. But then free competition must be restricted by certain conditions. It must, for instance, take place only between equals. For a lame man to compete with a racer, a poor retail dealer with a rich capitalist, a small peasant proprietor with a great landholder, can by no means conduce to the strengthening of moral power, and will lead to nothing else than to the supremacy of the material in the name of liberty, and to its inevitable possession of the rewards of victory. Nor will the assertions of Adam Smith hold good, that the welfare of society is best promoted by the principle of non-intervention, that every one who promotes his own interest gives an impulse to the interest of the whole, and that general prosperity is the natural result of individual selfishness. It is a notion untenable by its very nature, that a state of justice should ever be brought about by the satisfaction and exercise of mere natural impulse, when righteousness belongs to an entirely different world, and must originate from an entirely different side than that of mere nature and the natural man. On the contrary, we may even without, and prior to, the testimony of experience be convinced, that to let nature and its powers rule in moral relations can lead only to social confusion. Besides, experience has taught us, that while free competition has indeed abolished former monopolies and the evils therewith connected, it has brought into existence a new monoply, viz. that of *capital*, under the oppression of which countless numbers have fallen into a condition which does not essentially differ from that of the slaves of antiquity.

§ 62.

Capital does not mean the same as property or riches, so far as these are employed either in the defraying of necessary expenses or the procuring and contriving of enjoyments, or are even only laid by in the form of a collected store. Capital, on the contrary, is *productive* property, *i.e.* such as is applied to the production of fresh property in progressive alternation, and is therefore inseparable from *investment.* In the old heathen world, and in the Middle Ages, the use of capital was only to a small extent developed. In ancient times there were great, nay, enormous possessions, consisting chiefly in landed property and slaves, not in investments and stocks, although these occur, in their earliest form, in the ancient world in the disposition or " employment " *(occupatio)* of large sums of money. In the Middle Ages there were also large possessions, but these consisted chiefly in natural produce, and service which dependants were obliged to render to their lords and superiors. Capital could not attain development, because this was hindered by a mass of restrictions or particular legal appointments connected with the feudal system of the times, its guilds and corporations, its privileges and monopolies. Capital first made its appearance on a large scale in the commerce which was carried on in the fifteenth century with the East by way of Venice. The restrictions just mentioned were here removed. After the discovery by the Portuguese of a sea-passage to India, the brothers Fugger of Augsburg sent a whole expedition to the East, and, besides covering their expenses of 1000 ducats, made a net profit of 175,000 ducats. And this means capital and investment. Even Luther speaks of the mighty riches of the Fuggers, and tells us that they lent the emperor twelve tons of gold for his wars ; and that a Fugger, being once summoned for the payment of a property tax, replied that he did not know how rich he was, nor how much he possessed, and therefore could not pay the tax ; that his money was dispersed throughout the world, in Turkey, Greece, Alexandria, France, Portugal, England, Poland ; but that he would pay the tax for what he possessed in Augsburg.[1]

<hr>

[1] Luther's *Werke,* Walch'sche Ausg., XXII. 319.

It will not be without interest to mention here what position Luther took with respect to this new phenomenon. He is very doubtful about it, and thinks that it cannot be right, *i.e.* not according to God's commands. He uses the strongest expressions against *usury* and trading in interest, by which so many had already been brought to poverty. He equally blames the trading companies, then just introduced, as nothing else than monopolies; for these companies get goods of all kinds into their hands, do what they will with them, raise and lower prices according to their desire, *oppress and ruin all small traders, as the pike does the smaller fish in the water*, as though they were the lords of God's creatures, and free from all the laws of faith and love.[1] " Hence comes it that spice is so dear. This year they raise the price of ginger, next year that of saffron, etc.; and they know how to manage so as to suffer neither loss nor harm. For if at one time they lower the price of ginger, they will reimburse themselves upon saffron, and so forth; so as to be at all times secure of the largest profit." But this he argues is contrary to the nature of temporal possessions, which God has appointed to be subject to danger and insecurity. They have, however, found out how to make certain and constant profit with uncertain temporal wares. The whole world is impoverished by them, and thus all money must fall into and swim in their bag. " Kings and rulers ought to see to and forbid such doings; but they are, I hear, sharers and directors of them, and Isa. i. 23 still holds good: ' Thy princes are rebellious and companions of thieves.' They sometimes hang a thief who has stolen a whole or half-florin, and they transact business with those who steal and plunder the whole world: great thieves hang the small ones. If the companies are to remain, justice and honesty will be overthrown ; and if justice and honesty are to remain, the companies must fall. *A bridle must be put into the mouths of the Fuggers and all such companies.*" He also laments the luxury which has come into the country from India and Calicut, with these spices, these gold stuffs and silver vessels, things which are of no use but only for magnificence. He complains also of the deceptions of merchants, who put pepper, ginger and saffron

[1] Luther's *Werke*, Walch'sche Ausg., X. 119.

into damp cellars, that they may weigh the heavier; who adulterate their goods by artificial colouring, and such like practices. On the whole, he is of opinion that it would be far better to promote and extend agriculture, and to restrict trade, pointing at the same time to the fact that there is so much land still untilled.[1]

For the rest, it was just the Reformation which gave an impulse to the further development of capital, by mainly contributing to the overthrow of mediæval restrictions. Unfortunately, however, it did something more than this; for in its secularization of the property of the Romish Church, it by no means paid sufficient attention to what became of it in a social point of view,—though this was in some degree consulted by the foundation of hospitals and schools,—suffered property to be purchased under price by certain individuals, and really squandered it.[2] Not till much later, not indeed till the French Revolution, was trade entirely emancipated from the restrictions of law. It was then that free competition, which had already been advocated by Adam Smith, came into full play, and capital attained its full development. The liberal State, which delights in life and motion, in the conflict of forces, faithfully obeys the directions of Adam Smith not to interfere in the matter, and only takes care that private property and personal safety shall be unmolested. It confines itself, as Lassalle expresses it, to performing "the office of a night watchman," and in other respects follows the maxim of *laissez faire* and *laissez passer*. "Every one is now at liberty to become a millionaire." Thus an entirely new class is being formed in modern society, that of the millionaires, or of the *aristocracy of wealth*, a class in which modern Judaism takes a high position, exercising, like a Midgard serpent encircling the world, an oppressive supremacy over nations and rulers.

§ 63.

It cannot be disputed that free competition has contributed to the development of many forces and promoted the welfare of numbers. Nor can it be denied that capital is of greater importance to society, when extensive undertakings are in

---

[1] Luther's *Werke*, W. A., X. 394.   [2] K. Marx, *Das Capital*, p. 750.

question, when a general economic intercourse and exchange prevail, and when, in contrast to a merely national, a world-wide political economy is called into existence. But as little can it be denied, that free competition has diffused misfortune and poverty among a far greater number of persons, that thousands upon thousands have to fight for their daily bread a desperate battle, in which they at length utterly succumb to the stronger. And this fact it is that has produced the so-called *labour question*, which has now become world-exciting, and may well be called one big with the future destiny of civil society. In this respect we think first of all of the lot of factory operatives in the great manufacturing districts and countries, where thousands of poor workmen are in a state of absolute dependence upon some rich master manufacturer. These great manufacturers compete with each other, and the poor workmen also compete by " underbidding each other" (*i.e.* by asking lower wages) for the sake of getting work for their daily maintenance.

The relation between employers and employed is no longer a personal, but an impersonal one, a relation between two things, as is indeed shown even in the ordinary terms capital and labour, by which this impersonal contrast is expressed. The workman counts for just so much labour. And it is this labour-power which he sells for a certain time to his employer, who regards it like any other commodity. This newly arisen relation is distinguished from the slavery of the ancient world only by the fact that the slave was bound to a single master, while the workman is bound to the whole class of employers. As soon as the employer dismisses him, or closes his factory, the workman is left to live upon air; on this account he is obliged to seek work, and to take it wherever and under whatever conditions he can at the moment get it. His existence and that of his family is one of complete insecurity, and is exposed to all kinds of chance; he lives from hand to mouth, and has no sort of certainty about his future.

When, moreover, we look at the kind of life prevailing in factories, a life which has been often enough described, we find that the work, as already pointed out, is, in consequence of the manifold division of labour introduced by machinery, insipid and joyless, and one which blunts and destroys the intellect. For the workman is nothing more than a piece of flesh and blood machinery, inserted among the steel and iron portions, to work along with them. Family life properly so called, that foundation of a morally healthy human existence, is impossible in his case. As a rule, he is married and has a numerous family,—for the proletariate multiplies exceedingly, just as it was formerly said of the children of Israel, the more the Egyptians oppressed them the more they increased,—but a comfortable life at his own fireside he is utterly ignorant of. Not only himself, but his wife and children must work at the factory from morning till night, and that apart from each other. Just because machinery enables muscular power to be dispensed with, women and children—and even very small children—can be employed. Nay, the fingers of little children are, *e.g.* in lace factories, more skilful in tying threads than those of grown persons. The mother, being obliged to work all day long at the factory, becomes more and more unskilled in fulfilling the duties of a wife and mother, and totally inexperienced in matters pertaining to domestic life. She has to entrust such children as do not work in the factory to the care of the incompetent and neglectful, or to give them opium, brandy, and such things to sleep them. Nor does bodily health suffer less than mind and heart by this factory life. The rate of mortality among children and adults is a frightful one. Swarms of children especially are sacrificed to the steam-engine as to a modern Moloch. This mischief began at the close of the last century, when English manufacturers, representing to the Government that, under existing commercial circumstances, they were no longer capable of competing with foreigners, the otherwise great and highly revered William Pitt uttered these terrible words, the whole bearing of which he could then scarcely have contemplated: "Take the children." And they were taken, and devoted to a premature death. At all events, manufactures so flourished thereby, that free competition could be continued. That this is, however, a new heathenism, and that of the most flagrant kind, scarcely needs proof.[1] Adults die off in

---

[1] Reischl, *The Labour Question and Socialism*, Munich 1874, p. 72. Ch. l'érin, *Le travail des enfants employés dans les manufactures*, 1874.

their best years, not merely because their lives are shortened by scanty and sometimes unwholesome fare, but because factory work itself in a heated, moist, impure atmosphere, is evidently, in many respects, prejudicial to health. Malformation of the limbs, in consequence of the unnatural position to which the bodies of the workmen are in many instances confined, scrofulous and lung diseases, are the ordinary results of such employment. Large quantities of fine dust, *e.g.* in cotton and flax mills, are also constantly flying about, which being inhaled by the workers, cause affections of the chest, accompanied with spitting of blood. And this equally applies to the dust inhaled in the polishing of steel or gold.

Similar phenomena also appear outside the sphere of factory work properly so called. We need here only mention the young girls employed in dressmaking and millinery establishments, where the finery of the rich and aristocratic is prepared, and the often-discussed London needlewomen, who, according to Engel's description,[1] generally live in a state of great poverty in small garrets, where as many as possible are huddled together, and where during the winter months the animal heat of the inhabitants is often the sole means of warmth. These unfortunate creatures sit bent over their work, and sew from four or five in the morning till midnight, ruining their health and eyes in the course of a few years, and preparing for themselves an early grave, without being able, with all their industry, to procure the barest necessaries. The invention of the sewing-machine has made the lot of these poor seamstresses a still harder one. For the smallest and most imperfect sewing-machine can do as much as four or five needlewomen. Excellent, therefore, as this invention may in itself be, it at all events contributes in no small degree to diminish the need of hand-sewing, and to lower its price.

It is indeed maintained on the part of liberalism and capitalists, that these descriptions, and the still further details in socialistic works,—as, *e.g.*, that of Engel just named, a somewhat old (1848) but not therefore obsolete treatise, lately corroborated and continued by Marx (*das Capital*, Hamb., 2d ed. 1873),—are but one-sided and exaggerated views of the true state of affairs. None, however, of the facts stated by these

---

[1] Engels, *Die Lage der arbeitenden Classe in England*, Leipzig 1848.

authors has been weakened; and men whose intelligence and impartiality cannot be denied, declare that, much as has been done in particular cases for the improvement of the workman's lot, and much as noble employers, with hearts full of zeal for human welfare, have in this respect done and sacrificed, the great evil still very generally exists, and, in the name of philanthropy, absolutely demands a remedy.[1] It is also pointed out, that just in England, where the loudest complaints are heard, several enactments have been made on the part of the State to protect workmen against the caprice of employers, *e.g.* by means of an inspection on behalf of the State of the sanitary conditions of localities, especially with respect to ventilation and construction, also enactments concerning the hours of labour and the employment of women and children. But this appeal to Government orders is a condemnation of the whole system, and concedes that the State must not content itself with following the *laissez faire* principle, but must *by active interposition set a limit to the freedom granted*, and that therefore Adam Smith's theory, according to which the State must keep quite aloof from the matter, is untenable. What has, however, been as yet effected by the State in this matter is but a trifle, and, on the whole, of slight importance.

It is said that "the condition of workmen is their own fault, because, even when they have abundant wages, they do not lay by, but live only for the moment, following the maxim: A short life and a merry one; that they are addicted to two vices, to immorality—which is indeed promoted by the association of men and women at the same work—and to drunkenness. It is said that every Saturday afternoon, after the payment of the weekly wages, thousands of workmen are seen drunk; and lastly, that they are irreligious, and never go to church when allowed, being infected by materialistic and atheistic doctrines." All these reproaches may be well founded, and we will dispute none of them. But, we ask, is it to be wondered at if this is the case? And when we contemplate with horror the wild and godless nature which is developed by factory life, ought the prevailing feeling to be

---

[1] Comp. Schäffle, *Kapitalismus und Socialismus*, Tübingen 1870, p. 426. Plener, *Die englische Fabrikgesetzgebung*, Vienna 1871.

indignation and anger, and not rather the deepest compassion ? Is it the personal guilt of individuals which here encounters us, or the guilt of the whole civil community ? And is it so strange a thing that these people should be improvident, when they cannot lay by enough to secure themselves a permanent home and an existence under its protection, and that they should choose to procure themselves increased enjoyment for a few days, during which they consume what could have only afforded them help for a few weeks ? Is it to be wondered at, that they are addicted to the above-named vices, when pleasures of a higher and nobler nature are inaccessible to them ? Is it marvellous that they should lend an ear to the materialistic and atheistic doctrines of the age, if no one cares for their mental development ? For what has hitherto been done for them by Sunday and night-schools has not proved particularly efficient. And if they are without Christianity, for the inward appropriation and practice of which the needful time is scarcely afforded them, and which—and this applies especially to England—is often offered them in dry dogmatic formulas, and introduces them into sectarian controversies, in which they, of course, feel no interest, what else is there for them than the barren doctrines of unbelief and negation ?—doctrines which at all times find an ally in the heart of the natural and unconverted man, and whose correctness is also confirmed in their eyes by their wretched experience of the miseries of this life. They form, in opposition to the optimist view of life prevailing among the bourgeoisie and capitalists, a pessimist view of life. What Carlyle once said of the operatives in English cotton factories, applies to many workmen: "This world is for them no home, but a dingy prison-house of reckless unthrift, rebellion, rancour, indignation against themselves and against all men. Is it a green, flowery world, with an ever azure sky stretched over it, the work and government of a God ; or a murky, simmering Tophet, of copperas-fumes, cotton-fuzz, gin-riot, wrath and toil, created by a demon, governed by a demon ?" Byron, with his bitter satire on social relations, has found many readers among these English workmen, who, by means of the lectures and readings lately instituted for them, have been able to acquire a certain amount of education. The representations, too, of the life of Christ by Strauss and Renan, have not a few readers among the working-classes.

The sting which this social problem bears in it is still further envenomed, when we contemplate the multitudes willing to work for even the lowest pay, who are out of employment. There are thousands of individuals in the great cities of Europe, who get up in the morning without knowing whence they shall that day get the most scanty support, who often do not even know where they shall lay their heads next night, and will have to sleep in the open air. Many of these, when unable to procure some small chance occupation, pass their days in begging and stealing. This large number of unemployed poor leads us to another element of social misery, viz. *over-population*, whence arises a whole class of *supernumeraries*, of superfluous persons, *i.e.* of persons for whom society has no room and no use. Adam Smith's celebrated disciple, Thomas Robert Malthus (1766–1834), in his *Essay on Population* (1798), declares it an absurdity that every human being should, because he has come into the world, have a right to the means of subsistence. The poor man, he says, who cannot support himself and his family, did not before his birth ask society whether it would have him. If, then, he comes to the festive table of nature, and finds no seat and no cover laid for him, nature thus declares to him that he had better take himself off. Malthus is of opinion that we should always strive against a disproportion between the existing means of support and the numbers of the population, that nature itself opposes and remedies over-population by diseases, pestilences and war, by famine and starvation, and that it is folly to keep alive, by benevolent and provident institutions, the supernumerary population, and so to enable and encourage them to increase and multiply, and thus enhance the evil in question. Hence every one should be left to provide for himself, and the principle of free competition be strictly obeyed. He exhorts the proletariate, if they would not die of starvation, not to have so many children, whom they must afterwards provide for; and disciples of Malthus have moreover proposed to let the little superfluous children die a painless death by the fumes of charcoal! But certainly this thoroughly heathenish and heartless view will satisfy no one who still bows before the behests of morality and religion. It is difficult to understand how Malthus, who was originally a clergyman, could, while holding such opinions, preach the gospel to the poor. We by no means deny that the Malthusian view of the disproportion between the means of support and the number of the population, between food and the mouths requiring it, has often enough found sad confirmation in the actual state of things. But for our part, we cannot but persevere in the view that this disproportion is more the fault of man than of nature, that it must be contended against and overcome by moral means, and indeed by the efforts not only of individuals but of the whole community, by the better yield of lands now lying untilled, by a more equitable distribution of existing stores, etc.

The solution of the great problem which the individualism and political economy of Adam Smith have evidently left unsolved, has been attempted in an entirely opposite way, viz. by Socialism, although many socialistic experiments must be regarded as mere dreams and delusions. Any one acquainted with human nature will not find it altogether unnatural if the so-called supernumeraries, who are rejected from the great table of nature, should declare themselves to be those really entitled to places, and regard the capitalists as the superfluous who can be dispensed with, or that even if they are willing still to grant them a place, they should at all events desire an entirely different division of property.

UTOPIAN AND REVOLUTIONARY SOCIALISM.

§ 64.

While one-sided individualism, or liberalism, proceeds from that notion of *liberty* which the French Revolution developed, at the expense of equality, one-sided socialism arises from the *equality* which it, on the other hand, asserts at the expense of *liberty*. It desires to abolish unnatural distinctions among individuals, insists upon fellowship and brotherhood, and demands the same rights and the same property for *all*. The simplest way of attaining this seems to be to do away with all private property and private earnings, and to transform civil society into one great common household, in which neither this man nor that, but the whole community, is the great capitalist and employer, whose part it is to make an equitable distribution to all of both labour and profit.

The notion is an old one, and has already been frequently carried out in poetic descriptions—a circumstance sufficiently testifying to the fact, that it belongs rather to an imaginary world than to this earth. It is found so early as in Plato's books "of the State," and has frequently reappeared since his time in those numerous "political romances," which have developed socialistic and communistic views, and contained at the same time an indirect condemnation and satire of the imperfect and often unjust state of affairs actually existing. Among those, perhaps the most important is the famous work of Sir Thomas More, Lord Chancellor of England in the time of Henry VIII., concerning the newly discovered island of Utopia (1516).[1] Utopia (nowhere) is an island in the South Sea, surrounded on all sides by hidden rocks, and therefore inaccessible to any unprovided with Utopian pilots. This State, founded by a sage of the name of Utopus, and numbering one and a half million citizens, possesses a purely democratic government, with officials freely elected, and a head of the State holding office for life. Every forty persons form a *social group*, placed under common guidance; thirty such *groups* are under a *president*, and three hundred under a *chief president*. At the head of the general *administration of affairs* is a senate, which assembles under the presidency of the *head of the State*. Liberty is protected by the democratic constitution, while the main thought determining the whole is equality.

When one city in Utopia has been seen, all have been seen. It has fifty-four splendid cities, with straight streets running in parallel lines, all of equal size, all built on the same plan. The houses of each street are exactly like each other in arrangement, and lest the inhabitants should acquire a taste for, and take pleasure in private property, they are redistributed by lot every tenth year. Behind each house is a garden, the care and cultivation of which is committed to its occupant. Round each city lie well-defined plots of land, with dwellings and farm buildings, the farming of these fields giving occupation

---

[1] Rudhart, *Thomas Morus*, Nürnberg 1829, p. 122 sqq. Marlo, *System der Weltökonomie*, Cassel 1859, vol. I. Div. II. p. 449 sqq.

on an average to forty persons. The Utopians dwell alternately in the country and the city; and all, women as well as men, are compelled to undertake field work, with which they combine some kind of handicraft. They are obliged to work six hours a day, three in the forenoon, three in the afternoon, and the overseer watches to see that none are idle during working hours. The rest of their time is devoted partly to art and science, on which lectures are given to both men and women, and partly to recreation. If any one desires to take a journey, he has to obtain permission to do so. Wherever he goes, he is entertained free of cost, but is obliged, in return, to take his share in the kind of work with which he is acquainted. All the workmen, *i.e.* all citizens, without distinction, bring their productions to a general *warehouse* in the centre of their own quarter of the town, whence what every one needs is delivered to him. The government provides that the productions of the country shall be distributed in due proportions at the general *warehouses*, and itself carries on commerce with other countries, for the purpose of transporting elsewhere such special produce of the land as is not required at home.

The Utopians lead a happy life, understanding by happiness such a life as is appointed them by nature and reason only. They enjoy good health, and sickness rarely occurs among them. They have, however, hospitals outside the towns, in which the sick are tended. The Utopians retire to rest in the evening when the clock strikes eight, sleep eight hours, and consequently rise at four in the morning. Their dress is simple, tasteful and convenient, not subject to the changes of fashion, but settled once for all, and the same for all individuals of the same sex. Their meals are provided by different housekeepers in turns, and partaken of at common tables. During meals there are lectures or music.

The Utopians lead not only a moral, but also a religious life. They have magnificent temples, and a highly respected but not very numerous class of priests, a circumstance arising from the view that but few are fitted for this high vocation. They possess religious liberty, and are of various religions. But no one in Utopia can enjoy the right of citizenship who does not believe in a personal God and a life after death.

They strictly insist on the sacredness of marriage, and

adultery is very severely punished. They marry early, but over-population is avoided by colonization. Legislation is simple, and lawsuits uncommon; great crimes occur only as strange exceptions. These are punished by the offender being made a slave, and bound with golden fetters, for Utopians have a deep contempt for gold. All despicable vessels, chamber utensils, etc., are made of gold and silver, while those destined to more honourable uses are made of earth or glass. Pearls and diamonds may only be used by children as playthings.

Among the various Utopias, we may mention Fenelon's *Télémaque*, in which, in a series of imaginary pictures, he has anticipated the French revolutionary ideas, not merely of liberty, but of equality. We have also to name a Utopia which has recently appeared in Danish literature,—F. C. Sibbern's "*Aus dem Jahre* 2135," in which the talented author, who is chiefly known as an acute psychologist, sketches ideal pictures of the future. In this work, Europe appears as having entered upon socialistic and communistic conditions, from which ancient, *i.e.* the present, Europe, " with its unhappy system of property, its anxiety for and need of the means of earning a living, that constant source of the conflict of all with all, inseparable from the rights of property and possession, which pervades all life, and has issued in terrible injustice," is contemplated with horror. The transition to a better state of affairs is not, however, made to take place, as one might fear, by means of a violent revolution, but, on the contrary, by an event which is, at the same time, natural and supernatural. At the close of the nineteenth century, the human race in Europe, tired, mentally exhausted and paralyzed, in consequence of the unnatural state in which intellectual life, and all that gives value to human existence, were being gradually extinguished, sinks into a slumber. This slumber is followed by a revival, which brings with it a happier state of things.

Whatever may be thought of this work, full as it is of Utopian notions of equality and religious paradoxes, no one can read it attentively without perceiving in it a spirit of true philanthropy, a large - heartedness for human welfare and sorrow, nor without encountering a multitude of profound and striking thoughts. The retrospect at Old Europe, at free competition, at the lot of factory operatives, and the deplorable condition of needlewomen, at " the whole system of trade and business, that battle-field and scene of action where all are striving for the one object, of obtaining, at the cost of others, by oppressing and repulsing others, by injuring and wearing out their minds, or even exposing their lives to the powers of darkness and destruction, by all kinds of art and cunning, the greatest possible riches, without asking how it fares with others " (I. 249), is the occasion of many pertinent remarks. With the disposition and opinions which are said to prevail in New Europe, we can but sympathize, for then " the life of the soul will everywhere be esteemed more important and essential than the bodily life, so that intellectual prosperity will be no more wasted, nay, choked and destroyed, for the sake of gaining all kind of material possessions " (I. 133); for then the welfare of the soul will be the main concern, no soul will be any more misused or sacrificed, and least of all will great works or undertakings be carried on by the destruction of human souls (I. 112). With respect, however, to the new and more perfect state of things itself as here predicted, no greater value can be attributed to Sibbern's descriptions than he himself accords to the old English picture of " Utopia."

If we regard these Utopias as only pleasing dreams, in which a refuge is sought from the calamities of the times, the remark can scarcely be withheld, that such a life as that of the island of Utopia or the year 2135, must be extremely monotonous and tedious. The circumstances which are here conjured up are indeed idyllic, peaceful, harmonious, nay, paradisaic, but they are circumstances in which there is scarcely a trace of the struggle and battle of life, nor even of its sorrows. The abundant variety of relations which life furnishes, and their developments ever increasing with increasing culture, are here suddenly resolved into the very simplest relations, at all events into such as seem to be composed of extremely few elements. They are, so to speak, prehistoric circumstances, into which we are to be transported. History, historical development, historical conflicts and destinies, are out of the question in Utopia. Life runs on day by day in a very uniform circle of eating, drinking, sleeping, working, studying and playing music. As long, however, as we live upon earth, and have not arrived at the harmonies of eternity, which, moreover, will be far more various and many-toned than those of Utopian worlds, as long as we have still a history, we are ever relegated to the battles of life; and there is in the present struggle for existence an element which can never wholly disappear from life in this world. The importance to be attributed to all such romances rests mainly on the condemnation they pass upon the defects of existing systems; also upon their keeping alive the consciousness that a more perfect condition is to be aimed at, and laying down certain postulates, which the originators of these fancy pictures well know can be only approximately, and under great limitations, realized on this earth.

§ 65.

The matter is different when Utopian ideas are to be directly put into practice and realized, for they then become revolutionary, and threaten society with a chaotic confusion. This applies to *Socialism*, which has from time to time reappeared since the French Revolution to the present day. Pure *Communism* desires a continuous equal division of all material possessions, a complete abolition of the rights of property and inheritance. Socialism, in the special party signification of the word, does not indeed expressly demand the abolition of private property and hereditary right, though both are really weakened and overthrown. But it does require the abolition of all *private employment*. The directing superiors of society are to distribute to each his work, without reaping any advantage from it, for all profit comes to the society, which is to distribute it to its members. For this purpose, human beings must be divided into larger groups, consisting of a certain number of families, who live and work together in splendid dwellings (*Phalansteria*), specially constructed for the purpose. In these barrack-like buildings they perform all kinds of employment, among which, however, the industrial are the chief (Fourier). The revolutionary view of private property is expressed in the well-known saying of Proudhon: *La propriété c'est le vol.* This severe-sounding saying is declared, however, to contain no personal attack upon individual possessors of property. On the contrary, it is said to be an attack only upon the bad institutions and relations of society, the result of which is the general prevalence of injustice, and the exclusion of the majority from that share of property to which they have a well-founded claim. But the view of life on which the whole system is founded is not, as in the above-discussed romances, the ethic, but an essentially naturalistic and eudaemonistic one. Earthly enjoyment and the pleasures of sense are here esteemed the highest good, and the sole object of human life; of this supreme good, all must henceforth be partakers. Certainly this kind of socialism has come forward with a certain tinge of religion also; nay, it has appealed to Christ as the first socialist, who placed all men on a level. It has promised to give the world a new Christianity, by asserting, in the place of the dogmas which have hitherto composed it, the authority of the commandment: Thou shalt love thy neighbour as thyself. But the love of our neighbour thus proclaimed aims at nothing further than securing him the same share of sensuous pleasures which we desire for ourselves, a share in a complete carnal emancipation, including release from marriage and its sacred restraints. The deity here proclaimed is none other than nature, or the life of the all; and the inmost core of a radically irreligious mode of thinking becomes more and more manifest, and proves itself openly hostile to Christianity and the Church. How love to one's neighbour fares, was shown in the " Red Republic," which raised its head in 1848 and 1871, and which, though overthrown, is constantly keeping Europe in a state of tension and fear, lest it should again arise with its cry of: " War against palaces, Peace with cottages!"

This movement, notwithstanding the terror it inspires, has a relative justification in the presence of existing circumstances, as developed in all their injustice under the aegis of liberalism. It is undeniable that of all classes of society, the proletariate, the working or fourth class, must have most sensibly experienced that the French Revolution was far from keeping what it promised. The French Revolution proclaimed indeed *political equality*, but to this day the proletariate must have been again and again convinced, that of all the revolutions that have taken place since 1789, no single one has rendered even the slightest contribution to *social* equality, to an equal participation in the actual possessions of life, but that, on the contrary, the ordinary distinctions have in this respect remained the same.   It has found out that liberalism has, so to speak, fed it with formal political privileges, which are of no avail for the realities of life.   It is therefore owing to something having its root in the state of affairs, that the social problem is ever more and more coming into the foreground, and the political becoming of secondary importance.   The contrast may be popularly expressed as follows:—The political question is: Who is to reign over me?   The social: What shall I live on to-morrow? and so long as no satisfactory answer is given me to the latter, the political one is a matter of indifference, unless so far as it may help me to work and food.

But here revolutionary socialism falls, besides, into the great error of so understanding the principle of equality, that human individuality is completely suppressed thereby.   Its delusion is, that if the same education and the same external state of life were imparted to all men, all the differences now existing among them would disappear.   In this respect spurious socialism is agreed with its great opponent, Adam Smith, who, though an individualist, yet advanced no further in his conception of individuality itself, than to be able, when the division of labour is spoken of, to assert that "the difference between the most dissimilar characters, between a philosopher and a common street porter, seems to arise not so much from nature as from habit, custom and education.   By nature a philosopher is not, in genius and disposition, half so different from a street porter, as a mastiff is from a greyhound, or a greyhound from a spaniel, or this last from a shepherd's dog."[1] But this is by no means the case, as experience has a thousand times proved.   For we daily see before our very eyes, children of the same parents, brought up in the same family, develope in a totally different manner, both intellectually and morally. Hence it is an error to maintain, as this socialism does, that all men have the same wants and are susceptible of the same pleasures, and an equal one to assert that all can be used for one and the same kind of labour, and are capable of perform-

<hr>

[1] Smith, *Wealth of Nations*, I. 26.

ing work of the same value and quality. It is also connected with this principle of equality, to regard society, as this spurious socialism, agreeing herein with liberalism falsely so called, does, not as an organism, but only as an aggregate of individuals, brought together in a merely external and mechanical manner. When society is, on the contrary, regarded as an organism, as a body furnished with many and different members, a rich variety is exhibited therein, and it seems simply absurd to attempt to deny the distinctions of higher and lower capacities, of higher and lower classes, and to place, for example, the work of a porter on a level with that of an artist, poet, or learned investigator, the day's work of a factory operative with that of a statesman. And just as the kind of work is of an entirely different quality, so also is there an infinite difference in the wants of life, and the views of what makes life enjoyable.

The suppression of individuality comes forward most plainly in the abolition of all the *rights of private property.* Without personal possession, a personal life, properly so called, is utterly inconceivable. Every individual needs a certain amount of the things of this world to call his own, to dispose of, and to which, as his extended temporalities, he bears, so to speak, a proportion. Without such property the individual personality cannot attain its proper development. The personal existence or position in life remains without support so long as it lacks the means or instruments of its individual self-assertion, of performing its individual tasks and satisfying its individual requirements. In the one-sided socialistic State, personal enjoyment, properly so called, is quite out of the question, inasmuch as the individual cannot himself choose his pleasures, but must have them prescribed and distributed to him, either by the whole community or its leaders. The right of *inheritance,* moreover, is inseparably united with the rights of property. Without the right of transmitting his property, a person loses his interest in the future, and therefore also his interest in frugality, having no prospect that the fruits of his labour will profit his successors. Real personal work, too, such work as bears the impress of a man's special peculiarity, work which he has, as it were, stamped with his own image, with the talent bestowed on him by God, is out of the question. For work is here assigned to individuals from without, as seems good to a board of presidents.   Such a procedure must of necessity quench all love of work, and blunt all enthusiasm in any special art employment, the more so that the idle receives as much as the diligent, and that it is just individual talent and ability which finds neither respect nor appreciation.. To obviate the insipid uniformity of work, it has indeed been . proposed to let the workmen take turns at different employments, according to their desire and inclination (Fourier). But this is to overlook the fact that such a change of work is at variance with the division of labour.   For it is desired by means of the latter to ensure the attainment of proficiency in one or another special work, by confining one man exclusively to one kind of employment.   But how, we ask, will work be executed, if the same workman undertakes performances of the most various kind, and after a certain period has elapsed is transferred from one to another ?   It is said indeed in Sibbern's "*Year* 2135 :" "In the morning a tailor, at mid-day a cooper or turner, in the evening a waiter or musician—why should this not be done ? "   It may certainly be *done*, but the question is, *how* it would be done.   The same applies to his picture of life in *New Copenhagen*, p. 141 : " One might by chance meet the same man, the same woman, to-day at the cooperage or upholsterer's, and to-morrow as a public concert singer, or an actor, or instructor of youth in French, English, or Spanish." Now, we do not doubt that such things may go on capitally in Utopia, where it is also possible . that " professors " should go about at certain times of the day as letter-carriers, while the letter-carriers are listening to the lectures of other pro-fessors, for the mental nourishment and refreshment they require.   We doubt, however, whether this could go on in our actual world, and individuals could, in the midst of all this change of employment, continue to be individuals consistent with themselves.

How little an individual is cared for in this socialistic and communistic State is especially manifested by the fact, that family life is here almost entirely done away with. For, with the abolition of private property, family life is destroyed, and with it all the personal satisfaction which this affords to the members of a household.   Life at the home fireside, with its mutual and confidential exchange of thought, its mutual help and assistance, its special arrangements, its domestic regulations, in which the distinctive character or genius of every family is reflected, its exercise of hospitality, the arrival or departure of friends, its small family festivals, its benevolence to the needy (called the home poor), —all this must cease where many families live together in barrack-fashion at the expense of the State, and meet at great common meals arranged by superintendents, where all work together, and where children are removed from their parents and handed over to public care and education.

. The more the State system aimed at from this direction is realized, the more apparent will it be that the exact opposite to what is intended will be brought to pass.   This must be evident even from the fact that over-population, and then, again, want of sufficient means of support, will infallibly be its result. For wherever propagation is not to a certain degree restricted by a moral regard for provision for children and the whole family, where such provision is simply the care of society, which has to furnish equal work and equal profit for all, where no one is responsible for his particular household, there will the increase of population be unlimited.   (Men will, as Mirabeau expresses it, multiply like rats.)   The new inhabitants of the earth, thus numerously incorporated into society, who are mere consumers, till they can enter into the ranks of producers, will immensely increase the amount of wants; and instead of all enjoying equal prosperity, the end will, on the contrary, be, that all will be equals in poverty, want and misery.   The promised kingdom of happiness will be overthrown by starvation.[1]   But such a state must also introduce the opposite to what it aims at, even on the general ground of its quite overlooking one thing, viz. the inherent *sin* of human nature, or at best paying but very superficial regard to it. For is it really imagined that, in an industrial State, people will be contented with such a hierarchy of authorities, to distribute property, and assign to each his work?   It would betray a striking ignorance of human nature not to perceive that in a short time general discontent must break forth into

---

[1] Marlo, *System der Weltökonomie*, I. Div. 2d, p. 516.   Schäffle, *Capitalismus und Socialismus*, p. 201.

endless complaints at unjust treatment, and that reiterated demands for needful reforms would arise and call forth in their behalf ever-renewed revolutions.　Or is it supposed that all these workmen would work, each with the same fidelity and diligence as another, and that many idle and untrustworthy persons would not be found among them, who would nevertheless lay claim to the same enjoyments, in diametrical opposition to the reasonable saying, that "if any will not work, neither let him eat"?　If socialists are unceasingly hurling against the present liberal State the accusation that the rich live at the expense of the poor, *i.e.* of the workers, the complaint may undoubtedly be made against the projected State, that the idle are to live at the expense of the diligent.

ETHIC SOCIALISM.

§ 66.

We have hitherto been considering the two extreme tendencies which in our days stand opposed to each other; on the one hand, extreme individualism, which dates from Adam Smith, and which, while confusion is daily increasing, is really and essentially the system to this hour maintained and dominant in society; and on the other, extreme socialism, which threatens society with revolution.　Time will show how present circumstances will yet disentangle and develope, but we cannot but think that such a state of society must be aimed at as shall contain in principle the truth which is found in both extremes, and maintain the rights of both the society and the individual.　There is, however, as well as imaginary and revolutionary, also *a moral, i.e.* a Christian *socialism.*　Christianity paints no Utopias, describes to us no *perfect* conditions to be introduced in this world.　It teaches us, on the contrary, to seek perfection in another world; but it desires at the same time to help us to struggle against earthly care and want, so that the kingdom of God, and therewith the true kingdom of man, embracing, as it does, not only his spiritual but also his material life, may come upon earth and prosper.

Ethic socialism, as conditioned by Christianity, regards

human affairs, as they actually are, under present and earthly circumstances. It is *conservative*, it enters indeed into reforms and reformations, but not into revolutions. Hence it recognises the rights of private property and inheritance, together with the right of property to be accorded to corporations, foundations and institutions—a right which especially calls forth the greed of revolutionary socialism.[1] But it is at the same time *individualistic*, in the true meaning of the word, and it is so just because it acknowledges that law of solidarity which makes it the duty of the whole community to exclude no individual from its care, and does not, like liberalism, direct the individual " to help himself," and to compete as best he may. Its constant aim is the restoration of a social condition in which every one who is willing to work may really earn his daily bread. Christianity confirms and verifies the words spoken to man at his first departure from paradise: " In the sweat of thy brow *shalt thou eat bread.*" The curse which is in these words laid upon man's labour, viz. that it shall be combined with toil and exertion, a fact abundantly evident in all human labour, and even in that which is most intellectual, has frequently been dwelt upon. But we must not overlook the promise also given in these words, viz. that he who works shall really have bread. For it is by no means said: In the sweat of thy brow thou shalt labour, but yet shalt not eat. Christianity teaches us, on the contrary, that the labourer is worthy of his hire (Luke x. 7), and hence requires that a just and consistent proportion should exist between work and wages. It utters its sharp rebuke against the selfish employer (Jas. v. 14): " Behold, the hire of the labourers who have reaped down your fields, which is of you kept back by fraud, crieth, and the cries of them which have reaped are entered into the ears of the Lord of Sabaoth." And as must especially be insisted on, the Saviour of the world Himself teaches us in the Lord's Prayer to pray for our *daily* bread. But this implies, that if we only fulfil the conditions connected with the prayer, bread shall certainly and

---

[1] This includes certain instances of liberalistic greed, which on many occasions come to the surface, *e.g.* the demands set up, that the property belonging to the Church should devolve to the general treasury of the State. This is nothing else than a bad kind of socialism.

truly be given us. We should do well here to notice also, that the Lord taught us to make this request not only in an individualistic, but in a socialistic sense, "Give *us* this day our daily bread."   And in proportion as Christianity penetrates a whole nation will all thus pray with a feeling of their solidarity, and all *work* together for the fulfilment of their prayer. The obstacles to this fulfilment may indeed lie in the individual, in his idleness or extravagance, but they may equally lie in the civil society, in its bad or unwise enactments, which need a thorough reform that all may be fed. Daily bread indeed differs, nay, differs infinitely in the cases of different individuals. But when our Lord taught us to pray for daily bread, He taught us at the same time how to make this request, viz. in indissoluble connection with the other petitions of this prayer; and this implies that no one has daily bread in the Christian sense, unless he can, though continuing to live in straitened circumstances, both pray and *labour* for the fulfilment of the *other* petitions of the Lord's Prayer. To have daily bread only in such wise as to have daily difficulty in avoiding starvation, and the mind exclusively devoted to the struggle for earthly existence, without time or room for anything higher and better, cannot certainly be called having bread in the meaning which must of necessity be deduced from the Lord's Prayer. In thus speaking we by no means exclude or forget what must be considered as divinely sent trials, as mysterious dispensations. We are here speaking of those ethic view-points which the Lord's Prayer furnishes for the whole community, and its judgment on human requirements. And in this respect we say, that he only has daily bread in the Christian sense who is able at the same time to pray and to labour for the fulfilment of the first petition: "Hallowed be Thy name;" who therefore may hallow the day of rest and worship, *and is not obliged to do on Sundays either his paid work or service;* who is also able to work—both in his own soul and on those of others—for the second petition: "Thy kingdom come;" and who, while fulfilling his earthly calling, can within his own *family,* or in the circle of his nearest friends, be effectively promoting the coming of God's kingdom.

Consequently the question is to help the labourer to an

existence not differing materially from that of "the middle classes," to a real family life as the foundation of all truly moral personal life, to afford him the possibility of a somewhat assured future, and hence especially to assist him to procure himself the comfort of a provision for old age, and a resource against the times when he is out of work or sick. We well know that perfect certainty for this life neither is to, nor can, exist. ' But he whose existence is uncertain to such a degree, that he can in no sense reckon on the future (as, *e.g.*, the husbandman can, who in spring calculates beforehand on harvest, and in harvest on next summer), he whose external existence is utterly unsettled and insecure, without any stay or firm foundation, will also be devoid of true stability and firmness in his inner life, and will himself remain dissolute and unreliable. For this reason it is a special delight to us to see cleanly and well-ventilated workmen's dwellings built anywhere, families attaining in them permanent homes, and provident funds instituted. If all that has hitherto been done is far from entirely abolishing distress, still such institutions manifest an ethic thought which needs only to be further carried out. Besides this, however, not only the moral and religious, but also the *technical education* and improvement of the working man, must be provided for, so that he may cease to be a mere machine, and attain an understanding of, and an insight into the nature of the work in which he has to co-operate, and thus come gradually into such mental possession of leading principles and rules, as may make him capable of engaging independently in an undertaking himself.

§ 67.

If we further inquire as to the *means* by which the goal is to be reached, it is obvious to all, to refer to private benefi-cence, and especially to recommend a relation between em-ployers and workmen which shall be ruled by a spirit of humane and Christian love. It should certainly not be forgotten that no small number of employers have already made great personal sacrifices to help their workmen to an existence consistent with the dignity of human nature. But the performance of such important duties neither can nor ought to be left to mere individual inclination and intelligence, nor to mere accident, but must at the same time be aimed at by regulations and arrangements which bear a more general and reliable character. And in thus speaking we see ourselves led to the idea of an organization of labour, to the idea of *trades-unions*, but not in a Utopian sense, though even such Utopias have at any rate the merit of having first started such a thought, though in a sense in which its carrying out was absolutely impracticable. In behalf of the formation of such trades-unions, both self-help (Schulze-Delitzsch) and the State (Lassalle) have been referred to. Hence union-stores have been proposed, by means of which individuals should be able to obtain the necessaries of life at a cheaper rate, and also unions for production (co-operative stores), whose object it is that the workmen should themselves take in hand the industrial enterprise, should be at the same time both labourers and employers, and themselves enjoy the full profit of their labour. But here the difficult objection certainly arises : In what manner are these people to obtain the needful capital, and how are they to stand a competition with great capitalists ? To which must be added also the circumstance, that such joint undertakings can never succeed, unless they are so fortunate as to find qualified and intelligent managers. It is the sad delusion of many workmen, and one only too much fostered by Lassalle, that they can work as well without guidance and without authority ; that the relation of superiority and subordination is one which ought not henceforth to exist ; and that the State should, according to Lassalle's advice, bestow large capitals upon such many-headed combinations, although they may be devoid of a stable, capable, and trustworthy manager. The arrangement has also been proposed, of allowing the workmen to receive, besides their wages, a certain share in the net profits of the undertaking. Lastly, a settlement of the rate of wages by the State has also been demanded. All these expedients, however, require *State assistance*.

It must indeed be confessed, that with respect to the question before us, there is still much obscurity, much which has not as yet taken solid form, but is still seeking it. But the truth which, among the troubles of the times, has more and more come to the surface, and has from day to day more loudly and urgently raised its voice, is still this: That the *State*, in a matter so powerfully affecting the whole community, must no longer keep to its old *laissez faire* policy, no longer comfort itself with the thought that the world can go on of itself, but must perceive that it is a part of its duty to afford its energetic co-operation. If, however, the State should think it has nothing further to do than to follow the directions of Adam Smith, and to refrain from all interference, the question still remains to be considered, whether the liberal State would not, by its inaction, be guilty of the same neglect and disregard with respect to the rights of the *fourth class*, as the absolute State was before 1789 towards the *third class*, an inaction which entailed a whole series of fatal events; and whether the neglect which the liberal State would thus commit might not in these times also entail similar results, and the last state of things be, if not worse, yet quite as terrible as the first.

We are here confining ourselves to pointing out, in a general manner, the direction in which social reform in this department must take place, without surrendering ourselves to Utopian chimeras. For we cannot regard as Utopian the demand that *legislation* should afford protection to artisans, and to workmen in general. By this we do not mean to say that the State must draw up certain rules and regulations for them, but, on the contrary, that the workmen should be fully at liberty to devise such regulations among themselves, and that the State should afterwards sanction them. Thus statutes of union, rules of association, and enactments concerning labour, would be drawn up by the workmen themselves, and afterwards placed under the protection of civil law.[1] There would then appear under new forms, suited to the circumstances and spirit of the times, something corresponding to the guilds and corporations of former times, communities which, notwithstanding all the excrescences which certainly needed to be abolished, had in their day a beneficial effect upon the moral life and stability of the working-classes. Socialists are working against themselves when they attack whatever of corporate rights and regulations may exist in

---

[1] So Domcapitular Moufang in a speech to his electors (see Rudolph Meyer, *Der Emancipationskampf des vierten Standes* I. 71).

other classes. For it is not by a still greater destruction, but, on the contrary, by the more extended development of the corporate element in society, that the working-classes will be assisted. Nor are we able to perceive aught Utopian in an arrangement already introduced in many places with great success, we mean in the appointment by law, on the part of the State, of the day of work, *i.e.* of the number of hours of labour, nor in its taking the day of rest under its protection by prohibiting Sunday labour, nor in its laws concerning the employment of the labour of women and children, nor in its care that operatives should do their work in healthy rooms, and not be carelessly exposed to the danger of being mutilated by machines, etc.[1] We also find it by no means Utopian, but, on the contrary, an arrangement entirely in harmony with existing circumstances, and well adapted to obviate strikes and much of the mischief resulting from free competition, for the State, after due consideration, and at the request of the workmen themselves, from time to time to regulate the amount of wages. For it can scarcely be expected that the freely elected boards which have appeared in England can be very effective. By the means here indicated, the interests of workmen are placed under *legal* regulation, and they themselves are no longer without a legal standing in society, are no longer exposed to the caprice, to the arbitrary favour or disfavour of capitalists, and to mere chance. If the State has marine laws, commercial laws, and laws of exchange, why should it be unable to enact labour laws ? We also regard it as in harmony with the nature of circumstances, that the State should lighten the burden of taxation for the workman, that it should even, not indeed according to Lassalle's disproportionate demands, but to a certain and limited extent, afford them support, just as it affords it to many private undertakings for the common good, that it should, *e.g.*, when it is desired to set up co-operative associations, assist them by the purchase of machines, etc. Nor can we help regarding it as in accordance with justice and the public interest, that *the rule of money,* i.e. *of capital (the plutocracy),* should be in some

---

[1] A beginning worthy of notice has been made in Denmark also, by means of the law of May 23, 1873, "On the work of children and young people in factories," etc.

degree restricted, or, as Luther expressed it, that a bridle should be put into the jaws of the Fuggers and such associations, that a limit should be set to the stockjobbing mania and to usurious interest, and especially that the rate of interest should be settled. Usury was of old regarded as unchristian, a view which not only the Pope, but also Luther confirmed. In modern States, on the contrary, where competition enjoys unlimited freedom, all usury laws are out of force, and a rate of interest entirely given up. But a contradiction is undeniably involved in the fact that the State should *abolish* usury laws, and nevertheless consent on its part to enforce the fulfilment of pecuniary engagements, and thus make itself the bailiff of usurers, whose exorbitant demands it willingly helps to exact. Rud. Meyer remarks (in his above-cited work, I. p. 78), with reference to this matter, that the utmost concession which the State can in this respect make to liberalism is to say: Get as much percentage as you can, but I will only by the means at my disposal enforce for you the payment of four or five per cent. Different opinions may be entertained as to some of the details here alluded to. We bring forward no politico-socialistic programme, but, on the contrary, leave it to those possessing the technical talent to draw up one which, while it has regard to the special conditions and circumstances of every country, will at the same time be no less considerate of international relations. For it is easy to perceive that if effective reforms for the protection of workmen are undertaken in any one country, that country would not be able to stand competition with foreign lands, unless corresponding reforms were introduced there also. The need of such reforms will, however, so far as they are reasonable, undoubtedly be felt in all places. It is also evident that a change in the principles regulating one department of intercourse, will likewise introduce corresponding changes of principle in other departments of social life. The main question is merely this: If State assistance in general is set up as an ethic demand, from which the State cannot and must not withdraw, can essentially other view-points than those here pointed out be adopted, and activity exercised in essentially different directions from those described?

§ 68.

But we turn from the State-help to self-help. We are here thinking of that self-help which, generally speaking, every man must offer, and which no other can perform for him, the *self-education* through which every one can conquer his evil inclinations, and constantly work out and raise himself to a true moral personality. Hence the working-man and the whole proletariate confessedly need this self-help. But they must also be assisted; they are in want of direction and support. As long as they are attached to doctrines which deny Christ and God, and cannot be induced to renounce the pernicious idea, subversive of all morality, that man has only a mundane, and no supermundane destiny, and that the sole object of life is to pursue during its brief span the greatest possible number of sensual enjoyments, it will not be possible to help them. Their wishes will never be allayed, nor their desires quieted, and contentment, that radically necessary condition of being satisfied with life in *every* position, will never strike firm root in their minds. What alone can help them is Christianity—the Christian faith, the Christian view of life. For it is of very little use to exhort workmen, after the fashion of irreligious political economists, to contentment and moderation, to frugality and diligence, and at the same time to deprive them of all deeper moral and religious *motives* to these virtues, which in and by themselves are mere formal notions. There is, as long as we stop at the standpoint of the celebrated English philosopher and economist, John Stuart Mill (1806–1873), no higher moral principle to lay down for the people than that of *success*. But in presence of such morality, with all its preachification of moderation and economy, the workman will always be justified in exclaiming: "A short life, but at least a merry one; let us eat and drink, for to-morrow we die" (1 Cor. xv. 32).

If then Christianity, with its gospel for the poor, is alone able to help in this case, it is also certain that the *Church* is called upon to co-operate in the solution of the social problem. The Roman Catholic Church deserves all credit in this respect, even though, as is her nature, she carries on her propaganda among workmen. The very position which she has taken up with regard to the labour question, may well be one of the most effective means by which this Church may gain favour and success in the immediate future, and it is at any rate to her honour to have introduced into many workmen's clubs a better spirit, which attacks and overcomes atheistic notions, and to have supported their undertakings by both advice and action. The Protestant Church stands behind in this matter, the reason for which is partly found in the fact that we possess neither the same corporate independence nor the same material means as the Roman Catholic Church. But our Church must no longer keep aloof. A wide field is here opened for "*the inner mission.*" The word and preaching are not sufficient alone. An interest must absolutely be taken in the material prosperity of workmen also. They must be helped not only by Christian instruction and spiritual influence, but by actual and effective assistance besides. When our Lord and Saviour fed the five thousand in the wilderness, He did not feed them merely with His word, but gave them also bodily nourishment. And the poor need this twofold feeding as much as we do.

We have endeavoured in the preceding paragraph to show what we mean by Ethic Socialism, though we willingly admit that we have, properly speaking, only pointed out its *elements*, and not given a complete description. This it is for the moment scarcely possible to do without being betrayed into what is Utopian. A perfect state of things cannot be established as long as sin, transitoriness, and death abide upon earth. But we may, at any rate, expect improvement in proportion as an ethic judgment and treatment of social relations gains ground and penetrates. That unsolved problems will ever remain is what no reasonable man can doubt. To illustrate this fact by a single example: Suppose that all which we have, in the preceding pages, demanded for the improvement of the lot of the factory operative were realized, one very objectionable circumstance would still remain, viz. that all work in factories and by means of machinery is monotonous, unintellectual, and dull. It is, however, an ethic requirement that man should not perform his work as mere compulsory duty, or simply as the means of providing himself with support; but that he should fulfil his daily task with joy and pleasure, and put into it something of his own personal peculiarity, which is an impossibility in mere factory and machine work. Believing, however, in progress, even with respect to man's dominion over nature, we allow ourselves to add this question: Would it be a Utopian dream to imagine that a time may yet come in which machinery will again retire into the background, and handicraft come more to the foreground, when handicraft has, by a series of new inventions, succeeded in making machinery far more serviceable to it than formerly? The right relation between man and the machine is, that the machine should do man service by freeing him from the lower, the merely mechanical, the utterly intellectual part of work, while the state of things now is that man, on the contrary, merely serves machinery, and so becomes a piece of machinery himself. Is it then so monstrous an idea, that that which is in itself reasonable should one day become a reality? that handicraft, allied as it is to art, and yielding to its performers real delight and pleasure, should have a great future before it, in which mere factory work, properly so called, should be limited to colossal productions?[1]

And even if we imagine such a goal as already attained, we must still ever return to the general reflection upon which our Lord's saying, "The poor ye have always with you" (John xii. 8), is founded. At all times it will remain the duty of society to take care for its poor. We may, however, lay down, as at all times binding, the rule, that this care for the poor will only be a true and thorough one in proportion as it seeks to obviate not the want arising from poverty alone. It will fulfil its duty in proportion as it helps the able-bodied pauper to obtain such work as he is fitted for, and, on the other hand, opens appropriate sources for the stream of over-population. With respect to private benevolence, this—so far as it does not enter into an actual personal relation to the poor—will be best exercised by societies, and so far as they

---

[1] We can here only refer to the remarks of F. Reuleaux in his *Theoretischen Kinematik* (1875), p. 514 sqq., on the importance of low-power machines in the restoration of handicraft and the restriction of the machinery,—a thought often reproduced in the work, *Det gamle og det nye Samfund, eller Laugstvang og Näringsfrihed*, of Fr. Krebs (Old and New Society, or the Coercion of the Guild and Freedom of Trade), Copenhagen 1876.

can be again called into existence by guilds and corporations,
for they will at all events best know their own poor.

THE STATE AND PUBLIC MORALITY.

§ 69.

To the common weal pertains not only generally prevailing
prosperity, but general morality. The amount of culture and
civilisation found in a nation is not the only condition of
public morality, as manifested in the customs universally
current and ordinary among its people. Its other and more
special conditions are found in the moral principles which
govern personal life, the measure of justice and love, of
obedience and honesty diffused throughout the community,
and in the readiness shown to make sacrifices for the whole.
The character of the public morality is shown in the relations
which the different classes of society occupy towards each
other. The question here is, whether a just equality exists
in the midst of class distinctions, so that all the different
classes are united by the consciousness of their human and
national solidarity, or whether individual classes are oppressed
by others; or whether class distinctions are utterly effaced in
an undistinguishing equalization, in which each is indifferent
to the whole, and cares exclusively for itself, in which the
only remaining difference is that between possessors and
non-possessors of property, and the worth of an individual is
estimated according to his money. Public morality manifests
itself especially in the relation in which labour and profit
stand to each other; whether industry, combined with
moderation, is an all-pervading and predominant virtue in the
nation, or whether the love of pleasure and the pursuit of
enjoyment, with an attachment to luxury, have the upper
hand. But above all is its character shown in the relation
which individuals occupy to the arrangements and institutions
of the whole; whether, *e.g.*, the sacredness of family life and
of marriage is recognised and upheld, or whether the ties of
family are for the most part relaxed; whether marriages are
lightly entered into and dissolved; whether adultery is
regarded as an ordinary occurrence, and in public opinion no

longer involves loss of respect ; whether prostitution is of great extent in large cities ; whether law and the authority of government are respected, or whether a licence free from all authority prevails, so that every one does what he pleases, and a weak government tolerates such conduct ; whether legal offences and crimes are of frequent occurrence ; whether the people are, on the whole, still penetrated with reverence for religion and the Church, or whether unbelief, indifference and frivolity have the upper hand.   In proportion as the ties which bind individuals to these ordinances are relaxed, does a decay of morality set in.

It is in the nature of the case, that much of what has here been touched on can neither be commanded nor forbidden on the part of the State.   Still the State can and must, for its part, co-operate in the development and confirmation of public morality.   A mutual interaction always exists between the morals and the laws of a State.   As morals influence legis- lation, so does legislation in its turn influence morals (Montes- quieu).   Laws, *e.g.*, which, instead of making divorce difficult, facilitate it as much as possible, or laws on civil marriage which, by their formulæ, do to a certain extent contain an invitation to withdraw from the church celebration of marriage, as a non-essential and indifferent addition, cannot but have a disturbing effect upon morality.   For what is inculcated and sanctioned by the State the mass of the people regard as normal, and consider themselves morally justified if they act in accordance therewith.   The State works positively on the side of morality by extending help and protection to the Christian Church and Christian education, and negatively by opposing public scandals.   That the Christian State must protect Christian worship is self-evident.   It must, though respecting individual liberty, still issue orders concerning Sundays and festivals, forbid secular business and all noisy proceedings during the hours of public worship, and put a stop to theatres and public amusements in Holy Week.   If the modern State abrogates, or puts out of force, such appoint- ments, interwoven as they have become during the course of time with the life of the people, if, *e.g.*, it allows of public amusements on days of general prayer and fasting, which are appointed to enhance the consciousness of national sin and of

God's retributive justice, the motive of such abrogation or non-enforcement can only proceed from the standpoint of a non-religious humanity, which thinks it must not restrain the freedom of such as are alienated from the Church, and cannot do without their worldly amusements, and esteems it more important to gratify these than to ward off scandals from the Christian portion of the community. The same standpoint prevails when the State, as proprietor of railroads, suffers trains to run, and all the business therewith connected to go on, not only on Sundays, but even during the hours of divine service, thereby destroying respect for the Lord's day in the popular consciousness, and at the same time depriving its workmen of their day of rest—both in their families and in God. When the State itself sets such an example of disrespect for the holy day, it is no wonder that it is obliged, by lax and uncertain (and therefore easily evaded) enactments for festivals, to make concessions in other departments, *e.g.* with respect to field-work during the time of divine service.

With all the liberty of speech and conscience which the Christian State may grant, it cannot tolerate open *blasphemy*, open contempt for the Christian religion, whether its expressions are orally uttered in public meetings, or make their appearance by means of the press. And though it must allow *art* to develope according to its own laws, it cannot permit the public exhibition of such works of art as offend the general moral feeling, or the representation of plays in which holy things are profaned. In many cases it will be difficult to define the boundaries which may not be passed, and which will differ in different ages and at different stages of civilisation. There is, however, a certain limit, which must at all times be recognised as one not to be transgressed.

The toleration of houses of ill-fame, and gambling-houses, by the State can only serve to cause scandals. It is urged that the State makes concessions to the former, and places them under its supervision for the sake of warding off worse evils, of securing females of the better class from violence and seduction. But this implies that there must be a class of women, naturally those of the lower and poorer strata of society, destined to the service of sin, and appointed to become vessels of dishonour. And this is quite to fall back to the heathen view of slaves, who were considered. as having no other destination than to sacrifice their human dignity for the good of those in higher position. Such a view should be most emphatically opposed by the Christian State, whose duty it precisely is to prevent, in every manner, the existence within the civil community of such a class of unfortunate and despised beings, many of whom have surrendered themselves to such a condition amidst the temptation of want and poverty. Hence the close connection of this question with the labour and the proletariate questions discussed above. Christian societies for the " inner mission " have done much both to prevent the evil and to rescue the fallen, though the results are but of small amount when compared to the extent of the evil. But even if the State should think it impossible to do anything in this respect, it can at any rate abstain from formally organizing such a caste. And least of all should it, as in France, legalize it by granting licences to such houses for a money payment, and thus increasing its revenue by their taxation. If it is affirmed that immorality would not cease with the cessation of this State toleration, this is certainly a true remark, but one utterly beside the subject. For the question is not whether the government is to banish immorality from the world, but whether *it becomes it* to debase the moral notions of the people, and whether it *may* do this by legalizing immorality instead of branding vice as vice.

It also conduces to the undermining of public morality for the State to tolerate gambling-houses, where the players stake that on which their own subsistence and that of their families depend, and in their passion seek to ruin others for the sake of acquiring riches. Damage is also done to public morality when the State forbids indeed private gaming-houses, but itself keeps a public one, by placing itself at the head of lotteries, thus inviting its subjects to obtain wealth and property in an immoral manner, and at the same time seeking to improve its finances by such means. For the moral way to acquire property is work : " He that will work, let him eat." So far as property *comes* to us, it must be *given to us*, but we must not strive to obtain it without work, by seeking, by all kinds of arts, to conjure and enlist chance on our side, and by invoking the blind heathen goddess of fortune. The objectionableness of lotteries lies in the fact that, instead of working and humbly waiting for the gifts which Providence may bestow, a wheel of fortune is ingeniously prepared for the possible gain of individuals, and the certain loss of the many. The pernicious influence of lotteries is chiefly seen in the lower working-classes, who so easily succumb to the temptation of ceasing to work, and trying instead whether fortune will not favour them. And the justification offered for State lotteries is the same as in the former case, viz. that their object is to ward off greater evils, that the passion for gambling cannot be extirpated, and that it is better it should be under the regulation of the State. It is the same antinomistic argument which asserts that to prevent crime, crime must be organized, and sin thus avoided by means of sin. When number-lotteries are abolished, and class-lotteries allowed, the pernicious consequences are indeed diminished, because the working-classes are kept from gambling by the stakes being higher. But class-lotteries possess their temptations for those also who occupy a lower grade in human society, and are made more accessible to them by many well-known means; while to those of higher position, who are possessed of the means of joining in them, they furnish an immoral way of increasing their property. Hence it is unworthy of the State to afford these institutions the support of its name. It is also thoroughly inconsistent for the State to abolish number-lotteries and to allow the continuance of class-lotteries. For the assumption on which it proceeds is, that the love of play cannot be extirpated, that the persons in question will play, and that it must therefore take the matter into its own hands. Is there, then, any consistency in preserving the opulent from committing too great excesses in gambling, to the ruin of their property, by offering them the expedient of class-lotteries as a channel for their passion, and abandoning the poorer and lower classes to their passions and their fate? What is needed is the perception, that this kind of wisdom which would try to cure immorality by immorality, instead of by the fear of God and industry, is a false wisdom, and that the whole system must be given up.

TRANSGRESSION AND PUNISHMENT.—CAPITAL PUNISHMENT.

§ 70.

The *administration of justice* on the part of the State is of essential importance to public morality. Legal institutions are the foundation of the moral life of society, as well as of its external stability ; and where this foundation is shaken, where, *e.g.*, confidence existing in tribunals has disappeared in a nation, it may be regarded as a sign that public morality (the moral consciousness of the people) is undermined. For the administration of justice is not only of importance to individuals whose rights are thus personally secured, but to the whole civil community. For this reason, legal institutions must be absolutely maintained against all caprice and despotism. In the exercise of its penal justice, the State shows how strictly it understands law and justice. Its penal legislation, and the recognition and validity given thereto, is a nation's clearest expression of its consciousness of justice, and therewith of its moral consciousness of the authority of law, of duty and responsibility, of accountability and guilt.

The *penal law* of the State is founded not upon human compact and custom, but upon the fact that it is determined to maintain justice upon earth, according to the will of God, by external enactments and means. The ruler is the minister of God, a revenger to execute wrath upon him that doeth evil (Rom. xiii. 4). *The idea of punishment* is not hit in its centre when it is found merely in the objects of punishment, viz. that the criminal may be imprisoned, or that others may be deterred from committing like acts, or that society may be defended against criminals. If amendment is the sole object of punishment, the latter might be entirely dispensed with, upon the sincere repentance of a criminal, whereas we find that the penitent criminal, who has incurred the penalty of the law, has to suffer the same punishment as the hardened. In many cases, punishment may, it is true, conduce to amendment, but its first and essential object is by no means to be thus defined. And if to deter from crime is the sole purpose of punishment, then the criminal would be treated as only a means for the sake of others, and not for his own sake; and for the purpose of still more stringently discouraging crime, the severest punishment would always have to be chosen,—a proceeding which no one would approve on the part of the State. Finally, if punishment is only to serve as a defence against criminals, the State would do best for its own safety by sending *every* criminal out of the world without further ceremony, or at least by keeping him in life-long imprisonment, for in this case there is no principle by which to inflict degrees of punishment.

The first and essential view-point upon which all depends, and which furnishes us with the main element in the idea of punishment, is that *punishment must be inflicted for the sake of justice* (Stahl, Hegel, Rothe, etc.). Punishment is the reaction of justice against the infraction of some legal enactment, which latter thus asserts itself as a power even with respect to the transgressor. It is the law whose authority and sacredness have been violated, and to which satisfaction is offered by the criminal incurring just *retribution*. The penitent thief on the cross had a just conception of the import of punishment when he said, " We receive the due reward of our deeds " (Luke xxiii. 41). While the criminal suffers just punishment, this suffering—supposing he does not harden himself—will serve to arouse in his soul conviction of sin and repentance, and thus contribute to his amendment, while it will at the same time be useful in exerting a deterrent influence upon others. Moreover, it may be said that the State thereby protects itself against arbitrary crime. But the proper, essential and fundamental idea—if punishment is considered of and by itself—is this, that satisfaction is done to justice, so that " right may yet remain right " (Ps. xciv. 15) (judgment may return to righteousness, E.V.). Retribution must not be so understood as to make punishment correspond externally and literally to transgression (an eye for an eye, and a tooth for a tooth, etc.), which might lead to absurdity. The relation is not to be one of external but of internal likeness, *i.e.* the punishment must be *proportioned* to the actual nature of the transgression. Thus, even where restitution is demanded, but cannot be made in an exact and direct manner, it is usual to repay the estimated *value* of the thing.

Righteous retribution is not *vengeance*, which presupposes

passion and selfishness. On the contrary, it respects in the transgressor the dignity of human nature, and excludes all that is barbarous and inhumane. It cannot but be esteemed inhumane to enhance the punishment of death by tortures, or to impose such loss of liberty as degrades the criminal to an impersonal instrument, as is the case with galley slaves, or to inflict disgrace of such a kind as to undermine self-respect, and so to lead to still deeper demoralization, as, *e.g.*, by branding. It is barbarous to debar prisoners from all and any relation with human society and its blessings. On the other hand, it is a reasonable requirement, that prisons, though it is not their first and chief object to be reformatories, should nevertheless add to their main and essential purpose the teleologic task of amendment, and especially that they should allow Christianity access within their walls, that so our Lord's saying, "I was in prison, and ye came unto me" (Matt. xxv. 36), may be fulfilled. Our own times are giving actual proof how much may be done in this department to turn imprisonment into a real blessing. In contrast to the barbarous punishments of former ages, the penal legislation of the day is distinguished for its humanity. Testimony of this is in many respects furnished by the improved arrangements of prison life, owing to certain humane and Christian efforts (those of Howard, Mrs. Fry, and prison societies in different countries). On the other hand, it must be considered as among the darker features of the times, that humanity is often exercised at the expense of justice, and that there is a laxity and weakness in the administration of justice, which cannot but have a pernicious effect upon morality and upon the general condition of the public. When a decided inclination is manifested to declare great criminals not responsible, or when, to take an example from another sphere, despotic officials get off with a trifling fine, when—as Bishop Mynster expresses himself in his autobiography—legal penetration applies itself to so large an extent to the discovery of evasions and excuses for scoundrels, we have the opposite extreme to the rigorism of an earlier time. Fines, though not entirely to be dispensed with, are on the whole an ambiguous means of punishment. They are in general a real penalty only to the indigent, while to persons of better means, or those who have friends to pay for them, their only importance is that of a declaration of guilt. This, however, makes but slight impression upon many, when they see at the same time how low an estimation the State itself makes of their guilt.

§ 71.

The supreme and heaviest punishment is that of death. In former times this was inflicted but too frequently, and for widely differing crimes. The one-sided humanity of our days reveals itself by urging the total abolition of capital punishment. There is, however, one crime, viz. wilful murder, which calls, as it were, for capital punishment as its only corresponding penalty. Even so early as in Genesis (ix. 6) it is said: "Whoso sheddeth man's blood, by man shall his blood be shed, for in the image of God made He man." This saying of God was uttered long before the nation of Israel appeared upon earth, and was addressed to all mankind. The view expressed in these words pervades the entire Old Testament, while in the New the lawfulness of capital punishment is assumed in such passages as Rom. xiii. 4: "He beareth not the sword in vain, for he is the minister of God, a revenger to execute wrath upon him that doeth evil;" Matt. xxvi. 52: "They that take the sword shall perish with the sword;" Rev. xiii. 10: "He that killeth with the sword, must be killed with the sword." But apart from this, capital punishment originates in the very nature of the case. For if punishment is to be righteous retribution, and if crime and punishment are to be proportioned to each other, the deliberate destruction of human life *must* be punished with death. For life, which includes the entire existence, and not merely this or that single aspect of it, this or that blessing of life, there is among all conceivable values absolutely no other fitted to be a compensation, but just—life itself. The saying: Life for life, here holds good; no *single* part can be an equivalent for the *whole*. This truth is affirmed and confirmed even by criminals condemned to death, so far as they attain to true moral self-knowledge. For then they do not complain that injustice is done them, but as a rule desire to suffer death, from a feeling that it is thus only that they can atone for their guilt.

The opposition to capital punishment was during the last' century headed by the Italian Cesare de Beccaria (1738–1794). He considered capital punishment wholly unjustifiable, because not included in the original civil contract. For he thinks it inconceivable that any one should have consented to allow himself to be put to death, if he should put another to death, because no one is capable of disposing of his own life. It would be but fruitless labour to unravel the web of sophisms contained in this argument. We confine ourselves to the remark, that the State by no means originates in a civil contract, that it is not merely a human, but in its inmost nature a divine ordinance, that rulers are the ministers of God and of justice, and that the law of justice is equally binding, whether men approve it or not. Schleiermacher, too, opposes capital punishment as barbarous, and requires that rulers should smooth the way for its abolition by never signing and thus approving a death-warrant. This view he justifies from the following view-point: No one may inflict upon another a penalty which the latter would not be justified in inflicting upon himself. Now, no one has a right to kill himself, consequently capital punishment must be rejected.[1] We cannot approve this argument, which is akin to that set forth by Beccaria. We admit that the criminal must be capable of acknowledging the justice of his punishment, but that he should therefore dictate it himself, is in our opinion contrary to the nature and idea of the matter, because punishment must be prescribed by a higher authority. This subject must, moreover, be regarded not from an autonomic, but a theonomic view-point, not according to human self-legislation, but according to the legislation of God. The theory of punishment which opposes the penalty of death, generally proceeds from the view, that reformation is the end of all punishment, and consequently recommends imprisonment for life. But we, who maintain, on the contrary, that punishment is inflicted for justice' sake, cannot but adhere to the conviction that life-long imprisonment, or loss of liberty for the rest of life, is absolutely a thing not homogeneous, nor corresponding with life, for which it is no substitute. Nor do we think we shall succeed in abolishing capital punishment,

<hr>

[1] Schleiermacher, *Die christliche Sitte*, p. 251, Appendix B, 121.

except perhaps for a short time, until we can do away with murder. Goethe says: "If death could be abolished, we should have nothing to object; but it will hardly do to abolish the penalty of death. If this is done, we by and by recall it. When society renounces the right of inflicting capital punishment, self-help comes forward again directly, revenge for bloodshedding knocks at the door."[1] The Emperor Joseph II. abolished capital punishment in Austria, in place of which criminals were condemned to draw vessels up the Danube. But it soon had to be introduced again. At the beginning of the French Revolution capital punishment was abolished, in the name of humanity; we know, however, how soon and to what extent it returned. This spurious and sentimental humanity reared round that horrible barbarity, which was carried out by means of the guillotine.

In thus, however, making capital punishment indispensable, we confine ourselves expressly to *wilful* (*i.e.* premeditated) *murder*. We do not venture to extend it to political offences, except in cases where they are combined with murder, since there would otherwise be no sufficient cause for its infliction (comp. Rothe, *Christl. Ethik*, III. 890). But while we bring forward the element of righteous retribution as the essential and deciding element with respect to capital punishment, we are also desirous to give their full value to the other elements of the idea of punishment. For certainly the assistance of religion and the Church, exhortation and consolation, must be afforded to the criminal, with the object of his amendment. And if, as is proper, the execution takes place in public, it will also have a deterrent effect upon the people, to whom it should be no idle spectacle, but a means of awakening grief and penitence; the whole community being more or less involved in the guilt of having contributed, by the state of sin in which they themselves live, to make the criminal what he is.

With regard to *the right of pardon*, which is in all countries awarded to the ruler as one of his prerogatives, it must not be regarded as a right to act unjustly or capriciously, to release a criminal from just punishment, though it has often been so

---

[1] Goethe's *Wanderjahre*, Anhang, *Aus Makariens Archiv.* Comp. Harless, *Christl. Ethik*, 7th ed. p. 475.

employed.   On the contrary, it consists in the right to remit capital punishment in individual cases, on account of extenuating circumstances, *e.g.* of extreme youth, or the peculiar character of the temptation, which legislation and a court of justice are unable to take into account.

With the preceding remarks may be combined the question: If it is the undeniable duty of the State to punish murder, what position does it take up with regard to *suicide?* We cannot but regard it as a sign of the lax humanity of our days, when a burial, accompanied by full church ceremonial, is allowed to suicides as a matter of course.   The suicide sins not only against God and himself, but also against the Church, to which he causes great offence by disregarding and defying the commands of religion.   A reaction against such a proceeding on the part of the Church is utterly needful, unless it is itself devoid of religion.   A Church which grants a specifically Christian burial to the suicide, itself disregards the commands of Christianity, by manifesting indifference and lukewarmness in this respect.   That there may be in many cases extenuating circumstances to justify that argument of non-responsibility which has been so greatly abused, we would by no means deny.

THE CONSTITUTION.

Popular Rule by the Grace of God.—The Sovereignty of the People.

§ 72.

Public morality is in many respects a result of the constitution or organization of the State, and this essentially depends on the relation between rulers and subjects. Morality (the moral consciousness) is one thing in despotic and another in free States.   It is different in States where freedom and authority are in harmony, from what it is where liberty has been obtained at the cost of authority, and where the constitution bears within itself the germs of anarchy.   There are constitutions which exercise a beneficial educational influence, and others which have a demoralizing effect.   Christianity has prescribed no definite form of constitution, from which fact, however, it must not be inferred that it regards this as a matter of indifference. It has expressly taught us only that the State is a divine ordinance, and that the source of plenipotence or sovereignty must be sought in God. And upon this truth it grounds the view that rulers, as organs for the exercise of power, are such "*by the grace of God.*"

To declare that rulers are such by the grace of God is, if the Christian idea of God is assumed, more than saying that the power exercised by them is derived from God; it is also an affirmation that they themselves are of God, as having been called by God's providence, in the course of history, to be his ministers on earth. The designation, "by the grace of God," furnishes an inducement not to pride but to humility; and awakens the consciousness of responsibility before God. In its full sense, it can only be applied to rulers who are *legitimate, i.e.* who find themselves in possession of power, whether according to the order of historical tradition, or, where this has been interrupted, by the assent and co-operation of those who are the possessors of supreme power. A revolutionary government, or one which has attained power only by usurpation, can only be called a government by divine permission; and not till after a lapse of time will it be seen whether this permission can also take the designation of "grace." Rulers occur in history who might rather be said to rule "by the wrath" than "by the grace of God." Still power and authority always originate from God, even if the organs which exercise them are unfaithful or unwise stewards. "God must be very far from us," says Franz Baader in one of his letters, "or, to express it more correctly, our policy must be very far from Him, since He lets us commit such abominations."

The direct opposite to the view here stated of the authority of rulers is the notion of *the sovereignty of the people.* According to this, supreme power is originally found in the people, which possesses of its own right a superiority over the government. The people, that is to say, the masses, the majority of the moment, have not only the right to appoint their own rulers, who are accounted only the officials or agents of the people, but also the right to depose them at their own pleasure, and to put other ministers or agents in their places. According to divine order, government is to be *from above* downwards, here it is required to be *from beneath* upwards.

According to divine order, rulers and subjects form a contrast which is indeed to be harmonized into unity, but still a contrast, in which rulers stand above subjects. But the usual acceptance of the term, the sovereignty of the people, never reaches to a real contrast and a relation of superiority and subordination. Rulers and their authority are but a product of the popular will, by means of which merely seeming rulers and seeming authority, both reflections of the changing popular will, exist. When it is said on behalf of popular sovereignty that the king, or the government in general, exists for the sake of the people, not the people for the king or government, it is not out of place to observe that both exist to serve a higher authority and a nobler purpose, and are hence mutually for each other.

The idea of the sovereignty of the people apparently finds a support in the *republic* and the *elective monarchy*. But this can only seem so to a superficial consideration. For it by no means follows, from the fact that the people chooses the *organ* of power, that it is itself the source of that power, the supreme authority, and the head of the government. From the moment when the choice is made, the people are *under* their rulers, and may by no means arbitrarily dismiss them or treat them as inferior.

There is, however, a deeper sense in which the term sovereignty of the people may be understood. The one here indicated is, however, undoubtedly that inculcated and widely diffused by the democratic press, and with which many heads are filled, when self-government and self-management are in question. By the word we may mean, not the chance masses and chance majorities as opposed to king or rulers, but the people as an organized whole, *comprised in indissoluble union with its government*, a joint organism by which absolute *self-determination* is exercised within, and to which *independence* belongs without, *i.e.* with respect to other nations. In the latter case, however, it would be better, for the sake of avoiding ambiguity and misunderstanding, to use the more correct expression, the *sovereignty of the State*. The State, though certainly also to be regarded as a human, is nevertheless in its inmost nature a divine institution, invested by God with the highest earthly power; and rulers are the organs for exercising this power, a fact which does not, however, exclude the co-operation of the people.[1]

Constitutional Monarchy.

§ 73.

The often started question: What is the best kind of political constitution? has been variously answered by history. For this has shown us that now one, now another kind was best adapted to promote the public welfare of this or that people at a given time, without our being able to say that it is therefore absolutely the best, or that which most completely corresponds with the idea of the State. If Montesquieu's famous saying, that the vital principle of monarchy (as to opinion and feeling) is honour, of despotism fear, of aristocracy moderation, and of democracy *virtue*, be correct, it cannot but be decided that the democratic form of government, under which all, or at least most, must distinguish themselves by self-control and self-denial, is that which will be with most difficulty realized. Montesquieu also remarks, that it is under this form of government that the whole power of education is required (*c'est dans le gouvernement républicain, que l'on a besoin de toute la puissance de l'éducation*). In general, it can only be affirmed that that constitution will most approximate to the idea of the State, and thereby be most in harmony with the spirit of Christianity, which most perfectly exhibits the combination of liberty and authority; in which there exists a strong and powerful government to which all submit, while liberty finds at the same time the widest scope, and free citizens co-operate for the realization of the objects of government as willingly as for their own. In recent times it has been believed that the most complete reconciliation of authority and liberty is found in so - called *constitutional monarchy*, which would consequently be the most perfect

---

[1] During the rule of the Stuarts in England in the 17th century, Filmer (in his work, *Patriarche, or the Natural Power of Kings*) developed that one-sided view of "kingship by the grace of God," which made it signify the *unlimited* power of the king and the *unlimited* obedience of subjects, and was the occasion of Algernon Sydney's well-known *Discourses concerning Government*, in favour of popular sovereignty and revolution (Hettner, *Geschichte der engl. Litteratur*, p. 43 sqq.).

manifestation of the idea of justice in the State.   As to what is, however, the best kind of constitutional monarchy, opinions are widely different.   The many projects that have arisen, the experiments that have been made since the French Revolution, the constitutions overthrown as soon as set up, the many hastily run up political edifices, the continued revisions and constantly recurring transformations, sufficiently prove that the problem is not yet solved, and that in many respects it has not advanced beyond the tentative stage, perhaps because the road by which this solution is sought is one on which it can never be found.   When the English constitution is referred to as the best model, the remark has often enough been made in reply, that this constitution is a quite peculiar growth, which has, in the course of centuries, and under special circumstances, been developed in intimate connection with its excellences and defects, and cannot for that very reason be imitated by others founded on entirely different historical circumstances and natural conditions, nor by States which have to begin constitutional life from the beginning.   The English constitution has undoubtedly been during a long series of years relatively the best for the English nation.   Experience must show whether it will remain so for the future.   Besides, we are here treating of modern constitutions, which, compared with the English, can only be called improvisations, and are, as it were, of yesterday.   The relation in which they stand, on the one hand to reality, on the other to the idea, is always a question which may be variously answered, and whose future may, from a historical point of view, be very problematical.

§ 74.

Monarchy is the oldest and most venerable form of government, while the republic is of more recent origin.   Impersonal law rules in the republic; the supreme power of the State appears in monarchy in a living person.   The word "majesty" expresses a union of power, law, and graciousness; hence majesty is an object of reverence, dutifulness, confidence, affection, and hearty devotion.   Consequently monarchy has at all times had the greater attraction for the majority, for men feel the want of a personal authority, of an actual chief.

Louis XIV.'s celebrated and much attacked saying, "*l'état c'est moi*," may also be understood in a better sense than has been usual. The monarch is the State itself, since the authority of the State is concentrated in him, not, as Louis XIV. meant, for the satisfaction of his private inclinations, but for the good of the community; and though not the principle of the State, he certainly is its *central* organ.

Though monarchy may be either hereditary or elective, the former is much to be preferred. Such preference must be awarded it not merely because it avoids the disputes and party spirit connected with election,—a question of mere ways and means,—but above all, because of its full manifestation of the fact that the king exists not by the will of the people, but by the will of God, that the king and his authority are *given* us, that he is exactly the person whom we ought to have, that subjective arguing is in this matter of as little use as it would be to complain that we have not other parents than those whom God has given us, although those parents may have undeniable imperfections, to which we need not be blind, but by which our dutifulness must not be disturbed.

The perfect form of monarchy is by no means absolute, un-limited monarchy, not only because all kings and rulers, without exception, have one fault, viz. that of being *men* affected by human weakness, in both intellectual and moral respects,—a fault which representatives of the people possess in common with kings,—but because the idea of the State demands that all elements of its life should attain their organic development, and this is impossible under an absolute government. It is true that even under absolute monarchical government there may exist either independence of justice or good administration, but a higher requirement than this is involved in the decision that monarchy must be constitutional, or, as it is also called, "limited monarchy," one which is to find its true strength in its very limitation, or within certain boundaries. On the one hand, it is here in place to mention that, let the wisdom and discernment of the government be what they may, it needs the assistance of the experience and discernment existing among the people, which may, with respect to many questions, serve to modify its judgment. For a very different conception may be formed of the same object, when regarded from below, from what is formed when it is viewed from above.   On the other hand, too, this development appears inevitable.   For the greater the progress of the people in moral development, the more the idea of the State penetrates and is alive in the whole community, the more is the demand brought forward, that the relation of subjects should be combined with that of citizen, that the people should, by means of their representatives, co-operate in debating and deciding upon the laws which they are to obey.   This is the general thought which has led to constitutional monarchy.   We alluded above to Louis XIV. as a representative of absolute monarchy, and are thereby reminded of *Bossuet* and *Fénélon*.   Bossuet is an unqualified advocate of absolutism ; Fénélon, on the contrary, though not in a position under existing absolutist oppression to make his views public, was already a prophet of limited monarchy.   We are not thinking only of his Utopian ideas, as brought forward in " *Télémaque*," but more especially of his letters to the Dukes of Beauvilliers and Chevreuse, as well as to the Duke of Burgundy.   In these he portrays, in the most vivid colours, to the future king, the dangers and temptations of absolutism ("*il ne faut pas que tous servent à un seul ; mais un seul doit être à tous, pour faire leur bonheur*"), and already requires the co-operation of the Estates in the government, and lays down a complete sketch of a constitution (including, *e.g.*, a regular and public budget, the abolition of the privileges of the nobility and hereditary offices, freedom of trade, etc.). Political ideas which were realized at the Revolution in combination with the laying aside of religion and morality, are here found in the purest ethico-religious connection.[1]   In the time of Louis XV., Montesquieu further developed the constitutional idea, by means of the severance of the legislative, the judicial and the executive powers.

§ 75.

In carrying out the constitutional idea, a danger makes its appearance which must be overcome, unless the constitution is to fail of attaining its object.   We allude to the danger, that the inevitable contrast between people and government, whose

---

[1] Comp. Lamartine, *Fénélon*. Hettner, *Geschichte der französischen Litteratur im 18 Jahrhundert*, p. 27 sqq.

different kinds of views are in mutual opposition, should become a hostile tension, an inimical dualism, a party struggle between government and people. Modern constitutions being, for the most part, the results of a contest between princely power and popular liberty, it is but natural that this viewpoint, from which people and government appear as two contending parties, should in many respects continue to sway the opinions of both. This is especially manifested in the persuasion, which to this hour is very often the *sole* view-point from which many estimate this matter, viz. that popular representation serves as a *guarantee*, as a means of defence and security against the encroachments of the government. Guarantees always presuppose the existence of some sort of danger, against which protection must be sought; in the present case, that the government and the people are fundamentally hostile parties, who must, from constant and mutual distrust, keep a check upon each other, and that what is required is to maintain a certain mechanical balance between the contending parties. Without such a feeling of mistrust it would be impossible to account for the admission into the fundamental laws of many States of an enactment, by means of which the representatives can annually refuse, not only *extraordinary* imposts, but even the whole State-budget with all the regular taxes, and may, by virtue of this manœuvre, render impossible the fulfilment of its duties by the government, and bring the whole machinery of the State to a sudden standstill. By such means has it been sought to secure an effective means of coercing the government. We by no means desire, generally and in every sense, to deny the necessity of guarantees, which finds its reason in human fallibility, but are only maintaining that this must not be the sole and supreme view-point, and that, in the example adduced, it comes before us as a greed, so to speak, for guarantees, in its extreme one-sidedness.[1] It is this greed for guarantees, this spirit of mistrust, which serves to explain, *e.g.*, such an enactment as the following: that where

---

[1] Trendelenburg, *Naturrecht*, p. 464 sqq. The granting of taxes signifies a potent control, but not that one power should be able to lord it over the other, or over the whole community. Hence provisions should be made by law in a constitution for keeping this right of the legislature within such limits as the condition of the State requires, and for making an entire refusal of supplies illegal.

the king is allowed by the constitution to choose certain members of the Diet, or representatives of the country, he may choose only such as have before sat in the Diet, and been thus *chosen by the people* (¹), and who have consequently received their first impression from the popular side. This has been done to obtain security with respect to the king, because it was thought he could not be trusted, after examination and consideration on his own part, and consultation with his ministers, to choose in a right spirit.

But in proportion as the demons of mistrust prevail in the region of constitutional life, and continue to incite rulers and people to procure guarantees against each other, is this life afflicted with internal disease. The normal condition is at all events, that constitutionalism should present to our view an organism, in which the king represents the central member, in which all organs and functions co-operate for the health of the whole, and in which, lastly, the differences which do occur are but transitory and soon resolved into harmony and union. The sublime spectacle of genuine constitutional life is only afforded us where king and people feel themselves really united by mutual confidence, by joint responsibility, and equal readiness for the self-sacrifice requisite for enduring and fighting through whatever may await them.

§ 76.

When a constitutional monarchy is to be instituted, the first main problem consists in the due limitation of the rights, on the one hand of the king, on the other of the representatives of the people: the question is, whether the centre of gravity shall be found in the power of the king, or in that of the representatives, whether the truly monarchical or the parliamentary principle is to predominate in the constitution, whether—as Stahl expresses it—the king or the majority in the chambers is to govern. Where the centre of gravity is placed in the king, a co-operation may indeed be incumbent upon the representative body, but it cannot be co-ruler, or, more strictly speaking, cannot be ruler, *i.e.* really and actually, though not in title. Genuine monarchical government requires that the representative body should be either merely *consultative*, or, if possessing a *deciding power*, both for obstructing and promoting the proposals of the government, that it should yet be in such wise limited, that the actual initiative and decision should rest with the king, and that the ministers should be *his* organs, and not those of the representative body. Parliamentary government, on the contrary, requires that the power of the king should be placed in the hands of ministers, who conduct the government without any real regard to his will, but with unlimited regard to the will of the popular representatives. The ministers proceed from the parliament; and the king is obliged to accept them as the organs of the ruling majority. When they no longer possess the confidence of parliament, they must resign; and the king must appoint a new ministry. The definition: " The king is not responsible," according to its true meaning, by no means aims at maintaining *his dignity*, but only gives it to be understood, that not kings but their ministers are to be regarded as, properly speaking, *agents*. The veto allowed to the king is in many respects illusory. In many instances it is not he who says no, but the ministers, just as it is they too who dissolve parliament when necessary. When this form of government, in which the monarchical principle is reduced to a mere semblance and shadow, is recommended by an appeal to the English constitution as its great model, in which royalty, though surrounded with external splendour, has been in fact brought down to a minimum of power (of which indeed nothing further can be relinquished unless it is to be entirely abolished), and which has notwithstanding yielded such beneficial results to the nation, we must again repeat, that it is very questionable whether it could be imitated with similar results by such nations as are without those historical antecedents and conditions which are inseparably connected with the English constitution.[1]

Parliamentary government is gravitating towards republicanism. It must nevertheless be confessed that it still differs in many respects therefrom. It has indeed been said that so-called democratic monarchy, which however undeniably differs widely from the English constitution, is nothing else

---

[1] On the relation between the monarchic and parliamentary principle, comp. the full discussion by Stahl, *Philosophie des Rechts*, II. p. 321 sqq.

than a republic under the mask of monarchy, that it is
tainted with an internal falseness, in that it wears the outer
semblance of monarchy, but denies its power, and that the
more honourable course would be to proclaim itself republican.
But, much as may be said for this view of the matter, one
restriction must be admitted.   For even those monarchies
which are most limited, if they are hereditary, afford to the
whole constitution a *stability* which it would otherwise lack,
and which is not found in any republic, not to mention those
which are improvised.   Monarchy preserves the connection of
the historical traditions of the nation, and sheds over the
constitution the glory of historical reminiscences, even where
such glory is but the after-glow of past ages, now in the far
distance.   With respect to the above-mentioned dependence
of the king upon his ministers,—to which many add the
remark that " the king can do no wrong," because he can do
nothing at all,—some limitations must here be added.   For
under every constitutional government the character of the
sovereign, his personal convictions, his interest in affairs,
exercise an influence which ministers must in most cases take
into account.[1]   But, in any case, the king must at last give
in to a resolute ministry, unless he is willing or able to take
another in its place.   Still, even this state of things differs
materially from that which prevails in a republic.   It is,
however, very questionable whether those nations which have,
after the model of the English system, adopted parliamentary
government, have not, by displacing their centre of gravity,
put themselves into such a position, as to be building and
dwelling upon a soil more like shifting sand than the firm
and solid rock; and whether there are not nations for which
a constitution with more moderate popular rights and more
extensive royal prerogatives would better secure the welfare
of the community.

---

[1] Guizot, *Mémoires*, VIII. p. 86 : "Partout où la monarchie constitutionelle a
existé, la personne du monarque, ses opinions, ses sentiments, ses volontés
n'ont jamais été indifférents ou inactifs, et les plus indépendants, les plus
exigeants des ministres en ont tenu grand compte. Dès nos jours comme dans
les temps anciens, sous les ministères whigs comme sous les torys, dans les
rapports de Lord Chatham avec George II. et de Lord Grey avec Guillaume IV.,
comme dans ceux de M. Pitt avec George III., l'histoire constitutionelle de
l'Angleterre en offre, à chaque pas, d'incontéstables preuves."

§ 77.

The second constitutional problem concerns the composition of the body of representatives. The more the royal power has been limited, the more necessary it is that the people should be wisely organized as a political power. A representation of a people, truly worthy of the name, should be the flower, the noblest essence, so to speak, of its intelligence and morality. It must, moreover, be as *all-sided* as possible, by representing in the fittest manner all the various tasks and interests of social life. If, then, we seek for an ethic principle by which to organize national representation, the true one, as it appears to us, is that the actual spheres, the chief circles of social life, should be made the point of departure ; in other words, that classes and corporations should be represented. Without those intermediary organisms, classes and corporations, the people remain but an indiscriminate mass, which can be brought under no ethic principle. In the classes, on the contrary, those different callings and industries, which give to individuals their moral significance, appear. Corporations ought to choose, and it is only thus that the fittest, the most intelligent, and, with respect to character, the most trustworthy representatives can possibly be obtained. In classes and corporations a community of interests and views exists. If corporations choose men from among themselves, it may be presumed that they know those on whom their choice falls, and that they select the fittest and most trustworthy of those who best understand their interests. It may also be assumed that they who possess thorough information in one sphere, will be also competent to enter into legislative and administrative questions of a more general kind, which can never be taken for granted of those who dabble in everything, and are at home in nothing. Of course, it may here be objected that in this case a class-spirit, a corporation or guild spirit, will assert itself in a partial and one-sided manner. This is, however, a matter which must be met and overcome by increasing public spirit and progressive education, which will ever more and more contribute to make the interests of the community the living and present interests of individuals. It is true that the representatives of the several classes will look at the whole and the general chiefly through the medium of their class interests, and start from their own standpoint. But the very point to be aimed at is to ascertain how the questions under discussion are viewed by different social circles. And it is very certain that anything concerning which the representatives of particular social interests are agreed, will commend itself to the government as the expression of the general will of the nation. Partial notions will be corrected by the discussions themselves, or in the last appeal by the government and king, as the authority placed over all the classes, to maintain the balance between them, and to reconcile their several interests.

The truths here laid down are regarded by liberalism and democracy as mediæval views, unsuitable to the present age, which requires just *universal suffrage.* We are, however, by no means demanding a mediæval particularism, or that the single classes should have *exclusive* regard to their own special interests. We desire a really representative system, by which *the nation* itself may be represented, and its affairs managed in the interest of the entire community. But we maintain that a representation of classes is the only possible national representation. This kind of representation has also been advocated by the principal thinkers of the day (Hegel, Fr. Baader, Stahl, Walter, Trendelenburg, etc.). And time will show whether the perception will not be gradually arrived at, that the modern system, by which citizens are divided into certain merely local electoral districts, and a certain number of representatives allotted to each district, is not only very defective in practice,—as indeed present experience already superabundantly shows,—but also *false in principle;* and that the class system, though at present requiring, as must certainly be admitted, a *new and more varied development,* is the only one based on a true principle. At the same time, it cannot be denied that the grouping of classes and the relative position of the different groups in different countries, according to existing circumstances, need different modification. But this, as a technical and mechanical matter, lies outside our field of observation.[1] We are here speaking in only a general manner

---

[1] Comp. *e.g.* Trendelenburg in his above-cited work, p. 461: "The question would be to find an aristocracy of every business and calling, distinguished as such by their fellows, and to commit the election to them."

of the direction to be kept in view, and the object to be aimed at in the whole process of election, while desiring to secure to a chamber of representatives, or a diet, such a supply of intelligence and fitness, that the interests of the whole community, which include those of each class, may be really appreciated and understood. In universal suffrage — which starts simply from the assumption that the State is to be regarded as a collection of atomistic individuals, instead of a system of organic distinctions, within which each individual has the importance of a member—it depends upon accident whether the representatives consist of the best and most intelligent men, or whether they belong to the ignorant multitude. It is quite a matter of chance whether *all* the interests of the nation—not those merely which relate to the material prosperity of the several classes, but also art, science,. the Church, or even the interests of the poor and the lower class of labourers—will be cared for or not. For election. statutes contain nothing at all on such matters. It is ethically a radical detriment, a moral defect, a defect in the one-sided,. individualistic system, that the care of important moral departments in the national life should be left entirely to blind *chance;* that this kind of election should absolutely provide no guarantee that matters which concern the welfare of the whole community should be fully investigated and understood. It may be reckoned as one step at least in the direction of what is reasonable, when the contrast between town and country is made the starting-point in elections. We thus rise above hollow abstractions about the general rights of man to something real, something formed by nature and history. Even if this contrast is an insufficient one, we still attain thereby to that which looks like an organism, and to the first beginnings of a recognition that there are differences and inequalities which ought to be represented.[1]

---

[1] The words which Schiller in his *Demetrius* puts into the mouth of Sapieha are applicable to the abstract (not the organized) rule of majorities, the mere "sovereignty of numbers":—

"Die Mehrheit?

Was ist Mehrheit? Mehrheit ist Unsinn,
Verstand ist stets bei Wen'gen nur gewesen.
Man soll die Stimmen wägen, und nicht zählen.

§ 78.

Proof of the justice of universal suffrage has been attempted, by asserting that all regard to classes and class-distinctions must be utterly excluded, because only private and selfish interests, class-feeling and party-spirit, nay, what is really a system of caste, would thereby prevail, that every individual in the State ought, on the contrary, to feel himself a mere *citizen*, and that this is especially true of the representatives of the people. For, though chosen by the individuals of a single district, they are said to represent the whole people. Neither is it any single element, but the whole, that lives in them, and it is to be assumed of them that in their simple citizenship they understand not merely this thing or that, but all that pertains to the welfare of the people, while they are at the same time raised, as must be presumed, far above all private motives. This proof, however, is one in appearance only. A citizen *in abstracto*, or "in pure generality," is a fiction, a being never met with in actual life. As no one is a human being in pure generality, but only in a definite peculiarity, in which he is to express the general, so no one is a citizen in pure generality, but only in a definite occupation, in a certain circle of society; and it is only in his special calling that he will give expression to his general civil virtue. It is only through the medium of his class that he stands in relation to the State; only in this his objective definiteness that he has a political importance, and can be taken account of by the State. Even in daily life, when a man is spoken of, we are accustomed to ask: *What* is he? and this means: What is his trade or profession? On this matter Hegel has somewhere made the remark: People are accustomed to say of an official, an artisan, a manufacturer, a merchant, etc., he is something, and of any one who has no place in any social circle they say briefly he is nothing. But only one who is something, and understands something, is fit either to elect

Der Staat muss untergehn, früh oder spät,
Wo Mehrheit siegt und Unverstand entscheidet."
(Majority! What is majority? Majority is nonsense. Intelligence has always been with the few. Votes should be weighed, not counted. That State must perish sooner or later where the majority triumphs, and want of intelligence decides.)

or be elected.   And any one elected must represent, in the first place, that *sphere of life* within which he is something and understands something; and through this alone does he stand in relation to the whole, and is capable of gradually attaining a true understanding and right judgment of the whole.   We repeat that, when representation is in question, it is an organism and its internal distinctions which must be kept in view.   Only what is organized and organic *distinctions* can be represented.

How it really fares with pure citizenship, which pretends to be raised above all private and selfish interests, is unmistakeably shown wherever universal suffrage is introduced. For we there see that very class principle, which is denied in theory, assert itself in practice in the most pernicious form, one single social class striving, by the help of universal suffrage, to obtain the mastery for the purpose of carrying out its own selfish interests, and tyrannizing over the other classes in the name of pure citizenship and the good of the whole community.

§ 79.

Another seeming proof of the rightfulness of universal suffrage is usually advanced in the maxim, that because all are equal with respect to their human rights, they have also an equal claim to political rights.   But the leap to such a conclusion is an unlawful one.   Human and political rights differ widely.   The rights of man are universal and absolute; political rights are special and limited.   Human rights are *innate*, given together with the dignity of man as a being made in the image of God.   Every one—even the worst of criminals—has, as a member of human society, a claim to be protected by society from any infringement of his human dignity, and to be aided, as far as possible, to develope and work out his personality to an existence worthy of this dignity.   But the human total, of which the individual with all his rights constitutes a single member, does not exist in indefinite generality, but is *organized* by means of a whole system of distinctions, viz. the various spheres of life, in which different individuals are developed, each according to his station and special position.   And here come forward

those special rights, which neither are nor can be the same
for all, because they are united to certain *conditions*, and must
for the most part be *acquired* by individuals through their
own ability and labour.   To this special class belong political
rights, which can by no means be called general.   For it
must always depend upon certain *conditions*, and the fulfilment of certain duties, whether an individual possesses
political rights, while the dignity of human nature must, at
all times and under all circumstances, be acknowledged in
every man, without exception.   If all are equal in political
rights, why are not the suffrage and the right of being elected
granted to servants and beggars, who are undoubtedly
partakers of the same human rights as other men?   Why,
too, should not women have the privilege of both voting and
being elected?   For, as far as human rights are concerned,
women are certainly on the same level as men.   Some have
indeed, and with true logic, if the premises are acknowledged,
drawn this consequence, and been willing to admit women to
a share of the representation.   But the greater number of the
defenders of universal suffrage shrink from this, because they
have a foreboding that such a proceeding will bring to light
the entire unreasonableness of the matter, in other words, that
the principle laid down by them cannot be carried out to its
consequences without manifesting itself to every one as an
absurdity.   There are those, however, who do not shrink
from this.   It must also be granted that communists and
socialists have, under the premises laid down, logic on their
side, when they not only demand the extension of universal
suffrage to the proletariate also, but claim, together with
equality of political rights, *social* equality, and an equal share
in the advantages of property.   And it is undeniable that
there is very little use in conceding political rights to all
unless they can be assisted in obtaining such a position in
society as may make them capable—and for this the necessary
degree of education and intelligence is also required—of
an independent exercise of their political rights.

§ 80.

To avoid the mischievous effects of universal suffrage, by
which the power of deciding may so easily pass into the hands

of the rude and ignorant masses, a *census* has been introduced; in other words, a certain amount of taxable property or income is required as the condition of the right of voting. The idea on which this is based is, that property and money being the conditions for the acquirement of education and intelligence, consequently furnish a pledge that these will be found in the possessors of a certain amount of income. But this pledge is an extremely insecure one. Knowledge, culture, and trustworthiness are very far from being always and necessarily combined with material possessions, and it is very questionable whether real intelligence will, as a consequence of this arrangement, really get the mastery. Plato already makes the remark that it is not the rich who always furnish the best pilots. In our days, another circumstance, viz. the oppression which capital in so many respects exercises upon society, and the ever-widening gulf between possessors and non-possessors of property, gives additional difficulty to this expedient, by making it odious. A property qualification for the franchise evidently places itself on the side of capital, and excludes non-possessors, who are insisting—and certainly, in spite of their exaggeration, not without reason—upon social and political rights. And thus we are brought back to class-representation, and consequently to the right of the fourth class also to representation, the class which, as Fr. Baader expresses it, properly belongs (*gehört*) to that element of the population which *is not heard* (*gehört*).[1] Besides, class-representation is alone consistent with monarchy. Universal suffrage is year by year increasingly undermining monarchy, with which its *principle* is irreconcilable. For if the State is nothing more than a heap of individuals living together in democratic equality, what reason can be found in a system carried out upon the principle of equality for the utterly isolated inequality of *a single person* and a single family standing in such a relation of superiority to all other individuals and families, as actually exists in kingdoms? Where the democratic principle of equality prevails, it seems as if only a

---

[1] In the remarkable article: "On the existing disproportion between the non-possessing or proletariate class and the possessing classes of society, with regard to their produce both in intellectual and material respects, viewed from a legal standpoint, 1835" (Fr. Baader's *Sämmtliche Werke*, VI.).

president, elected to exercise supreme authority for a period
in the name and by the order of the people, could be admitted.
And even supposing that, for the sake of avoiding too great
vacillation, some fragment of kingship should be retained, it
would still stand upon a very loose foundation.　The case is
altogether different when the principle of the organism, a
system of class and corporate distinctions or separations,
pervaded throughout by the contrast of superiority and subordination, is made the point of departure.　For then the
monarch is the ultimate point of union, who himself belongs
to none of the classes, but for that very reason does in his
predominant and exalted position perceive and protect the
interests of all classes of society.　This circumstance manifests
at the same time how preferable a monarchy is to a republic.
For in a republic the different classes of society and their
interests are—notwithstanding their supposed equality and
the talk about universal citizenship—constantly warring
against each other, and are each in turn striving to get the
upper hand.　It is this internal strife, with its party spirit,
which destroys republics.　Kingship, on the contrary, is a
power raised above these contentions and fluctuations, one
whose natural interest it by no means is to favour any one
class above another, but, on the contrary, to watch over the
interests of all.　And only then does it fail to fulfil its office,
when it takes the part of any one class—*e.g.* the hereditary
nobility, or the aristocracy of riches—against the others, and
thereby brings itself into a perilous dependence, nay, places
not itself alone, but the whole State, in a dangerous position.[1]

§ 81.

The *political problem,* whose solution is contended for not
only in print, but also in actual life, is regarded by many as

---

[1] Stein, *Communismus und Socialismus*, I. p. 64: "There is no power on earth
which can shake it (monarchy), so long as it appears as the power presiding over
the movements of society, and promoting the development of *all its classes,*
for then it will be to all classes the only element which will find its own
perfection in the highest development of each."　And, p. 68: "*As long as there
are classes, groups, ranks, and consequently contrasts in society,* so long will the
present and future *of states* depend upon the monarchical principle.　If it should
be possible for them to cease, the time for this principle will be past."

the question: Monarchical government or republicanism? which of these is to come off victorious? We think, however, that the question must be expressed in a more universal form; for though the contrast between monarchy and republic forms one element of it, still the world-wide struggle by which the times are agitated is that between *liberalism* (individualism) and *socialism*. The latter, in contrast with individualism, puts not the individual but the community in the first place, and starts from the demand that individual liberty should be restricted within the community, and identified with its interests. The political problem is essentially one with the social, and can only be solved together with and by means of the latter, and not apart from it.

Liberalism may be defined as the *moderate* carrying out of the principles of the French Revolution. Its fundamental thought is individual liberty and equality of rights, by means of emancipation from a state of political guardianship, from the oppressive fetters of monopolies and privileges. In its first enthusiasm it hoped, by carrying out its principles, to create a condition of things in which the State should henceforth exercise no kind of oppression upon individuals, in which merit alone should be successful, and prosperity and culture should, by the unrestricted operation of every faculty, be universally diffused. Now, if it would be unjust to deny that liberalism has brought much of this to pass, yet it has, on the whole, shown itself more powerful in destroying than in constructing and perfecting, and has in a great degree contributed to the disorganization and dissolution of society. This has been because its conception of liberty is only *negative*, because it strives only for freedom from restrictions and limitations, but is not adapted for fashioning anything. It has in many countries annihilated the political importance of classes, and introduced a popular representation consisting of individual atoms. It has undermined monarchy, by transposing the political centre of gravity to such representation, and by making the king, as far as possible, the mere executor of the will of the nation, *i.e.* of accidental majorities. In its religious indifferentism and purely individualistic view of religious liberty, it has co-operated in banishing religion from public life, by creating creedless (*bekenntnisslose*) legislatures, in which, *e.g.,* Jews are placed on a level with Christians, and has mightily promoted the present ascendancy of the Jews. To this must be added, that it has delivered the Church into the hands of creedless legislatures, and that while it has on all sides introduced a superfluity of individual liberty, it has in many places withheld from her the freedom which was her due, or has forced upon her a constitution after its own image, viz. a rule of majorities incompatible with her very nature. And while in its one-sided struggles for emancipation it aims at dissolving the connection between Church and State, and thereby weakens the importance of the Church as an educational power, it also does everything to destroy the connection between Church and school, nay, to start creedless schools, and that in the interest of " culture " and " national enlightenment." From culture and enlightenment it expects everything. But without intending it, it has by its optimistic faith in the power of civilisation and enlightenment, and its empty notion of toleration, afforded the most powerful impetus to the Romish Church and the Romish propaganda, which are always fishing in the waters of liberalism. In the social sphere it has introduced free competition, which is the chief point of its social order, its focus, and at the same time its dark point, its *partie honteuse;* for while it has abolished all other monopolies, it has introduced the monopoly of capital, and that oppression of the labouring and non-possessing classes which this involves.

Another characteristic of liberalism is that it is inconsistent, and stops half-way in carrying out its principle. Its crowning inconsistency may be said to be the fact, that while it has abolished the political importance of classes, and claims equal rights for all, it has nevertheless laboured, and still labours, to create a special class with political importance and influence, viz. the so-called " third class," *the bourgeoisie.* In its interest liberalism has striven to weaken both sovereign and nobility; in its interest it seeks to withhold from the " fourth class " the rights it is struggling after; and in its interest it is that, now in its hour of need, it invokes the aid of monarchy against the enemy which from day to day threatens to be too much for it, and would find support in its contest against democracy in the power of the crown. But many other inconsistencies, some of them good and praiseworthy, occur in liberalism. To be consistent, it would have to make civil society an aggregate of free and equally privileged atoms. This is, however, opposed by actual life and reality. And many of the adherents of liberalism being not only men of the most honourable character, but also of the highest intelligence, it naturally appears in a great variety of intermediate formations. Hence its principle is often tempered and alleviated by sounder views, belonging to another sphere of thought, and giving evidence of notions of organism. These intermediate formations, however, of which literature shows us many, we are not here able to discuss. We are considering liberalism only according to its principle and its results. And to this very day individualism is the *prevailing* principle of its legislation and public acts, as well as of its entire mode of thought, even granting that this principle may be outwardly clothed in some modification or other.

The real contrast to liberalism is not formed by that ultra-democracy which demands a consistent carrying out of principles, and may consequently itself be designated as liberalism carried out. The difference between liberalism and ultra-democracy is one not of quality but of quantity, a difference of degree. The true contrast to liberalism or individualism is socialism. The *community* is the contrast to the individual, and it was easy to foresee that when one-sided individualism had prevailed for some time, a reaction in a socialistic direction must set in. This reaction appears chiefly in the form of radicalism, which passes an unpitying sentence upon liberalism, and lays before it not only a political problem, but especially that great social problem which liberalism is incapable of solving. The future does not belong to liberalism, but to socialism, while it is as yet uncertain what form the community will assume, after the inevitable contests now impending have been fought out.

We do not presume to predict the future, but speak only of possibilities, being well aware that it is in this sphere by no means possible to draw certain conclusions as to historical reality from what is possible or conceivable. It is conceivable that what we have laid down as an ethic demand may come forth as a final result, viz. real monarchy with a class constitution, in which, consequently, *the fourth class* will attain a satisfactory position not only in political, but also in social respects.   For we must emphatically insist that any new constitution, which is to be permanent, must be based upon a new social foundation.   It is, however, also conceivable that an attempt may be made in a socialistic spirit to realize a republic; nay, there are those whose political and social ideal for the future is a world presenting the great spectacle of a confederation of republican States.   Then, too, all work is to be executed in each separate State by federations, or organized unions and groups; and the present difficulties arising from the contrast between rich and poor are to be for ever abolished; and, lastly, political representation is to take place according to groups, and kingship to be replaced by presidency.   Even a Marlo (*i.e. Winkelblech*) has thoughts moving in this direction. He seems to have entirely lost faith in the future of monarchy. To the liberalists and capitalists, who in their contests with socialism cling to monarchy, he says, speaking of its fate in France: " When the head of Louis XVI. fell upon the scaffold, all the nations of Europe trembled, and the eyes of millions were filled with tears of grief.   It was felt that this act in the world's history meant far more than the fall of a crowned mortal, that it was the fall of the legal ideal of ages, the settlement of accounts between the present and the past.   When Bonaparte lost the crown, which he had seized by violence, they, who had been the admirers of his greatness, were plunged in mourning; when Charles X. descended from the throne of his fathers, his fate awakened the same emotion as when a venerable ruin is overthrown; and when Louis Philippe vacated the throne which he had obtained by intrigue, the world rejoiced at the bankruptcy of a too successful sharper. This is the history of the French monarchy, and in presence of such a history the plutocracy thinks to find protection under the shadow of a newly erected throne," etc.[1]   Napoleon III., Sedan and the present French Republic could not yet be spoken of in Marlo's work.   If he had lived to see these things (he died before 1860), they would have furnished him with fresh arguments.   We make, however, the general remark, that the examples adduced have for us no force at all.   We acknowledge, indeed, that the principles of the Revolution

[1] Marlo, *System der Weltökonomie*, Cassel 1848, I. p. 425.

could not but lead to democracy and to the abolition of monarchy. But we do not recognise the necessity of these principles themselves. The events which followed the revolution only prove that kingship or imperial regime, when built upon the principles of revolution, is not a durable institution, and that this is equally the case when it is based upon those of ultramontanism. The fate of monarchy in France cannot be regarded, without further ceremony, as typical for countries and nations which are of an entirely different character from the French, which have come through a very different historical development, and built on other foundations.

And if this whole idea of a socialistic republic proves, so soon as it is actually carried out, a mere Utopia, there is only a third possibility left, viz. for the disturbed and chaotic state of affairs to be brought to rest by *Cæsarism, i.e.* by the restoration of interrupted social order and the despotic repression of individuals by a single absolute ruler, whose autocracy is founded upon his power, a modern Nimrod, a mighty hunter of men. Should this really take place, an historical Nemesis could hardly fail to be recognised in the fact, that when men would not have a true monarchy they were forced to receive a tyranny, when they would not have fathers they had to accept taskmasters. Under all circumstances, it must be regarded as certain, that liberalism is daily approaching its dissolution. Even in case it should for some time longer maintain its power and ascendency, it will only be able to do so by compromises with its opponents. It is strong and effective only when it agitates and is in opposition. But the opportunity for this is over, and this work is now undertaken by other hands.

CIVIL VIRTUE.

§ 82.

Under every constitution, whether monarchic or republican, absolutist or constitutional, and however numerous may be its defects, the individual must maintain his *civil virtue.* In the preceding sections (Div. I. § 8) we had occasion to consider "civil righteousness" as an expression for *all* personal morality at a certain stage of development. We are here considering civil virtue as a single element, both of personal morality and of the morality of the community.

Its foundation is *patriotism.* This may be more particularly defined as an affection for the country, "the spot of earth" where first we opened our eyes to the light of this world, where our mother-tongue was first heard and first put into our mouth, where we grew up and learned what home meant. It is not, however, merely love for our native land as such, for certain districts or fields, certain meadows and forests, certain lakes and coasts, viewed from a merely natural view-point. It is love to the land as the land of our *fathers,* the land which they have bequeathed to us, which they have tilled and planted, and on which they have left their mark. Consequently it is at the same time love for a certain nation, for its nature, and for its peculiarities, which finds its plainest, its "most speaking" impress in a certain language, a certain form of speech, by means of which we became conscious of ourselves and received our intellectual inheritance. As love to the land, the nation and the language, it is at the same time love for the *history* of the nation, for its past memories, for its heroes and great men, whom we may call our own, for its traditions, manners and customs, its artistic and literary creations—and for all these, not as a past which is closed up from us, but as the presuppositions of that present life which is the continuation and completion of the past. And because the State and its enactments, as these have been in many respects determined by the national peculiarity, exhibit the most comprehensive form of a people's historical development, patriotism attains its full moral character when it is love for a certain *State,* its stability and historical future, love for a certain civil community within which the various human industries are developed just to certain special and characteristic limits.

§ 83.

Civil virtue has both a social and a political character. In its social aspect it is shown when an individual worthily occupies some position in his own class, and makes it his glory to perform with ability and uprightness the duties of a calling in which he serves not himself only, but the whole community. No one ought, however, to be wholly engrossed in the business of his own calling, but should develope a feeling for the vocations of others and their importance to the whole. Socio-civil virtue shows itself chiefly as a lively interest in the common welfare, which it also seeks on its side to promote by individual efforts (*e.g.* by voluntary associations for the relief of material or intellectual wants, or for the restoration of material or intellectual possessions). But it is especially manifested when the upper classes have both a heart to feel for and a readiness to effect the improvement of the lower and less favourably placed classes. The socio-civil virtue of the latter appears in the form of industry and unenvying contentment.

In its political aspect, civil virtue appears in the submission of *subjects to rulers*. And here indeed it is seen in the form of obedience to the laws and institutions of the State, including a willingness to render to the latter the imposts which are its due (Rom. xiii. 1–7). It appears as dutiful obedience to the authority of the State, and readiness to take part in the defence of the country under the direction of its rulers. The promotion of dutiful obedience to rulers is the aim of the apostolic precept to make *intercession* for them (1 Tim. ii. 1), "that we may lead a quiet and peaceable life in all godliness and honesty," which is only possible when rulers afford protection against crime, and maintain order and external peace. But the subject relation must develope into the *patriotic*, and this implies that the idea of the State itself (the State as *the whole*) is active in the individual citizen, and that he affords his voluntary and independent co-operation in realizing its aims. It belongs to civil virtue to abide by the principle: "Obedience to existing laws," but to that also which is connected with it: "The right to require better laws." But though the possibility of co-operating for this purpose is afforded to all by free constitutions, it does not follow that all can take an equal share in political life. To active participation in its stricter and formal sense—to a share in the representation, to the office of a minister, to political authorship—only very few are really called. But public spirit and political intelligence should prevail more and more in all, and these, where they really exist, will manifest themselves in various ways, both in word and deed. The distinguishing feature of civil virtue is justice, founded upon patriotism, inasmuch as the fundamental idea of the State is that distributing and even-handed justice which secures to every citizen and to every relation of life that which is their due. Hence genuine political interest cannot be conceived of without a deep social interest, an interest in all those matters which are necessary to a healthy national life. Without a lively sympathy in social conditions, and a thorough devotion to social duties, citizenship is an empty formalism, a hollow enthusiasm for a form of government, or its mere shadow.

§ 84.

Political parties are generally divided into that of *Conservatism* and that of *Progress*. Civil virtue must strive for the union of both, while opposing both spurious conservatism and spurious progress (radicalism). That which is evil must not be maintained, but care should be taken to replace it by something better. Great intelligence and *patience* must be shown in efforts for reforms, lest the evil be made worse, or the wheat plucked up with the tares. Under a bad or an imperfect form of government, we may certainly labour in a legitimate way—to smooth the path for a better; but nevertheless we must continue to work with *patience* and *fidelity* under existing imperfect arrangements. For good may be effected even with bad machinery, if only we work in a right spirit. In dangerous times, when even the existence of the State is threatened, whether by external enemies or internal discord and dissolution, political virtue will manifest itself in the form of the *courage* which is not overcome of evil, but continues to oppose it while leaving the issue in the hand of God. It was said of one of the ancients, that the State passed a vote of thanks to him for not having despaired of the safety of his country in the midst of great danger. The Christian, indeed, knows well that there is but one kingdom, viz. the kingdom of Christ, of which it is true that it neither can nor may be despaired of in any sense of the word. But never should he doubt that faithfulness to duty, carried out to the uttermost by labour and conflict for his earthly fatherland, will have its importance with respect also to the heavenly country. It is in those times of great calamity, which arouse that genuine feeling of equality, in which both high and low willingly make the greatest sacrifices for the common cause, that patriotism shows itself to be such, in both a political and social aspect.

§ 85.

The more political life is developed, the more are *public characters* also developed. What has just been said of political virtue, will be manifested in them in more strongly marked form. It is in the nature of things that they must be men of strife, and it is just in political strife that the greatest temptations and dangers to character are found. The apostle says (2 Tim. ii. 5) that "if a man strive for masteries, yet is he not crowned unless he strive *lawfully*" (or duly). This saying applies also to political contests. To embrace a party is not in itself reprehensible, if he who does so chooses his side after mature consideration, and while he espouses certain views and tendencies, still remains open and accessible to better information. But there is also a reprehensible kind of party spirit. A man cannot be said to strive lawfully who does no justice to opponents, and is hardened against truths coming from the opposition camp; nor can he be said to strive lawfully who sacrifices his own convictions, his own conscience, to benefit his party. Nor can it be called striving lawfully to use unfair means for external party ends, *e.g.* by means of agitation to convert the ignorant multitudes into the blind instrument of party leaders, or to procure by bribery a majority in the chambers, a trick which has been practised even by the governments of great States. All this is immoral and a dishonest kind of striving, which can gain only soiled and worthless laurels. If a public character is to keep pure and upright, he must possess moderation and self-control as well as justice, and be capable of practising resignation. He must know how to accommodate himself to a minority, nay, to stand alone, to dispense with popularity, to bear misconception, unjust and dishonouring attacks, things quite inseparable from public life. To be able, however, to practise such resignation, he needs to find a support within.　　Such a support has been not infrequently found by great statesmen, amidst the vexations of their career, in stoicism and in contempt of the world.　A Christian finds his in the kingdom which is not of this world, and which, while it raises him above the world, enables him at the same time to continue the contest.

Public characters may be divided into men *selon les circonstances,* and men of principle.　The former are those who make their principles conform to circumstances, hang their cloak according to the wind, and in stirring times run through a whole multitude of political standpoints, directing their efforts towards what is at any time attainable—what seems to them "most expedient."　The men of principle are those who, on the contrary, control and use circumstances according to their principles, and, when they are unable to do this, know how to wait.　Political genius is ever found in the ranks of the men of principle, whether their principle is that of justice or of power (Macchiavellians).　Talent is, however, more exhibited by the men of circumstances (of political incompleteness).

It is often urged in behalf of this absence of political principle, that we ought to keep the happy medium.　As there is a middle-way morality, so there is undeniably a middle-way policy, which is in itself justifiable, nay, necessary.　But if this is to mean anything more than a policy of circumstances, a mere system of accommodation, a balancing between extremes, there must be in the background some definite principle to set up the highest standard to be aimed at.　In modern historians, who at the same time give instruction in politics (*e.g.* Thiers), we more frequently meet with mere middle-way politics, devoid of principle, and·trivial middle-way morality.

PUBLIC OPINION.—THE PRESS.

§ 86.

Wherever there is political life, there also will be found that *public opinion* which is the expression of prevailing views and tendencies.　Public opinion generally contains, from its very commencement, an element of truth, because the true, the good and the right work instinctively in the human conscience. Nay, there are cases in which public opinion is the expression of the social conscience, with which it must, in other respects, by no means be confounded (comp. General Part, § 120). In general, however, public opinion is affected with this limitation, that the amount of truth found in it is for the most part of an incidental and obscure nature. There is a confused mingling of truth and falsehood, right and wrong, reason and passion, wisdom and folly. And opposing party views often make it hard to say what public opinion is, or to speak of it as united. Hence there is good reason for both esteeming and despising public opinion ; and every one who would effect anything in the service of truth and justice, must occupy this double position with respect to it. No government can dispense with the duty of listening to public opinion, of receiving hints from it, and, in many cases, of seeking its support. But the government which makes itself the slave of public opinion, which has no other compass to steer by, and which consequently dares not, in certain cases, have or follow any other opinion, shows that it is neither fit to govern, nor qualified to become an authority.

The task of separating the germ of wisdom and the delusions of folly found in public opinion, points back to the higher one of understanding one's age, of possessing a true knowledge of the *spirit of the age*. All here depends on distinguishing between the spirit of the age and the spirit of history.[1] The spirit of the age is the confused and obscure mixture. It has, indeed, a presentiment of that new thing which is striving to come into existence, but its notion of it often more nearly approaches a caricature than an ideal, and it always " holds the truth in unrighteousness." The spirit of history is by its very nature the spirit of the divine government of the world, of providence, of the divine counsels, the spirit which so often ' shines in the darkness, but the darkness comprehends it not " (John i. 5). That the spirit of the age not only differs from that of the divine government of the world, but may be decidedly opposed to it, may, we think, be best shown by referring to the Jewish nation in the days of Christ. The

---

[1] Comp. Hirscher, *Christl. Moral,* II. p. 219. Rothe, *Christl. Ethik,* III. p. 431 sqq.

Jews were, indeed, conscious that the time had now arrived in which Christ must appear. But they deluded themselves into expecting a Messiah according to their carnal imaginations, a Messiah who should break the yoke of their Roman oppressors and raise them to national power and glory. When, then, the true Messiah appeared among them in the form of a servant, they rejected and crucified him, and thus showed that, though impelled by the *spirit of the age*, nay, wholly filled thereby, they misconceived the *spirit of history*. And not the people only, but the leaders of the people, who thought they stood on the high places of the age, the Pharisees and Sadducees, misunderstood the spirit of history—misunderstood and misconceived that which was at that very time to appear, that which the age required, that new thing which was destined to give a new form to the world.[1] The same experience is repeated with respect to many social questions, from the highest to the lowest, under many forms and in every variety of light and shadow. An indefinite notion or anticipation of something to come, something to bring about a better state of things, is indeed ever stirring in the masses, but its real form is veiled by false ideals of every kind. Hence what are called the "wants of the times" must not be regarded as such without further question. For the wants of the times are of two kinds, what the times desire and what they really need. It often happens that invalids desire a remedy or diet exactly opposite to what they really require.

To understand one's age is certainly one of the most difficult of tasks (comp. "*Can* ye not discern the signs of the times?" Matt. xvi. 3). And he only would be capable of understanding them perfectly who could observe them with the eye of eternity. Only an approximate comprehension can be spoken of in sinful and limited man. Nor is this possible in a Christian sense, otherwise than by viewing the appearances and events of the times in the light of the divine word. Most politicians are now indeed estranged from the Christian points of view, and the Christian mode of judging. And yet they must have been well able to convince them-

---

[1] From a discourse of the author on 1 Cor. xv. 58 : "Servants not of the spirit of the age, but of the Lord" (Martensen, *Hirtenspiegel*, 40 Ordination Discourses. Deutsch, v. A. Michelsen, Pt. 2, p. 38, Gotha).

selves that, however ingenious their calculations concerning the times may have been, the *sum total* shows plainly enough that they committed an arithmetical error when they omitted taking into account the religious and ethical factor.

§ 87.

Public opinion, which we are now chiefly considering in its relation to political and social questions, but which, instead of being confined to great and important matters, extends also to the slightest and most trivial, has for its main organ *the press*, and especially the periodical and newspaper press. The latter not only gives expression to prevailing public opinion, but seeks by its so-called "leading articles" to influence it. It is the spirit of the age which speaks and is expressed in newspapers. Not inaptly have they been called the *second-hand* upon the clock of history, for they have respect to the moment, they work for the moment, and aim at producing a momentary effect. They have their importance with respect to the characteristics of the present; but any one who would become acquainted with his times from them alone—and this certainly applies to a great number of individuals, who derive their information from no other sources—will obtain only a superficial and phenomenal knowledge. It is of very little use to keep gazing at this second-hand when we do not even know the historical hour in which we live, nor its real meaning. For the latter purpose the clock must be viewed from a higher standpoint.

From what has been said it is evident that we by no means regard the spirit of the age exclusively in a bad sense, and that for this very reason, that it is a mixed spirit, a spirit made up of heterogeneous elements, and may be of very varying quality, in proportion to its relation to the spirit of history. That a spirit of the worse, nay, of the worst kind, speaks in so many newspapers, results from the fact that many who make it the business of their life to entertain and guide the public by means of the daily press, belong to the class whom Riehl calls "the literary proletariate," persons who, furnished with a superficial education, seek in this way to gain a living, and whose interest it is to feed opposition to and discontent with existing social and political circumstances, regarding themselves as they do, whether rightly or wrongly, as neglected and injured by the State and society. There are also newspapers in which the spirit of the age indeed, but one of a better quality, is found, and whose columns consequently exhibit pure elements of the spirit of history. Examples might easily be adduced of articles bearing the stamp of uncommon intelligence, and being in their popular form of no less importance than more learned productions. Great authors have sometimes been—though indeed but for a short time—newspaper editors. In general, however, it may be said that just because the daily papers work only for the moment, and because those who are entirely devoted to this employment as the business of their lives, are obliged to furnish information, and give their judgment on it day by day, and must, amidst the manifold accumulations of matters concerning which they have to enlighten their readers, work with unceasing haste, and under the influence of the passionate emotions, the varying frames of the moment, from which no one can keep entirely free, and which scarcely let them take breath,—that for these reasons the views they express cannot possibly be mature and enlightened.

Hence the value of the press must neither be over-estimated nor undervalued. It is undoubtedly a power in society. Its power rests upon the fact that it speaks to a great number at once, "as in a great popular assembly," and that its sayings are daily reiterated. Its power depends upon the power of repetition; for if the same thing is said over and over again, the multitude at last believes that it must be true; and thus it may become of terrible force in opposing government. And lastly, its mighty influence rests not only upon the circumstance that it speaks about the present and the passing moment, which is always an advantageous introduction, but also that it ensures immediate comprehension, its popular language and flowing statement being directly comprehensible to any one, without his needing to break his head in studying them. If this is somewhat ambiguous praise, still this daily communication to the public is the necessary requirement of circumstances, and is, at a certain stage of national cultivation, indispensable. First, the daily news is needed, the accounts of the latest events, important and unimportant, great and small. Then also the articles, which are partly the echo of those daily discussions which we like to see publicly confirmed, and partly exercise an educational and transforming influence upon them, and may therefore thus produce not only pernicious but also beneficial, purifying and reforming effects. Especially do recent occurrences, both foreign and domestic, demand discussion and investigation. And though all will agree that a mature judgment can only be formed after a lapse of time, still the moment has its claims. The still recent occurrence demands an immediate discussion, and this reproduces the first impression and the first judgment. It is under this point of view, namely the *provisonal*, that the utterances of the press—with of course the necessary exceptions—must, on the whole, be regarded. And this is indeed the more necessary, the more important and complicated the subjects of which it treats. Its judgments must only reckon as sentences from which there is an appeal to a higher court, in which they may often be not merely more accurately formulated, but often reformed or even reversed. With respect, for instance, to domestic policy, the representation of the people, assuming it to be wisely constituted, forms a higher court of appeal than the press. Under the above-mentioned point of view, however, the utterances of the press have, in their discussion of public affairs, their own importance, as a single element in the entire process of thought and conviction concerning them.

What has been here said concerning the importance of the press in the political and social departments, applies also in the scientific and æsthetic. For what are all the notices and criticisms of scientific works which appear in the daily journals but purely provisional judgments, given according to first impressions, nay, too often given by novices, whose crudities are none the better for being dressed up in the phraseology of connoisseurs, to whom there is nothing new under the sun!

What must be required of the press is, a love of truth and moral independence. Much falsehood is daily propagated in the world by means of the press, not only by false and partial views, which may indeed arise from human infirmity, but under false lights, and by much dishonest silence concerning anything which might be inconvenient to one party, and advantageous to the other. To use Goethe's expression, they try to "*secretiren*" (*i.e.* set aside) their opponents or those who are not quite sympathetic. When we demand moral independence, we mean independence and candour, with respect not only to the government, but also to the public. Even the newspaper organ of a one-sided view extorts from us a certain amount of respect if it continues faithful to itself amidst the changing humours of the public, and can put up with remaining in a minority, because it still continues to serve a definite cause. But those organs, on the contrary, which surrender themselves as slaves to the public, which hang out their cloak to the wind, or place themselves at the disposal of capital, or of the highest bidder, make themselves despised. It must certainly be confessed that it is in many cases very difficult for the daily press to maintain its independence. A newspaper exists only by means of its subscribers. Now, when these desire to read nothing but their own opinions, and wish to see only their own tendencies favoured in the paper, and give notice that they will cease to subscribe if a contrary course is adopted, what is an editor to do? He is evidently in a position of temptation. A newspaper is in the most favourable situations when, by the worth of its contents and the attractiveness of its style, it makes itself indispensable to the public, and exercises such an authority over it that even opponents are not willing to dispense with it, and hence feel obliged to keep to it, even though they read in it all kinds of things that do not suit them.

§ 88.

The liberty of the press must be allowed if the press is to fulfil its vocation. This liberty, however, must not be in every respect unrestricted and irresponsible. Enactments concerning the freedom of the press are among the most difficult problems of legislation, if they are to avoid two extremes. On the one side, it is evident that the more the freedom of the press is restricted and curtailed, the more difficult does all free opinion on public matters become. It may even be asked whether it is not much better that false and pernicious doctrines should be openly and publicly expressed, and consequently be publicly refuted, than that they should be forcibly repressed, and glide about, as it were, in darkness, disseminating themselves like a deadly poison, against which, though it more and more infects the political organism, there is no kind of remedy; whether much that is evil does not lose its sting by being openly expressed, and thus, as it were, ventilated; and whether people, when they have thus disburdened their hearts, do not become less malicious? But, on the other side, it cannot be concealed that experience is very far from confirming the maxim, that the press is its own corrective, and that its own reaction against degeneration is sufficient. The corrective is often lacking, even when a multitude of papers and journals are in existence; and the rectifying word is often expected from them in vain, or else does not appear till after the lapse of a considerable period. Erroneous and pernicious views, subversive of State and Church, of religion and morality, continue to exercise an influence, because these are by no means addressed to those classes only who are capable of comparing them with other views, and of deciding for themselves, but also to the unlearned and ignorant masses, upon whom the very circumstance that such views *can* be publicly stated has a certain imposing effect, and imparts to them an appearance of corroboration. Another mischievous effect of the freedom of the press, obstructed only by the very slightest restrictions imaginable, is the influence it exercises upon the style of writing and the prevailing tone. For continued experience shows that the greater the freedom granted by legislation, the worse and the more audacious does the tone of the greater part of the daily press become. The saying of Goethe to Eckermann will always hold good, that "an opposition which is not obliged to keep within certain bounds, grows flat," in saying which he also specially brings forward the fact, that a press legislation, which imposes certain restrictions, forces the opposition to be *intellectual*, by forcing it in many cases to express itself in an indirect manner, instead of doing so with coarse simplicity. He refers to the example of the French, which undeniably proves that no press legislation can prevent a talented author from openly saying what he chooses, if he understands how to say indirectly what he must not say directly. In this respect, however, it must not be forgotten that the indirect mode of expression will be understood chiefly by the educated, while the multitude require undisguised statements.

On the whole, it may be said that the laws of the press must always be suited to existing circumstances. The measure of freedom which can be borne depends upon the nature of the whole political and social, in a word, the whole moral condition. When "liberty for everything that springs from the mind" is demanded, and therefore (as Grundvig expresses it) "liberty for Loke as well as for Thor," the measure of freedom conceded to Loke must still be limited by Thor's possession of his hammer. Or, to speak without figure, the measure of liberty to assert itself in public allowed to the bad, the false, and the treasonable, must always be regulated by the measure of power which may be supposed to be present in the good and the true to attack and oppose it. A censorship is justly odious, because even truth is thereby exposed to the danger of arbitrary suppression. And yet there may be times and situations in which censorship is an indispensable necessity. Several modern constitutions, indeed, expressly forbid the re-introduction of censorship. Such determinations, however, by which it is intended to bind beforehand the hands of subsequent legislation, testify more of freethinking than of wise foresight. "It may easily happen," says the Danish statesman, A. S. Oersted, "that civil order and security may be sacrificed, if the constitution prohibits not only to the government, but also to the legislature, the employment, in any case, of the censorship or of any other repressive measure, whereby society might be secured against the attacks of a violent press ; and it is worthy of remark, that those unpleasant events which have taken place in other countries—where it has been found necessary to procure protection against the dangers to which society was exposed by the unrestrained freedom of the press, liberty to hold public meetings, and similar privileges, recently accorded by the constitution, by placing towns and districts in a state of siege—have nevertheless been unavailing warnings against such enactments. When, however, an evident necessity commands it, the constitution will be disregarded, nor will even the mischievous excuse be made that unforeseen circumstances have happened."[1]

How differently under different circumstances the expediency or inexpediency of the unrestrained freedom of the press may be judged of, may be seen from the following expressions of opinion, preserved in Gejer's "Bluebook" (*Saml. Skr.*, 1 Abth. Bd. 7, p. 181):—

M. Thiers, the liberal journalist, says in 1830: "No danger is combined with the unlimited freedom of the press. It is only *truth* which produces effects. What is false does no harm, and only destroys itself by its violence. No government was ever overthrown by libels."

M. Thiers, the minister, writes in 1834: "The insurrections, both at Paris and Bordeaux, were caused by the press. On the whole, it is the press which has effected all this deplorable mischief."

DIFFERENCES BETWEEN THE GOVERNMENT AND THE PEOPLE.
—DISPUTES.

§ 89.

Not only may rulers abuse their power, and not only may the people make unreasonable demands, but such occurrences may also arise under an existing political constitution as to make it no longer suitable, and to justify the demands of the people for reforms, new arrangements and improvements.

A state of tension and disputes may arise between a government and its subjects, which, instead of finding a peaceful solution, may issue on the contrary in a *Revolution*, in a violent overturning of the existing order of society, for the purpose of thereby introducing a more satisfactory state of affairs. Most revolutions proceed from beneath, by means of insurrection and arbitrary self-help on the part of the people. There are, however, also revolutions proceeding from

[1] Oersted, *Aus der Geschichte meines Lebens und meiner Zeit* (1851), I. p. 61 sq. (Danish).

above, the so-called *coups d'état*, which involve breaches of the law and of the constitution on the part of the government.

A revolution is under all circumstances a moral abnormity, and as such reprehensible. It can never be normal to annihilate the State and existing institutions for the sake of amending them, nor can it be normal that one single portion, one factor of the body politic, should put itself in the place of the whole. But, this being generally admitted, the question has from of old been again and again started, whether in certain cases it is not justifiable to make use of a political antinomism, because before a higher tribunal it would be unjustifiable to allow the existing state of affairs to continue. In the times of the English Revolution under the Stuarts, Anglican theologians, who sided with the before - named Filmer, absolutely denied this justification, would allow no such "certain cases," and condemned all revolutions, without exception or restriction, nay, maintained that no cruelty or licentiousness on the part of the king, who indeed acted by divine right, could justify violent opposition on the part of the people, but that all must be endured with passive obedience and absolute non-resistance.[1] Those texts of Scripture which treat of the duty of obedience to rulers formed the starting-point of their reasoning, while the fact that the rulers spoken of in the New Testament, being heathens, were both evil and tyrannical, was especially dwelt on. It must not, however, be forgotten that Scripture equally says: "We ought to obey God rather than man" (Acts v. 29). Suppose, then, that a government should require its subjects no longer to profess, *i.e.* to deny, the Christian faith, or to take part in religious ceremonies repugnant to their conscience, or should demand of them something contrary to the Decalogue: in such cases we should not only be justified, but bound not to obey, which is really equivalent to opposition. Hence it follows, as a direct inference, that opposition must at any rate be confined to passive, and never extend to active resistance, which would resort to the use of force against rulers, and seek to abolish the existing state of the law. Such is the strictly defined doctrine of non-resistance—a doctrine which has been brought forward with many exaggerations

---

[1] Macaulay's *History of England*, vol. III. chap. 9.

and excrescences with which we are not at present concerned. We may here refer to the example of the apostles, who, though they continued to preach the gospel in opposition to the prohibitions of the authorities, patiently submitted to the sufferings which were the result of such conduct. After this pattern did the Christians of the first centuries act, when they would not sacrifice to heathen deities, or burn incense before the image of the emperor, but then also patiently suffered the martyrdom which was the result of their refusal. From this we may deduce the rule that, when conscience compels, and representations and remonstrances can effect nothing, we must do what we cannot help doing, but must then submit without opposition to civil punishment, and so make known our acknowledgment of the legality of government and of existing judicial enactments.

On the whole, it must be confessed that passive resistance is the moral and normal condition both for individuals and nations. We can entirely adopt the words of a highly esteemed jurist, that respectful and persevering remonstrance, manly forbearance and steadfastness, are the weapons by whose employment against an unjust government, a people must give proof of its sense of law and justice, and its political maturity, and that such conduct will at length, though perhaps slowly yet surely, gain its end.

The condemnation of active opposition will always find its support in the thought, that it cannot be called allowable and right forcibly to annul the State, to suspend the laws, and partially to reintroduce a state of nature ; that it is not justifiable thus to suspend the supremacy of all moral principles to an incalculable extent; for where legal institutions are abolished, many moral restraints are dissolved, and free scope is given to unwisdom and passion. Nor can it from a moral point of view be esteemed right, that he who in a dispute constitutes but one party, should be the judge in his own cause, and himself carry out the sentence. All of which is the same as saying that the use of bad means is necessary for the promotion of a good cause, nay, that God to help the oppressed needs our sin, our transgression of His own command, and can in no other manner succour the oppressed, if they only patiently await the Lord's good time.

§ 90.

And yet there is a thorn left in our mind. We cannot get rid of the " certain cases." No one would maintain that all revolutions are of one and the same character, and the question presses itself upon us : whether there are not cases and circumstances *in which the boundaries between passive and active resistance can be no longer maintained*, in which the self-help of despair appears, and the notion of *self-preservation* comes into force ? For if we say that a revolution is in no case justifiable, as was so long maintained in the times of the Stuarts by Anglican theologians and strict Tories, until they were themselves exposed to the tyranny of James II., and henceforth altered their view and their exposition of Scripture, then we say that prevailing injustice and infringements of law, nay, sins which cry to Heaven, must always take their course unchecked, and meet with no further opposition than protests, to which no attention is paid; that a nation must receive injuries, nay, insults to hearth and home, with passive obedience ; that even though country and kingdom should be ruined, the national spirit, the mother-tongue, the popular life should be stifled and die, the once existing historical right must never be sacrificed to the ideal right; that a nation must in quietistic and fatalistic waiting for the help of Heaven let itself be torn by the most ruthless ill-treatment, without venturing, in dependence upon the help of Heaven, to use its own strength. Then the question presses itself on us, whether the appeal to God's command, to the duty of submission to authority, is here really in place ? whether a nation is not really absolved from the duty of obedience when rulers, by continued deeds of violence, *annul themselves as rulers*, themselves abolish the state of law, and by making mere force prevail over law, introduce the rude state of nature, that is, just the state of things in which we are directed to self-help.

It is from this point of view that earnest thinkers, who can by no means be accused of revolutionary sympathies, have been led to the conviction, that there are cases and circumstances in which revolution is lawful. So the above-named A. S. Oersted, who, in the *History of his Life and Times*, says (I. 55): " I found (by continued reflection) that, though a consistent carrying out of the principles of legal science (whose part it is to show what external legislation can forbid or allow) never can permit opposition to the constitution, the law and its organs, yet that, notwithstanding the great moral importance which the maintenance of existing institutions must have, there is a limit to its binding power, which must give way so soon as what is still called the State is corrupted to such a degree as absolutely not to correspond to its idea and moral purpose, but only to serve for the protection of violence and injustice, and the suppression of law and liberty.

Niebuhr expresses himself still more strongly. He says, in his lectures *On the Revolution Era:* " The exact error (of the French nation at the beginning of the Revolution of 1789) lay in the question concerning revolution in general. Here the maxim : Necessity knows no law ! undeniably applies. They who mistake this give the word for what is most horrible. When a people is trodden under foot and ill-used to death, without hope of improvement, like the Greeks under the Turks, when no woman's honour was secure, and the Pasha fetched the daughters and sons out of the houses of the Christians, when no vestige of justice was to be obtained from the tyrants, and religion was persecuted, then supreme necessity existed, and rebellion against the oppressors was as just as possible. Any one who could here be mistaken as to the lawfulness of insurrection must be a wretch deserving to have men's backs turned on him, and to be spat on, and such newspapers as the Frankfort journal merit the highest detestation. Even when oppression does not go so far, but still the people are ill-used, as the Protestants were under Louis XIV., and the Irish Catholics within the times of octogenarians, then necessity knows no law, and the oppressed cannot be blamed for taking arms. Any one defending himself against such a tyrant as Cæsar Borgia does well; he is fighting against a wild beast. But such cases are rare and easily decided. It is another question, whether it is right to resist the supreme power on account of endurable grievances such as those were which existed in France before the revolution." [1] This question Niebuhr answers in the negative. He condemns not only the horrors of the French Revolution, but the Revolution itself, as

[1] Niebuhr, *Geschichte des Zeitalters der Revolution,* I. p. 211 ff.

an unlawful rebellion against lawful authority, as an unjustifiable insurrection.

§ 91.

But even if the lawfulness of self-preservation is admitted, the great question still remains : What measure of injustice must be full before self-defence may be carried out to active resistance, and to what extent may the latter be employed? Such questions lead us into the region of casuistry. For though we have just heard that the rare cases in which revolution is justifiable are easily recognised, and that it is therefore not difficult to draw the line between lawful and unlawful revolution, between endurable and unendurable oppression, still there must be cases in which this is by no means so very easy, in which, if we had to give our judgment in answer to the question, whether a revolution ought or ought not to take place, our thoughts would accuse and excuse one another, and it would be difficult to arrive at a decision. Meantime the knot is not so much untied as cut through by actual revolution, which is not a simple work of moral freedom, but just as much a natural event, a process of nature, a catastrophe in the moral world. *The curse of every revolution* is, that not one is the work of justice alone, but is at the same time, and none the less, the work also of excited passions, which had long brooded in obscurity, and now when opportunity arises, burst forth into flames, whose extent and effects no one can calculate or control. It is because revolution proceeds from the complications which sin has produced in human society, both in times past and at the present hour, that its lawful, its morally justifiable element, is overgrown by its unlawful element, its vindication of justice inseparable from the transgression of law, its moral enthusiasm from the selfishness of natural heathen passions. Its lawful element must be sought in a certain amount of necessity which justifies self-help and self-defence. Where, however, self-defence must be employed, we no longer find ourselves in a purely moral region, which is always limited by legal institutions. Self-defence and arbitrary self-revenge are indigenous in a state of nature where club-law prevails. And if it is difficult for men, even in personal self-defence, to maintain due moderation, and not to overstep the bounds, how much more difficult is it when whole masses are directed to self-help and self-defence! for rashness and vehemence are the characteristics of the multitude. If, then, a revolution is ever beneficial in its results, it will be scarcely possible for any one who participates in it to maintain an unviolated conscience. Even those great heroes, who exercise in the midst of revolution a salutary influence, and perform deeds of deliverance, do not escape that lot of moral contamination and transgression which constitutes the tragic element of their fate. He who delivers his native land by tyrannicide, is none the less pursued by the shade of the slain. But we must not forget that if the self-help of revolution involves an immense responsibility, no less rests upon those who by their misuse of power drive a people to extremities. Revolutions afford us a glance into those depths of sin, where crime from above and crime from below meet our view; but amidst all, the judgments of God are executed, whether upon the sins of rulers or of the people.

§ 92.

Those revolutions are absolutely unjustifiable which are occasioned not by actual oppression, but by the mere desire of innovation. There is much truth in the saying, that when a whole nation unanimously rises and rebels, great and important reasons for such a procedure must exist. Nevertheless, Mynster's saying also holds good, that " there is in decaying nations a desire for change for the mere sake of change, for secret machinations and conspiracies for the mere sake of secrecy. The unlawful is often dearer to such people than the lawful."[1] The Romance nations may serve as examples. The existence of an appetite for change and innovation, which needs a revolution from time to time as a public diversion, points to a *blasé* condition of the general consciousness, to an inward emptiness and hollowness, for which life has lost its earnestness, the salt its savour, in which family life is dissolved, and that satisfaction which the citizen should find in the performance of the daily work of his vocation, work which can prosper only in quiet and peaceful circumstances, is a

[1] Mynster, *Blandede Skrifter*, III. p. 246.

thing unknown. Life being here passed without a sense of duty, and without love, the customary becomes disgusting, and the weariness of mental idleness begets, besides other evil lusts, the lust of revolution, in the midst of whose whirl and confusion the emptiness of existence may be forgotten. To such nations, the favourite saying, " They are not yet ripe for freedom," cannot properly be applied. They must rather be designated as " over-ripe," for they are, for the most part, in a state of mental rottenness.

Revolutions, whether more or less justifiable, may be mostly considered under two chief view-points. They are either purely *national* or *social*. By purely national we mean those where a whole nation, in all its social classes, suffers under undeserved oppression on the part of unjust rulers, and is thereby forced into active resistance. As an example of such a national rising, we may cite the insurrection of the Netherlands against the foreign yoke of Spain under Philip II. Their national rights, and the privileges which had been conceded them, were violated, and those very numerous inhabitants of the land who had embraced Protestantism were deprived of their religious liberty, persecuted as heretics by the Inquisition, and condemned to the flames. The noblest of the land, if they refused to degrade themselves into instruments of tyranny, were thrown into prison and executed. All felt the injustice and contempt with which the nation was treated, and all classes of society, even those which were otherwise at strife between themselves (the nobles and the commercial class), stood opposed like a wall to the foreign tyranny. It is difficult to understand how a merely passive resistance, which, moreover, had long been practised in vain, could be carried out against a fanatic government, obscured by Jesuitism, and with absolutely no understanding of, or sympathy for, the people, whose peculiarity and independence it was, on the contrary, striving to destroy. In spite of the darker side, which is inseparable from every revolution, the insurrection of the United Netherlands is one of the most justifiable revolutions which history has to record. This is true also of the Greek war of liberation, 1821–29, which must be placed upon an entirely different level from other recent revolutions.[1]

[1] Thiersch, *Griechenlands Schicksale vom Anfange des Befreiungskrieges.*

Social revolutions, which proceed from an internal strife between different classes of society within the same nation, differ from purely national revolutions. The former occur when individual classes are oppressed by others, and the government sides with the ruling classes, because to do so coincides with its own one-sided interests. This was the case in French society before 1789. Royalty and the court, surrounded with the greatest splendour and magnificence, and devoted to a life of unlimited enjoyment, made common cause with those elements of society which were equally addicted to luxury and magnificence, viz. the nobility and higher ranks of the clergy, who both passed their days in idleness. With these royalty was, so to speak, cemented. When Louis XVI. ascended the throne, there existed but one real distinction in French society, viz. that between the noble and non-noble, the privileged and non-privileged classes. This distinction split the nation into two parties, and royalty was found in the one instead of standing over both. Access to the highest posts and offices was open only to the nobles. Of all profits and possessions the nobles took the best for themselves, while all *burdens* were laid upon the non-noble. To this was added, that intelligence, knowledge, culture, were, on the whole, not found among the nobility, whose merit chiefly depended upon their birth ; that the labour necessary to procure them enjoyment had to be performed exclusively by the oppressed class, which was, at the same time, the more intelligent. Hence the contrast between nobles and non-nobles was also one between non-producers, who were nothing but consumers, and producers, who were excluded from consumption. The consumers appealed to their chartered privileges, to their historical rights ; those excluded from enjoyment, whose labour was chiefly devoted to furnishing the means of enjoyment to the court and nobility, appealed to the rights of men, to ideal justice. It was from this side that the great French Revolution, which, according to its proper nature, was a social one, proceeded. The result was, that *the third class* attained supremacy, and that royalty combined more and more closely with it, as was especially manifested by the July monarchy of 1830, hence called also the citizen-monarchy. The contrast between nobles and non-nobles, privileged and non-privileged, has now lost its importance. In these days, however, the contrast between possessors and non-possessors (capital and labour) has raised its head, a contrast which at any rate involves the *possibility* of a fresh social revolution. For the rest, we by no means desire, by what we have here said of the revolution of 1789, to express an opinion that, in the manner in which it was carried out, it was either a justifiable or a necessary revolution, but merely to point out its social character.

§ 93.

A revolution proceeding from beneath can only be justified by necessity, and thus holds good also of the so-called *coup d'état*. The more or less justifiable *coups d'état* aim either at preserving the whole State from dissolution and destruction, as far as this can be done, by the overthrow of the entire existing constitution, as *e.g.* Bonaparte's on the 18th Brumaire. Or, their object is a social reform, which could not take place under the existing constitution, because the ruling classes of society are exercising an undue oppression of the other classes, and opposing urgently needed reforms. The highly advantageous revolution which took place in Denmark in 1660, by which the king assumed absolute power, thus contributed to social reform. After the undue oppression exercised by the nobility, both upon the sovereign himself and the third class, this change in the constitution seemed to be at the same time the emancipation of royalty and of the burgher class. It would unquestionably have been more beneficial if the king—as was reasonably expected—had at the same time granted to the country a class-representation adapted to the then existing state of society. For then the official hierarchy and the bureaucracy, concerning both which complaints were subsequently made, would have found their necessary counterpoise.

An example of an unjust and unwise *coup d'état* is furnished by the attempt made by Charles x. of France, which led to the July revolution of 1830. Nothing less was contemplated than a reaction, by which the whole state of society was to be gradually brought back to that of 1789, and which must have been viewed by the whole nation as an attack directed against itself. We will not, however, here examine how far the Revolution of July was itself necessary.[1]

§ 94.

Since even such revolutions as may be called justifiable are abnormal phenomena, and have incalculable results, the question has often been discussed : By what *means are revolutions to be obviated ?*   It is not difficult to state these means, but very difficult to bring them into actual application.

They may be all summed up in the one universal remedy : Christianity, or, in other words, that the Christian State and the Christian people should be a truth.   If the irreligious State be insisted on, revolution is always standing at the door ; but we lay emphasis on the words : the Christian State must become *a truth.*   For that mere appearance of it, upon which reaction has often sought to support itself, is of little avail ; and to endeavour to make a people Christian by compulsion is the surest way to revolution, as the English Revolution of the 17th century sufficiently proves.   But in proportion as Christianity really pervades a nation, its opinion, disposition, and manners, its social and political institutions, will reverence and defer to *authority,* to rulers, to law and order, be active among it, and the notion of the sovereignty of the people, so far as the rule of the masses is meant, be rejected as a phantom.   However vigorous may be the desire for liberty, there will be beside it, in such a people, the consciousness that progress can only take place in the way of conformity to law, and that it is better to suffer injustice than to commit it.   Where Christianity is the power ruling over minds, there will be far more moderation and contentment with what exists, than where Christianity is absent, for the very reason that it teaches us to seek our supreme good in a super-mundane state, and directs us to the kingdom of God and the heavenly citizenship.   We are not, indeed, ignorant that it is this which has so often brought upon Christianity

---

[1] Mynster, *Meddeleser om mit Levnet,* p. 236 : "It must be fully acknowledged that the French Revolution of July 1830 was both justifiable and conducted with great moderation, and that it was undoubtedly necessary, unless everything was gradually to return to the state of affairs before 1789."   Other voices (Niebuhr, Hegel) have, however, declared against the July Revolution.

the accusation of political indifferentism—of indifference to the concerns of civil life. But such indifference is no necessary result of Christianity. On the contrary, experience shows that Christianity has exercised a most decided influence upon civil affairs—upon the form and development of the States. Certainly, Christianity does, at the same time, awaken and maintain the consciousness of the finiteness and *relativity* of the State and of earthly civicism, and of the imperfections ever found in them. A Christian may, indeed, labour for a political ideal, for the reformation of the State and of earthly civil affairs ; and yet, his position to these relative matters being a purely relative one, he will combine with his efforts the conviction that every constitution, even though not good, is endurable if we can live under it " a quiet and peaceable life, in all godliness and honesty " (1 Tim. ii. 2). The case is far otherwise when men seek their satisfaction exclusively in the things of this world. For since, by reason of their destination for eternity, they are compelled to seek after *absolute* satisfaction, and are seeking this where it is not to be found, they live in a state of continual discontent. This discontent, whose cause is the lack of religion, combined with dogmas hostile to religion and theories of popular sovereignty, produces revolutionary tendencies in the minds of many in these times. They take up a pessimist position with regard to all that exists, and surrender themselves to spurious optimist expectations of a state of prosperity to proceed from its overturn. From this selfish unrest, these unsatisfied earthly desires, an inward flame may be kindled, which will break out in revolutionary efforts.

Where Christianity manifests itself as a real power, it acts on the one hand in opposition to revolutionary tendencies in subjects, while on the other its fruit is that rulers will reign in righteousness. But the righteousness required for obviating the evil of revolution is not to do justice merely to what exists, but also to what is originating, to that which is developing in the times. We need, says Baader, not merely *stationary*, but *evolutionary*, which differ greatly from *revolutionary* governments. All evolution which is not supported, finds itself a vent in revolution. One chief means, therefore, of preventing the latter is for the government to place itself at the head of reform. Hence it must be owned that there is profound truth in the opinion expressed by Stein, with regard to the social problem, in his famous work, *On the Socialist Movement in France*, that the genuine, most lasting and most popular sovereignty is the *sovereignty of social reform;* that sovereignty must come forward *against* the will of the ruling classes *to elevate the lower, and hitherto socially and politically subject classes;* and that there is no higher or more divine mission for royalty than this. He adds: "All sovereignty will henceforth become either an empty shadow or a despotism, or will perish in republicanism, unless it has the moral courage to be a sovereignty of social reform."[1]

WAR.—CONSTANT PEACE.

§ 95.

Under the influence of Christianity there has been formed, in opposition to national selfishness and the right of the stronger, an international law, which requires that the mutual relations of nations shall be determined according to the principles of justice and Christian humanity. Especially since the era of the Reformation have efforts been directed towards the formation of an international jurisprudence (*e.g.* the celebrated work of Hugo Grotius, *De jure belli et pacis,* 1629). None the less, however, does the history of Christianity, even down to our own days, display a series of transgressions of law committed by one nation upon another. "*Wars* and rumours of wars" (Matt. xxiv. 6) are constantly heard of in Christendom. The true vocation of war, however, is to serve as a means of preventing injustice and violence by physical force, and of extorting what justice demands.

War is one of the most powerful testimonies to the corruption of human nature, one of the greatest calamities and plagues of this world. It is, however, a necessary evil, and one based upon a divine ordinance. For rulers "bear not the sword in vain," and must use it against the external as well as the internal foes of society. It is in the fact that

[1] Stein, *Geschichte der socialen Bewegung in Frankreich,* III. p. 46–49.

the sword is given by God to the ruler, that the reason and justification of war consists. For it would be very one-sided to maintain that the sword was given only to protect the State from attacks arising within, and not from those which penetrate it from without.

But it is just because this God-given sword is delivered into the hands of sinful men, that it may be so fearfully misused. Only that war is in accordance with the divine ordinance which is carried on with the weapons of righteousness and in the cause of righteousness. Merely personal and dynastic wars must be condemned, for it is not right that a nation and a State should be degraded into means for merely personal interests. It is only for the sake of the whole State, and to defend the State as such, that war may be carried on. Wars of retaliation, and wars of conquest, whose aim is a mere extension of power, are also indefensible. Undisguised selfishness, with its prudent calculations, is never just. A just war must proceed from objective violations of justice, and must at the same time have *sufficient* justification; for not every transgression of justice is a sufficient cause for war. That alone is a just war which has a sufficient cause, which is waged for the supreme and most important possession of the people, for altar and hearth (*pro aris et focis*), for that which is in a spiritual as well as in a material sense necessary to the existence of the nation. Or that by which other nations suffering oppression are succoured, for by a concert of States the individual State is not relegated to a selfish perception of its own interests only. When it has been insisted that a just war can be only a war of defence, and not one of attack, a non-practical distinction is made, for defence cannot in many cases be separated from attack. On the other hand, it may well be said that a just war must always be one of defence or protection, whether a nation is protecting itself or another from oppression; and this may often necessarily involve an attack upon a hostile or injurious power, which it is designed to render harmless. It is from this view-point that a *religious war* must also be regarded, notwithstanding all the objections of that widely disseminated religionless policy, which in its indifferentism thinks that all religious contrasts are equal, that they utterly vanish in the presence of humanity and civilisation.   Positive religions cannot be at once banished from the world, and a war of religion, though certainly not justifiable, if undertaken for the purpose of propagating the faith by means of the sword, is so, if waged to *protect* the rights of an oppressed religious community.

Since war brings with it so many horrors, and he who begins it takes upon himself so enormous a responsibility, a war should never be commenced till everything has been tried that may lead to a pacific solution of the dispute.   In the carrying out, too, of the war itself, the principles of humanity must be applied as far as possible, and all needless cruelty avoided.   Stratagem and mutual deception cannot in this respect be condemned, since both sides are agreed in employing against each other not force alone, but craft, together with all the artifices of war.   But Christian humanity demands that, since war is carried on for the sake of peace, a department must be left, within which confidence may be felt, the truth spoken, and where it would be esteemed *dishonourable* to deceive the trust reposed.   And where Christianity has true professors, there also—as we have seen in recent wars—will Christian love practise its works of mercy towards the prisoners and the wounded. Since the Church and its offices accompany the combatants ·to the field of battle, the higher kingdom, the kingdom of peace, is among them.

Besides, we must, as Luther says, look at war with manly eyes, and not think only how great a calamity war is, but also what great calamities are to be put an end to by means of war. And if a one-sided pessimist view regards only the many terrors and devastations of every war, the horrors of the battlefield, the sorrows brought upon families, the towns burnt down, the cornfields trampled on, and the demoniacal passions let loose, we must not overlook the fact that war has also its arousing and purifying effects.   It arouses a slumbering patriotism, and calls citizens from the luxurious enjoyments of peace, and from petty and selfish interests, to sacrifices and self-denial for the common cause. It awakens in many a lively consciousness of the perishableness and insecurity of human affairs, teaches many to pray, and humbly to submit to the Lord of Hosts, whose just judgments may be executed upon earth even by means of war.

§ 96.

Every State laying claim to independence must possess an army; for an army is the physical force by which a State must maintain both its internal and external security. And just because an army must, in all its operations, act as a physical force by mechanical means, nay, because war is carried on by the action of the great machine to which an army has been ever increasingly developed, obedience and *subordination* are the main virtues required in the military class. Obedience indeed, to be of true inward value, must be inspired by love for king and country; for it is this which excites the enthusiasm of heroism, and impels to that willing self-sacrifice in which the warrior makes the saying of the Redeemer: "Fear not those who kill the body and cannot kill the soul" (Matt. x. 28), in quite a special sense, his motto. Still, however highly we may esteem heroism and enthusiasm, they are both unproductive when once they cast off obedience, and renounce patient submission to the many privations which the soldier has to put up with.

Every vocation has its ideal, poetic, and also its prosaic side; but there is hardly one in which the ideal and the prosaic appear in such sharp contrast as in that of the soldier. War has its times of great crises, its days of enthusiasm, exaltation and victory; but it has, too, its days of defeat and retreat, when the question is to be satisfied with the consciousness of duty performed and courage maintained, even under the oppressive feeling of humiliation. And then come, too, the purely prosaic, not days only, but weeks, in which nothing of importance takes place, when, often amidst great privations and grievances, time creeps on in empty, vacant monotony, while further orders have to be waited for. Henry Steffens, who took part in the German war of liberation against Napoleon i., relates in his autobiography that during such a period of waiting he fell sick through weariness, and at the same time was made nervous by the endless chatter of his numerous comrades which by day, and their endless snoring which by night, deafened his ears; and that Gneisenau said to him on this occasion, "Weariness is a necessary element of our present method of carrying on war," but at the same time consoled him with the fact that perhaps as early as to-morrow he might experience something which would satisfy him for a long time.[1] The exercise given to obedience and subordination furnishes an essential element in the ethic value of both the weariness and enthusiasm, the poetry and the prose of war.

Among the contrasts inseparable from military life, is that between life upon the battlefield and life in hospitals. The latter is of no less importance to the development of the inward personality than the former. While on the field of battle an earthly object and an earthly victory are striven for with self-sacrificing devotion, battles are fought and victories gained in the hospitals—not indeed by all, but yet by many of the wounded and dying—whose importance belongs to the kingdom which is not of this world![2]

§ 97.

A soldier's obedience is essentially obedience to the king as supreme head of the State. The *military oath*, where monarchy is a reality, must be taken to the king, and to him alone, not to "the king and constitution." The suspicious feature in this form of oath, which may be designated as a product of the Parliamentary system, consists in the circumstance that the army is thereby transformed from an obeying to a *reasoning* power. For it is invited to investigate the limits of kingly authority in its relation to the constitution and the popular representation. By this oath, moreover, it is involved in endless reflections, which must have a paralyzing and perplexing effect, obedience being made a hypothetical matter, to be rendered, viz., "so far as" the king maintains the constitution, or "so far as" the representatives maintain the constitution. It is mischievous to import a formula so

[1] Steffens, *Was ich erlebte*, VIII. p. 73.
[2] Compare the excellent little work, *Der Seelsorger im Kriege*—Reminiscences of a Danish Military Preacher (1876, Danish).

full of disturbing reflection into an oath, to be taken by a class whose very nature it should be not to reason. It is, however, equally mischievous to dispense with any military oath. The omission of this solemn act blunts the feeling of the importance of the matter, and at the same time leaves the whole question of military obligation open and undecided, as a matter which may still be a subject of discussion, *i.e.* makes it the very thing which it ought *not* to be.[1] The official class is quite differently circumstanced from the military class. The former should certainly take the oath to the king and constitution, not perhaps because in their case the above-mentioned "in so far" is specified, but because it is their very vocation to apply the constitution to the special cases occurring in official life.

The introduction of universal *compulsory defensive service* must be regarded as an advance. For all the sons of a country are called upon to defend their native land. A more elevated spirit, and one which opposes barbarity, is imparted to the army when its members are taken from the most widely differing strata of society. But there is good reason for the demand that the clerical class should be exempt from military duty, this class having to work more directly for the kingdom which is *not* of this world. To misconceive the importance of this demand, is to misconceive the clerical vocation.

§ 98.

There are Christian *sects* (Mennonites, Quakers) who regard the calling of the soldier as incompatible with that of the Christian, and hence refuse to perform military duty. They appeal to the command of the Lord (Matt. v. 39): " Whosoever shall smite thee on the one cheek, turn to him the other also," etc. This view arises from not distinguishing between the community of the saints—the kingdom of higher and spiritual righteousness, in which a disposition in conformity with the gospel is to prevail, and where the precepts of the

---

[1] The question whether the sovereign, or a parliamentary majority, is the supreme authority in *military* affairs is instructively illustrated by the recent history of Prussia. (Comp. *Aus dem Briefwechsel Friedrich Wilhelms IV. mit Bunsen*, by Leopold von Ranke, p. 196 sqq.)

Lord find their application to individual circumstances—and the State as the region of external justice, in which law and the sword must prevail. To deny the lawfulness of war is the same thing as to deny the State. But the State cannot cease as long as we are upon earth. And a Christian must live at the same time in two kingdoms: in the kingdom of the higher righteousness, and in that of external (legal) justice, in which, by reason of continual unrighteousness and transgressions, justice must be promoted by external means. Nor can it by any means be proved that Scripture intends to abolish the State and the military class. To the soldiers who came to John the Baptist and asked: What shall we do? he did not say that they should resign their service, but, "Do violence to no man, and be content with your wages" (Luke iii. 14). Christ did not bid the centurion at Capernaum to give up his post, nor did St. Peter speak in such wise to Cornelius when he baptized him (Acts x.). It is everywhere assumed that this calling is compatible with reception into the Christian Church.

In opposition to the view in question, it must further be remarked that the sword which is used in battle is not the sword of the murderer, but one given by God to execute justice upon earth. In war, too, it is not individual against individual, but those general powers,—nation against nation, and State against State. The combatant should know that he is subserving a divine ordinance. It is not his business to investigate whether the war in which he is fighting is a just or an unjust one. The responsibility lies upon those who have resolved upon war. His concern is to show fidelity and bravery, though certainly it is the happier case when he and all his brothers in arms can be penetrated by enthusiasm for a righteous cause. On the question whether a soldier can be in a state of salvation, Luther utters a noble thought. In the prayer which he advises a soldier to make before battle, this passage occurs: Let him thank God that he is certain that his service is no sin in God's sight, but an act of obedience well-pleasing to God; but let him not hope to be saved because he is a soldier, but because he is a Christian, who trusts not in his own works and deeds, but in the Lord Christ who died for us. "If thou wilt add thereto (to this prayer) the Creed and Lord's Prayer, thou canst do so, and rest content.   And then commit thy soul and body to God's hands, draw thy sword from the scabbard, and strike in God's name."[1] In contrast with this, Luther also describes the heathen frame of mind before battle: Contempt of death and defiance, hope of glory and fame, expectation of a good booty, and in some cases, hope, too, of new love affairs and adventures.   We may here also mention the soldiers of Napoleon, their heathen "*gloire*," and their exclamations, even in death, of " *Vive l'Empereur !*"

<h3 style="text-align:center">§ 99.</h3>

War is waged for the sake of peace, and it has been already often asked : Whether the time will ever come when war shall cease, and *perpetual peace* prevail between the nations of the earth ?   It is, however, a delusion to suppose that war can ever be abolished, for then we must know also how to banish sin and injustice from the world.   Scripture, on the contrary, tells us that in the latter days there will be terrible wars upon earth, nation rising against nation, and kingdom against kingdom, amidst great tribulations (Matt. xxiv. 6 sqq.).   And yet the same Scripture speaks also of a time when the wolf shall lie down with the lamb (Isa. xi. 6), when sword and bow shall be broken, and the sword be beaten into a ploughshare (Isa. ii. 4 ; Mic. iv. 3).   It tells of a militant kingdom on earth, when Satan shall be bound, and the kingdom of Christ shall alone prevail (Rev. xx. 4).   If we may only represent this golden age as a transitory one, which will be again driven away by wars and rumours of wars, when Satan is to be again unbound (Rev. xx. 7), continual peace still remains an ideal, which must be unceasingly contended for in the consciousness that the earthly kingdom of peace, which may be approximately realized in separate periods, but always only on a lower stage, points as a mere type to its heavenly antitype.   It is this which is the destiny and ultimate goal of man, and is in contrast with every earthly kingdom, a kingdom *that cannot be moved*, because it is not merely a kingdom of happiness, but also of salvation (comp. General Part, § 47 sq.).

[1] Luther's *Werke*, X. p. 621

The means by which the earthly ideal of peace is to bo striven for, is an alliance of Christian States for the maintenance of peace according to the principles of Christian love and justice, and hence a state of things in which policy is determined by morality, and all Macchiavellian maxims arc condemned and excluded.[1] After Napoleon, with his selfish policy, which despised all international law, was overthrown, this notion was embraced by the Holy Alliance (1815), to which Fr. Baader gave an impulse by a representation which he made to the three victorious monarchs, Alexander I. of Russia, Francis I. of Austria, and Frederic William III. of Prussia.[2] The Holy Alliance declared in the documents of its institution, that it agreed to take, as the *sole* standard of its mode of acting, the precepts of religion, precepts of justice, love and peace, which, far from being applicable to private life alone, should, on the contrary, exercise *absolute* influence upon the decisions of rulers, and be the guides of all their proceedings. It declared that rulers are to be regarded as only the *delegates of Providence*, and that the Christian nation, of which they and their peoples constitute parts, had in deed and in truth *no other* sovereign than Him to whom alone power belongs as an attribute, because in Him are all the treasures of life, knowledge and infinite wisdom. It further solemnly acknowledged, that their duty to God and to the nations they governed commanded them, as far as in them lay, to give the world an example of justice, concord and moderation, and henceforth to direct all their efforts to the *promotion of the arts of peace*, to the increase of the internal prosperity of their States, and to the *revival* of those *religious* and *moral* feelings whose supremacy had, amidst the calamities of the times, been but too much destroyed.[3] All was referred to the Christian revelation, a fact implying that confessional distinctions (Greco-Catholic, Roman Catholic and evangelical-Protestant) must be no hindrance to peace.

[1] Comp. Kant, " Zum ewigen Friede," *Werke*, vol. XII. Rosenkranz' edit.

[2] H. Thiersch, *Ueber den christlichen Staat*, p. 182. Comp. Baader's article on the need, introduced by the French Revolution, for a new and more intimate alliance in politics and religion.

[3] Görres, *Die heilige Alliance und die Volker auf dem Congress zu Verona*, 1822 (*Politische Schriften*, vol. V. p. 47).

The Holy Alliance has been derided, and its deriders, and
all who do not believe in a moral order of the world, and
those who regard Christianity as only fitted for private and
domestic use, have certainly had the satisfaction of seeing
that quite other and unholy principles were but too soon
adopted, and that the actual course of transactions and
events formed a striking contrast to the principles expressed.
They have had the satisfaction of finding that the Holy
Alliance was gradually and imperceptibly dissolved, and that
the treaties of 1815, and the whole system of States founded
by that Alliance, now belong to the things of the past.
Nevertheless, the thought itself is a great and a true one.
The mistake which the Alliance committed in the carrying
out of its principles was unmistakeably this, that the
sovereigns who inaugurated it placed themselves upon the
standpoint of Conservatism, and opposed progress, in opposition to Baader's warning, that a government must not be
stationary but evolutionary. Also, that in their tendency to
assert the rights of *legitimate* authority, in opposition to
revolution, they ignored the rights of liberty, and did not
reflect that social life in its normal condition is based upon
the union of authority and liberty. To such a degree did
the fear and horror of evolution possess them, that they saw
in every voluntary popular movement a revolutionary impulse and "demagogic machinations," and therefore, as far as
they were concerned, gave support to the view, that the Holy
Alliance was at bottom a confederacy of sovereigns against
peoples, a view which Napoleon I. expressed at St. Helena
in the words: " *C'est une alliance des rois contre les peuples!* "
This gave rise to a liberal and liberalistic opposition, with its
demands for constitutional government, guarantees for the
people, etc., nay, even with extravagance and fanaticism (Sand's
Assassination of Kotzebue). Mutual mistrust was now developed, and peace was again disturbed by wars and revolutions. We must also agree that Görres was in the right
when he frankly declared, first in his work, " *Europa und
die Revolution*," and afterwards in that on the Congress of
Verona, that the misfortune of the Alliance was that it came
too late. For if the Christian and just principles of the
Alliance had been made the standard at the Congress of

Vienna, which took place shortly before, much which was there decided on must have been settled otherwise. The partition of Poland, which evidently resulted from an *unholy* alliance of the same three powers who concluded the Holy Alliance, would thus have been declared null and void, and Poland restored according to the principles of justice. Then, too, would a demand have been made for the restitution of Finland; nor would Denmark, as Görres also expressly states, have been punished with such disproportionate severity (by the loss of Norway), for doing only what all other nations did, etc.[1] Whatever may be thought of the above-mentioned historical and other examples, this maxim will not at any rate be disputed, that it was a misfortune for the Holy Alliance that its Christian policy was not brought into existence till after a system of States had already been arranged, and an edifice according to heathen policy erected. Though all this may, however, be said, the great importance and truth of the thought itself cannot be thereby abolished; it necessitated, so to speak, its own acceptance by the inherent power of truth. For it is upon Christian foundations alone that the peace of the world can be built, and not upon the system of the so-called "balance of power," a purely mechanical and fundamentally a selfish system, based upon no higher motive than self-elevation. The balance-of-power system makes no inquiries concerning right and justice. Its aim is no other than to prevent any one power in the system of States gaining a supremacy which would be a menace to the others. It is a mere substitute for justice, and by the favour of circumstances is transformed—as experience shows—into a policy of great powers, which in many cases but ill accords with justice.

The present time may be designated an interregnum in international respects; for nothing is settled. This much, however, is certain, that there is no prospect that the principles of the kingdom of peace will prevail in the immediate future. But though the Holy Alliance can only be regarded as a transitory and quickly vanishing meteor, it yet belongs to those ideals which, we know, will return, because they are of the truth, and the human race cannot dispense with

---

[1] Görres, *Ueber den Congress von Verona*, p. 56 sqq.

them. A time will come when this ideal will again rise in the political heavens; it will show itself to the nations, after they have been tired out and used up by a policy of so-called "interests," which is in its very nature a policy of power, and the right of the stronger.

THE IDEAL TASKS OF CULTURE.

ART AND SCIENCE.

§ 100.

Culture and civilisation develop in the life of nations in connection with political and social efforts. Civilisation may be understood as culture in its application and effects upon the civil community and its arrangements. The innumerable advantages which culture has, by a series of inventions and facilities for controlling external nature, bestowed upon States and the civil community, have been justly extolled. Its chief blossoms, however, have from of old been found in *art and science*, which do not, as the manifold other tasks of culture, aim at any direct advantage, but whose value is found in themselves. We may, however, speak in an ideal sense of the advantage of art and science. For in its art and science a nation possesses an intellectual capital, which must by employment be made to yield the profit of diffusing *human education* among the people.

There are various kinds of education—professional, technical, political, social education, etc. By human education, in the full meaning of the term, however, we understand a developed feeling, a lively interest, an open eye, an open ear, an open heart for the human in all its forms. Next to religion and moral goodness, there is nothing which is to such a degree capable of developing in us the universal-human, of making us partakers of universal or all-sided humanity, as art and science; nothing which can in like manner set us free from those intellectual restrictions with which we often go through life, as though we had bandages on our eyes, or were hemmed in with mental fences, which make a free look around and free movement towards all sides impossible. It is true that history shows us ages in which a high degree of æsthetic and intellectual culture has accompanied a decay of morality and religion. And hence we might perhaps be induced to conclude that, if men are not the better for them, art and science had better be dispensed with as mere intellectual luxuries. But the periods alluded to, with a culture separated from personal life, lacked the noblest element, nay, the very core of human cultivation, and were pervaded by inhumanity. Genuine human cultivation is nothing else but culture, determined and animated by the moral and the morally religious. Culture without morality is without worth, or is at most of very ambiguous worth. But, on the other side, it must be said that though morality maintains its undoubted worth with but a slight degree of culture, still it is in such a case restrained within bounds, which prevent its due and full development. And thus the phenomenon is often repeated, that men who are religious and Christian, but of defective education, manifest not merely want of taste, but also actual narrowness, give their judgment about things which they do not understand, embark in all kinds of undertakings for the reformation of the world, or at all events of their own nation, in short, in tasks which are above their capacity. In their observations and arguments the middle terms are always wanting, a sure mark of the uneducated. They forget that to bring the kingdom of God into effective relation with the world, it is not sufficient to know the kingdom of God, but that it is also necessary to know the world and human nature, in which this kingdom is to be planted. It is, however, by means of a right use of art and science that we take possession, in an ideal manner, of the world and its manifold life.

While art and science have an educational effect, they afford at the same time an elevated kind of delight, which is combined with an exaltation above the visible and actual. Art has this advantage over science, that it is capable of charming most men; while science is only for a comparatively smaller circle—a circle which is, however, by means of the increasing prevalence of education, constantly enlarging.

ART.

Art and Humanity.

§ 101.

All *art* is affected with the limitation that the beautiful ideal world which it represents is but phenomenal, has existence only for the imagination. But not the less does this imaginary world contain " the essence," so to speak, of the actual world, and the anticipation of the world to come. It is the actual world which is brought before our eyes in art, but the world as it is beheld by artistic genius, to which applies in the highest sense what was said of the human spirit, that it is a " born idealist," and which everywhere seeks out, draws forth, and portrays in individual forms the idea, the essence, the inmost truth of existence. Artistic genius is akin to Prometheus, in saying which we need not let our minds dwell upon his *plunder* of the fire, though the artist often lets himself be tempted to carry off the divine spark as plunder.

The subject of art is man and man's world. The different arts denote different stages in the realization of the ideal of humanity, from architecture, which builds and adorns a dwelling for man or a temple for the deity whom man worships, sculpture, painting, music, up to poetry, by means of which man and human life attain their most perfect representation. It is poetry which must be chiefly had in view when the importance of art with regard to the moral life is in question, and what applies to poetry applies also, with the necessary restrictions, to the other arts. Poetry expresses chiefly the interests of the human heart, for all the harmonies of the world's life, and also all its discords, its sufferings and its sorrows, find their echo in the breast of the poet. At the same time, however, we behold in the mirror which the poet holds up to us, an intuitive representation of human life as it is, with its events and fate, its ways and doings, its characters and passions, behold under variously changing forms both the Iliad and the Odyssey of life, its tragedy and its comedy. It is by all these that the poet gives us his answer to the question: What is life? and gives it us, as it were, in a dream, to which we willingly surrender ourselves.

§ 102.

Art must not be regarded as a kind of chance gift which has fallen into the lap of certain favoured individuals as their special portion. It is, on the contrary, intended for the whole human race, for all nations, and it consequently accompanies the race through the whole course of its historical development. Hence we distinguish between ancient (heathen) art and Christian art—a distinction which is based upon their respective different views of the ideal of humanity, of the nature and destiny of man; and these must in their turn be referred to differences in the religious principle and the idea of God. We need only name, by way of example, the notions, providence and fate, guilt, moral responsibility and retribution, which are so differently understood in the ancient and the Christian world. What a difference is there between Æschylus and Shakespeare! And, again, within the Christian world, how different are Shakespeare and Calderon, the Protestant and Catholic poets! Of the view-point from which Goethe and Schiller regarded humanity, and of the influence this exercised on their poetry, we have already had occasion to speak.

When it is required that all modern art should, as such, be *Christian art*, it cannot from the standpoint of Protestantism be meant that art must be exclusively religious, and place itself directly in the service of religion, nay, of the Church. There is indeed a sacred art, called into life by Christianity, as a component part of public worship; and this by no means belongs exclusively to the Roman Catholic Church, in which it is mingled with secular accessories of all kinds. For Protestantism, too, has its sacred art, as is especially testified by its hymn poetry and sacred music, *e.g.* Sebastian Bach's passion music of St. Matthew. But through Protestantism art was emancipated from her comparative dependence upon religion and the Church, and entered on a freer and an independent career as secular art. In saying this, however, we by no means assert that it ceases to be

Christian art, assuming that the Christian ideal of humanity, together with the Christian view of the world and of life, does not cease, even though unexpressed, to be that which gives definite form to all those images of life and the world which art brings before us. This is the case with Shakespeare, though he deals with exclusively secular subjects, and his drama is, properly speaking, the secular drama. Shakespeare forms in this respect a contrast to Calderon, who chiefly works with religious and sacred materials, derived partly from Scripture and partly from legends, but who, for this very reason, cannot, like the Protestant poet, lead us into the midst of stirring secular life.

§ 103.

The ideal of humanity is not merely the subject of art, but art itself is an individual, effective contribution towards the realization of this ideal in the life of the nations. All art is and must be *national*. It is to be an individual representation of the general human. But national peculiarity is the first great main peculiarity, in which the general human attains form. Of this, poetry offers the clearest proof. The true poet sings for his *nation*. It is only by means of language that he can address it; and only what a nation is capable of appropriating by means of its own dialect can become its property. It is the *spirit* of this definite language which comes upon the poet, and, freed from prosaic dust, unfolds its wings through him, its chosen organ. It is this spirit which inspires his words, and it might justly be said that it is not so much the poet who has great command of the language, as the language which has, on the contrary, great command of him. The reason that Oehlenschläger is so great as a Danish poet is not only because, on his appearance at the beginning of this century, he added much that was new and great to our poetry, and brought us back to our own most ancient and original poetry, our sagas and myths, and thereby also to the first sources of our northern mental and spiritual peculiarity; but also because a new world of speech, a new well of language, which has since poured itself forth through various channels upon the nation, was suddenly opened by him.

The greatness of Oehlenschläger cannot possibly be duly recognised in Germany, because in his German works he has made use of a language already brought to perfection by great original poets. Though we certainly do not overlook the incalculable importance it is to a nation that the subjects of its poetry should also be national, that the history of its fatherland should live in poetic representations, still the national element in poetry and art is not shown only by their dealing with national matters. On the contrary, all subjects which are, generally speaking, adapted for poetic treatment, can and must be treated nationally, in accordance with the character of the people, with their natural mode of thought and inclinations, those inborn tendencies of heart and mind whose peculiar emotions have found expression in the formation of the language.

But in thus laying stress upon the national, we would equally insist upon the generally human element. The national, apart from the human, is merely the particular, is natural one-sidedness, is rough and unpolished, and rife with all kinds of peculiarities and bad habits. The enthusiasts of national poetry make the peculiarities of a nation their special aim ; they require, *e.g.*, that its past ages and their power should be depicted by the poet in all their wild rudeness, and thus enveloped in misty haze, and expressed in only half intelligible language, should be set before the people as a means of national revival. Unconsciously to themselves, they change poetry into historical antiquarianism. What we desire, however, to have in a popular form is not the ancient, but the human, the ever present, that which can speak to *us*, who belong to the living history of to-day, who have reached the stage of development now occupied by culture and humanity. This is the sense in which we recognise the justice of the demand that all poetry should be *modern:* International intercourse has induced nations to endeavour to appropriate each other's poetry, for the sake of possessing and enjoying the universal-human in a greater multiplicity of forms. No poet is more national than Shakespeare. If, then, he is nevertheless appropriated by all other nations, this proves that it must be a great universal-human, ever present value, which gains for his works a place not only in the national literature of his country, but in the literature of the world.

There is, however, one thing in poetry which belongs exclusively to the individual nation, and which the best translation can but imperfectly render, and that is the language. The language is as indispensable to poetry as it is to the nation itself. A national poet may sometimes successfully attempt to express himself in a foreign tongue. But he can speak from the depths of his heart and soul in only one. Baggesen—and this is true also of Oehlenschläger—felt greatly attracted by German literature, and obtained no small amount of appreciation as a German poet; nay, even composed poems in French. Still he designates—

> "*Der Heimath Töne*—keinem Deutschen abgelernt—
> Darin der Dänensprache Quellen rieseln "[1]

—as the purest that ever resounded from his harp, and as that which he hopes will gain *distinction* from his countrymen in after times. It was these tones which he so often remembered with sadness, and for which he longed, in his labyrinthine wanderings through foreign lands and amidst foreign literatures.

§ 104.

If inquiry is made as to the effects produced by art, whether upon nations or individuals, the answer to such inquiry has already been given in the preceding pages: it *gives pleasure and it educates.* But the pleasure which art affords is not purely intellectual but æsthetic. It is a pleasure, in the beautiful and the sublime, caused by imagination and feeling,—an elevation of soul by the harmonies of existence, while even its discords and contrasts are either resolved into harmony, or are tending to such resolution upon the heights of art. Pleasure is the direct effect produced by art; education only the indirect. Hence pleasure is the first thing we seek in art. We need this pleasure as an inward refreshment, a release from the pressure of business, from labour amidst the dust of reality. We know well, indeed, that delight and times of refreshing are also found in religion.

---

[1] *The Tones of Home*—to be learned by no German — through which the springs of Danish language find a channel.

But we cannot always remain and live directly in this loftiest interest, though it must always be present in the depths of our being, cannot always be solemnizing this worship as such. During our life on earth, with its many duties, we are permitted also to stay awhile in these mid-regions, and to find in them a strengthening for future work. And what we assimilate in art, becomes fresh material for us to work up in the development of our character.

The educational effects of art consist in its enlargement of our horizon, and its development of our feeling and interest for all that is human, and therewith for all that exists. It educates us to look at actual life with clearer eyes, developes our *organ for the poetry of life and of existence itself*, which is a presupposition of our receptivity for the poetry of art. And the more we learn to have an open eye for the poetry by which we are at all times surrounded, and which is inherent in reality, the more we know how to draw from those same sources from which poets and artists draw,—which by no means implies that all are called to be themselves poets and artists, though it certainly means that there is in every human being a poetical element to be developed,—the more elevated a life shall we lead, and the deeper will be our experience of the infinite richness of this earthly existence, whose sorrows, griefs and poverty have their poetry no less than its joys. This effect of art in developing our organ for the poetry of actual life, and bringing us back to this ever gushing fountain, is of most essential importance. Who will deny, for example, that one who has become intimately acquainted with the creations of painting has thereby had his eye educated to perceive, both in nature and in man, very much which escapes others? In like manner, it may be taken for a sign that poetry has exercised her educational power upon us, when an organ has been set free within us, by whose means we see and feel much in the world, in our own life and circumstances, which we should not otherwise see and feel, at least not so clearly, not in the same mutual relation of the finite and infinite, of the temporal and eternal. It would be a misconception, which we think we have sufficiently guarded against, to suppose that this means that we are to regard our whole life æsthetically. What we mean is this, that poetry and a poetic view of things by no means dwell only in the works of poets, but belong to existence itself, and penetrate, so to speak, the whole of it; and that a man who has, in no sense of the word, a feeling that this is the case, is very far removed from a perfect human life, and also incapable of a deep view of religion, which by its numerous images and parables is constantly directing our attention to the poetic element which our earthly existence of and in itself already contains.

Another chief effect of art is, to educate by *instructing*. From of old it has been called " an instructor of the nations." Without instructing directly, art, by means of its pictures of life, proclaims practical wisdom, and does this, as far as the majority are concerned, far more effectually than philosophy, whose teaching is expressed in general ideas addressed to the understanding. Still we must expressly remember that all works of art must not be required to be instructive. There are works of art and poems (*e.g.* lyric) which afford us the pleasure to be found in every work of art, without imparting any kind of instruction, in other words, without in any way giving prominence to the moral. Such, nevertheless, exercise an educational effect, by purifying the feelings and developing a sense for form. Music does not instruct, but it certainly educates. It has an ennobling effect upon heart and mind, developes a feeling for rhythm and harmony, and thus cultivates an understanding of the harmonics of the universe, and of the harmony which should fill the human soul. The importance of music in general education may be perceived especially by the fact that it is from music we borrow our expressions, when speaking of objects belonging to quite other spheres ; as in our use of the words harmony, unison, in tune, out of tune, keynote, and tact. Besides all this, there exists a relation of reciprocity between art and education. Art educates, but to appreciate and find pleasure in a work of art, we must already possess a certain amount of education.

Art and Morality.

§ 105.

Much has been said on *the relation between art and morality.* This question has chiefly been raised with respect to poetry, and in poetry with respect to the *drama* and *fiction*. It is superfluous to remark that there must be no direct moralizing. But when, on the other hand, we hear it asserted that morality has nothing to do with poetry, and that moral considerations are quite beside the mark in æsthetic criticism and judgment, we must protest against such an assertion, because it is really equivalent to saying that actual life has nothing to do with poetry. Truth is the main demand to be made from art of all kinds; we mean that higher ideal truth which is already contained in the realities of things, but is brought out by the poet, and indeed purified by him from the accidental obscurities by which it is clouded in actual life. If, then, truth is to be demanded of the poet in his delineation of human passions, and if it must be insisted that he should give no unpsychologic descriptions, portray no passions which do not occur in actual life, it is equally necessary that, when the subject of a poem requires it, the moral should be represented as it really is, that is, according to its truth, and that he should not represent the moral law and the moral government of the world as different from what they really are. If it be required of the poet that he should understand how to give a vivid representation of the illusions of human life, of the struggles and rivalries of mankind for so many objects of only imaginary value, it must equally be demanded of him, that he should know and be capable of describing that which alone has true and absolute value in human life. It may, in the strictest sense, be asserted that every drama, from its beginning to its end, contains a moral. For all human actions do of necessity presuppose a norm, a rule to which they conform, or from which they depart; and there is nothing which can be represented, whether as criminal or as ridiculous, or as an object of irony, otherwise than under this assumption. Hence every dramatic poet enforces some kind of morality. This is especially evident when what is represented turns on moral problems, great collisions in life and their solution. In this case the poet's task does in and of itself produce the absolute demand of moral truth. Morality, then, becomes a chief moment for æsthetic judgment. If the morality is false and wrong, if the poet either does not understand the matter which he proposes to deal with, or comes forward as a false prophet, proclaiming, by means of his poem, a painted lie, his work, viewed merely as a work of art, and therefore as a whole, is a failure, even supposing it to be in other respects not without æsthetic excellence.[1]

We by no means carry our demand so far as to require, however, that every poetic work should deal with great moral problems. There are dramas in which the moral element is not brought into special prominence, but just hovers above the surface, and which yet have their poetic value. What must, however, be absolutely insisted on is, that the artistic treatment should never insult morality. We do not mean that art must not represent the immoral as well as the moral, for this is, on the contrary, indispensable, if art is truly to reflect life as it is. But immorality must not infect and be inherent in that view of life and those opinions which the poet desires by his work to promulgate; for then he would injure morality, and violate that moral ideal to which all human life, and therefore art itself, must be subordinated. Plays and novels which depict virtue as that mere conventionality and Philistinism which is but an object of ridicule, or which hold up to our admiration false and antinomian ideals of virtue, representing, *e.g.*, the sentimentality of a so-called good heart as sufficient to justify the most scandalous moral delinquencies or "free genius" as privileged to sin, which paint vice in attractive and seductive colours, portraying adultery and other transgressions as very pardonable, and, under certain circumstances, amiable weaknesses, and which by means of such delineations bestow absolution on the public for sins daily occurring in actual life—such plays and novels are unworthy of art, and are as poison to the whole community.

Equally with all untruth must all impurity ($\dot{a}\kappa a\theta a\rho\sigma i a$) be excluded from art. Purity and chastity are requirements resulting from the very nature of art. But it is just because art is so closely connected with sensuousness, that there is such obvious temptation to present the sensuous in false independence, to call forth the mere gratification of the senses. The sensuous must, however, be always subordinated to the intellectual, for this is involved in the demand for *ideality,*

---

[1] Comp. Sibbern, *Æsthetik*, Pt. I. p. 104 sqq. (Danish).

in other words, for that impress of perfection given by the
idea and the mind in every artistic representation. And
even if æsthetic ideality is present in a work of art, it must
be subordinated to ethic ideality, to the moral purity in the
artist's mind, a purity diffused throughout the whole. If, too,
the sensuous is presented in only an æsthetic ideality, there
are still cases in which the æsthetic effect is an impure and
obscure one, that is, in which at the same time some moral
or religious offence is given, and the harmonious impression
which art should produce upon the mind is thereby destroyed.
It may be difficult in individual cases to draw the line, and
much may have to be decided according to circumstances.
Still, in general it may be said, that the more a poet or
painter addresses himself not to individuals initiated in art.
but to the masses, to the *people*, the more he aims at producing by means of his work impressions and effects which
are to be transferred into *popular life*, the more strictly must
purity and chastity be insisted on, that the right impression
may not be missed. Goethe's *Romish Elegies* may be cited as
an example of great æsthetic ideality, combined with an
absence of ethic ideality. They will hardly produce a pure
and undisturbed effect upon any except a small circle of so-
called "pure connoisseurs," mere, nay, so to speak, bare æsthetics,
who find enjoyment in turning from the moral world of
Christianity to heathenism and heathen art, as it flourished
in the period of the ancient world's moral decay.[1] In its
highest forms, poetry is related not merely to morality, but
to religion. The poet becomes the prophet, shows us, as it
were, the mountain sunlit peak of the highest view of the
world and of life, and gives utterance to the deep things of
heart and mind. The farther, however, the human race
advances, the more will the contrast which distinguishes men
from each other, whether in philosophy or in life, the contrast between faith and unbelief, that " deepest theme of all
history," as Goethe called it, be reflected in poetry also, that

---

[1] The fact must not, however, be overlooked, that Goethe did not here lay
aside all regard to ethic ideality. For he subsequently thus expressed himself
to Eckermann, "If I had written my *Romish Elegies* in the same measure as
Byron's *Don Juan*, they would have been vicious." This saying contains an
acknowledgment of the connection between the æsthetic and the ethic, though
only on the formal side.

is. in those poets who stand upon the high places of intellect, whether in the realms of light or of darkness. In these will be more and more clearly seen the contrast between a poetry in which the poet is working for the kingdom of light, and weaving a robe of beauty for heavenly truth, and an infernal demoniacal poetry, equipped in all the charms of genius, all the magic of æsthetic ideality, like Lord Byron's, but in which the poet is labouring only for night and death, and thus weaving " the veil of Hecate." The nearer we approach to the last times, the more will this contrast be developed, while nevertheless the multitude will in all ages seek nothing more in poetry than amusement and æsthetic enjoyment, and there will in all ages be poets who in their productions will aim at nothing higher than driving away the ennui of their readers.

The Theatre.

§ 106.

We cannot speak of the import of art in human life without speaking also of the *theatre.* Dramatic poetry, that highest form, that flower of art, receives its consummation on the stage, and is not, so to speak, otherwise complete. The representation of a dramatic work of art is assisted by every other art, by music, painting, sculpture and architecture, which co-operate with poetry to produce one great united effect. The *æsthetic* importance of the theatre necessarily arises from the development of art itself, which here reaches its climax, attains that point of union in which all the effects of art are comprised. Many objections to the ethical importance and value of the theatre have nevertheless been raised, objections which, if insuperable, would lead to an irreconcilable contradiction between the æsthetic and the ethic.

A glance at history will show that the question as to the moral worth or worthlessness of the theatre has been differently answered at different times. The primitive Church opposed the theatre, that is, the heathen theatre, which was involved in the general moral decay of the times. The later Catholic Church itself carried out theatrical representations, the subjects of which were taken from the Bible. In the Protestant

Church, the theatre has been at one time attacked, at another defended. From a purely human standpoint, the theatre was most strenuously attacked by J. J. Rousseau. And there are not a few who at the present day entertain objections to the stage, whether on moral or religious grounds. It is, however, a fact, that the theatre has been admitted among all cultivated nations, nay, has become in some sort a necessary of life.

From our standpoint we cannot concede the existence of an irreconcilable contradiction between the ethic and the æsthetic. On the other hand, we admit that among the objections brought to bear against the stage, there are some which challenge serious moral reflection, and raise difficulties by no means easily obviated. Many of the objections are indeed of such a nature that they may for the most part be raised against all art, and apply rather to degenerations of art and its enjoyment than to the matter itself. Of this kind is, *e.g.*, Rousseau's opinion, expressed in a paper to d'Alembert, who thought the erection of a theatre at Geneva desirable, viz.: The theatre excites the passions without moderating them; it purifies those passions which one has not, and, on the other hand, inflames and cherishes those one has; arouses in the heart of the people, especially the young, those impulses and desires which are incompatible with morality. It promotes effeminacy and the pursuit of amusement, and makes men confound the transitory emotion caused by a play with moral principles and actions. The stage is not an institution for serious men, but for idlers and loiterers, who seek here a place of refuge, where they may forget themselves and their duties, and get rid of their time. If men need recreation, there are far nobler pleasures both in nature and domestic life. To which we reply: Effects like those described may certainly be produced in many theatrical audiences, but they may be also met with in the lovers of art in general, and especially in *novel-readers*, among whom are many idle persons, who really desire nothing else than to forget themselves and their duties, and to kill time. But the fault lies not in art nor in the stage, considered in themselves. It is to be attributed partly to those false tendencies which appear in the decline of art, *e.g.* when the stage places itself at the disposal of sensuality, and brings itself to a level with those common public amusements, which may be of a very ambiguous nature. The fault may, however, also lie in the individuals, who are incapable of appropriating what art offers them. Art educates, but it also presupposes education; and no one can profit in a moral respect by a work of art, if he is himself unable to place the ideal world of art and real life in their true *relation* to each other. In art the rule holds good: to see and not to touch; not to want to get palpable hold of that which can be appropriated only in an ideal and contemplative manner. If we want to transpose plays and novels into actual life, and put them directly into practice, we grasp at a shadow, and fall into the water, like a child snatching at the moon, whose image it sees in the stream and takes for the actual moon. When we remember the thoughtlessness with which children and young people are taken to theatrical amusements which are unfit for them, we must from such a view-point admit that there is in Rousseau's objections much which parents and tutors would do well to lay to heart. It is true, too, of nations, that they must possess no small capital of moral development and moral earnestness, if the stage is not to have a pernicious effect, to be degraded to a mere means of gratifying the passion for vain and empty amusement, and continually furnishing fresh food to all that is combined therewith.

§ 107.

Objections more nearly touch the matter itself when they are confined to an attack, not so much upon the performance of dramatic works of art, as upon the lawfulness of a *class of actors* and of a *standing stage.* An actor class, a class of men making this art their exclusive vocation, first came into existence during the 17th and 18th centuries, and that in connection with the standing drama of larger towns, where theatrical exhibitions were given every evening, or at least at regular intervals. Before that time plays were only performed on extraordinary festive occasions, and the parts taken by persons whose business was by no means acting; thus, *e.g.,*

at the time of the Reformation, by the citizens and the scholars
of grammar schools. The deeper motive for the formation of
a special class must be sought in the higher artistic requirements of modern dramatic poetry. The actor class first
appeared in the form of strolling players, who at last formed
permanent or standing theatres. It is to this class of actors,
and these permanent theatres, at least in their present state,
that objections are made by Protestant moralists and by
eminent men among them, who by no means deny the
importance and lawfulness of dramatic poetry itself, nor even
of occasional theatrical performances. Thus Rothe's *Ethik*,[1]
e.g., contains a sharp attack. He finds permanent theatres—
where performances must be given to excess for the satisfaction of a passion for amusement, and where resort must be
had to a mass of inferior, nay, bad pieces, for the purpose of
appeasing its cravings—destructive to art, which is thereby
more and more estranged from its ideal vocation, pernicious
to actors, who get accustomed to what is commonplace or bad,
nay, are obliged to aim at pleasing the public, and lose moral
dignity in this mode of life, and ruinous to the play-going
public, which more and more sinks to a moral standpoint not
much better than that of its actors. This is shown by the
immense importance attributed to all the appointments of the
stage, to the petty theatrical clapping and empty theatrical
criticism with which they are so constantly received, all of
which is so entirely different from Schiller's " moral institution."
In contrast with the corrupting practice of the day, Rothe
then sets forth a very ideal view, of which the only difficulty
is how it may be satisfactorily realized. For he thinks that
a time, though distant, may be looked for when the entire
theatrical system will undergo a thorough reformation, and
permanent theatres and an actor class no longer exist; when
only on special and solemn occasions, on national holidays,
etc., classical pieces will be performed before the whole
people, for the special purpose of calling forth great national
remembrances, when the parts will be undertaken by those
individuals who, in all classes of society, are most gifted in
the mimetic art; when to appear upon the stage will be
found incompatible neither with the dignity of a man nor the

---

[1] Rothe's *Christl. Ethik*, III. p. 747 sqq.

modesty of a woman, but be rather esteemed an honour and a distinction (he would, however, except unmarried ladies). In this way, he thinks, the stage will attain its true national importance, and exercise a far-reaching influence in reviving national consciousness.

We cannot help regarding this view as too ideal, and thinking that it leaves reality too much out of the question. Even granting that theatrical representations given by amateurs could in past times produce an effect, we still doubt if they could do so in the present day, when permanent theatres and the performances of real histrionic *art*, have made us acquainted with far higher pretensions. At such representations we should certainly have good reason to exclaim: Good people, but bad musicians! We cannot return to the *naïveté* of an earlier age, and would rather dispense with the whole thing, and confine ourselves to the reading of dramatic works. But however frequently such reading may be recommended in contrast to the stage, one thing must not be lost sight of, viz. that modern dramatic literature has for the most part been called into existence by the permanent stage, and that we by no means owe to it only the mass of inferior pieces to which it has undoubtedly given rise, but also classical works, whose authors not only received their chief impulse from the standing stage, but also intended their productions for public representation. We Danes should certainly not possess, at least not to the same extent, either the dramatic works of Holberg or Oehlenschläger, of Heiberg or Hertz, if theatrical performances had been restricted to special festal occasions and to amateurs. And would the Germans, we ask, without this were taken for granted, possess the tragedies of Schiller? Or can it be supposed that the greater part of Shakespeare's plays would have been written, unless he could have composed them for repeated representation?

In judging of this question, it must not be forgotten that a relation of reciprocity exists between the stage and the dramatic author, and that the question concerning the existence of the stage radically coincides with the question whether dramatic poetry itself is to attain maturity.

We do not understand how Rothe can at the same time inculcate it as an important duty to labour for the institution of a good national stage, and yet suppose that such labour could succeed, if plays are to be acted only on special festive occasions. We are both fully agreed that a superfluous number of theatres in the same town is highly objectionable; that the State should renounce its *laisser aller* in this matter, and impose some limits. But if there is to be a national stage for the æsthetic education of the people, it must necessarily be permanent, and one where performances are being continually repeated. Classical works cannot indeed be always represented. But art offers also a lighter kind of recreation and lighter productions, which, though not calculated to be immortal, nor fitted to make deep and lasting impressions, may nevertheless contribute to innocent amusement and refinement.

§ 108.

Against the lawfulness of a class of actors, Schleiermacher alleges that though every human talent ought to be cultivated, and therefore that also of acting, yet that not every talent is to be raised into a vocation.[1] He greatly doubts whether the histrionic art, at least as it was practised in his time in Germany,—for he has regard only to the German stage, —is *independent* enough to build a vocation upon, which could only in one case be worth the trouble, viz. if the actor were an independent continuation of the author. This is the case, in his opinion, on the Italian comic stage, where the comic piece furnishes only the leading ideas, which are then carried out by the actors, who, as improvisatori, continue the work of the author. In this case, he considers it worth while to devote oneself to the profession. Without passing any judgment upon the pieces which Schleiermacher had in view in his days, we still cannot be persuaded that the art of acting is in itself so unimportant and dependent, even though an actor should not fill the part of such an improvisatore. We maintain, on the contrary, as a matter of experience, that not till its performance on the stage is the work of an author fully understood, that the actor—and this is his special duty—can bring forward and

---

[1] Schleiermacher, *Die christliche Sitte*, p. 675 sqq.

give substance to what was merely hinted at or not fully carried out by the author, and that he can, besides, cover or conceal by his representation what is perhaps faulty on the part of the writer. Such work surely deserves to be called independent. It assumes the deepest and subtlest penetration into the creation of the author, not only in its details, but especially in its entirety; and without being an improvisatore, who is always more or less dependent upon accident and frame of mind, and may very often lose himself in trivialities and mere reminiscences, the true actor becomes the ideal continuer of the author, by giving his work its full completeness. There are representations on the stage to which the works of even distinguished authors bear the relation of the bud to the full-blown flower. Not till they appear upon the stage is *their maturity attained*, and their intrinsic fulness apparent. Of course, we are here speaking of the highest efforts, the supreme attainments of dramatic art. But that the art of acting is in itself too unimportant, as *art*, to be chosen as a vocation, is a view to which we can attribute no weight. And we cannot but think that those distinguished men who are of opinion that classical dramas could be successfully represented by amateurs of various classes of society, and that only on special festive occasions, have not sufficiently considered the matter from the side of its artistic claims.

On the other hand, an objection has often been urged from an ethic view-point, which we cannot but esteem as the gravest,—we mean the objection raised with respect to the many dangers to character by which this class is surrounded; and, at any rate, an element of truth cannot be denied to prejudices against the class of actors, which have been handed down from old times. We have now in view not merely the dangers threatening them from the side of sensuousness, but are contemplating chiefly the danger to his mental life incurred by the actor, who, constantly absorbed in other characters, nay, making them entirely his, thereby forfeits his own; who, constantly living in the *appearance*, loses the inmost truth of his personality, and becomes devoid of peculiarity, " a sounding brass and a tinkling cymbal,"—as Heiberg says of an actor in his poem, " A soul after death." It is no sufficient answer to this objection to appeal to the dramatic author, who also must live in the various characters of his own work ; for the author needs not to change himself into his work, but, on the contrary, to retire behind it, while the actor has himself to become the work of art. It is this " epideictic " (or ostentative) element, this constant *making a show of himself* to please and to gain the approbation of the public, which makes his position so different from that of the author. And what increases the danger is, that the actor cannot, like the author, work alone, but must do so in conjunction with others, and that it is often very difficult for a nobler nature to resist the influence of common surroundings, and not to be himself also drawn into all the vanity and arrogance, the envy and clap-trap, the not only petty, but also malicious intrigues by which it often finds itself encompasssed.

If, then, the above-mentioned dangers and temptations were insuperable, and the actor must, for his art's sake, sacrifice his dignity as a man, judgment must be given against the stage. For then to be both an actor and a Christian would be absolutely incompatible, and the Church would have to insist that an actor who desired to be a member of the Church must renounce his profession, in saying which we cannot but recall the excommunications of actors in former times. Then no Christian, nay, no earnest moral man, could enter a theatre, for a spectator co-operates in the entire undertaking,—a fact not sufficiently considered by those who, while they regard the calling of an actor as a very pernicious kind of life, are nevertheless constant frequenters of the theatre. It would be well for them to consider that authors, actors and spectators are *jointly responsible* for the existence of this institution, and that even a spectator must take account with himself as to how far he can, with a good conscience, participate in it. No one, however, will be able to prove that the dangers alluded to are insuperable. For even if it may, with good reason, be said that a moral risk is incurred in choosing the profession of an actor, it must not be forgotten that many other callings also are connected with moral risks, while yet it is by no means asserted that loss must therefore necessarily ensue, and never gain. Even if we feel inclined to agree with a celebrated performer, that " a respectable actor is worth three times as much as any other respectable man,"[1] this is only saying that unusual dangers have to be overcome, and that there are menacing rocks and reefs, on which many have suffered shipwreck. On these dangers themselves we subjoin a few remarks.

To bring up children to this profession is objectionable, especially as it cannot be known whether they possess the requisite talent, nor whether their natural dispositions afford a prospect, at least, of their being one day able to endure the moral trials which await them. Such a venture should not be allowed, because the free choice of the child is thus anticipated, and he is launched, at an immature age, upon a dangerous sea, without any certainty that he will navigate it safely. The art must be chosen freely. And in this matter it will be of the greatest importance whether the artist, when he first enters upon this course of life, is of good moral character, at least bears within him the groundwork for such a character, or whether, at the commencement of his career as an actor, he is without such a foundation. In the latter case there will be but little probability of his overcoming its dangers, and much, on the contrary, of his being easily absorbed both by his art and by vanity, and the more so the more talent he possesses. For the greater the talent, the greater the temptation. As the class of actors originated from the strolling players, who in their vagabond kind of life had but a loose kind of morality, devoid of any firm foundation, and as their art still consisted very much in jugglery, and they themselves formed, on the whole, a sort of artistic proletariate, it was but natural that, even on this account, a prejudice should have been formed against the whole race of actors, a prejudice which to this very hour has never entirely disappeared. But the facts that a *class*, in the full meaning of the term, has been developed from this proletariate, that actors are enrolled in the civil community, and have become true artists, that their class has been recognised by the State, nay, the stage itself made a matter of State-care, that the conditions of an artistic existence are secured to them,—all these must be regarded as a great social advance, of decisive importance with respect to the question in hand. For the

[1] *Seidelmann's Leben*, by Rötscher, p. 254.

more actors participate in the same education and the same social rights,—circumstances involving the same *demands* in a human and individual respect on them as on others,—and the more the pupils of this profession proceed, not from an artistic proletariate, but from morally developed and ordered social circles, the more *possibility* will there be of a moral foundation.

Starting, then, from the assumption that one who devotes himself to the histrionic art stands upon the foundation of personal morality, he will by no means find in the practice of his art only dangers which he has to resist, but also means which he may use for that development of his personality which is incumbent on him. For his art offers him an effective means for moral self-knowledge, as surely as a general transposition into the character and the moral condition of others is one of our most efficient means of self-knowledge; that is, if—for all depends on this—we, while thus mentally transposing ourselves, descend also into the depths of our own being. In the practice of his art he is forced to exercise self-command by controlling both his organs and his own particular frames and feelings—an effort which, presupposing the moral foundation spoken of, is of importance not merely with respect to art, but also to actual life. His calling is also specially fitted to exercise him in self-denial and resignation. How often, for instance, is there a painful contrast between the actor's own mood, and that in which he has to carry out his part on the stage! How many an actor and actress could in this respect tell us of mental struggles and heartfelt grief of which few have even a conception! Again, while the dramatic artist may feel great delight when his performance is successful and appreciated, yet whether this appreciation is given or withheld often depends upon mere accident. In this respect his position is different from that of other artists. The poet can quietly wait for the approbation which is for the moment withheld, and console himself with the thought of posterity. The actor must either obtain approbation at the moment, or it will escape him for ever, for, as Schiller says, " *Dem Mimen flicht die Nachwelt keine Kränze.*"[1] And he must be satisfied with the consciousness of having striven after his ideal to the best of his power.

[1] "Posterity twines no garlands for the actor."

We cannot, then, side with those who think that the stage must be reformed by the abolition of the class of professional actors and the permanent stage. On the contrary, it seems to us an actual duty to purify and cultivate the stage as much as possible, in the spirit of art and morality, and to concede to actors in general, so far as this has not been already done, the position of artists, with full and independent rights, treating each individual, however,—and this applies to all men in all classes,—according to his own personal worth.

§ 109.

While thus admitting the lawfulness of the stage, *as long as* it submits itself to the strict and serious requirements of the ideal, we now turn to the special demands which must be insisted on if it is to answer its end. And these are the same which we have already brought forward with respect to art in general. The drama must be national. Whether a nation can have a national stage or not, depends upon its possessing national dramatic authors, especially writers of comedies. When a nation is without the latter, it can only have a national theatre in a very limited sense. This must give constant performances ; but tragedy, which represents life at times of elevation, cannot frequently appear, while comedy in its various kinds must form the staple commodity. Rothe's complaints in his *Ethik*, that a German national theatre is still only in the far distance, and that there is so great a number of second-rate pieces, should, in our opinion, be exchanged for the wish that a great writer of comedies, fitted to exercise a purifying influence, would arise in Germany ; an event which would certainly obviate many of his complaints. For the rest, a national theatre should not perform only patriotic pieces, but the national element in the histrionic art should be shown in that whole mode of conception and representation in which the national genius finds expression, and which is also impressed upon its appropriation of what is foreign. It is essential to the national character of the theatre that the *language* should be heard in its fullest purity, that the stage should furnish, whether in the delivery of poetry or conversation, an example of the most perfect *pronunsiation.*

We say designedly "national" and not "popular." For it is by no means the language of the masses and of every-day life which ought to be heard on the stage, except in those special cases where comedy involves it.

And as we demand from all art *truth, i.e.* ideal truth, and not the coarse realism from which it is the vocation of art to deliver us, as we also require from all art purity or chastity, we also make the same demands from the histrionic art. The latter demand must be especially insisted on with respect to the stage, because of its higher power of producing impressions. For here all is active personal representation, so that much cannot possibly be suffered on the stage which might be put up with in the reading of dramatic poetry, where it hovers before us in the undefined outlines of the imagination, only half visible or audible, while on the stage it is completely present to both eye and ear. From this view-point we are obliged to say that the dramatic and the theatrical are by no means one and the same. The theatrical is the dramatic fully embodied. The latter without the form which it receives upon the stage is a mere shadow hovering before the mind, in which much is left to the reader's own conception.

The demand for purity and chastity extends not merely to what is sensible, but is generally applicable, when restriction within certain limits is in question. Hence it holds good also with respect to stage representations of what is sacred and religious.

§ 110.

It cannot be asserted that the religious element must be in every sense excluded from the stage. It can give no offence, if it has *for us* no other signification than a historical or mythological one, *e.g.* in the *Iphigenia,* where heathen ceremonies and heathen divinities are represented. And historical dramas, in which Christianity and the Christian Church appear as *historical powers,* are equally unobjectionable. The doubtful element enters when those matters in Christianity and the Church, which are still *of present authority with ourselves,* and upon which our own personal communion with God is based, are made subjects of theatrical representation. However difficult it may be, in special cases, to draw the right limits, it may be said in general, that it is repugnant to religious reverence, to the feeling of our dependence on God, to see the sacred history of Christianity, or Christian worship itself, brought upon the stage. When other arts, such as music and painting, adopt these subjects, no offence is felt. The offence results from the personal representation, the impersonation which identifies the artist and his work.

Mediæval Catholicism certainly did not take this view of the matter, for in the so-called "miracle plays" it gave representations, not indeed upon the actual stage, but still in a theatrical manner, of the gospel history, as is still done at Oberammergau.[1] With respect to such representations, it must, however, be remarked that their object was by no means the production of a work of art. These plays were developed from the Roman Catholic worship, in which sacred and secular are everywhere intermingled. They were a simple mingling of the religious and the æsthetic, and their object was both to instruct and admonish the congregation, by placing the gospel history before their eyes. In these spiritual plays it was by no means mere amusement that was aimed at, but also the edification of souls and the glorification of the Church. It was fundamentally the same viewpoint from which also certain Protestant theologians of the seventeenth century proceeded, when they demanded that *only* sacred subjects should be represented upon the boards of the playhouse, and all secular plays excluded.[2] They desired to keep the stage in dependence upon the Church, without perceiving that they were thereby secularizing the sacred. Self-conscious Protestantism, on the contrary, which understands its own principle, makes a fundamental distinction between art and religion, the stage and the Church, and demands that each should keep within its own limits. It is not indeed to be denied, that many Protestant Christians also have been able to witness with interest, nay, even to a certain degree with edification, the simple and popular Passion Play at Oberammergau, in which Christ, Judas, Peter, Caiaphas, Pilate,

---

[1] Hase, *Das geistliche Schauspiel.* Hagenbach, "Kirche und Schauspiel," in Gelzer's *Protestantischen Monatsblättern*, vol. XIX.

[2] Hase, as above, p. 314.

and the other characters are represented by honest peasants, who, according to the assertion of a famous comedian (Ed. Devrient), are said to have distinguished themselves by their excellent acting. Nevertheless, Protestant seriousness will never be able to reconcile itself to a theatrical representation of our Lord in our public worship, and least of all to its being offered to a modern audience by way of *artistic enjoyment.* In the first place, the Saviour of the world is a subject *incommensurable* with art of any kind, one utterly transcending the power and resources of art. We take, however, no offence when an artist paints a Christ, or a Thorwaldsen represents Him in sculpture. For the painter and sculptor make no claim to show us the *whole* living present Christ, but only a single aspect of His being, and aim by their works of art only at reviving the historical *remembrance* of Christ.[1] But we feel repugnance as soon as a sinful man presumes to represent to us the whole living present Christ, in His personal and living appearance, by exhibiting himself just as he is, and to produce upon us, by an *artistic illusion*, the impression of His perfect *holiness.* The impression can be none other than an offensive one, nor can we resist the thought that this sinful man would do better to care for his own salvation, and place himself in that one relation to Christ which alone befits a sinner, than to juggle with what is sacred, and to pollute it with common and unclean hands.

But we go further, and maintain that all sacred history— with the exception of certain secular elements in the O. T.— is incompatible with the stage, and also unfitted for *dramatic* treatment. For a dramatic treatment of sacred history cannot be carried out without embellishments and additions. But this history, the foundation of our faith, is to be appropriated just as it is given, and embellishments and additions in this region must be regarded as a profanation. Even in ecclesiastical history there are characters who have produced so decided an impression on the minds of men, that a mixture of truth and fiction concerning them is unendurable, a remark which applies especially to Luther. Apart, however, from the fact that his magnitude is an incommensurable one for the dramatic artist, we can but regard it as a mistake to place

[1] Schleiermacher, *Die christliche Sitte*, p. 632.

him upon the stage, as has been done by Zacharias Werner
in his well-known drama, *Die Weihe der Kraft* (1807).

If we now turn from the sacred facts to Christian worship,
this, too, if dramatically represented, will not fail to excite a
feeling of repugnance. A picture or a poetic narrative, in
which Christian worship or Church ordinances are depicted,
excites no offence, because such representations produce only
the impression of a remembrance of something distant or
absent. But when such things are directly and personally
represented upon the stage, it appears a profanation. And
why? Because God Himself is involved as the *near* and the
present in this acting, which is an imitation of personal
devotion, of communion with God. The personal relation
of a sinful man to God must not be a subject of illusion, but
only of personal reality; and the holy God, who is thus
assumed as present, must not be used as the means of an
æsthetic amusement. In an æsthetic point of view also, it is
obvious that it is the art of representation itself, which again
destroys the illusion in which it aims at placing us, and the
impression becomes neither a purely æsthetic nor a purely
religious one, but an impure mixture, a mish-mash of the two,
a fact forgotten by many authors, who delight to mingle the
directly religious in their theatrical pieces. For it is a main
point in all artistic illusion, not to excite in the spectators
any association of ideas by which the illusion is destroyed,
and the dream, as it were, dispelled. But the religious masque
upon the stage, which brings religion far too near, rouses us
from our dream, compels us, against our will, to think of the
contrast between appearance and reality, of "the sounding
brass and tinkling cymbal," of the second commandment:
"Thou shalt not take the name of the Lord thy God in vain,"
and to remember that the fire must not be stolen from God's
altar. Schiller has often been blamed for the mistake he has
made in his *Maria Stuart*, in bringing the sacrament of the
altar upon the stage, and Goethe justified for preventing it.
According to our opinion, the absolution should also be ex-
punged. It may perhaps be asked whether what is here
said must be extended also to prayer, and whether this too
should be excluded from the stage? In our opinion, it should
be. A dramatic author may indeed find occasion to intro-

duce a prayer. In Shakespeare's dramas certain single prayers are found, though he is, on the whole, sparing and abstinent in their use. But here, too, the difference between the dramatic and the theatrical makes itself felt as soon as prayer appears upon the stage. On the whole, we abide by our maxim, that direct personal intercourse with the holy God is a thing which no one may by a *personal* act merely imitate. The holy God must not be invoked in mere appearance, not even when this is done under the mask of art; for it is, after all, to take His name in vain. Art is here overstepping its boundaries, and presuming to encroach in disguise upon a region which must be only entered in religious seriousness and reality. The praying mask upon the stage will only produce a mixed effect, half æsthetic, half religious.

It must, however, be admitted, that the same degree of offence does not exist as in the case of the Sacrament, because of the more *subjective* character of prayer, and also because there are in the latter a multitude of shades by which the offence may be lessened. Hase remarks that " prayer is the natural note of the anxious or of the relieved soul," and there are moments in tragedy in which it cannot be dispensed with. We think, however, that at such moments it would be more correct only to intimate prayer in a *symbolic* manner, so that there should be no actual praying on the stage. On the whole, it must be said that prayer is the less offensive on the stage in proportion as it only breaks forth as the natural note of the soul, as a momentary cry of distress, as an exclamation of joy; in other words, the more it expresses the merely psychological and human side of prayer, while the objective and divine, that which belongs to the revelation of God, is repressed. On the other hand, the more the God of revelation is invoked, and the prayers of the Church, the public and regular worship of God, recalled to mind, the more offensive does it become. The Lord's Prayer on the stage is absolutely an offence and a scandal.

Nor can we help reckoning the use of hymns from the Church service on the stage as offensive and unpermissible; and regarding the introduction of Luther's hymn, " Ein feste Burg ist unser Gott," in the opera of the *Huguenots*, as a profanation. That such an abuse should give no offence to

Protestant consciousness, but rather have gained much approbation, is only a testimony to the irreligious humanism of this age of modern Judaism and heathenism. Hase indeed thinks that it is not much to be wondered at if the Church is robbed of a spiritual song by the world, when the Lutheran Church, at the time of the Reformation, appropriated so many secular melodies and national lays ; he admits, nevertheless, that it is not edifying to hear the same song to-day on the stage, and to-morrow at church.

What we desire, then, to see excluded from the stage is all *direct* appeal to God. The religious element may be indirectly present, nay, must make itself the more felt, in proportion as the author's view of life and the world, by which the whole piece will be pervaded, is serious. Tragedy should, moreover, exhibit the divine government of the world, and fill us with fear and reverence for those unswerving laws of righteousness to which human life and human actions are subjected. But, in entire opposition to the ecclesiastical and theological view of former times, that only sacred subjects should be represented on the stage, to the exclusion of all that was secular, because thus alone could men be instructed and improved, we adhere to the view, which may be regarded as that of modern times, that the proper sphere of the stage and of dramatic art is precisely *secular* life, in its full variety of human characters and interests, whether foolish or serious, in the innumerable collisions and situations occurring in actual life. It is more especially tragedy and the higher drama which are exposed to collisions with religion, because they so nearly border upon it. Comedy, which does not aim at the sublime, is that form of the drama least threatened with such collisions.

§ 111.

We conclude these remarks on the theatre by repeating that, just because the effects produced by the stage may be pernicious to much else and much more than mere taste, nay, may be in the highest degree ruinous to souls, and because there is not the remotest prospect that the theatre will be done away with, or that people will let themselves be deprived of it, it must be an interest of society that every possible effort should be made to make and keep the stage an artistic institution, for the ennoblement of popular life, so that these "boards which mean the world" may not at least mean it in its worst sense, and that a wholesale poisoning of the people may not go forth from this "moral institution" (comp. Special Part, I. § 18), for which great poets have laboured. The tendency towards what is evil has existed in all ages, and certainly exists in no small degree in the present day ; and a time will come when complete decay will appear in this department also, and the complaint of the fathers of the Church, that the theatre is a temple of evil spirits, be renewed. But as long as it is still possible, we should make every effort to maintain and protect those forces which may refine and ennoble the nations.

In opposition to pietism, we say with Steffens: "When pious zeal condemns all dramatic art, such condemnation manifests either an intellectual narrowness, which arrogantly assumes a right to judge of matters of whose value it is ignorant, or an uncertain and struggling mind, which perceives danger to itself, but can for that very reason pass no general judgment. If you would detect the dangers of the drama, you must esteem, nay, love the genuine drama. Love alone possesses a purifying power; it would not abolish, but ennoble."[1]

As far as concerns the individual who is desirous of making art contribute to the development of his personality, we add the remark that art is a generous wine, which, used in its due proportion, revives and invigorates, but when immoderately partaken of, enfeebles and enervates, produces an æsthetic quietism, and unfits for practical life. This due proportion must be determined by each for himself: "All things are lawful unto me, but all things are not expedient: all things are lawful for me, but I will not be brought under the power of any" (1 Cor. vi. 12). We refer our readers in this respect to what was said (see the General Part, § 133 sq.) in another connection on the permissible. An excess of theatrical amusement, when it becomes a habit and a necessity, is generally a sign of shallowness and a love of shows.

---

[1] Henrich Steffens, *Von der falschen Theologie und dem wahren Glauben,* 1831, p. 197 sq.

Those who daily frequent theatres " to kill time," do not reflect that it is in truth themselves, their own mental life, which is killed with time by these ever-varying shows, which being but imperfectly comprehended, produce no effect, afford no nourishment. The more the mind is filled with these empty shows, the more vacant and indolent it becomes, the more it loses of vital power, of mental forces and germs, which are choked in so desolating a flood. But as weakening and enervating an effect as is produced by an excess not merely of theatrical pleasures, but of the pleasures of art in general, is also the result of an excess of art *criticism*. This at least engenders that mental pestilence by which so many are in these days stupified and made incapable of finding any real enjoyment in art, because their minds are devoid of love for, and true devotion to, its creations, and have forfeited all originality and simplicity. No one, however developed he may be by reflection, can, unless he has in the depths of his own spirit a fund of originality and simplicity, from which he may derive vigour and delight in creative effort, be a true poet or artist, and this is equally true of the power of true appropriation. It holds good of the kingdom of art also, that, in spite of all our reflection, we must become as little children, if we would enter it. There are many who need not only to be counselled to observe moderation in their enjoyment of art, but who are just as much in need of advice to diet themselves strictly with regard to their criticism of art, by which they inwardly weaken and undermine their powers, while a salutary abstinence would enable them to attain to an enjoyment of art which might be a true means of strength and refreshment. Criticism exists for art, and not art for criticism. And the position to be taken up first and foremost with respect to a work of art is that of receptivity and self-surrender, in other words, to let it effect in us what it can, and give us what it has to give, and what we are in a condition to apprehend. Not till after this can criticism, which indeed is not to be dispensed with, take up its fitting position.

SCIENCE.

Science and Humanity.

§ 112.

While it is the mission of art to create a world of beautiful and individual forms, in which truth is seen in image and parable, the task imposed on science is to investigate existence, its nature and laws, for the purpose of knowing truth as truth. The scientific instinct is as deeply implanted in human nature as the artistic, and the two are closely related. Both aim at ideally taking possession of both external and internal reality, and ideally rendering it back again. Of poetry and philosophy we may say with the poet:

> " Ein Spiegel mit zwei Namen,
> Verschieden nur durch Schliff und andren Rahmen." [1]

Science embraces whatever exists, the visible and the invisible, the world of nature and the world of mind. From of old, however, the deepest thinkers have always perceived that not the physical, but the ethical world is the higher, and that the central point of human inquiry, and the enigma of human life, is man himself. The wisdom of the ancient world closed its career by racking its brains over the ideal of humanity, which it was always seeking, but never finding; and despairing of itself, it sank, worn out and exhausted. Christianity, which solved the enigma by the personal *ideal of humanity,* who descended from heaven, which teaches us that only in God and in His revelation does the enigma of human life find its solution, has given to science a new development, not only by emancipation from the restrictions of the ancient world, but also by the power of eternal redemption. Just as there is a contrast between ancient and Christian art, so is there a corresponding contrast in science; for the relation of man to God, to the world and to himself, has been wholly changed by Christianity.

§ 113.

Christianity, by emancipating men from the limitations which were peculiar to the ancient world, opened a new horizon,

[1] One mirror with two names, differing only in cut and frame.

and made possible the *universal* character of science, its free movement in all directions. Not only did the new view of life and of the world which Christianity introduced, penetrate the world of thought in various ways like leaven, but Christianity itself brought forth a new science, *Theology*, and a Christian philosophy connected therewith. A strife has often been kindled between theology and the Humanists, *i.e.* the adherents of the merely human, by whom it has often been asserted that theology, which developes its knowledge from faith, and is itself a believing knowledge, is therefore no science at all, inasmuch as science must be independent of faith, and be developed apart from all assumptions. Without entering farther into the details of this strife, we would merely remark, that it is a great delusion to suppose that any kind of human *knowledge* exists without *faith*. To all knowledge there is a corresponding faith, and to all faith a corresponding knowledge. He who does not choose to believe in God and in His revelation, must believe in the world, in reason, in nature, and develop his knowledge from this assumption, while he who believes in God and His revelation, developes a knowledge corresponding to such belief. The much discussed contrast between faith and knowledge is misunderstood when it is viewed as a simple contrast, as though on one side were faith, and on the other mere knowledge, apart from all assumption. It is, on the contrary, a compound contrast, a faith with its corresponding knowledge being opposed to another faith with its corresponding knowledge. It is a conflict not between two, but among four, there being two allies on either side. The fact that all human knowledge must be based on faith is one appertaining to the bounds set once for all to human nature, to our position as created spirits, to the creaturely character of our existence, to our not being like the Creator, capable of deriving our knowledge from ourselves, but having to rely upon something given, which, being the foundation of our thought itself, is never entirely within our comprehension. All science, without exception, goes back to certain first postulates, whose truth cannot be forced upon us by any demonstration, but is only directly evident, and can only be grasped with a *direct certainty*, which is nothing else than faith, whether it be religious, moral, or scientific faith. The conflict which has in our days been waged concerning the truth of Christianity, and the value and authority of theology, is not a mere conflict concerning the notions by which men have tried to exhibit truth, but is, in fact, one concerning human certainty with respect to Christianity. Since certainty, however, especially with respect to religious truth, is conditioned by man's personal relation thereto, by his will, the reconciliation will never be attained in a *purely* theoretical way.

Naturalism is based upon articles of faith, which, though anything but proved, serve it as the presupposition of its arguments. The first of these articles of faith may be thus stated : Nature, as it at present exists, is the same as it has in all time and ever been; no disturbance, nothing that cannot be accounted for, has ever been introduced, and this nature is the alone conceivable. This can, however, by no means be proved, and no one can—as even enlightened natural philosophers allow—prove the necessity of the present constitution of nature. Necessity is inferred from mere actuality, and a view of the world is constructed upon this blind faith. The remark, too, is here in place, that so-called " exact experimental science " is full of hypotheses converted into articles of faith. We merely refer to the faith in *atoms,* by which a *confidence, a persuasion of things not seen,* is expressed. For who ever saw an atom ? who ever saw an *eternal* atom ? We may also refer to the belief in *matter.* We see, indeed, things which we call material things; but matter itself, *eternal* matter and its infinite divisibility, has no one seen. Also, to faith in time without end or beginning, in the never ending, never beginning chain of causes, or to faith in the many millions of years said to have been required for the formation of the sphere, etc. Such notions, outstripping and outflying all experience, sufficiently show that the exactness so much appealed to is but very relative, and that the experimental science which in our days contends against faith and Christian speculation (the science of faith), is itself interwoven with faith and metaphysics. The question then is, whether these metaphysics are worth anything, and whether these hypotheses suffice to explain what is to be explained ? It may certainly turn out that the imperfections and chimeras of

this doctrine are no fewer than those of Christian speculation.
The ingenious physicist Lichtenberg (1742–1799) made in
his days the remark, concerning the geological hypotheses
with which he was acquainted, that two-thirds of them
belonged rather to the history of the human mind than to the
history of the earth.

§ 114.

All sciences were in the Middle Ages dependent on theology, and this was in its turn dependent on the Popish Church
as an external authority.   With the Reformation, the long-
prepared emancipation took place.   The liberated human
mind broke up for itself new paths, asserted the importance
of the secular sciences, and also the right of every one to
read with his own eyes what is written in the book of
nature.   It was first and foremost in theology itself that the
emancipation was accomplished, by its freeing itself from the
false authority of the Pope and of human doctrines.   It
bowed to the authority of Scripture, not only as the written
word, but because it approved itself to the conscience by the
power of divine truth.   Truth, evidencing and proving itself
to be such to the religious consciousness, and itself producing
certainty in the heart of man, is the principle of the Reformation and of Protestant theology.   And in all secular sciences
is reiterated the demand of Protestantism, that truth should
prove itself by its own light and its own power to the candid
mind, accompanied, however, by the corresponding demand,
that the inquirer should place himself in that due relation of
subordination and obedience to the subject, apart from which
neither direct certainty, nor a certainty strengthened by
means of the scientific process of thought, can arise in the
mind.   Hence, too, it is only under the ægis of Protestantism
that *philosophy*, as a seeker and inquirer after truth, can go
its own way, and carry out its reasoning through a whole
series of experiments, to discover by this means the ultimate
principle, that thus a true philosophy, one which shall explain existence, may *start* from this point of departure.   If,
however, the thinker's own heart has recognised in Christianity
the truth and the source of all certainty, he will henceforth
no longer aim at a philosophy which is *inquiring* and working

itself out through a series of subordinate standpoints, but will
then endeavour, from a right and luminous beginning, to
explain existence in the light of Christianity, *i.e.* in the light
of truth itself.[1]

§ 115.

It is true of science as of art, that not only is the ideal
of humanity its object, but also that it does itself represent
one of the constituent members in the realization of this ideal
in the life of nations. Of science, too,—with the exception
of the exact sciences, in which the diction employed is a
matter of indifference, because higher and intellectual matters
have not to be expressed,—we require that it should be
national. This requirement certainly seems to involve a
contradiction, since science, and especially philosophy, must
express that which is universally valid—which really holds
good to all thinking minds. But it is in human nature that
the universally valid, "*pure* reason," as it is often called, can
be only thought and spoken of in definite language ; for it is
only in the element of language that we can think, and
outside of language lie only those purely mystic regions, in
which nothing definite is any longer thought. The fact,
however, that we are confined to one definite language, sets a
limit to this universal validity, so that in this respect also it
is true, that the one light shows itself to different nations in
different refractions, without therefore ceasing to be the one
light. The same philosophic opinion, however, by being
expressed in different languages, undergoes certain changes,
especially in respect of the subtler definitions, the particular
language not always containing corresponding terms ; and even
when it furnishes such, they will yet exhibit a different
shading. In view, too, of the variety of languages and the
limits of each individual language, the saying holds good,
" Our knowledge is fragmentary " (E. V. " We know in part "),
because our language, even though the most cultivated, is
still but fragmentary. And it might well be said, that if we
are to have a perfect philosophy, we ought to have a universal
language, as mankind had before the confusion of tongues, or

---

[1] Comp. the author's article, "Vom Glauben und Wissen " (*Jahrb. f. deutsche
Th.*, 1869, 3).

to be capable of thinking with the same facility in the
languages of all cultivated nations, so as to be able to master
ideas in all their different shades. But this not being the
case, we must insist that in this world of partialness every
nation should fulfil its universal human task, and therefore
the scientific part of this appointed task, in the *peculiarity*
given it by God. As the poet sings for *his own* people, so
too should he whose vocation is that of a teacher of science
desire to bring truth before *his own* people, whether he is
heard by a larger or a smaller circle. That scientific truths
should be stated in a manner harmonious with the genius of
a nation's language and its natural talents, is an indispensable
condition for their appropriation, and a sign also that what is
communicated has attained actual vitality in those who communicate it.

§ 116.

To remedy in some degree the limits set to the comprehension of science by the use of a national language, scholastic,
Græco-Latin words or technical expressions are employed.
These are, so to speak, elements of an artificial universal
language, and have the advantage of designating the abstract,
that which is secreted by the rich abundance of life, while
in the national tongue, too often expressing only the idea on a
single side, much circumlocution is needed to give expression
to the general. Words, too, derived from foreign living languages, have been adopted or imitated, because the foreign word,
the comprehension of which may at a certain stage of international intercourse be assumed, expresses a shade of the idea
which escapes the mother tongue. The use of these foreign
words must indeed, as the mother tongue advances in development, be as far as possible gradually diminished. But they can
never be entirely dispensed with, because no single language
is capable of expressing everything in words of its own.

But it is not only in scientific treatises, but in ordinary
literature also, that the use of foreign words can never be
entirely done away with. The words of Holberg on this
subject, in his *Moralischen Gedanken* (Rode's edit. p. 402),
will always hold good against a one-sided purism. He there
says, among other things: "If it be asked to what purpose

is the great solicitude shown by certain of our grammarians to purge our language from all foreign words, it may be answered, that they serve no other purpose than that of making our language difficult, not only to foreigners, but even to natives. For well-known words, which every one understands, are discarded, and either newly-invented ones, or old ones long out of use, take their places. And if we are not exactly forced either to invent new or to revive obsolete words, we are often obliged to use the same word, although it does not suit one place as well as another. I grant, indeed, that no European language is so poor that we cannot make ourselves understood in it. But if we try to express our meaning with emphasis and elegance, we soon feel a deficiency, for it is one thing to make our meaning understood somehow, and another to express ourselves in the fittest and most adequate words, as those nations can do which have many words to choose from, and are able to select from three or four that which best fits a certain place, just as builders choose the stone best adapted, not merely for carrying up a building, but also for adorning it. We see that the most cultivated nations have borne this in mind, and thus brought their languages to the greatest perfection. For the greater the progress in science and eloquence, the greater need is felt to employ appropriate foreign words. It is advantageous to promote friendly intercourse among nations, but this is not done by making our language difficult and incomprehensible to our neighbours, which, on the contrary, shows a kind of misanthropy; for it looks as if we held inspections of our language for the sole purpose of henceforth making our neighbours, who could formerly read our works, merely able to peep at them in a purblind manner. This seems, indeed, to be the special object of some writers; and that no one may doubt their intention, they have even exterminated certain letters, as if to show that though they cannot altogether dispense with foreign words, they will make them incomprehensible by a change of letters. Thus, *e.g.*, since the words 'doctor,' 'character,' 'academy,' cannot be got rid of, they are written 'dokter,' 'karakter,' 'akademy.' Surely this is a monomania of patriotism!"

These remarks of Holberg are unquestionably applicable in these days also, whether we consider on the one hand the fanaticism for purity, or on the other the unprincipled orthography in which some indulge. He concludes, however, with the remark, that he does not want to quarrel with any one on this matter: "I desire only to account for my own mode of writing, and to point out that when I use convenient foreign words, I do so with due consideration; and, moreover, that I intend to stick to such principles, notwithstanding all the criticism with which they may be attacked."

An opinion involving and recommending the happy medium was already expressed by Leibnitz (1646–1716). At a time when German literature had attained but very inconsiderable development, Leibnitz complained that the intelligence of the Germans was enfeebled, because their mother tongue had so greatly fallen out of use, and so many foreign words, producing only obscure, confused and approximate notions had been introduced. He declared that they would gain greater accuracy, clearness and certainty, both in their thoughts and transactions, by a more thorough use of their native language. It cannot be denied that Leibnitz, who, however, rarely employed his mother tongue in his own works, expressed in these words a truth which all nations would do well to lay to heart. Nevertheless, while grieving at the dreadful hotch-potch found in literature, by the intermixture of foreign, and especially of French words, he adds—in entire harmony with Holberg—"I do not mean, that we should be such puritans in speech as to shun with superstitious horror a foreign but appropriate word, as though it were a mortal sin, and thereby weaken ourselves and deprive our language of proper expressiveness." He compares speech-puritans to invalids afflicted with the disease which the Dutch called the "*Perfectze-Sucht.*"[1] We may add that this puritanical sect, in their zeal for purity of language, bring about quite as sorry a hotch-potch, partly by the introduction of their self-formed artificial words, which being quite removed from the genius of the language, make an entirely foreign impression, and partly by an intermixture of words long obsolete, which are incomprehensible hiero-

<hr>

[1] Leibnitz, *Unvorgreifliche Gedanken betreffend die Ausübung und Verbesserung der deutschen Sprache.* (Guhrauer, *Leibnitz's Deutsche Schriften,* I. p. 455, § 16.) Comp. Pichler, *Die Theologie des Leibnitz,* I. p. 47.

glyphs to most readers, and which by the unintelligible, half-intelligible and confused notions which they occasion, likewise weaken the reader's understanding.

Goethe says (*Works*, xxxii. p. 221): "To purify, and at the same time to enrich our mother tongue, is the concern of the best brains. Purification without enrichment is mostly an unintellectual work, for nothing is easier than to disregard matter and attend to expression. The man rich in intellect fashions his word-matter without caring what elements it consists of; the unintellectual may well speak with *purity*, since he has nothing to say. How should he feel what a sorry substitute he lets pass instead of a well-defining (pregnant) word, when this word was never alive in him, because he has thought nothing about it ? " In his *Leben* (beginning of Book 7), Goethe discusses the true revolution which had taken place with respect also to language in German literature, as he knew it in his youth. It was required that, in opposition to the undue intermixture of French words, language should henceforth be pure and natural, plain and universally comprehensible. " By these praiseworthy efforts, however, door and gate were opened to our broad, native flatness, nay, the dike pierced through which the floods were presently to flow. Good brains, free, up-looking children of nature had therefore two subjects on which they might practise, against which they might strive and vent their displeasure; these were, a language disfigured by foreign words, forms of words and turns, and the worthlessness of those works which had been careful to abstain from this fault; and it struck no one that, in opposing the one evil, the other was called upon for assistance." That Goethe in his own works avoided both extremes, need hardly be mentioned.[1] On the whole, it may be said that the more a people increases in culture, the

---

[1] Fr. Schlegel (*Works*, VIII. p. 157) gives a catalogue of the foreign words occurring in Goethe's *Wilhelm Meister*. He does not attach any blame to it, but asks whether such words as Equipage, Engagement, Negligé, Mantille, logiren, arrangiren, applaudiren, Route, Douceur, respectiren, Calculs, secundiren, tractiren, undelicat, Indiscretion, etc., might not easily be exchanged for quite as good German words. Single expressions may always be contended about. The question of more general interest is, whether Goethe, in the choice of these words, was not guided by a *principle* which he had adopted with due consideration.

more will its language acquire of purity and copiousness, and thus render the use of many foreign words superfluous. It is, however, a great mistake to think that the use of such words should cease. With increasing culture foreign words are not only got rid of, but also introduced. Holberg's remark, that the more progress nations have made in science and eloquence, the more they have felt the need of employing " apt " foreign words, is a thoroughly just one. For increase of culture is inconceivable without increase of that national intercourse, that reciprocal action, that mutual interchange with other cultured nations, which gives rise to the reception of new foreign words, and the formation of new words under foreign influence. The cosmopolitan element is ever asserting itself in the national.

§ 117.

The demand for nationality involves the demand that each nation should cultivate that side of science which accords with its vocation and special endowment. There are nations which are more disposed to physical or historical than to philosophical studies, and *vice versa*. All are not called to the same kind of intellectual work. But all are called to a mutual giving and taking, on which account *international* intercourse in science is absolutely necessary, if the human race is to fulfil its vocation, and the individual nation is not to fail in its own, by shutting itself out from the general stream of culture. This international intercourse is indeed less in the natural sciences, but in intellectual knowledge it is essentially conditioned by the fact that all cultivated nations possess *one and the same school, one and the same foundation of culture,* in that classic literature of the Romans, which furnishes them with common *assumptions*, common points of contact, and common information for their mutual understanding. Even this circumstance may show how irrational is the demand made in certain quarters for the abolition of classical literature as the foundation of higher education ; for this would be to abolish and put out of use that very element which, next to Christianity, is the chief condition for a mutual under- standing among the nations, and an exchange of thought on all matters of a higher order. If we conceive both Christianity and the classical literature of antiquity got rid of, the nations would no longer be able to understand one another on intellectual questions, but would in their intellectual isolation and national pride and prejudice sink back into the confusion of Babel. Nay, not a nation would then be capable of a truly intellectual comprehension of itself, as a *member* in the totality of the race.

§ 118.

The effects produced by science upon a nation are not direct but indirect. It is by a thousand channels that science influences general culture and promotes true popular enlightenment. That science is unpractical, can be the assertion only of the short-sighted, who can perceive none but direct effects. And yet the natural sciences show, for the most part in an entirely direct manner, that science is practical. Every movement, too, in philosophy, every real philosophical system, exercises an influence upon general opinion, upon the prevailing direction of thought and mind. Whether the higher science favours a merely physical tendency alienated from the moral, or an ethical, or a partially logical one, this will soon be reflected in the various regions of society. Philosophy, both in a good and in a bad sense, works like leaven, and by the progressive development of culture will the boundary between what is written for scholars, and what is written for men of general information,—the boundary, as the French say, between science and literature,—become a more and more fluctuating distinction.

The more general the conviction becomes, that science is in truth a vital matter, and that the very core of life and of things is in question, the more will the demand for *popularity*, or the general intelligibility of scientific statement, assert its claims. Popularity must not indeed be obtained at the cost of profundity. But as in science we need to be warned against a spurious popularity, which serves only to diffuse shallowness, so also should we guard against a spurious profundity, which often, without being aware of it, is only cracking empty nuts, a subtle profundity which so loses itself in refinements and hair-splitting as never to hit the centre for want of simplicity of sight, or a meditative profundity in which the thinker will indeed descend into the depths, but in which, too, he will lie there without power to raise himself again. Popularity does not mean that everything can be understood by every one irrespective of the different degrees of culture which each has attained, a mistake in which those seem to be involved who demand that science shall be "popular." General intelligibility will always be but comparative. Such comparative popularity, excluding all *unnecessarily* aristocratic ways in science—for it can never be absolutely democratic—must be recognised as a demand of humanity. True popularity is *humanity in the communication of truth*, a due consideration for those who are to be taught, painstaking efforts really to impart it to those who are capable of receiving it. Genuine popularity is also the test of genuine profundity, for as a rule the saying holds good, that " what is obscurely said is obscurely thought."

We have a model of true humanity in statement and diction in the Greeks, who had the good fortune—a good fortune affected indeed by a great limitation—to possess a language in which they could philosophize without needing to make use of foreign technical words, and who could express all they wished in their mother tongue. Even in the discussion of the most difficult problems they exhibit just the right degree of general intelligibility. Not that everything is in their case easy to understand, or capable of being understood by all; but that it must, on the whole, be confessed that when what is said is not, or is only with difficulty understood, this results from the difficulty of the subject-matter itself, and not from the manner in which it is stated, and that in this respect everything is done to meet the reader half-way. Though it may justly be remarked that the form of dialogue, in which Plato has imparted his philosophy, cannot be imitated by ourselves, because we have no Socrates whom we can make the chief speaker, yet this very form might remind us that science should be developed by means of a long conversation, which we moderns have to carry on by the organ of literature. The object is to arrive at a mutual understanding; and *humanity* demands that mutual assistance should be rendered for such a purpose. The opposite course. namely, utter regardlessness of the reader, is inhumanity Certain philosophical works give us the impression that the author, far from thinking of any kind of dialogue with other thinkers, or any relation of reciprocity with them, is apparently concerned only with what he perhaps calls "the matter" on which he desires publicly to hold a monologue in unintelligible language. A more *humano* manner and form of philosophizing has therefore been recommended by great thinkers. By Schelling, for instance. In his remarkable dialogue "On the Connection of Nature with the Spiritual World" (Clara),[1] such expressions as the following occur: "Are these horrible technical terms indispensably necessary? Might not the same thing be said in a manner generally intelligible? Must a book to be philosophical be utterly unenjoyable?" "I would much rather see the philosopher with the social wreath in his hair, than presenting himself to the world with the scientific crown of thorns, like a martyred *Ecce homo!*" We are here reminded of Pascal, who says: "When we meet with a natural, unconstrained style, combined with excellent matter, we are beside ourselves for joy, for we thought, perhaps, we might find a distinguished author, but we have now found a *man.*" "I would give nothing for a philosopher who could not make his fundamental view intelligible to any man of general education, nay, if it came to this, to any tolerably clever and intelligent child. And what is to be the end of the present severance between the learned and the multitude? Truly I see a time approaching when the people, who must become more and more ignorant of the highest matters, will arise and call scholars to account, saying: You ought to be the salt of the people, why then have you not salted us?" etc. For the rest, even Schelling has not in his latest work (*Der Lehre von den Potenzen*), "On the Doctrince of Forces," succeeded in quite freeing himself from foreign technical words; and for the reasons stated above, scarcely any one will be able to do so.

[1] Schelling's *Werke*, 1 Div. vol. IX. p. 86 sqq.

THE SCHOOL.

§ 119.

If the rising generation are to share in general culture, and even in science itself, they must in every nation be *educated*, and this is the office of the *school*. Since, however, the preponderating majority of the people are not to directly devote themselves to science, though all should participate in education and general improvement, there must be different kinds of schools: the national school, the middle school (*Realschule*), the grammar school (*gelehrte Schule*), and the high school or university. In every grade of school the instruction should be determined by the *education*, by a regard to the whole man, in whose development intellectual culture constitutes but a single moment, which must be subordinated to the whole. The aim of all education should be to form the will and intellect for the universal human. But no one should be educated to be a man in a merely general sense, but to be one in a definite occupation within the sphere of social life, or, if the particular occupation cannot as yet be more nearly determined, at least he should be educated for a definite circle of callings, among which the growing youth will, at a subsequent stage of maturity, have to choose one. Hence instruction must at every stage of school life aim at general education, and that with respect to the special occupation or business.

The National School.

§ 120.

The national or elementary school must impart what is universally necessary in human education. This universal element may be defined as the scantiest, but as correctly as the most important and most excellent. Christianity and the mother tongue are the main subjects of the national school. With these must be combined writing and arithmetic, and as far as possible something of drawing, the latter for the sake of cultivating that sense for a clear and definite apprehension of the phenomena of the natural world, upon which Pestalozzi

so much insisted, when he, with undoubted justice, declared
words, forms (*i.e.* of sensible objects) and numbers to be the
chief formal means of all human education. To the above
named are to be added, though certainly only in the most
general outlines, somewhat of geography and history, especially of the native land. But instruction in Christianity
and the mother tongue must be the chief matter, to which all
else must be absolutely subordinate. For Christianity and
our native language form the foundation of human culture,
the key to all further power and knowledge. By means both
of Bible history and the Catechism are the highest divine and
human matters imparted to children, a sacred tradition and
instruction, which must be communicated as such, and which
contains that which children must learn *by rote*. But that
which is in the first place to be learnt by rote, must be incorporated in the mind and heart; the child's religious *organ*,
his religious disposition, must be cultivated; and for this
reason, practice in the singing of hymns must be combined
with religious instruction. How much an able and Christian
teacher, who has a love for children, can in this respect effect,
not only in the cultivation of their intellects, but also in
their religious development, and what a lasting blessing such
instruction may be, experience has frequently shown.

In our days, when—as Tegnér had already occasion to
remark—"the intention seems to be to make the national
school as learned and the grammar (*gelehrte*) school as unlearned (*ungelehrt*) as possible,"—a circumstance connected,
as he justly adds, with the over-admired levelling system,
which would screw up the education of the common man, and
lower the education of the other classes, for the sake of thus
bringing about the desired equality,—there are many who
desire to banish religion from the national school, or at least
to keep it quite in the background. This is done for the sake of
gaining time and opportunity for more advanced instruction
in secular studies, or for the admission of a greater number of
such subjects. But nothing is a greater mistake than to
overload national schools with elements which can by no
means be there assimilated, but must remain in the mind as
undigested fragments. On the other hand, it is essential to
proper human development, that during the first stage of

education religion should hold the first rank, and that secular subjects may be at a later period independently developed. Either the national school must be essentially a religious or Christian school, in other words, its characteristic feature must be that religion is its first and most important matter of instruction, or it becomes a nonentity, a collection of elements without a governing unity. Many are of opinion that religion, being a thing not to be taught but to be lived, is too good to be made a matter of instruction in schools, that it is only profaned by teaching and learning by rote, and that it must be relegated entirely to the family and to instruction for confirmation. But not to speak of the many families to which it would be of very little use to relegate religious instruction, we must repeat, in opposition to this sentimental view, the truth that Christianity is by no means only to be lived, but must also be taught, that it is both doctrine and historical tradition (which means more than mere Scripture history), and that the Christian State is bound to take care that this doctrine and tradition be brought within the reach of all.

§ 121.

Instruction in the mother tongue should not only be of a kind to enable children to read with intelligent emphasis, with logical accent (so often lacking in rural schools), but should also make them acquainted with matter which may have an ennobling and cultivating effect. A good *reading-book* for national schools is one of the most difficult and important of pædagogic problems. What literature in general is to us, the reading-book should be to children, and certain portions of it should also be of a kind to be read with pleasure and instruction by older people. Its contents should be taken from all circles of existence, and be suitable to the age and capacity of children. They must embrace what is in a human respect most worthy to be known and appropriated by all, whether from nature, history, or human life. The portions should be partly selected from the national literature, partly composed—for which great skill will be needed—for this special purpose. A good reading - book will imperceptibly supply the young with that general culture which is at this stage always possible, and which would be vainly aimed at by an accumulation of various separate departments. The reading-book must aim at an *equal* cultivation of the different intellectual powers of the young. In former times a one-sided stress was laid on the cultivation of the intellect. In ours, an opposite partialness has in no small measure found acceptance, in the desire to influence chiefly the feelings and imagination. The reading-books are filled with a superabundance of fables, legends and wonderful adventures, and seek, so to speak, to feed children on cakes and sweetmeats—which must be regarded as a deformity in æsthetic education. Our aim is not exclusively that children should be pleased, but that they should be educated.

§ 122.

As children must not be overloaded with intellectual matter in national schools, so neither should the teachers themselves in their preparation at the training schools (*Seminaren*). Christianity should here be the main subject, together with the native tongue and the national literature, of which a survey should be given in connection with the history of the native country. Other subjects should indeed be taught thoroughly, but not in too great quantity, and with a full consciousness that they stand in the second place with respect to importance. Teachers who know a little of everything and nothing thoroughly, are always without a real inward stay in the exercise of their calling. For in the daily work of patience and perseverance, in which the teacher must at the same time exert a personal influence, he needs a central point, a centre of gravity. There must be some one thing in which the teacher is grounded and up to the mark.

In school discipline two extremes are to be avoided. Formerly children were kept in slavish fear, and the rod was constantly over their heads. The authority of the schoolmaster was that of a tyrant. In the present era of humanity, liberty and popular efforts, an inclination to lawless freedom prevails in schools, many desiring that children should only learn what they like, only work when they are inclined, and that the teacher should in other things be governed by their wishes and moods, so that the free play of their intellects may not be obstructed. But schools based upon such a view of human nature, being without authority or obedience, abolish themselves as schools. Authority and willing obedience, firmness and love, can and must be combined. To the same category of lawlessness belongs also the desire that compulsory attendance and school restraints should be done away with. Without restraints, a school, as human nature is constituted, cannot attain its end, as experience—though this might and should have been known prior to all experience—has abundantly proved.

§ 123.

That the *oversight* of schools should be exercised by the clergy is the only *natural* state of things, as long as national schools are to continue national (*i.e.* as long as Christianity is their foundation and central point), and not to be changed into something else, no one knows what. The often heard demand for the liberation of education from the Church means, in the connection in which it is made, nothing else than its liberation from religion, or, in other words, that religion is to be at least placed in the background and deprived of its leading position in instruction. For if this is not the meaning, one cannot comprehend the importance of every other oversight except the clerical (*e.g.* that of itinerant lay school inspectors). Any other oversight can be of importance only if a rank is to be conceded to secular instruction which does not become it, or if elements are to be admitted into the national school which are utterly alien to it. In the best case, and with the most favourable disposition, religion is but allowed to remain as one among many subjects, and the clergy permitted to take the oversight of it. But the very thing to be contended against is, that religion should here be treated as a separate subject. It is religion which makes a school a national school, where *instruction* still goes hand in hand with *education.* And an oversight of the religious instruction which does not extend to the whole school, and especially to the *relation* existing between religion and other subjects (*e.g.* history and instruction in the mother tongue), cannot be **what in a** national school it ought to be. To those who would do away with, or at least diminish, the authority of religion in the national school, we would put the as yet unanswered question: What is to give it its characteristic stamp, its individual signature, if religion is no longer to do so? For in all instruction, and in every school, there must be something central, to which all else occupies a position, and which bestows upon it its importance. The middle school receives its peculiar character, its stamp, from natural science; the grammar school has long received its from classical literature; and in like manner the national school from religion. What, then, is to take its place? and what new stamp is to be impressed upon the national school? It will soon be evident, that to make the national school a grammar school, will be to uncharacterize it, to render it useless, and to introduce a system of mis-education. Absence of characteristic and mis-education have already begun to appear in grammar schools, in consequence of the frequent efforts which have been made to render them non-classical by banishing or infringing upon their teaching of Latin and Greek. The reform of parish (*communal*) schools has been constantly discussed with the object of promoting "popular information," so far do these champions of culture overlook the fact that not the information, but the *education* of the people, must be placed in the first rank. It is only when the education of the people is made the chief view-point, that the national school appears in its true light. The State must, above all things, demand that its future citizens shall be educated to "fear God and honour the king" (1 Pet. ii. 17), and the efforts of the national school should be specially directed to the laying of this foundation. As a school of religion, it closes with confirmation, and, indeed, in many places, as in Denmark, with the completion of the fourteenth year, or even between the thirteenth and fourteenth. How many kinds of secular studies is it thought possible to teach to children of this age? And which branches of knowledge are to be those chief branches, for the sake of which itinerant lay inspectors are needed, because the clergy are said not to be proficient enough, or not to have time enough, to take the oversight thereof? It is on the teacher, however, that all chiefly depends, and what is best cannot be had to order. The vivifying effects promised from the new formalism, with its numerous reports, tables and schemes, will still fail to make their appearance.

On the other hand, the idea of schools *for carrying on education* (*Fortbildungsschulen*), schools in which secular instruction may be further matured, should by no means be rejected. For an age when the people, in the widest sense, are called to a share in political life, further secular education than is possible in elementary schools is certainly desirable, and here we are fully justified in speaking of the need in these times of increased popular education. These supplementary schools may be supposed to be of different kinds for different ages. But it is by no means easy to find the correct form for these establishments, some of which, especially in Denmark, have even assumed the name of high schools (*Hochschulen*). As long as mere lectures are given in them for incitement and entertainment, without the pupils being obliged to do any mental work, or make any intellectual efforts, the form is not found. For education and knowledge are not attained without *labour and effort*. Nor is the form found until the matter and the extent of what is to be taught have been definitely determined in proportion to rank and calling. A general education, without relation to a definite calling, and unconnected with preparation for it, will only make the young purposeless and visionary.

§ 124.

Midway between the national and grammar school is the middle school, the purpose of which is to initiate the young, and especially those who are to belong to the trading and citizen classes, in such acquirements as may be of direct application to the position in life which awaits them. The greater the importance attained by the industrial class in our days, the greater also is the importance to be awarded to the middle schools. Christianity and the national literature and history must here, too, have their place. But natural science and the modern languages form the characteristic speciality by which they are distinguished from all other schools.

The Grammar School.

§ 125.

The *grammar school* receives its specific stamp from ancient classical literature. The studies in which the young are to be initiated are called the " humanities," and this word awakens the idea of human culture and human improvement. Genuine culture may indeed be attained without an acquaintance with Greek and Roman literature; but genuinely *scientific* culture cannot be attained without this foundation. Greco-Roman antiquity fully exhibits that form of humanity to which the race was able to raise itself independently of Christianity, shows us a model culture, complete and finished in itself. Its literature is an inheritance which has been bestowed, not on this or that single nation, but upon the human race. To appropriate and understand this inheritance is a main con‐ stituent of all scientific culture, by reason not only of the *historical* importance of these works,—inasmuch as apart from them we should certainly have no historical consciousness of the development of the race, — but also of their internal nature.

The study of the ancient languages, simply as such, is in and of itself a very important means of scientific culture,. because it developes the logical sense, the study of these ancient languages—which on the one hand are so fully de‐ veloped in their internal structure, and on the other lie so far‐ from the sphere of our ideas that it needs severe labour to‐ make them our own—being, together with mathematics, one‐ of the best means of training students to think accurately. We are, however, very far from exclusively regarding formal and exact training as the chief object of the grammar school. The study of the ancient languages must be inseparably united with the study of ancient classical literature. By this study a sense for the classic, for what is perfect both in form and matter (apples of gold in cups of silver), will be developed. By a profound acquaintance with these works, not only will a sense for form, a sense for harmony, lucidity, proportion and calmness of statement, so different from the crudity, affectation and restlessness of modern times, be developed; but we shall also experience, and this often imperceptibly, the influence of a matter familiarizing us with ideas and ideals which must be ranked among the most profound and substantial thoughts and creations of the human mind, and which, together with the form under which they are imparted, impress upon the soul a stamp of *ideality*.

We must, however, here obviate the misconception, that we desire to give the literature of classical antiquity the highest place, and are aiming at making our youths Greeks and Romans. The grammar school receives its character and stamp from ancient literature only so far as to recognise it for what it really is, namely, the assumption of Christian culture, and of a modern national literature essentially influenced by Christianity. This literature also belongs to the humanities, and Christianity itself is in the highest sense not merely a *divinum*, but also a *humanum*. To expunge Christianity from the grammar school, would be to change it into a heathen institution, against which the objection so frequently raised against classical studies on account of their heathen character would be a valid one. It might, too, be difficult to point out the importance to us of an acquaintance with ancient literature, unless it were placed in *relation* to our own times and lives.

§ 126.

The principle of the grammar school, its determining thought, is not the principle of pagan, but of Christian humanity. But just because we would have a scientific comprehension of Christian culture, we must be acquainted with its *presuppositions*, and receive them also as an element of our own culture. As the New Testament cannot be understood without the Old, neither can the world of modern culture without Greek and Roman literature, which is, so to speak, the Old Testament of culture. What the law is in the Old Testament, a schoolmaster to bring us to Christian liberty, classical studies are to general intellectual culture. By the study of grammar, the young are made familiar with the laws of thought. By ancient poetry is developed a sense for that strict law of beauty which prepares the way for the higher and free form of beauty found in modern art, in art as determined by Christianity. The prose works of antiquity contain a picture of the public life of ancient times, of their heroes and orators, of the struggles of their political parties, etc., and afford us a preparatory acquaintance with political law and the nature of civic community in general. By the contemplation, too, of the moral life reflected in these works, by the pictures here given of great characters,—many of whom may be esteemed the forerunners of the higher ideal of humanity revealed in Christianity; a Socrates, *e.g.*, may be fitly regarded as a John the Baptist from a heathen standpoint,—the young become familiar with the moral law of heathenism, and with the moral ideal which hovered before it. But as surely as the Christian principle of humanity should be that on which these schools are based, so too must the Christian ideal of humanity be constantly set forth as the true. It is the task set before the grammar school, not to obliterate the distinction between Christianity and paganism, but, within its own province, and in proportion to the intellectual development of its scholars, to make them conscious of this distinction, and also to draw their attention to the points of contact between ancient and modern times.

Hence we must also require that parts of the New Testament in the original should be read. The authors of the New Testament, who wrote among the ruins of classic antiquity, are the classics of the Christian religion. *Religious instruction*, which need not consume much time, must be continued at *all* stages of the grammar school. Christianity is not a mere matter of feeling, it is also a religion, a view of life and the world, into which the young must as much be introduced as to the religions of antiquity, its myths, its view of life. We therefore regard it as nothing but a blunder to give religious instruction a place in only the lower forms, and to exclude it from the upper, for the sake of gaining more time for natural science. For the *human* culture of the scholars will remain to a great degree incomplete, unless at the same time that they are initiated in pagan views and opinions, they are also made more thoroughly acquainted with those Christian ideas of religion and morality which would lead them to look at antiquity in another light than the pagan. Besides, such an omission would, in a purely intellectual respect, have this result, that the young would be without an essential condition for hearing philosophical lectures at the university, which must always *assume* an acquaintance with these Christian ideas and conceptions, and the mental activity therewith connected. Thus is one great factor of human culture withheld from them; and if they are unable to obtain elsewhere the instruction which it was the duty of the school to afford them, they come, so to speak, *wall-eyed* to the university. Such a school is an edifice in which one of the main supporting columns is damaged—a damage, a vandalism, pointing back to a humanity devoid of religion.

§ 127.

That ancient classic literature has now served its time, and is henceforth no longer necessary as the foundation of scientific culture, is an assertion repeatedly made by the so-called " realists," who, appealing to the practical, to what is serviceable in life, refer, in opposition to humanism, to the immense advance made by the natural sciences, to their great importance in the present day, their influence on modern life. Less advanced realists desire that at all events grammar schools should grant to the natural sciences an equal rank with classical studies. In opposition to this demand, we remark that physical science finds its true place in the middle (*Real*) school and in the larger realist institutions. But mind is higher than nature, and though mind is present in nature also, we must still constantly maintain that the manifestation of mind, whether in man or in history, is something far higher than its manifestation in unconscious creation. Physical science makes us acquainted with man in only a very insufficient manner, and belongs to the humanities only in a very periphrastic sense. The culture which it bestows will never be of equal rank with classical culture, not to mention the notion of supplying its place. And the grammar school, which is at home in the world of *language* and *mind*, which seeks its strength as well as its limits in this world, does well to guard against false compromises with realism, and not to let too much physical or other realistic matter be forced upon it. Such compromises would make it unfaithful to its proper calling, change it into a strange hotch-potch, where no distinction can be made between chief and accessory studies, where everything and nothing is learnt, and where what loses most is precisely classical education. Such a hotch-potch, where everything is of equal importance, only serves to make its over-satiated pupils indifferent to everything. Their powers being dispersed over a variety of subjects, to each and all of which the same attention and interest are to be shown, they are taught to like nothing, to admire nothing, they are brought to a *nil admirari* in the worst sense. The powers of youth ought, on the contrary, to be concentrated on what is important; "its powers must be *spared* for what is great." [1] It should be so educated as to love and admire in an intellectual sense.

§ 128.

Classical education has been attacked not only by realists, but by *Romancists*, who are indeed agreed with us concerning the supremacy of mind and history, but maintain that modern national literatures are now so developed, that if they were only dealt with in connection with their antiquity, and the land from which they sprung, we should possess in them a foundation of scientific culture which would reduce classic literature to subordinate importance. In the place of classic antiquity, we are directed on the one hand to the glories of the Middle Ages, on the other to the old pagan times of the north, with their strength and heroism. No single modern language, however, with its corresponding literature, can be pointed out capable of serving as a foundation for *general* education. For to be such it must be *common* to all cultured nations, and adapted to furnish the points of departure and contact for mutual scientific intercourse among nations. And for this purpose there is absolutely nothing but the ancient classic literature, to which the indisputable privilege of *historical necessity* can be accorded. For this reason we cannot agree with those who—though more in the indefiniteness of imagination than in a definite school plan—direct us Scandinavians to the old northern literature and mythology as a foundation for scientific culture. For, however great the importance we attribute to it, it still lacks the feature, on which all here depends, of *universal historical* importance, which, according to

[1] **Fr.** Thiersch, *Ueber gelehrte Schulen,* III. p. 340.

the will of Providence, must be at once accorded to Greco-Roman literature and mythology.   Nor is our ancient literature the expression of a *culture* developed to its climax, and capable of exercising a preparatory discipline as the presupposition of that modern culture determined by Christianity.   Highly as we estimate the northern mythology, with its profound symbolism, with the Thor, Balder, and Ragnarok myths, still it never had a *Homer* to glorify it in the forms of beauty and art.   And ready as we may be to acknowledge that the northern mythology is, according to its inward significance, more elevated than the Greek, inasmuch as it is ethic, and gives expression to a view of a conflict between good and evil, with a victory in the distance, and is thus predictive of Christianity, while the Greek is only æsthetic ; still such an acknowledgment must be limited by a nearer view, which will show us that northern mythology must rather be called præ-ethic than ethic, that mind and nature are here found only in disturbed fermentation, and that the contrast between Ases and Jettes is only a contrast between the powers of nature, where neither good nor evil has that truly spiritual and moral character which was long after expressed by Shakespeare, the hero of northern poetry and of the northern view, the poet who is far more serviceable to life.   Nor was our northern poetry followed, as its result, by an historical period, with a fully formed social life, with a series of thinkers, orators, artists and poets, who, under the sway of these mythic pre-suppositions, developed the pagan feeling and mind, according to the possibilities latent therein, till they were all exhausted ; and this is just the very particular in which old Greece and Rome are so instructive, showing us as they do præ-Christian civilisation, its bright and its dark side during a cycle fully lived through and completed.   What was brought to an end in the north by the destruction of champion life was by no means a completed civilised world.   It was Christianity itself that had first to bring civilisation to the northern Barbarians, who certainly were destined for a great future under its trans-forming influences, but who, for that very reason, so to speak, had fortunately for themselves no completed past in which their life germs, their possibilities, had exhausted and lived themselves out beforehand.   It seems too questionable to insist on taking as a foundation for general culture a mythology whose deeper intellectual meaning was not rediscovered till the present century, and was during all the intervening centuries lying enveloped, as it were, in clouds, and totally useless—a literary experiment which reminds us of a one-sided preference for the Romance languages.

We do indeed consider it desirable that our northern literature and mythology should, without prejudice to more important subjects, be brought, in our grammar schools, into due connection with the study of our modern national literature. If this is done within due limits, it will serve to strengthen a consciousness of the peculiarity of the northern races, by leading the young back to the first roots, the first sources from which our language and mental peculiarity have arisen. With regard to the sum total of human culture, our ancient literature, like the mediæval literature of each of the modern nations, is only a more or less important speciality, a thing peculiar to each separate people. But the *general* foundation common to all modern nations, the presupposition of all Christian literature, is and remains the Greco-Roman literature, on which account Christianity, wherever it comes, always brings with it the elements of classical culture.

The University.

§ 129.

University education is developed upon the foundation laid in the grammar school. The university embraces all the sciences, as a complete organism, an intellectual unity, a whole, in which each separate science only obtains an importance by being treated as an individual member of the one all-comprising science. Hence there is good reason for filling up the first academic year with philosophical studies. The task of the university is a practical one, inasmuch as it educates officials for both the Church and the State. But just because they, who are to become instructors, or to take part in the conduct and administration of public affairs, should not only be in possession of a certain mass of information, should not be satisfied with mere routine and tradition, but have principles at command, and be also capable of applying them in an independent manner—just because of all this is the task of the university also a theoretical one, and science must be cultivated with due thoroughness, as it cannot otherwise be what it ought with respect to life. A complex of special schools, internally unified by no directing spirit, and in which only practical instruction and knowledge directly applicable in life are imparted—such a complex is no university. It does not become one until the different branches of science are so treated, that all special knowledge is referred to that which forms the union of all we know; in other words, when they are treated in a philosophical spirit. We might even simply say, if the expression is taken seriously, when they are treated with spirit. For spirit is inseparable from idea, and where the idea is operative, the view-point of union and totality will be so too, though in different manners according to the nature of the subject. The one light will then illuminate even what is most special. The retrogression in philosophical studies, which is everywhere seen in these days, is no promising sign. For it testifies that the desire for truth is weakened, and that a mistrust of all higher knowledge of truth, and consequent despondency, have induced men to walk in the broad path of sensible perception, without reflecting that it is the most uncertain of all.

What has been said above applies also, with certain minor distinctions, which this is not the place to define, to the *study of theology*. The Protestant Church cannot be satisfied with clergy who have had only a traditional education, a mere training for the clerical office. However the relation between theology and philosophy, or that between faith and knowledge, may be defined, none of such definitions, it matters not which, can be made, without deeper investigations, leading into the whole region of knowledge. And every conception or form of theological science, which is not to stop at external tradition, must, by means of a train of active thought, refer its separate details of knowledge to a comprehensive and connecting whole.

§ 130.

Among the various attacks which have of late been directed against the continued existence of universities, the most important seems to be that derived from the art of printing and a constantly extending literature. It is said: In times when the art of printing did not as yet exist, it was obvious that eminent men, possessed of ideas and knowledge, should combine to establish certain homes of the sciences, where youths desirous of knowledge might assemble to appropriate the treasures which such men could personally impart. But now, when scholarship and ideas can be and are constantly imparted in the most convenient manner, universities must be regarded as obsolete institutions, which no longer correspond to any real want. This objection would have weight if literature and the university lecture were quite of the same kind. It is based, however, on an entirely mistaken view of the nature of the academic lecture.

In proportion as a work is a really literary production, as it approaches to being classic, will it bear a stamp of comparative finish and completeness, and of having smoothed off the marks of the workshop, designed as it is to be appropriated by more mature thought. The university lecture, on the contrary, introduces the disciples of science into the workshop itself, and gives them inducements to intellectual labour. The university tutor communicates to his hearers not merely his knowledge, his information, but lets the knowledge of which they are to partake grow before them, and, as it were, re-originate, by having regard solely to the stage of knowledge on which they are standing, and consequently to the yet unconscious knowledge, or non-knowledge, or seeming knowledge, which they bring. Step by step he leads them to the stage of information at which those classic works of literature may be *understood*, conducts them to a comprehension of the standpoint from which such works are *produced*, by educating their *organ* of perception, and developing their talent for scientific investigation. And this he does whether his lectures are of an edifying or of a reflective and critical character, or whether they exhibit a union of both, and are thus of the highest kind of academic lecture.[1] For, as the elder Fichte expresses himself in his book, *über das Wesen des Gelehrten*, the author needs only a single form wherein to express his thoughts; but the academic tutor, on the contrary, must use an infinity of forms and turns, to produce an instructive and educational effect upon his hearers. And if all scientific instruction should partake in some measure of the dialogue form, this applies in a special manner to the academic lecture. For though the teacher is here the only speaker, still his lecture must often so far assume the form of a dialogue between himself and his hearer, who is about to appropriate what is lectured on, as to pay due regard to the objections, doubts and questions which would naturally arise from the latter.

The more an academic tutor confines himself to the mere communication of positive information, delivered by means of dictation, the more weight must be allowed to the above-mentioned appeal, to the help afforded by books. But the more free, the more animated by his own spirit, his lectures are, and the less the living voice and entire personality of the instructor can be accounted non-essential and indifferent, the weaker will this appeal be. The remark that the number of eminent tutors is always very small, is not of decisive importance. For the main point is, that the university has in and by itself its lawful idea, its peculiar task, which can in no other way be fulfilled. That there is always in the carrying out a distance between the ideal and the reality, that there are more and less fruitful periods in university life, is a circumstance which applies in all departments, without its being a reason for the abolition of this or that institution. It applies indeed in a special manner to literature itself. We may also mention the mutual intercourse between teachers and taught, and the common intimacy of the students, as a moment which can never be replaced by literature. They who have gone through a genuine university career, will not be talked out of their conviction, that they received and learned in this spring-time of life what they would never have learned from books alone.

[1] Schleiermacher, *Ueber Universitälen.* "No university tutor can be of real service who is entirely devoid of either of these qualities, namely, enthusiasm and clear thought" (*Philosophische Schriften.* I. p. 576).

§ 131.

The *academic liberty* of students means their freedom from actual business pursuits, freedom to devote themselves exclusively to the idea, to the appropriation of and search after truth. It is not freedom from discipline, nor from the exertion of thinking, but is inseparably combined with that *honesty* of study so emphatically insisted on by Fichte, which does not cease on all occasions when direct utility no longer appears, does not skip necessary branches of knowledge because they seem dry and tedious, a kind of study which has been rightly designated as slovenliness, as epicureanism in learning. Truly honest study also excludes that so frequently occurring Philistrosity, which inquires only after the serviceable, the directly practical, and desires no thorough, no well-grounded knowledge.

But while the intellect is maturing, the *disposition* must also be cultivated; and to the university is committed the responsible task of co-operating indirectly, from the view-point of the highest good, of the destiny of man, of the supreme aim of human life, in the formation of character. Neither the State nor the Church can be served by men of mere intelligence, possessed only of an impersonal knowledge and skill, perhaps even led by means of the university into endless doubts, into an empty and barren criticism, induced only to be ever learning and never coming to the knowledge of the truth (2 Tim. iii. 7), and thus acquiring a certain laxity of character. They need personalities, *men* who are not simply knowers and doubters, or even non-knowers, but men of energetic *will*, who bring with them from the university that which can strengthen both will and character, nay, impart vigour to the whole man. What has been said applies pre-eminently to the study of theology, which should lead a young man to the right practice both of Melanchthon's saying: *Pectus est, quod theologum facit,* and of Luther's: *Oratio, meditatio, tentatio faciunt theologum.*[1]

§ 132.

Liberty of teaching, i.e. liberty in the investigation of truth and in its communication to his hearers, is the chief element

[1] Comp. B. J. Fog, *Ueber das theologische Studium*, p. 27 sqq. (Danish).

of tutorial freedom. The State should here bear in mind that science can only flourish in an atmosphere of freedom. It must, as far as possible, trust that scientific errors and partialnesses will be corrected by science itself. Time and patience must be exercised with respect to one-sided tendencies, and the State should beware, above all things, of interfering with a clumsy hand, and had better leave thinking minds at liberty to go their own way. How much important knowledge would have been lost to mankind, if the inquiring mind had been fettered by the constraint of an external law! Besides, when an attempt has been made to impose such fetters, they have, as history teaches, been soon burst through. But however emphatically freedom of instruction may be insisted on, the case is quite altered when the region of candid and serious inquiry is forsaken, when the professorial chair is abused for agitations in a purely external and practical direction, when, *e.g.*, atheistic and anti-christian doctrines are proclaimed, with the plainly expressed practical intention of attacking and undermining the religion of the country; when antinomian doctrines, whose aim is to do away with marriage and the family, or to bring about the abolition of property, to extol communism and to promote revolutionary movements, are promulgated. Under these circumstances the State may not remain indifferent, but must protect both itself and its academic youth against such attacks.

The philosophic faculty is that which must claim the largest amount of freedom of teaching. For the theological faculty the limits must be narrower, because no one can here be a teacher unless he knows himself to be in full agreement with the fundamental doctrines of revelation and of the Church, though he should by no means be bound to the letter of the symbol as to a slavish yoke, and though the history both of orthodoxy and rationalism shows that freedom of teaching in the theological faculties exhibits at different times a different and, in general, a very changing character. But philosophy being the searching science, which brings everything to the test, it is inevitable that a variety of standpoints should here supereminently appear. And if philosophy is to exist at all, it must be allowed to err and to teach defective views. They who cultivate it must have a right to say: Thus far are we capable of coming by the way of reflection; we here submit the results we have arrived at. If any one can carry the matter farther, he is welcome. Of course, the State will always reserve its rights with respect to these results, when they have a practical side. And since the conflict with the greater community always falls back upon the question: What is that which causes *offence?* and since the notion of what is offensive and revolting is different at different times and under different states of society, even the sincere inquirer after truth will at times be in danger of being a martyr,—a circumstance which belongs to the tragic side of science, and has been illustrated by a series of historical examples since the days of Socrates. If, then, the State, for the sake of obviating on its side, as far as possible, so unjust a martyrdom, yields ever so much to the demand for emancipation, and grants ever so much freedom, it must still at all times be required that one who is appointed an academic teacher by *the State itself,* should in his communication of truth, and in his mode of communicating it, conscientiously respect the community, whose youth he has bound himself to instruct within his own sphere, and to educate for the service of this community, and that he should treat with forbearance and respect whatever it esteems sacred and venerable. If he cannot accommodate himself to this, he had better not allow himself to accept a state-appointment, but make use of the freedom of the press for the diffusion of his views, and prefer to exist in Socratic independence.[1]

[1] It may here be appropriate to mention Spinoza, who would accept no appointment from the State. As appears from the letter in which he declined the appointment to Heidelberg, he seems to have had a consciousness and a feeling that his philosophy was not adapted for human society as a whole, but only for solitary thinkers. It applies also to other systems than that of Spinoza, *e.g.* to the purely sceptical and purely pessimist systems, that they are not fitted for society as a whole, but only for self-isolating individuals, on which account they are far more fitted to be communicated in a literary manner than in official academic lectures, especially when students are obliged to hear such professors. For the rest, it is in many cases very difficult to draw external boundaries, and every attempt made in this respect has entailed great inconvenience. Hence much must here be left to those *moral* restraints which the tutor must place upon *himself.* In a work left by Sibbern, and published after his death, entitled *Moralphilosophie som Retsindigheds-og Tilbörlighedslære,* it is very truly said (p. 110): "Let him who delivers lectures as a commission from the

THE CHURCH.

THE CHURCH AND THE KINGDOM OF GOD.—EDIFICATION.

§ 133.

What art and science possess only in image and thought, religion possesses as actually existing in personal reality. But it is only in the Church that religion attains corporeity. The Church, too, works for the ideal of humanity, by working for the culture and care of the new man, for the implantation of the kingdom of God in the realm of human nature, for the edification of the flock of Christ.

"*I believe in the Holy Ghost, the holy Catholic Church.*" When this confession was uttered for the first time, it was an absolute novelty to the world. By this article of our Christian faith, we profess to belong to a community whose origin is not of this world, not from the soil of nature or culture, but from above, a new creation, a divine institution and ordinance, a dispensation appointed for the dispensation of the means of grace, a pillar and fortress of the truth, destined to be the depository of revealed truth throughout the ages. Its destination is to comprise all the nations of the earth as one great family, and to carry on to perfection the whole body of believers. The Church is at one and the same time a visible and an invisible body. It is invisible inasmuch as it is a community of saints, a new manhood within the human race, a society not merely of professors but of believers, who, dispersed throughout the world, and separated from each other, are yet one in Christ. It is invisible also because pervaded by invisible forces and influences of grace; and, finally, because Christ, its heavenly head, is invisible. It is, on the other hand, visible inasmuch as its invisible nature makes itself manifest in the world, and its existence is conditioned

State, well consider that he may not say everything which he might otherwise be fully justified in expressing." Of himself Sibbern says : "In my book, *The Year* 2135, much is said which I never have, and never could have, allowed myself to say in academic or other lectures,"—a statement which suggests very fertile and practically applicable thoughts concerning academic *tact*, and the regard due to academic *youth* entrusted to the guidance of a teacher appointed by the State.

by the *historical* manifestation of Christ by means of the word and the sacraments, the means of grace appointed by Himself. The *Confession of Augsburg* defines the Church as " the assembly of all believers, among whom the gospel is preached in purity, and the holy sacraments administered according to the gospel." In saying this, however, it defines the notion of the Church only in its narrower import. In its wider meaning, the Church comprises all *the baptized ;* for little children also, and they who are weak in the faith and in sanctification, if baptized, belong to the Church, though they do not belong to the community of saints.

The Church is not the same thing as the kingdom of God. It is the main earthly instrument, the central *organ*, for the extension of the kingdom of God. But the kingdom of God itself is a far more comprehensive notion than the Church. The kingdom of God is older than the Church, has existed from the beginning of creation, and will abide in glory when the Church as such has disappeared. The kingdom of God comprises all forms of the kingdom of humanity. Its object can only be obtained by the co-operation of all circles of human society. But the special activity of the Church for the promotion of this object is directly *religious.* Though the Church, directly or indirectly, exercises on her part an educational influence, it is yet in accordance with her destination that the influences proceeding from her should bear a higher character than that of culture.

§ 134.

In contrast to the educational influences of art and science, those proceeding from the Church may be termed *edifying.* Under the notion of edification we comprise all that promotes communion with the Lord and the intercommunion of believers. It is a figurative expression, but owes its life and form to this very circumstance. It is the house, the temple of God, which is to be built up of living stones (Eph. ii. 19 sqq.; 1 Cor. iii. 10 sqq.; 1 Pet. ii. 5). The task of building points to laying the foundation, that foundation once laid, which is Christ, the foundation of the apostles and prophets, the foundation laid in the heart, even faith; and everything is edifying which can help to establish human life on this basis. Edification includes in itself both the community and the individual. It is the Church which is to be built up, the great temple, called also the "body of Christ," which consists through the mutual connection and assistance of the members. But the individual is not to be merely one of the members in the great temple, but also an independent temple of the Spirit of God. Hence all, too, is termed edifying which contributes to the sanctification of the individual, which helps me personally in the affairs of my soul, of my salvation.

The spiritual temple is not to be built in height and depth only, but also in length and breadth (Eph. iii. 18). It is not only to be raised from its deep foundation to soar heavenwards, as the church tower is seen by bodily eyes to rise above the lower dwellings of earth. It must also be extended in *breadth*, for it is to expand, to spread itself over the whole human race; nay, every circumstance of human life is to be sanctified by Christian faith, by receiving the consecration of the gospel. Finally, it must be built also in *length*, for it is to continue and stretch through all time, from generation to generation, and not to attain its completion till the end of the days. To attempt to build up a mystic temple of humanity in its height and depth, its length and breadth, but without Christ as its foundation, is to grasp at a shadow instead of a substance, and to build a mere castle in the air, a *Fata Morgana*. Other foundation can no man lay than that which is laid, viz. Christ. The invisible edifice which we are building finds its visible image, its emblem, in the tabernacle, in Solomon's temple, in the Gothic church of the Middle Ages, and in the New Jerusalem of the Apocalypse.

We do not, however, overlook the fact that the work of *Christian* edification itself is going on also outside the Church and its forms; for the Christian religion extends beyond these, though it must always maintain its connection with the Church. There is, however, much Christian piety which, without wearing the Church form as such, co-operates in the work of building the temple of God, and proves itself to be in every moral circle of life a directly edifying power. The spiritual temple, as the end and object of edification, is co-extensive with the kingdom of God, which will remain when all earthly forms of association shall have disappeared. The Church itself, as a form of earthly association, is a mere means for preparing the saints for that state in which the words: " Behold, the tabernacle of God is with men, and He will dwell with them, and they shall be His people, and God Himself shall be with them, and be their God " (Rev. xxi. 3), shall be in their full sense accomplished.

§ 135.

Edification depends upon a co-operation of divine grace and human freedom. We are built up by God the Lord, but are also to build up ourselves into a spiritual house (1 Pet. ii. 5). It is the Lord who will Himself build His Church, as he said to St. Peter ($οἰκοδομήσω$ $μου$ $τὴν$ $ἐκκλησίαν$, Matt. xvi. 18), " I will build my Church ; " while elsewhere it is said : " Build up yourselves." It is the result of this human factor in the work of edification that the holy Catholic Church appears in a variety of particular Churches, of confessions, which have variously fashioned their doctrine, public worship and church discipline. Very especially does the human factor appear in the government of the Church and in its relation to the State, concerning which the Lord prescribed nothing, and which can be only indirectly regarded as pertaining to the work of edification. These varieties are, however, anything but indifferent. Their respective values depend upon the degrees of acquaintance with the plan and sympathy with the mind of the heavenly Architect possessed by the earthly builders, upon their right use of the means given by the Lord Himself in the word and sacraments for the edification of the Church, on whether they have built on the one foundation wood, hay and stubble, or gold, silver and precious stones (1 Cor. iii. 12). Hence it is through the human factor that there is always in the Church a difference between its ideal and its reality.

§ 136.

Connected with the difference here shown to exist between the divine and the human factors of edification, is the distinc-

tion laid down by many (Harless, A. Oettingen) between the
Church and church polity (*Kirchenthum*)   There is one
Church, not many.   But the one Catholic Church appears in
a variety of polities.   By church polity then, or, as it might
be called, church system, we understand the *ecclesiastical
organization* under which the Church has at different times
appeared, and which not only sets forth what was taught by
the Lord, but also comprises, as ecclesiastically valid, binding
and obligatory, in other words, as *legally* normative, the
doctrines formulated by men, with the form of worship and
the institutions therewith combined.   Such church polity is
necessary if the Church is to spread and maintain itself in the
world, and especially if it is to become national ; but it must
not be confounded with the Church itself as the Lord's institution.   Church polity is capable of change and improvement ;   the church, as Christ's institution, is perfect and
unchangeable, is at all times the same.   Church polity has
in itself only relative authority, and must be tested according
to the absolute authority of the word of God.   Much in
church polity is of only transitory value, and may be regarded
as a merely temporary scaffolding to the work of church
edification, but does not form part of the temple itself.   The
value of a church polity consists only in its being a setting
for the Catholic Church and the Lord's means of grace, His
word and sacraments, in its leading souls to these, and to that
saving faith which appropriates them ; and it must never
usurp authority over the word and sacraments, put itself in
the place of the divine institutions, or place its own institutions on a level with them.   This is indeed often done by
some single church polity giving itself out to be exclusively
" the Church," and desiring to bind the conscience to its
institutions as to a divine command.   This is a confounding
of the Church and church polity, or, if the term is preferred,
church system, and seems to have been, at least partially,
what Sibbern, whom we have so often mentioned, means
when, with polemical pathos, he speaks so frequently of
" *Christenthümelci* " as something essentially different from
Christianity, and Grundtvig, when he calls our Lutheran
Church, in opposition to the holy Catholic Church, a civil
institution.   When such an attack is made, it must not, how-

ever, be overlooked—always excepting such a distinction between our Lord's ordinances and ours as is ever right and
lawful—that it is a mere empty imagination to suppose that
the holy Catholic Church will ever be able to come forth in
the world without a church polity, a church system, being at
the same time formed, without this "civil institution," or, to
express it more correctly, without a legal ecclesiastical organization ; and that it would fare very ill with a Church if the work
of man were to be in every sense excluded from it. It would
be a sign of spiritual death, a proof that the Church was
deficient of all independent appropriative and reproductive
power.

Besides, however correct the distinction in question may
be, we shall nevertheless undoubtedly continue to speak of
the Lutheran Church, the Romish Church, etc., and not merely
of the respective church polities or church systems. The
formal confession, and the forms of worship appertaining
thereto, may be regarded from another view-point than the
predominantly ecclesiastical and legal, viz. from the *religious.*
But we shall always be constrained to say, that the different
particular Churches are only true, in opposition to seeming,
Churches, so far as they represent the holy Catholic Church,
and serve as its expression. And if we Lutherans prefer our
Lutheran Church to every other, the reason is, that we regard
it as that Church which expresses in the comparatively
most perfect manner the œcumenical or universally Christian,
without arrogantly claiming to be in an *exclusive* manner
the Catholic Church itself. What appertains to the latter
can only be determined by the New Testament and the oldest
genuine tradition.

§ 137.

Different ways of viewing the relation existing between
the divine and human factors in the work of edification, will
have for their result differing opinions concerning the
historical development of the Church. The Roman Catholic
Church has a falsely optimistic view of itself and its own
really remote historical antecedents, and regards with an
equally false pessimism all other phenomena of church

history. This its false optimism is based upon the circumstance of its regarding and authorizing all its human institutions and doctrines, whole heaps of hay and stubble, an
endless quantity of mere scaffolding and outworks, including
much mediæval rubbish, as directly divine means of grace
and salvation, and, during the progressive development of its
institutions and doctrines, looking at the reality as in every
particular point in perfect harmony with the ideal—an
optimism which culminated in the Vatican Council and the
dogma of infallibility. This Church possesses in the Pope a
supreme authority both in doctrine and discipline, in which
the ideal and the real are commensurate. The contrast to this
optimism is formed by the pessimism exhibited by the sects,
which regard the entire development of church history as a
failure, national churches as a Babel, as mere human work, as
civil institutions with a Christian appearance, etc., while they
hold an uncommonly optimist view of themselves as those
among whom alone true Christianity is still to be found.
Irvingism, whose true elements we by no means ignore, cannot
be absolved from a false pessimism, when it regards the
Reformation of the sixteenth century as a mistake, and the
Church as having to such a degree departed from her destination that the Lord was in consequence obliged in the latter
days to institute a new infallible authority in the Church,
and for this purpose to send not only apostles, but also to
restore other church officers of the apostolic age.

The Evangelical Church, conscious of her infinite distance
from the Lord, regards herself and her work of edification
under the apostolic view-point: "Not as though I had already
attained, either were already perfect; but I follow after, if
that I may apprehend that for which also I am apprehended
of Christ Jesus" (Phil. iii. 12). But the Christian optimism
with which she regards the course of church history is founded
on the Lord's promise to His Church, that "the gates of hell
(the powers of death) shall not prevail against it" (Matt. xvi.
18); upon the fact, that in the midst of every corruption, the
tie which by the means of grace unites the Church to her
invisible Lord is never absolutely broken, and that the Holy
Spirit, as the Spirit of reformation, is ever and again working.
She has the comforting confidence, that although the Lord has

sometimes let men go their own way, He has never been unfaithful to His word, "I will build my Church;" that in spite of all that men have built amiss or neglected, and though He may have removed the candlestick of this or that particular church, yet *His work, His Church-building*, has been continually advancing; that the different ages of the Church are under His guidance, and that His plan for His Church will in any case be realized, whether with, without, or against the will of man.

THE CHURCH AND HUMANITY.

§ 138.

The Church, in working for the kingdom of God, is working also for the kingdom of humanity, which attains its perfection only in the kingdom of God. It is inconceivable that the Church and the world should in and of themselves be irreconcilable contrasts; it was the Church and nothing else which introduced into the world the true ideal of humanity. This she did by her proclamation of Him who is the Son of Man, and who requires of us that we should put off the old man and put on the new. Nevertheless, and just because there is in the Church as well as in the world so much of the old man, conflicts have frequently arisen between the Church and humanity, whether because the Church asserted a false principle of authority, or because the advocates of humanity contended for a false emancipation. The Romish Church, indeed, during the Middle Ages deserved well for its human education of the nations. But the more they advanced towards liberty and maturity, the more did this Church misconceive the relative rights of emancipation, and the relative independent value of secular life, and seek, like a jealous mother, who will not allow that her children are of age, to keep the nations under the restraints of authority. Since the time of the Reformation she has been reactionary, and has taken up a hostile position towards the religious liberty which has been granted, as well as towards scientific and political liberty—a hostility which has in our days found full expression in the "Syllabus" of Pius IX., in which, *e.g.*, it is condemned as an error that Protestants should claim freedom of worship, and that the Catholic Church should not possess the right of employing secular power. By this and cognate propositions, the Romish Church has placed herself in irreconcilable opposition to modern humanity and the progress of culture.

Though the Evangelical Church also has frequently misunderstood her position with respect to humanity (we need but refer, *e.g.*, to the contest between Götze and Lessing), still her principle involves a recognition of the relatively independent importance of emancipation and secular life. This principle, however, by no means requires an approbation of false emancipation, or an entrance into false compromises with a humanity devoid of, or even hostile to religion. Just as strenuously as she opposes the advocates of the papacy, must she also contend against those who are carrying on the so-called "battle of culture;" for these protest not only against the Pope, but also against the gospel, nay, against all religion, and aim at setting up, by means of naturalistic and pantheistic assumptions, a self-dependent kingdom of civilisation, an omnipotent State, to be itself a proper God on earth. Just because the Evangelical Church has to maintain the true ideal of humanity, must she oppose the false ideal in all its manifestations; and the spiritual struggle against an atheistic, anti-christian, nay, a demoniacal humanity, has in our days become one of life and death.

THE CONGREGATION AND THE MINISTRY.

§ 139.

The work of edification must be carried out by the co-operation of *pastor* and flock. The existence in the Church of Christ of a clerical office and a clerical class is founded on an *intrinsic* necessity. This necessity must, however, be understood in a Protestant sense. The Romish Church, starting from unscriptural assertions, attributes to the clergyman (the priest) supernatural properties, which are stamped upon him independently of his personal character, in virtue of his ordination, distinguish him from the laity, and constitute him a mediator between them and Christ. The Evangelical

Church, on the contrary, insists on the priesthood of all Christians, their equality before God, and their vocation to show forth the praises of Him who hath called them out of darkness into His marvellous light (1 Pet. ii. 9). In so doing, however, Protestantism by no means refuses to recognise a special ministerial office, not merely for the sake of maintaining church order, but also because Holy Scripture plainly shows it to be the Lord's will, that there should be at all times an appointed ministry for the preaching of the word, the administration of the sacraments, and the guidance of the flock. With respect, however, to the *organization* of this ministry, especially to its different grades, to the distinction between pastors (priests) and bishops, all this is left to historical development, and therefore exists according not to divine, but human appointment (see *Art. Smalcald.* p. 351 in Hase's edit. of the *Libri Symbol.*). *The ministry of the word* itself, however, exists according to the express command of the Lord (see Matt. xxviii. 18-20; Mark xvi. 15; 1 Cor. iv. 1 sqq.; 2 Cor. v. 20; comp. *Conf. August.* V.), and does not depend upon any resolution of a congregation or a majority. And though the pastor is the servant of the flock, yet he is above all the servant of the Lord, and must—whether it please his congregation or not, whether it accords or not with what is at the time called " the prevailing spirit of the Church" —preach the word of the Lord, that word which is exalted far above himself and his people, and which will one day judge both himself and those who hear him.

The evangelical clergyman appears also as the servant of the Lord in the *administration of the sacraments.* He ministers, however, at the Lord's Supper, not as a sacrificing priest, but as one who dispenses the Lord's gifts to the people. In *confession* he comes forward not as one exercising authority over consciences, and therefore binding them to compulsory confessions, not as a judge imposing penances and remitting temporal punishments, but as a minister of the gospel, announcing the forgiveness of sins according to the Lord's word and promise, warning, counselling, reproving, comforting, as a brother or a father in Christ, those who entrust themselves to his guidance. The essential equality of clergy and laity is moreover shown in the Protestant Church by the abolition of

compulsory *celibacy*, by the fact that we have a married clergy.
The Romish Church extols the celibacy of her priests, as
making them independent of secular concerns, of the cares
and troubles of family life, which would but too easily withdraw them from things eternal, and make them incapable, in
times of danger, of sacrificing everything for the cause of the
kingdom of God.   We willingly grant, with the apostle, that
at times and " for the present distress," as well as for certain
individuals, celibacy may have its advantages, and independence be an advantage (1 Cor. vii.); but as a general rule
we cannot make it binding.   For a far greater intimacy can
prevail between a flock and its pastor if the latter has himself experienced married and family cares ; and there are many
matters concerning which, as being unacquainted with them,
an unmarried man could not be suitably applied to.   The
pastor may also, by a truly Christian family life, both in
prosperity and adversity, be to his people an example, which
may far more conduce to their edification than if he were
placed upon the heights of a supposed ideal sanctity, whence
he would look down upon marriage and a family as things
profane.   It is more possible to an evangelical than to a
Romish clergyman to approach the apostolic description of a
bishop.   For a priesthood bound to celibacy will never answer
to the words of St. Paul concerning the bishop, as the husband
of one wife, having believing children, and given to hospitality
(Titus i. 6, 8).   Nor, with all respect for the many estimable
clergymen of the Romish Church who have kept their vow of
celibacy, can the fact be denied that much immorality among
the clergy has been and still is the result of their enforced
celibacy—a striking testimony to the Scriptural saying, " It
is not good for (the) man to be alone."

EDIFICATION IN PUBLIC WORSHIP.

§ 140.

The edification of the assembled flock in public worship
takes place by the use of the means given by the Lord
Himself, by His *word* and *sacraments*.   The elements of
edification in the Evangelical Church are prayer and singing

(in the latter the whole congregation prays aloud), the proclamation of the word of God, or preaching, and the administration of the sacraments. The thoroughness of the edification depends upon the due relation between word and sacrament.

In the preaching of the word, for which Holy Scripture serves as foundation, not only should words *about* the Lord be heard, but words proceeding *from* Him, by means of His ambassadors, to the world and to His Church, words from Him who is Himself present where two or three are gathered together in His name, and who will make His word effectual by means of the Holy Spirit (Matt. xviii. 20; Luke xxi. 15).[1] But while preaching more or less depends upon the personality of the preacher, the Lord *alone* carries on His saving work in the sacraments, and the human peculiarity of the minister retires. The preaching of the word addresses the self-conscious part of the human being, the heart and conscience; the sacrament embraces the whole undivided man, body, soul and spirit, and extends its effects to the unconscious part of our being also, to the inmost natural side of life. And while the preaching of the word addresses itself to all, our Lord here performs His saving and redeeming work on the individual, receives the individual into His flock in the sacred laver of baptism, and thus establishes His Church in him, makes the individual a partaker of the communion of His body and blood, so that a direct and sacred contact and meeting takes place between the Lord and the believer in the Lord's Supper. This implies that the Church cannot be edified by the preaching of the word alone. And wherever this is attempted, wherever the sacraments are placed under a bushel, it is found that faith, notwithstanding all that may be in the deepest sense calculated to establish and support it, will be deficient in stability. This can never be present except where the Saviour is the sole worker, where His Church founding agency in baptism, His nourishing, refreshing, redeeming efficacy in His Holy Supper, operate independently of human gifts and human limitations. Or, in other words, where edification is confined to the preaching of the word, the spiritual nature of faith is without its true

[1] The author's *Dogmatics*, § 245.

corporeity. We may see this in many who seek their edification exclusively in hearing the word, especially from this or
that favourite preacher, while they are negligent or indifferent
in the use of the sacraments. Their piety gives the impression
of something purely spiritual without corporeity, without any
firm and distinct form, and very often bears the marks of
indecision, hesitation, carelessness and intermission. On the
other hand, however, we must also most emphatically insist,
that where the notion is entertained that the Church can
be edified by the sacraments alone, and the saving agency of
the Lord by means of the preaching of the word dispensed
with, there faith will be without real heartiness and appropriating power, and wanting in vitality and growth ; and there,
too, will a false security and facility be but too quickly
adopted, and mere externalism and bodily service, which
dispenses with true spirituality, be introduced into public
worship. The Romish Church is full of examples of such
bodily religious service, devoid of inward life and spirit.
Hence we maintain that, whether for the individual or the
congregation, true edification is not effected through the
preaching of the word alone, nor through the sacraments alone,
but through the word and sacraments in combination. We
are well aware that there is also such a thing as an extremely
superficial edification, an unspiritual religiousness, a religion
of mere habit, even where both word and sacraments are used.
But we maintain that a *living faith* can only attain its full
development when it does not put asunder what God has
joined ; for it is only through both the means of grace that
we are partakers of a whole and complete Christ.

Nevertheless, we may say with Luther, that preaching is
the chief part of public worship, *i.e.* in this sense, that
without it Christ cannot attain a form for us, nor can we
possibly attain to faith in Him, cannot follow Him, nor, to
speak generally, can our Christian life be a self-conscious
personal life. Without it we understand neither the nature
nor importance of the sacraments nor their right use, nor are
capable of truly appropriating them. For this reason the
preaching of the word is the main part of a clergyman's duty.
And though we cannot from good preaching infer, without
further ceremony, the good condition of a congregation, still

second-rate or dead (faithless and spiritless) sermons will always afford a presumption, that if life is not quite extinct in the flock, it still cannot come to a healthy development, because an essential condition of growth is wanting.

§ 141.

The task of Christian preaching is misconceived when it is placed only in instruction and information, when the preacher is regarded as only a teacher of religion, or a teacher of the people. It is not popular theology which is to be delivered from the pulpit, but the gospel, the word of eternal life, as flowing from its original source, though the preacher must be well furnished with theology as a prerequisite and condition. But a preacher should no more compete with a scientific theologian than he should compete with a poet in the art of poetic treatment. In both cases he would fall short, and satisfy neither the educated nor the uneducated. Though no preaching can dispense with the light of thought and knowledge, yet all—even what may unintentionally and by reason of the diction of Scripture be of a poetic nature—must be subordinated to edification, which is what is sought when a congregation assembles, not only by the simple, but also by the well-informed and learned. The task of Christian preaching consists in its being of such a nature as to testify that it proclaims to *hearts* that sacred truth to which the preacher himself stands in a relation of *personal* dependence, and with which he is personally filled. That this way of diffusing and corroborating truth should be esteemed inferior to the way of science, must on no account be admitted. On the contrary, we maintain our assertion, and extend it to *all* truth which concerns our relation to God and His government of the world, that it must stand the test of being addressed to the heart and conscience, and that it will be false in one respect or another if it is not capable of proving itself to be truth to the *conscience*. But it applies very especially to *saving* truth,— which did not come into the world as a collection of propositions, but as the revelation of eternal life, and as a message to man from the God who is Himself eternal life, and desires that man should surrender his heart to Him,—that the first and supreme *self-evidence* is given to the heart, the conscience and the will, to the personality, and that all scientific discussion thereof is but a secondary matter.

An old heathen teacher of rhetoric somewhere speaks of the orators of antiquity,[1] and after enumerating a series of names forming the crown and flower of Grecian oratory, Demosthenes, Æschines, Lysias, etc., continues: "To these must be added Paul of Tarsus, of whom it is to be noted that he was the first to bring forward doctrines without adducing evidence." The old orator seems to have got an impression of what was the peculiarity of Christian preaching. We who are well acquainted with Paul of Tarsus know that though he was indeed capable of furnishing evidence to the reason, yet in his preaching he appealed to another kind of proof, speaking "not with enticing words of man's wisdom, but in demonstration of the Spirit and of power" (1 Cor. ii. 4), and "by manifestation of the truth commending himself to every man's conscience in the sight of God" (2 Cor. iv. 2), declaring that "after that in the wisdom of God the world by wisdom knew not God, it pleased God by the foolishness of preaching to save them that believe" (1 Cor. i. 21). What we require of Christian preaching may be expressed as follows : it should not so much *prove* truth as hold it forth, direct attention to it, and place it vividly before men, not so much prove that error is error, as evidently expose its intrinsic emptiness and hollowness, and bring to light its evil results. The preacher, too, in his exhibition of truth, must above all hold forth Christ, or, to speak more correctly, must so prepare the way for Christ that He may manifest Himself to souls. In this lies the power of Christian preaching, this is its mystery, by which even a less gifted and simple preacher, far inferior in knowledge and education to many of his hearers, may produce powerful results. "We have this treasure in earthen vessels, that the excellency of the power may be of God and not of us" (2 Cor. iv. 7). We are mistaken, if we suppose that in consequence of the greater erudition and education of the day, Christian preaching is superfluous, or at all events to be confined to the more ignorant. Whatever advances the world

---

[1] In a fragment, which some attribute to Longinus (born at Athens about A.D. 213). Comp. Sibbern, *Æsthetik*, IIL p. 136.

may make in enlightenment and education, the preaching of the gospel will ever have the same effects as at first, whether upon the learned or unlearned, if it only remains true to itself, and desires to be only what the Lord intended.[1]

§ 142.

So far as regards its relation to the world, to the spirit of the age and the culture of the times, Christian preaching should in this era of humanity be ever seeking in the human points of contact for the Christian ; thus following the example of the apostle at Athens, who not merely reminded the heathen of what certain of their own poets had said, but also referred to their altar to " the unknown God," that he might better proclaim to them the God of revelation (Acts xvii.). The men of these days manifest more feeling for the human than the divine, hence the Christian preacher will often feel induced to bring forward the human side in the manifestation of Christ, that he may thereby lead to the Divine, to dwell upon the moral miracle, that he may lead therefrom to the physical (by which the corporeal nature is governed and glorified). Still, respect to the human must never seduce him into false accommodations, false compromises with the humanity of the day. Christian preaching should bear the impress of humanity, but it is to be also a stumbling-block and an offence. Wherever the gospel is faithfully proclaimed, it will still as ever be a sign which will be spoken against, a sign for the falling as well as the rising again of many.

It is true that the offence taken may be the fault of the preacher, or of ecclesiastical tradition. This point of view has been especially maintained by *Rothe* in favour of the educated classes of these days, who have turned away from the Church. It is said to be mostly the fault of the Church itself, for having disguised Christ in a garment of dogma and ascetic maxims, in which the present age can neither recognise nor receive Him, a garment suited only to the necessities of an earlier date, but now obsolete, for preaching Christianity in the conventional language of former times, instead of letting it speak the language of the day in which alone it could find acceptance.

[1] Mynster, " Ueber die Kunst zu predigen " (*Blandede Skrifter*, I. p. 81).

He maintains especially, that not ecclesiastical dogmatics, not doctrinal definitions of the Trinity, of the nature of Christ, etc., such definitions being only secondary, only human work of merely relative value must be preached, but the *ever new facts* of Christianity, or the living Christ Himself. This must indeed be acknowledged to be true and just, though there are not many now who preach the dogmatic formula of the Church as such, instead of the gospel according to Holy Scripture. But what Rothe—whose opinion of church doctrine we cannot here further discuss—does not, or does not sufficiently, bring forward and insist on, is that when this is done, the offence is by no means obviated. It is these very facts upon which Rothe lays so much stress that give offence to many among the educated. "The supernatural" is to multitudes the stone of stumbling. And Christian preaching cannot yield one of those facts which are briefly summarized in the Apostles' Creed. It must, by all the means at its disposal, prepare the way for them, that they may have access to and find acceptance with men. But the circumstance will at all times repeat itself, that these facts, or the living Christ Himself, exert upon many the most profound and powerful attraction, and verify themselves as redeeming and saving facts to their souls, while on others they act repulsively and arouse opposition, because in the *last* resort they *will* not accept them, as indeed our Saviour said of Jerusalem, "*Ye would not*" (Matt. xxiii. 37). For this every preacher must be prepared, however conscientiously and thoroughly he may try himself, to see whether the imperfections of his own preaching may not be a hindrance to his hearers. Rothe himself has, on other occasions, especially in his sermons, expressed himself to the same effect. But we are unable to share the optimistic view which he lays down in his *Ethics,* viz. that a time will come "when no intelligent person will any longer doubt the reality of that supreme miracle, which is also the central point of all human history, of the Divine Redeemer, Jesus of Nazareth."[1] Should this be possible, Christianity would cease to be Christianity; for it will be "hidden" from and inaccessible to the "wise and prudent" (Matt. xi. 25), that is, the intelligent as such, and reveal its glory only to those who place themselves as "babes"

[1] Rothe, *Christliche Ethik,* III. p. 1020.

before it, and become intimately acquainted with it by an act of free surrender,—a truth which Rothe in another connection also admits, and which, with his deep Christian faith, and his view of faith, he cannot but admit.

"Art thou he that should come, or do we look for another?" (Matt. xi. 3). There is much contention about the answer to this question. There are intelligent and learned men who desire indeed to have a Christ, but not Him who stands before us in the gospel, surrounded by the glory of the supernatural, which to their science appears as legend and fiction, nay, as mere myth, from which, by the help of criticism, the actual Christ must be separated and appear in His true form, namely, as a certainly highly gifted man, a religious ideal, and though not the absolute, yet still the relatively highest ideal known to us. Such a Christ would undoubtedly give no offence to the natural man. Only, we maintain, such a Christ can never be proclaimed as the Saviour of the world. A Christ whose form had first to be discovered by theological criticism—a criticism which after the course of a few years alters its views and represents as worthy of belief what it a short time since branded as incredible, or *vice versa*—such a Christ cannot be an object of faith, nor of *absolute* devotion and love. He will exist as more or less a hypothetical, nay (in a historical sense), an ambiguous character. Since we possess no other sources for the history of Christ than our gospels, the announcement of Him must always fall back upon these, just as the texts of our sermons must always be taken from them. But, then, how can *faith* in His Person be spoken of so long as this Person itself hovers before us in a mythic or a fabulous garment, the work of superstition, and we contemplate it with doubt and denial, waiting for the acuteness of our theologians to free the so-called actual historical Christ from all these coverings? How can there be any faith in Christ if the historical Christ is only to be expected as the result of critical investigations? For the historical Christ will be either undiscoverable, or He must be given us from the beginning. In contrast to the self-contradiction of requiring faith in a person whose real existence, whose life in this world, can be only an object of scientific hypotheses and researches, it is the duty of Christian preaching to testify, that He is come who

should come, even Christ, conceived of the Holy Ghost, born of the Virgin Mary, the crucified, risen, ascended Christ, who attests Himself to the heart by His word and Spirit. The more fully we surrender ourselves to Him, the more capable do we become of reproving the errors of the times, by the Spirit of truth whom He sends to us. In these days it is especially incumbent on Christian preaching to wear an apologetic character, to be armed for offence and defence on the right hand and on the left (2 Cor. vi. 7).

In its relation to believers, Christian preaching must strive to build up the Church from first principles to perfection (Heb. vi. 1). It is true that we never outgrow these first principles, that sin and grace and justification by faith must be always preached, for this fundamental Christian consciousness must be incessantly renewed from the living source. But besides this, the Christian preacher, who is placed over a congregation, should regard it as his duty to be able to say with the apostle : " I have not shunned to declare unto you all the counsel of God " (Acts xx. 27). And it must be regarded as a defect when a flock and its pastor remain year after year at the same stage, without any progress in knowledge and practice being perceptible. There are also certain articles of faith which should, with regard to the special character of the times, be specially brought forward. In our days, *e.g.*, there is obvious need that the prophetic teaching concerning the last things and our Lord's Second Advent should be dwelt upon. The more decidedly the signs of the times show that the day is at hand, the more important is it that the view of the world and of life prevailing in the Church should be developed in this direction also.

§ 143.

The essential characteristic of preaching is found in its being a testimony, and this applies also to that *spiritual song* in which the congregation testifies to its faith in thanksgiving, praise and prayer. Together with the faithful proclamation and reception of the word, hymns and songs form a main element of edification. Silent congregations are not a good sign. The chief requirement of a good hymn is not only to be poetical, but that the poetic element should be entirely subordinate to the purpose of edification, should contribute to and be lost sight of therein, that it should be unpretending, free from all self-chosen conceits, from that independence which belongs to secular poetry. All this applies equally to hymn tunes. If it is objectionable for a sermon to be brilliant at the expense of edification, it is equally so for hymns to sparkle with ingenious trickery or fantastic turns, to the injury of that poetic purity which is in this department an indispensable qualification, and to forfeit the characteristic of lowliness and piety. This is to betray a self-consciousness, a self-pleasing which comes of evil.

It belongs also to a good hymn that it can be sung by all, and it must therefore be congregational and orthodox. Nothing is less compatible with a hymn than the merely *individual*, or more out of place than for the general Christian element to acquire, through the poetic mannerism of the style, a flavour of the poet's peculiarity, which is thus forced upon a congregation. From this point of view it may—*cum grano salis*—be said, that a good hymn should be so colourless as rather to resemble the lilies of the field than the pomp and glory of Solomon, though the latter may be far more attractive in the eyes of the multitude. The motley is in this case the objectionable ; and if it has been said that " the motley is better than the pale," we may answer that neither is to be recommended, but that in certain cases the pale is the better of the two.

It is among the advantages of the Lutheran Church to possess a treasury of sacred song, which has in the course of years been continually increasing, and which by its depth and sincerity of feeling will be able to edify the Church from generation to generation. It may be said of the Danish Church that she is poor in theology, but rich in spiritual songs, and that she can in this respect — if not from the days of the Reformation, still from those which follow it— bear comparison with any other division of the Evangelical Church.

THE SUNDAY.

§ 144.

In the evangelical obedience of the third (fourth) commandment, "Remember that thou keep holy the Sabbath
day," Sunday, as the first day of the week, has taken the
place of the Jewish Sabbath, for regularly recurring solemnization by the Church. "The Son of man is Lord also of the
Sabbath day" (Matt. xii. 8), and He came not to destroy, but
to fulfil it, and to bring it to perfection. Though we cannot,
in this respect, appeal to any definite saying or command of
the Lord, still it is unmistakeable that this is the day which
the Lord hath Himself made, viz. by His resurrection, by His
appearance in the midst of His disciples when He delivered
to them apostolical authority (John xx. 19 sqq.), and by His
outpouring of the Holy Ghost on His Church. Already in
the Apostolic Church the Sunday was esteemed holy as "the
Lord's day" (Rev. i. 10 ; comp. 1 Cor. xvi. 2). That the
Christian Church could choose any other day for divine
worship, or that this day should ever be abolished by
Christians, is a thing inconceivable. As the Sabbath of the
Old Covenant served as a memorial of the completion of the
work of creation, so does our Sunday of the completion of the
work of redemption, while at the same time it prophetically
points to the future rest which God hath prepared for His
people (Heb. iv. 9). Each returning Sunday renews to the
Church the call, "Remember that Jesus Christ was raised
from the dead" (2 Tim. ii. 8), and the remembrance of all
connected with it, and reminds the world of the eternal
destiny of man.

§ 145.

Apart from religious considerations, periodical days of rest
are necessary, especially for the working-classes ; and even
though not moved thereto by the Church, the State would
itself have been forced to recognise the necessity of introducing a periodically returning day, set apart for the recreation of mind and body, for release from the turmoil and
burdens of earth, for some sort of elevation from the dust

of life's prose to its poetry. On nearer inquiry it might be shown that exactly every seventh day was preferable, since every other period of time would prove either too long or too short. This secular aspect of the day of rest forms among Christian nations a *moment* in the solemnization of Sunday, and in itself — apart from the crying abuses so usual in our days—a justifiable moment. Sunday being, according to the evangelical view, a day of holy joy, the joy must extend also to the secular side of life, which must be seen with marks of ideality and festivity. Ideal life, which is at other times fettered by the pressure of labour and the prose of the temporal, must on this day of release move more freely even in its secular manifestation.

The Sabbath is made for man, and not man for the Sabbath (Mark ii. 27). The rigorous view of tho sanctification of the day, which understands the command rather in the letter than the spirit, requires that the whole day should be strictly devoted to religious exercises; that not only work of every kind, but all and every secular amusement, should be excluded, so that three or even four attendances at church may take place on one Sunday, and the rest of the day be employed in either private or family devotion. It cannot be disputed that this is an unevangelical way of regarding the matter. While tho religious frame of mind suitable to Sunday should be the joy arising from the gospel, the day is spent in an ascetic and hypochondriacal spirit; and vacancy of mind and tedium cannot fail to result from such an excess of sermons, hymns and liturgical devotions, which but too frequently surpass the capacity, and especially the mental receptivity, of those who engage in them. The fact is overlooked, that, of edifying matter as of mental nourishment in general, no greater quantity should be received than we are capable of assimilating; that the enjoyment of art and social intercourse by no means come of evil, if, be it well understood, they are in harmony with the Sunday frame of mind, and do not tend to destroy it,—a condition which in most cases each must decide for himself. Nor must it be forgotten that works of urgent necessity, and (after the Lord's own example) works of mercy to the sick and suffering, are certainly lawful on this day. We admit that during holy week all public amusements should cease, because at this time religious seriousness, the seriousness of sin and atonement, attains its climax, and should be brought home to the consciousness of all, and that it must be called a profanation, a sign of the decay of public morality in a Christian people, when, in contrast with the earnest piety of former times, public amusements are in these days permitted in holy week, without exciting any energetic opposition. But what is true of holy week does not therefore apply to ordinary Sundays.

It is in England and Scotland especially that a rigorous view of this day prevails, though indeed with various modifications. And however much may be urged against such a view from the standpoint of evangelical liberty, still we cannot but honour a nation which places itself, in its relation to the divine and the holy, under such a discipline as a protection against the danger of being swallowed up in that great machinery of the world, by which it is surrounded and in many respects threatened. Besides, there is in these days far less occasion to contend against too rigorous a view of the keeping of Sunday, than against that lax, indifferent, and in its broad and bad sense worldly view, which exercises so widespread a sway with regard to the celebration of holy days. The liberty of individuals must not in this respect be restricted by any external law, but it may be generally asserted, that no one can be a true Christian who does not feel the need of spending a holy day in communion with the Lord and His Church, and that Christianity without Churchmanship (*Kirchlichkeit*) is but shadowy and formless. And if the State would make any kind of claim to be a Christian State, and a Christian nation and national Church are still taken for granted, it must on its part take the holy day under its protection, and thereby maintain among the people the consciousness that human life has an eternal destiny, and that agriculture, trade and worldly business by no means constitute the ultimate and highest end of life. All public labour and business must be forbidden, even though Jews and heathens feel inconvenienced, and exceptions should only be permitted in cases of the most urgent necessity. It is also the duty of the State to restrain the rough, immoral pleasures which have got the upper hand on this day. Lax rules for the observance of Sunday, which admit of numberless exceptions, blunt in a people the feeling of man's eternal destiny, the consciousness that this life should be lived for higher than earthly interests, while they support and cherish the notion, that to live for earthly wants, temporal profit and sensuous enjoyment is the chief and most important affair. The demand which has, with good reason, been made in these days for stricter rules for Sundays and festivals, is closely connected with the labour question, so frequently discussed in the foregoing pages. For workmen must be protected against that arbitrariness of employers which would make Sunday labour compulsory, even though such compulsion is but indirect, the matter depending upon so-called "free contract." This applies especially to work in factories and on railroads, by which thousands are deprived of both the day of rest and holy days. The objections which have been urged from the economic standpoint cannot be taken into consideration in presence of the divine institution and the eternal destiny of man. A whole nation can just as well as an individual dispense with Sunday labour, cases of exceptional and urgent necessity excepted, if it makes arrangements accordingly. "Six days' work with a blessing from above is worth more than seven without."[1] We might also well do with many fewer Sunday trains. England is in this respect a speaking example; for the strict sanctification of Sunday has by no means injured that country in economical respects.

SPECIAL PASTORAL CARE.—CHURCH DISCIPLINE.

§ 145.

The work of edification will not be confined to times of public worship nor to the assembled congregation. *Private and special pastoral care* begins in preparation for confirmation, the clergyman here entering into a personal relation with the individual, which may, under God's blessing, be subsequently further developed and strengthened. But in its narrower meaning, special pastoral care extends to the desponding, the erring, so far as these are accessible to the

[1] H. Thiersch, *Ueber den christlichen Staat*, p. 133.

exhortations of the Church, to the sick, the sorrowful and the dying. The rules for these various duties, so far as they can be laid down, belong to pastoral theology. In this place we only mention that a pastor should not only possess a knowledge of human nature, and be acquainted with different states of mind, but must also have a heart open and *enlarged* towards his flock. "Our heart is enlarged," says the apostle to the Corinthian Church, "ye are not straitened in us" (2 Cor. vi. 11). He must be able to put himself in the place of others, and to become, in the right sense, all things to all men (comp. 1 Cor. ix. 22), that he may by all means save some. To this must be added a special gift of love and patience, cultivated by constant intercourse with souls. It is, however, one of the darker aspects of our Protestant Church, that the care of souls, especially in large cities, cannot be exercised to anything like the extent it should, the numbers of the clergy being very disproportionate to the numbers of the population. "The harvest truly is great, but the labourers are few" (Matt. ix. 37).

§ 146.

Church discipline, as a partial and temporary deprivation of the benefits of the Church in the case of such of its members as have given cause of *scandal* to the rest, may be regarded from the view-point of pastoral care, inasmuch as it is an educational and purifying act, exercised upon the part of the Church upon the individual, whose *improvement* is its object ("That the spirit may be saved in the day of the Lord Jesus," 1 Cor. v. 5). This is not, however, the only view-point for Church discipline. It is also to be regarded as a reaction of the community against the scandal in question, a necessary moment of the Church's *self-assertion* ("Put away from among yourselves that wicked person," 1 Cor. v. 13). There are offences which the Church cannot tolerate without degrading herself and being unfaithful to her Lord. When, however, we describe church discipline as only a partial and temporary exclusion from the benefits of the Church, the reason is, that it does not become the Church to make the Lord's institution of baptism, the promises of which extend throughout life, invalid. For, even supposing a man to break and be unfaithful to his baptismal covenant, the Lord remains nevertheless faithful. The Church must never regard the tie between the Lord and the baptized man who has fallen into sin as absolutely broken, though it is indeed loosened. It is the Church's duty (contrary to the assertion of the Novatians) to receive again the fallen, if they repent, and the saying of Christ, "Let him be to thee as a heathen man and a publican" (Matt. xviii. 17), is not to be understood as excluding the receiving back of the sinner. In the exercise of discipline by the Evangelical Church, it has been brought forward as a main point, that the civil and ecclesiastical provinces must not be confounded, and therefore that church discipline must involve no civil disgrace,—a demand which can, however, only be valid in a purely legal sense.

The Romish Church can, in consequence of the authority exercised by the Catholic priest in the confessional, use discipline to a far greater extent than the Protestant Church. It is true that this may sometimes have a beneficial effect; but the compulsory character of this confession, the priestly directorship here assumed, and the consequent penances inflicted by the priest and prescribed by the Church, are wholly irreconcilable with evangelical principles. The slight amount of church discipline exercised in the Evangelical Church—for its entire disappearance is an untrue assertion, refuted by experience—has sometimes called forth, on the part of the Christian clergy and laity, an opposition to national churches, combined with an inclination to depart from them and to form smaller communities, which should be separated by their purity from the churches of the masses, where so much—as they say—"must pass through the coarse sieve." Complaint is especially made that in national churches "a clean table," that is to say, the table of the Lord's Supper, is not to be found, because in these so many unworthy guests appear at the altar. And it certainly cannot be denied that there are in this respect certain imperfections among us, which cannot be overcome. This must not, however, be said in defence of an ecclesiastical laxity, indifferent to that which not only *may*, but *should* and *must* be overcome. If the parable of the tares among the wheat (Matt. xiii. 24–30) is not intended, on the one hand, to exclude a wholesome discipline corresponding with the actual circumstances, no discipline will, on the other hand, be capable of abolishing the truth expressed in this parable, that the Church, as long as it exists in this world, will ever remain a *mixed* Church. A church discipline carried to extremes can scarcely escape the *Donatist* heresy, which dreams of an absolutely pure Church and an absolutely pure table. And all rigorous discipline, carried out, as it always is, with very fallible human vision, will always run the risk of excluding the *publican* instead of the *Pharisee* (Luke xviii.). However many small communities men may form, the difficulty of keeping them pure will soon set in, especially if they extend themselves, as every community aims at doing. Even at the first Lord's Supper, at which only twelve guests were assembled around the Lord, tares were found among the wheat; a Judas Iscariot was among them. A conscientious clergyman may indeed often feel much distressed at having to administer the Lord's Supper to those whom he regards as unworthy, without their having given just such open and *provable* offence as to enable him to exclude them. One thing, however, should be well considered, viz. that it is by no means the clergyman, as the steward of the mysteries of God, who is alone responsible, but that all they also who require and receive the Lord's Supper are *individually responsible*. Upon this individual responsibility of the members of the Church, the minister must in many cases depend. It is his duty to bring to the consciousness of his flock this personal responsibility. And that not for the first time in the address at confession (*die Beichtrede*), when it might be too late, when those assembled certainly show by their mere presence that they confess themselves sinners, but when in many cases such a confession may be a superficial one. He must, by means of his Christian testimony in general, and especially by his repeated testimony concerning the import of the sacrament, awaken and strengthen such a consciousness. This testimony must not, however, be of a kind to repel the penitent, instead of warning the impenitent from the Lord's table; the former requiring, on the contrary, to be attracted and comforted by the gospel of the Lord's Supper. What is above all things desirable, and to be striven after by all the means at command, is, that such a spirit should prevail in the Church, such a general judgment be formed, and such a voice be raised concerning the scandal of any abuse of the sacramental celebration, that the really unworthy would excommunicate themselves.

FOREIGN AND HOME MISSIONS.

§ 147.

The Church is *universal*, and is to be built up of the whole human race; it has the Lord's command to form all nations into Christian nations, hence it is directed to carry on and extend missionary work, until the gospel shall be preached to all nations, and then shall the end come (Matt. xxiv. 14). History shows us that the work of missions has its fruitful and its unfruitful seasons; also that its fruits are of various kinds, not only with respect to the spirit and power in which the work is carried on, but also in regard of the nature of the peoples who are its objects, whether those to whom the gospel is brought belong to nations of a highly gifted or of a meanly endowed nature. No one heathen nation must, however, be excluded from missionary efforts, even though every time is not the favourable, "the acceptable time," for the purpose (2 Cor. vi. 2).

The relation between the Christian and the human is shown in missions, on the one side, by the fact that Christianity cannot be brought to uncivilised nations, unless we bring them civilisation—for without a minimum of culture, Christianity cannot be truly appropriated, nor the Christian Church attain its development; on the other, by its bringing to cultivated nations a new culture, and introducing a transformation of the old. Missions are most successfully carried on by such Christian nations as possess colonies and extensive commerce. The recent development of culture has, by its many means of intercourse, facilitated in a great degree the connection between the different parts of the world, and thereby promoted missionary undertakings, thus at the same time bringing near and hastening the last times, in which the gospel will be preached to all nations. With this is connected also the mischievous circumstance, that commerce often brings European civilisation to the heathen, without at the same time bringing them Christianity, or without seriously concerning itself in the cause of the kingdom of God—a state of things entailing very undesirable results.

One main question in missionary activity is: Should Christianity be brought to heathen nations in the form of a definite *confession*, or should only the *original* pure gospel and the Holy Catholic Church be brought to them? Of course the latter is the chief matter. As soon, however, as a church constitution, with a definite order of public worship, is to be formed, the confessional element inevitably comes forward, although it may be confined to the simplest and most easily intelligible rudiments. Another question is, whether special missionary institutions should be organized for the conversion of the Jews? The general view is, that this is superfluous, because the Jews live among us, in daily contact with Christians, are also sharers in a cultivation essentially influenced by Christianity, and because Christian churches are open to them as well as to others. The question, however, is pressed upon us, whether in these days of apostasy, in which not only many Christians have fallen from the faith, but the majority of Jews also have become unfaithful to the older revelation and fallen into unbelief, such missionary institutions would not be at all events important, especially if they would set it before them as their task to quicken among the Jews the consciousness of their destiny as a *nation*, and thus at the same time encourage the consciousness of the revelation from which they have fallen away, in order thereby to lead them to Christianity. We do not, however, overlook the fact that the conversion of Jews can be but sporadic, until the hour strikes for that last great missionary work to the Jews, which the Lord has reserved for the last days, when Israel—after the fulness of the Gentiles has come in— shall be converted as a whole, as a nation (Rom. xi. 25 sq.), when their eyes shall look upon Him whom they have pierced (Zech. xii. 10; Rev. i. 7), when that great sign and miracle will appear, that all Israel throughout the world shall, to the astonishment of all, join in the song: "Blessed be He that cometh in the name of the Lord" (Matt. xxiii. 39), and then, in a higher and spiritual sense, the corruption of the Gentile Church will be judged.

§ 148.

A special gift is necessary for exercising and carrying out missionary work, "a faith which can remove mountains" (Matt. xvii. 20, xxi. 21), which, in its zeal for Christ's glory, and in heartfelt love for those who sit in darkness and in the shadow of death, can, by preaching, acting and suffering, by heroic courage and untiring patience, conquer obstacles often immense and to human eyes insuperable. The apostles, who, by the power of the word alone, removed the mountains of the heathen world, are in this respect our examples, as, *e.g.*, St. Paul when he says: "In journeyings often, in perils of waters, in perils of robbers, in perils by mine own country-men, in perils by the heathen, in perils in the city, in perils in the wilderness, in perils in the sea, in perils among false brethren, in weariness and painfulness, in watchings often, in hunger and thirst, in fastings often, in cold and nakedness" (2 Cor. xi. 26 sq.); or when he says: "To the weak became I as weak, that I might gain the weak" (1 Cor. ix. 22). Not without reason has it been remarked, that among the natural qualifications which are generally perceived in one going out as a missionary, are included an inclination for travelling in foreign and unknown lands, a taste for adventure, and a love of the marvellous. These, however, are natural dispositions, which must be sanctified by being entirely subjected to the obedience of Christ. An interest in the wonders of nature and in the phenomena of heathen civilisation—an interest for which many of the Jesuit missionaries have (as Peruvian or Jesuits' bark, among other matters, reminds us) been distinguished—must be entirely subordinated to an interest in the gospel. And if any one should, by God's grace, even make the experience that his faith can remove mountains, he must still say to himself with the apostle: "Though I have all faith, so that I could remove mountains, and have not charity, I am nothing."

§ 149.

Foreign missions are mostly carried on by voluntary associations, and this is true, in an exclusive sense, of Home missions (*die innere Mission*). The name and notion of the Home mission point, in the first place, to an agency which aims at opposing the heathenism within Christendom itself. But though this is certainly among the tasks of Home missions, it still by no means exhausts their object. Their object is, by works of loving service, to care for those in Christendom who are sick, suffering and dying, and who cannot as such be adequately reached and tended by the clergy, because their means and powers are insufficient. While the Church opens her doors and invites all who are willing ("Come, for all things are ready," Luke xiv. 17), the Home mission aims at *seeking* and saving the lost. The parables of the lost sheep and the lost piece of money find here a special application. It aims, *e.g.*, at the recovery of neglected and morally corrupted children, and forms prison associations (especially for the care of released criminals), Magdalen and other institutions. Nor are its efforts confined to the recovery of the fallen. It desires also to share in the work of *prevention* and *preservation*, by its so-called "creches" for infants, by asylums for growing children, by Sunday schools, by quarters for itinerant artisans, who, since the abolition of guilds, are exposed to so much temptation, by lodgings for young women, etc. The Home mission desires to afford not merely temporal, but spiritual aid to the poor; and the present socialistic movement has, by means of the labour question, set before it the great task of co-operating in the restoration of the true and Christian relation between labourers and employers, and promoting the sanctification of Sunday. It desires to take care not only of the poor, but of the sick (by deaconesses' institutions); hence its agency is not confined to the lower classes, but includes all.[1]

The Inner mission is one of the most hopeful signs of life in the Evangelical Church. It is a testimony to the revived strength of the gospel, to its divine power unto salvation, but at the same time to its power of relieving temporal necessities.

[1] Lehmann, *Die Werke der Liebe.*

Christianity and humanity are here in closest union. What Vincent de Paul aimed at in his days, in the Romish Church, is now to a far wider extent aimed at in the Protestant Church (Wichern). In its first beginnings it was called forth by the existing needs of society, and its enduring task is to investigate and bring to light those diseases of popular life which must be thoroughly understood if their cure is to be effected. It proceeded from a deeper view of the state of society—a view to which a sea of corruption was present, in whose depths thousands upon thousands were sinking, and the need of sending out lifeboats made itself felt. The Church and its institutions had neither adequate power nor means of coming to the rescue, even where the will might exist. Hence it was the *laity* that must help, by a voluntary *diaconate* (in the widest sense of the word); and an abundance of various powers and gifts, which had hitherto been lost to the community, was called forth and brought to light by the Inner mission. In these voluntary associations, one of the best forms of *individualism* is manifested. But the Inner mission will never be able to perform its task unless it co-operates with and is rooted and grounded in the Church as the objective existing community, with its stable and historical institutions. And great harm is done to the good cause—which is certainly the cause of the Lord and of His kingdom—when a false individualism is developed in the Inner mission, an arrogant boasting of universal priesthood, with a depreciation of the clerical office, and a pietistic, self-constituted system; or when, on the other side, the servants of the Church think they may look down with contemptuous indifference upon the efforts of the Inner mission. The question here is a practical inculcation of the scriptural doctrine of diversities of gifts and one Spirit (1 Cor. xii. 13 sq.).

A contrast to the Inner mission is in our days formed by a widespread tendency, which desires to relieve the needs of suffering mankind by purely human efforts, but without Christianity. We are well acquainted with the gospel of the good Samaritan, and desire nothing less than to deny the truth that much good may be done in this way also. A difference in principle is, however, here in question. The

Inner mission starts from the thought, that the ultimate reason of all human misery is sin, and that bodily and spiritual suffering can only be relieved when man is redeemed from sin by the gospel of Christ. This cannot be admitted by so-called "pure humanity," which, if indeed it does not declare war against it, leaves such a view out of question, as a thing quite immaterial. The Inner mission, however, cannot, without being unfaithful to itself, deny its principle; and when, *e.g.*, it is proposed to the deaconesses' institutions that they should place themselves upon a purely human standpoint, and carry out from this their care of the sick, they are asked to give up their own proper nature. Certainly they ought not to press Christian piety upon others, but they must carry on their work in the spirit of love to Christ, and where a receptivity and a need for it are found, must have a word of comfort and edification in readiness. The Inner mission will be well able to compete with "the efforts of pure humanity." For, without desiring to deny the value of eminent individual examples, to which we may here be referred, we maintain that self-sacrificing and world-conquering power is on the whole not on the side of "pure humanity," but of the gospel. It is a fact that in public calamities, *e.g.* war or pestilence, it is not to rationalistic, but to evangelical preachers, that the people flock to receive encouragement and consolation from their testimony, their ministrations; and that at such times the great preponderance of those works of love with which devotion, self-sacrifice and personal danger are combined, is found not in "pure humanists," but in positive and Christian believers.

§ 150.

With the efforts of both foreign and domestic missions are combined those of the Bible societies, whose aim it is to disseminate the sacred Scriptures among the people, so that there may be no house, no cottage in the country without a Bible. The Bible societies, however, can only answer their intention when their agency is carried on in connection with the preaching of the word and Christian worship in general. Scripture when isolated can effect nothing, and it cannot be denied that many illusions have been combined with the agency of Bible societies, and that many accounts of the great effects said to have proceeded from them are the results of high colouring and empty appearance.

The English Bible Society has done great service in the diffusion of the Scriptures. It would do still greater if it would diffuse a full and complete collection of the sacred books. As long as it adheres to its view, that the Bible must only be distributed without the Apocrypha, a measure which excludes a highly important *historical* middle term between the Old and New Testaments; as long as it continues from this standpoint to diffuse the Bible in Lutheran countries, where by its ample means it overcomes all competition, and thus banishes the Scriptures in the form once peculiar to these countries, and appertaining to the confessional system of Lutheranism; as long as it thus exerts itself to force upon our people its own private (and by no means universal) view of the inadmissibility of the Apocrypha into the entire Bible, so long will a great deficiency affect its work, and this work itself be an *imperfect* one. The society will consequently not deserve in every respect the praise of that love which, in its desire to be of service, seeketh not *her own* (1 Cor. xiii. 5), since, as far as this point is concerned, it seeks, on the contrary, to rule foreign Churches.

THE RELATION TO OTHER CONFESSIONS.

§ 151.

We can in these days only belong to the universal Church by being members of one of the various *confessions* in which that Church has individualized itself. The normal relation to our own Church finds its natural model in our love for our native land. As this love is opposed on the one hand to that national hatred which will not under national variety recognise the universal human which binds all nations together, upon the other to that hollow cosmopolitanism which ignores national individualities, and overlooks the fact that mankind exists only and solely in these, so it is with love to our own Church as our ecclesiastical native land. It is inseparable from fidelity to the possession and inheritance bestowed by God; it preserves, defends and developes the special and peculiar gift entrusted by God to this very community (as, *e.g.*, the Lutheran Church must faithfully preserve and develope the deeper apprehension of the Lord's Supper), and must not sacrifice it in favour of a spurious unity. True confessionalism is at once both polemic and peaceful, and faithful to the truth in love, in the midst of the struggle which is only engaged in for the sake of peace. It recognises in other confessions both that general Christian element on which they too are founded, and that special gift of grace bestowed upon them by the Lord, and is ready to learn from them—ready both to impart and receive.

Hence there must ever be within the different Churches a tendency towards *union*. "There shall be one flock, one shepherd" (John x. 16). Whether this saying of Christ will ever be realized in any form of Church, *externally* representing unity, is very doubtful. The much striven for union between Lutherans and Reformed can only be called a church union in a very imperfect sense, so long as the disputed points of doctrine have not found their unity in a definite confession, acknowledged by both sides.[1] But union on a large scale cannot be spoken of till Catholics and Protestants are united. Of this there is but little prospect. The Roman Catholic Church regards herself as directly one with the holy universal Church, and other Churches as distortions of the true Church; hence she can require but one thing—not that they should come to an agreement with her, but that they should repent and return to Rome. The Vatican Council and the dogma of Papal Infallibility have removed any such prospect to a still greater distance. It is not her many and diverse dogmas, but the one dogma of *authority*, the infallible Pope and the infallible, irreformable Church, that forms the main obstacle to union. How long the Lord will in His wisdom and long-suffering tolerate this human statute, this *idol* in His Church, He only knows. But a union of heart and mind is more and more taking place among believing Christians, including also many Roman Catholics, who, though not capable of breaking with their confession, feel themselves inwardly united with all

[1] Comp. Rothe, *Christl. Ethik*, III. p. 1095.

those who believe in the gospel. A disposition is being formed not to lay stress upon what separates Christians, but upon what is common to and unites them. This will be greatly promoted by the common struggle against unbelief and negation, as well as by the persecutions of the last times. Amidst confessional separation, by which Christian life is passed in different households,—in the different apartments, so to speak, of the same great house,—Christians will ever more and more perceive that what most deeply unites them is the simplest and the plainest, is that which was delivered from the beginning, which even children can appropriate, in which also the wisest and the simplest are on a level. Amid the various confessions of faith, the common banner under which they fight will be above all the *apostolic symbol*, the baptismal confession, the testimony of the original facts. But true union cannot aim at obliterating true peculiarities. It must appear as a *confederation* in a great Church alliance against the unbelieving world.

A transition from one confession to another should only take place as the result of most serious and conscientious research. Efforts whose aim is to induce individuals to pass from one confession to another are but objectionable *proselytism*, when they arise rather from a selfish interest in adding new members to one's own Church, than from an interest in the conviction of the individuals in question; also when deluding means of conviction are resorted to, and souls are blinded by sophisms and false representations of the confession it is desired they should forsake, and thus led away from the region of their own probation, a course of procedure which is the ordinary one with Romish and Jesuistic proselytizers.

THE RELATION TO THE STATE.

§ 152.

When the notion of a Christian State finds acceptance, the necessity for the existence of a Christian State Church, or, as, for the sake of expressing the freer relation to the State, it is now called, a Christian National Church, is thereby admitted. History shows that there are two extremes, which have both proved equally pernicious; one, where the State is placed in false dependence on the Church, a state of things which prevails where the Papacy succeeds in realizing its ideas; the other, where the Church is placed in a false dependence on the State (Byzantinism or Cæsareopapy). Both extremes are based upon a confusion of the spiritual and secular power. It has hence been demanded that a complete severance should take place, that the Church should not encroach upon the domain of the State, while on the other hand the State should not encroach upon that of the Church. That the evangelical, and especially the Lutheran Church, fell, by reason of the Reformation, into a one-sided relation to the State and to rulers,—who, on account of the necessity of the times, and till further arrangements, assumed the so-called "supreme episcopate" (*Summepiskopat*), *i.e.* were, as supreme bishops, to possess and exercise ecclesiastical supremacy, not only in external and mixed, but also in internal affairs,—is a fact which is generally acknowledged. In the present century an evangelical sovereign, ruling the most powerful of all the Protestant States of the Continent (Frederick William IV. of Prussia), expressed a wish to be able to resign his ecclesiastical rule into "the proper hands." Since 1848, when freer political constitutions, with creedless and religionless diets, were introduced, the supreme episcopate of sovereigns became still more inadequate for the protection of the rights of the Church, although they must maintain and administer this ecclesiastical power until it can be transferred into the proper hands. Though the ruler renounced his sovereignty, that is to say, in the sense of absolutism, this did not abolish his supreme episcopacy, which, as an independent annexe to his royal power, is of far older date, and this he is absolutely unable to share with a creedless diet.[1] It has, however, been urged as a demand not to be refused,—unless an evil territorial system, oppressive to the Church, is to prevail,—that the constitution of the Church should be so organized as to allow it a right of independent

---

[1] Where the supreme episcopate still prevails, the normal state of things is for the king, as *summus episcopus*,—which he can only be as being esteemed the supereminent member of the Church (*præcipuum membrum ecclesiæ*),—to have his special *ecclesiastical* organ (*e.g.* an *Oberkirchenrath*, as in Prussia, or some such dignitary), while as ruler of the country he has his *secular* organ in his

decision in its own internal affairs, and a right of joint decision in all mixed questions, *i.e.* those which fall as much within the province of the State as the Church. The form in which such an organization has been attempted at the present day, and in which it has been in many places actually realized, is the *synodal form*, according to which not only the clergy, but also the Christian laity, are summoned to common action. One chief task, and also one chief difficulty, consists in making Church representation a *reality*, and in preventing all mischievous predominance of majorities. Nor must its Church character be falsified by treacherous compromises with the spirit of the age, made with the intention of conforming the representation of the Church as far as possible to the liberalistic and democratic model, thus bringing about only a pretended representation (*repræsentatio ecclesiæ spuria et factitia*), and falling into Scylla by avoiding Charybdis. The evangelical synod must, as an indispensable *presupposition*, stand upon the basis of the *confession*.

The synods of a single national Church cannot form dogmas, for a representation of the greater body of the whole Church, to which the several national Churches belong, and with which they are united by a common faith, is needed to lay down new definitions of doctrine—for which our age is utterly un-adapted and inadequate. The synods of a single national Church must confine themselves to the more modest tasks of endeavouring, upon the foundation of the confession, to promote church life, and the right position and efficacy of the clerical office in the Church of their particular nation, and under the given circumstances; of revising the liturgy from time to time, whether on the whole or in single instances (*e.g.* the question of a new series of pericopes for preaching); of seeing to hymn-books and catechisms; and of discussing questions of both discipline and finance. The matters to be dealt with at such synods being of no great extent, and differing herein from the orders of the day at political diets, they might assemble at

constitutional minister. That a creedless minister, dependent, moreover, on the diet, should be his organ for the internal affairs of the Church, such as doctrines and liturgy, is a monstrous idea, which leads to the purely territorial system. On this whole question, comp. the author's work, *Den danske Folke-kirkes Forfatningsspörgmaal, paäny betragtet*, 1867.

longer intervals, *e.g.* every seventh year, even if at first more frequent meetings should be requisite. In the interval a committee or ecclesiastical board might undertake the decision of administrative questions in combination with the minister of public worship. Too much must not be expected from such synods, and loss of time in useless and fruitless discussion is inevitable. Their great importance consists in the fact that the Church possesses in them an *organ* by means of which she can, when necessary, both speak and act; while, where no such organ exists, ecclesiastical legislation comes to a stand-still, and the Church is obliged to remain with old, and in some instances obsolete laws. Where such an organ, whether in a synodal or consistorial form, is continually withheld from the Church, and the supreme episcopate at the same time is not energetically maintained and exercised, the end must at last be, that the national Church will fall entirely into the unlawful and "improper" hands of creedless ministers and political diets, or even that the entire connection between Church and State will be dissolved.

§ 153.

In contrast with the efforts which are made for the maintenance and further development of national Churches, there is at the present day a movement which desires the total separation of Church and State, and would resolve the national Church, which is based upon parishes and their mutual connection (the parochial system), into independent congregations, whose principle is the unrestrained liberty of *individuals*. This demand proceeds not merely from unbelievers, but also from believers. They who, in the interest of faith and of the gospel, urge the entire separation of Church and State, have regard in so doing to the apostolic Church and the state of the Church during the first three centuries, in which faith, even amidst persecutions on the part of the State, developed such noble and mighty powers, and at the same time, dwell upon the evils, the worldliness, the hypocrisies, connected with a State Church. They consider the transition of the Church into a State Church, which took place under Constantine the Great, a declension from its ideal, a transition to a corrupt condition.

This view-point has been vindicated with much power and eloquence by Alexander Vinet, who was also induced, by the force of circumstances in his native land, especially by the despotism of the civil authorities, who desired to tyrannize over the Church, to become the spokesman of the liberationist idea, for the realization of which he was filled with enthusiasm, nay, for which he lived, and from the diffusion of which he confidently hoped for a new reformation, a regeneration of the Church. With this his idea of the free Church, as the Church of personal Christianity, of personal conviction, he combined a very limited notion of the State, requiring from it nothing further than the protection of life and property; and demanding from social morality, the care of which is to be incumbent on the State, nothing more than external propriety and decency. We, who attribute to the State a higher ethic significance, and therefore require that, if it is to fulfil its vocation, it must be a Christian State, cannot be persuaded that the State Church can, in principle and nature, be of evil. However great the mistakes for which Constantine may be blamed, we cannot but maintain, without therefore shutting our eyes to the many inconveniences and defects which have in the course of years been brought to light, that it was through him that the Church entered upon that course in which she first became capable of *fully* carrying out her mission; that the State Church—or let us call it the national Church—is a thing which must and ought to exist, a thing which, despite all false individualism, must be maintained and defended.

Vinet, and all who occupy his standpoint, value the national Church at too low a rate, because they entirely overlook its *educational*, its pædagogic importance to the people. In desiring a flock of only personal believers, of those independently convinced, they forget that there are but very few who have really independent conviction, and that, at all events, the majority must be educated and brought up to it by being first placed under the influence of tradition and authority. The advocates of the free Church, by desiring only a flock of awakened and regenerate men, abandon the great multitude of the young and ignorant, who, unless some one takes them up, fall a prey to irreligion and all kinds of errors. Vinet's

Église libre has indeed had no small diffusion among the educated; but who would take charge of the lower classes, and especially the rural population, unless the clergy of the national Church did so? Experience, too, has everywhere shown that the high expectations which were formed of free Churches have by no means been fulfilled. It was supposed that when once the Church was free from the oppression of the State, a pentecostal season, like that of the period of first love during the first centuries, would again dawn. It has, however, been found that the pentecostal spirit, with its tongues of fire, does not appear, because its appearance "has been announced," that not merely external, but also internal conditions, which cannot be brought to pass at any moment, are indispensable preliminaries. No trace of extraordinary gifts of grace is discovered when we attend the public worship of free Churches, even if we are so fortunate as to hear "sound doctrine which cannot be condemned," and to find an irre-proachable administration of the sacraments. Without dis-paraging the free Churches, we think we may assert that there is by no means a higher life, a more thorough and serious Christianity in them, than in the national Churches, though the nature of the case involves the circumstance, that so long as the free Churches number only a smaller proportion of members, the weaknesses and defects, which always affect the mixed Church—for the Donatist dream of an absolutely pure and holy Church is never realized—will not appear in them in the same proportion and extent as in the national Churches.

H. Thiersch, in his excellent work, *Der Christliche Staat*, p. 235, gives remarkable testimony concerning the separation of Church and State. "I was," says he, "filled with youthful enthusiasm for the separation of Church and State. I thought I saw it rapidly approaching with the march of events. I hailed it as a deliverance from the paralyzing oppression of state-churchmanship, of police-churchmanship, which was heavy upon us in the sultry time before 1848. I expected that a new prosperity would spontaneously arise for the Church when it was liberated from the State. I hoped for the disappearance of hypocrisy and pretended Christianity, for a strengthening of Christian life and work. The object of my study and admiration was Christian antiquity—the time before Constantine. I hoped that the Church, separated from the secular power, would again become what it had been in the days of the martyrs. I thus found myself on exactly the same standpoint as Vinet."

" The experience of life, continued investigation, and maturer age have brought me to a more enlightened view."

§ 154.

But a separation of Church and State is not demanded in the name of religion only, but in that also of irreligion. Political and humanistic self-sufficiency has discovered that the State has no need of the Church, that the State as a legal institution is self-sufficing, that a country and kingdom are best governed without religion (*l'état est athée et doit l'être*), and that religion must be a private matter without influence upon public life. A widespread effort is also manifested (as already shown in the foregoing pages) to banish Christianity and the Church from public life, in proof of which we will only point to religionless diets, civil marriages, creedless schools, the purely civil system of poor laws, in which the co-operation of the clergy is sometimes entirely excluded, sometimes reduced to a minimum, the confiscation of Church property to the pocket of the State, whereby the clergy, where national Churches still exist, are changed into mere State officials, and other cognate ideals, to which purely civil burials are to be added.

We must, however, regard it as an impossibility that the irreligious State should ever be a reality, unless chaotic conditions, absolutely devoid of authority, first set in. Law and morals can be no *powers* in society without the binding and constraining authority of religion. There is one question to which we beg an answer, viz.: whether any State can dispense with an oath? and whether an oath, as a religious act, can have any actual meaning, without taking for granted a whole series of religious ideas?

§ 155.

Rothe's view of the relations between Church and State, which we can but briefly touch on, is very peculiar. He desires, indeed, that for the present the attempt should be made to maintain the national Church. But his idea is that the Church as an institution, as an arrangement and establishment, a power which in public life exercises an influence upon society as such, must recede and disappear in proportion as the State, which is in his eyes the only moral kingdom, developes; that the Church must submit to the law of history, and say to the State: Thou must increase, but I must decrease! In thus speaking, however, it is by no means Rothe's opinion that because the Church is to decrease and disappear, Christianity will also decrease. On the contrary, the golden age of Christianity will then first truly set in, the kingdom of God pervade the whole moral world, and Christian morality universally prevail. As long as the Church exists there is a relative contrast between religion and morality, and so long the one does not ensure the other. But their aim and destination, according to Rothe, is to be completely one, and this would render a special sphere for religion superfluous, though even then he finds himself obliged to let a minimum of cult (word and sacrament) still exist. On the other hand, the office (" the clerical " office, as he calls it) seems to disappear, because all will then be taught of God. The movement tending to this end began, according to Rothe, with the Reformation.

We certainly admit that through the Reformation both the State and morality were emancipated to self-dependency, placed in a relative independence of religion. But we maintain, *with* the Reformation, and *in opposition* to Rothe's view, that a certain relative contrast will always exist between the religious and the moral, though morality and religion are, in their inmost nature, one; that Sundays and working days, prayer and work, will at all times alternate with each other, and that both Sunday, with its public worship, and the clerical office will always maintain their independent importance. Rothe's error, in our view, consists in the fact of his regarding the entire absorption of religion by morality in secular matters as the climax of human development, or in his carrying out

the parable of the leaven in a one-sided manner, while omit-
ting to do justice to that of *the pearl*, which is thought of as
differing from all other possessions. As the leaven is dissolved
in the mass, and abolished as a separate element, so is religion
with Rothe resolved into morality, and, so to speak, only
tasted by means of the moral, without being enjoyed as a
separate and independent possession. But this is looking at
only one side' of the question. The other, namely the independence and self-existing excellence of religion, its *tran-
scendence* of all earthly possessions, of the State and moral life
in the State, are expressed in the parable of the pearl, which
holds good no less than that of the leaven.

If we test Rothe's view of the decrease and dissolution of
the Church by experience, it is indeed so far confirmed, as
the above-named tendency to banish the Church from public
life shows. But, on the other hand, experience by no means
confirms his optimistic expectation, that in proportion as this
takes place, Christian morality will more generally prevail,
and the kingdom of God more leaven the whole lump. We
willingly grant that churchmanship and Christianity are by no
means co-extensive, that among non-churchmen there are not
a few men in whom "unconscious Christianity" is found.
But as far as Rothe's optimistic view of the morality of the
present generation, which, in spite of its anti-churchism, is
said to be pervaded by the Christian leaven, is concerned,
such a view can be only shared by those who make too little
account of the effects of the old Adamic and anti-Christian
leaven, and at the same time form too high an estimate of
irreligious humanity, and view the latter through an idealizing
and embellishing medium.

§ 156.

However threatening and numerous the signs which seem
to announce the dissolution of national Churches, they should
not beguile or deter us from doing our utmost to uphold them.
That a time will come when this dissolution will occur, we
know from the sure word of prophecy, and its occurrence
cannot astonish us. But we must not incur the responsibility
of promoting it, and thus hastening the last days (the close of
this earthly dispensation), with their inevitable tribulations.

There are but two periods in history in which the free Christian Church is normal: the *first* and the *last* time, and both are periods of persecution. In the whole intervening period national Churches are normal, and free Churches to be regarded as exceptions. There are still, however, many Christian and conservative elements among the nations; reverence and adherence to good traditions still exist, and efforts for the continuance of national Churches must by no means be regarded as hopeless. We would, with Thiersch (*Der christliche Staat*, p. 89), designate the object to be striven for as the *sure stability of a national Church, combined with religious liberty.* A national Church must be capable of bearing the presence of formations of another kind, and differing from her own. She will be able also to learn even from the sects, inasmuch as these often represent, as in a mirror, a moment of truth, which has hitherto been neglected in the existing Church. For the rest, the future of national Churches is inseparable from that of Christian States. They stand, fall and rise again together.

CONSUMMATION OF THE KINGDOM OF GOD.

§ 157.

The social circles we have hitherto been considering are the earthly forms, by means of which both the whole human race and individuals are to be fashioned and educated for the kingdom of God, that they may be ripened for that holy kingdom of love which is also the kingdom of righteousness, truth and beauty. But the end set before mankind cannot be attained on earth, and the earthly form which the divine kingdom assumes must at last be burst through and broken off as a temporary covering, when it has fulfilled its temporary end. Here below, the kingdom of God, which would prove itself to be that of true humanity, still remains only *one to come.* The period when it will be a *kingdom come*, its *consummation*, can only commence by the abolition of the whole present earthly dispensation, which, with its material sphere of time and space, is but "a temporary arrangement." In this earthly dispensation, the kingdom of

God must continually contend with the false kingdom of the world, and the tares grow together with the wheat. That great alliance of nations which we call Christendom, is not to be regarded merely as an earthly type, a shadow of good things to come ; but also as a Babel, a kingdom of confusions, with all its false churchmanship, false politics, false prophets, producing a Charivari of voices in contradiction with themselves and each other; with that complete hell upon earth formed by the influences both of human selfishness and evil spirits, with the whole poisoned and pestiferous atmosphere which we breathe, and which is but very slightly improved by partial crises and purifications of the air. All this must one day be put an end to. The world's history is not of itself sufficient to be the world's judgment. A last and final judgment, a crisis must take place, by means of which the transition to *a perfectly new order of things, another dispensation,* may be accomplished.

However little it may agree with the notions of the day, its fancies for making the best of this world, its naturalistic, humanistic and super-civilised Utopias, we nevertheless look for the last day, the day of the Lord. For He who is the Head of His kingdom will Himself return with His kingdom, for judgment as well as for redemption, as we acknowledge in the Apostles' Creed when we say of the Saviour who ascended into heaven, who sitteth at the right hand of the Almighty Father, that from thence He shall come to judge the quick and the dead. This day of the Lord, however, will elapse in a series of catastrophes and periods of time, concerning which the prophetic Scriptures give us farther details. To this "sure word of prophecy" (2 Pet. i. 19) the Church is referred for the understanding of the signs of the times, for the recognition of the last times and the last things, not that it may surrender itself to fantastic delusions, and the unfruitful researches of a vain curiosity, but may know what it has practically to prepare for and to encounter. Certainly, prophecy concerning the last times is, to those who seek to interpret its details, a word hard to be understood, because so much is figuratively and symbolically expressed, because things nearest at hand and farthest off are crowded together, because here " a thousand years are as one day, and one day as a thousand years" (2 Pet. iii. 8). But independently of the varying explanations of details, in which we are for the most part left to conjecture, but which will become plainer to us in proportion as we draw nearer and nearer to their fulfilment, we may name as settled points, which social ethics can and must embrace, these three events: 1. The great apostasy and the antichrist; 2. The golden age and reign of blessedness on earth; 3. The perfect kingdom of heavenly happiness and glory. Much of what is here spoken of has received partial anticipatory fulfilments, continually repeated, since the beginning of the Church. We are now, however, concerned with the last and *complete* fulfilment.

THE GREAT APOSTASY AND THE ANTICHRIST.

§ 158.

It is decidedly and plainly predicted in the prophetic Scriptures, that evil must attain its supreme manifestation upon earth before the Lord comes. In the last times, a great and widespread *apostasy from Christianity* will take place, and Christendom become a complete Babylon. The national Churches will then be in a state of corruption, because false doctrines and unchristian church government will have got the upper hand. Babylon is called a whore, because she has broken the covenant with the Lord, in contrast with the believing Church, the faithful spouse, who cleaves to the Lord, as the bride to the bridegroom, continues in the covenant and waits for His coming. Babylon, Christendom corrupt both in Church and State, sits by many waters, and speaks in her heart, and boasts: " I sit a queen, and am no widow, and shall see no sorrow." The waters in prophetic diction signify the nations; and Babylon thus includes the varied multitude of the nations. Worldly luxury, combined with wealth, trade and extensive commerce, exercises a widespread dominion; ungodliness and debauchery accompany it, for Babylon is the abode of all unclean spirits. But in " one hour," *i.e. suddenly*, Babylon will fall, a sudden catastrophe will ensue, an overthrow of the social condition, of this whole world of culture and civilisation, with its sham Christianity. Then will antichrist and the antichristian kingdom be manifested. This designates a still greater degree of wickedness than Babylon, even the climax of apostasy, the consummation of evil on earth.[1] In the Revelation of St. John, antichrist is represented as the beast which rises up out of *the sea* (xiii. 1), the sea of nations with its roaring waves. We should here, however, remember that the beast in the Revelation does not so much designate an individual as a power pervading all history, a political power which arises from the turbulent, anarchical multitude of nations,—a view which does not exclude the notion that this power may in the last days make its appearance in a single individual. At all times there have been many antichrists (*i.e.* opposers of Christ) in the world; but according to the saying of St. Paul (2 Thess. ii. 3 sqq.), all the antichristian and Satanic powers will at last be concentrated in a single human being. The Middle Ages for a period saw antichrist in Mohammed, the Reformation era in the Pope,—a view which seems in our times to have received special corroboration from the Vatican Council (July 18, 1870), when Pius IX. placed himself in the temple of God in Christ's stead, and said of his poor, perishable, human words: "Heaven and earth shall pass away, but my words shall not pass away." At any rate, the Pope as such bears within himself great antichristian elements, and certainly belongs to Babylon, which in its narrower signification is the corrupt Church. According, however, to the features drawn in Scripture, antichrist can be only understood as a worldly tyrant, a despot, after the pattern of Antiochus Epiphanes, a ruler who founds a secular kingdom, a universal monarchy. He is called " the adversary " (viz. of Christ), the man of sin, the wicked one (the lawless), because he exalts himself above all law, whether human or divine. His appearance is marked by Satanic signs and wonders. He denies that Christ is come in the flesh (1 John iv. 3), which the Pope does not do, exalts himself above all that is called God, or the worship of God, and gives out that he is God (2 Thess. ii. 4). His ally is the false prophet, who is described in the Revelation (xiii. 11) as the beast out of *the earth* (*i.e.* the ordered, *cultivated* world, in opposition to the beast out of the sea,

---

[1] Rev. xvii. xviii.

nations in a state of turbulence). The false prophet, or the beast out of the earth, is like a lamb in appearance, but speaks like a dragon, speaks poisonous, seductive and deceitful words, brings forward such proofs against the Christian faith, that, if it were possible, the very elect would be deceived, and think that Christianity had been but a dream which Christendom had dreamt through a series of centuries, but from which it had now awakened to be as God.[1]

Then will great tribulations befall believers, since all who do not receive the mark (the sign and word) of the beast, who will not do homage to the antichristian world-power, must suffer martyrdom, while the multitudes live in worldliness and security. None who have not received the mark of the beast may buy or sell (Rev. xiii. 17), *i.e.* have the rights of citizenship; for such there is no longer room in the world. Antichrist founds a new state religion by strong delusions, into which the Lord suffers all to fall who have not received the truth in the love of it, that they might be saved (2 Thess. ii. 8), a Cæsareopapy of the worst kind, a world religion, which ends in the worship of the image of the beast, *i.e.* of the human spirit which has apostatized from God and made itself God. It is called a beast because it denies what is truly human, and with all its culture and civilisation is more and more tending to bestiality, to rude force and carnal lust. Antiquity furnishes us with foreshadows in Nebuchadnezzar, who set up his image for adoration; in Alexander the Great, who desired to be esteemed the son of Zeus; in the Roman emperors, before whose images incense was offered; and in more modern times in Napoleon I., who, though he complained that in these days such a thing as passing for a son of Zeus was no longer possible, had no hesitation about being called on certain occasions " the saviour " of the world and of the human race, and ordered that expressions of adoration concerning himself should be inserted in his catechism. Those who think it extravagant to suppose that such things, which as yet we know of only in the form of prognostications, should ever become a well-defined reality, cannot yet have directed their attention to the many antichristian elements with which the times are big. All who have any degree of skill in placing

<hr>

[1] Comp. Auberlen, *Der Prophet Daniel*, Basel 1854.

the signs of the times in the light of God's word, will not mistake the fact that those elements are more and more showing themselves from which the false prophet is to be developed: atheistic, materialistic systems, denying God and the existence of spirit, and based upon a purely physical view of existence; an æsthetic literature, which by its poetry, fictions and romances diffuses the gospel of the flesh among the masses, and upsets all moral notions; a daily press and journalism, which often proves a prelude to what is predicted in the prophetic word (Rev. xvi. 13), viz. that out of the mouth of the dragon and out of the false prophet shall proceed three *unclean* spirits like *frogs*, those creatures of the swamp, the morass and the mire, whose croaking, powerless as it is in itself, nevertheless produces a sound which penetrates to a distance and is heard all around, repeating the same thing day after day, and who are therefore well adapted, by their eloquence, to delude men, such as they now are, and to bring them into the right disposition, the right state of mind for the service of antichrist. Nor can the political state of the times be misunderstood, especially the prevailing tendency to banish Christianity from public life, to undermine all authority, and to break with all historical tradition, as furnishing many elements from which antichrist may one day emerge.

Not false democracy, then, will be the last of the historical events which is to precede the coming of the Lord, though many are of opinion that the Red republic will be so, because the beast is described as *scarlet* (Rev. xvii. 3). The last development will be *Cæsarism*, an absolute despotism. We may, however, well say that both are but different appearances of the same potency. The Cæsarism of the last days will certainly be scarlet, and revolution is the inevitably necessary presupposition of antichrist. The Apostle Paul has told us (2 Thess. ii. 6) that antichrist cannot come till a power, not further defined by the apostle, but a hindering power, well known to his readers of those days ($\tau\grave{o}$ $\kappa\alpha\tau\acute{e}\chi o\nu$, $\acute{o}$ $\kappa\alpha\tau\acute{e}\chi\omega\nu$), one which " withholdeth," and which he looks upon as beneficent, conservative and preserving, is taken away. By this withholding power we understand the good spirit still active in heathenism, the moral powers of life, and, above all, the moral *legal* institutions, which even in the heathen world are an object of reverence to men, lawful authorities, historical institutions, and good traditions among the nations, the only things which contain in them a power of resistance to a state of lawlessness. Not till all this, which also has its personal depositaries and representatives, is taken out of the way by war and revolution, and a state of things in which there is absolutely no authority comes to pass, can the beast, according to the full sense of prophecy, rise up out of the sea, seize the sceptre, and appear as the all-ruling power.

The believing Church is directed, during this whole period of tribulation and continuance of the antichristian government, to the words : " Here is the patience and faith of the saints " (Rev. xiii. 10). The parable of " the wise and foolish virgins " (Matt. xxv. 1–13) will then be fulfilled in the widest sense. While the Lord delays His coming, while believers are surrounded by the material powers of persecution and the spiritual delusions of the false prophet, they are tempted to become spiritually faint and wearied, and to slumber and sleep, with lamps burnt down and going out. The question therefore is, when at midnight the cry is made : " Behold, the bridegroom cometh, go ye forth to meet him," to have oil for their lamps, that they may not be shut out as unfit to meet the Lord, because they have suffered both the Spirit and His light to be extinguished. The question is to adhere to the prophetic word, and to take heed thereto, as to a light shining in a dark place (2 Pet. i. 19), which has faithfully told us of all before, that none of these things may, when it happens, come upon us unawares.

THE GOLDEN AGE.—THE CONSUMMATION.

§ 159.

If what has just been alluded to—an evening red with blood--were to be the final close of human history, the pessimist view of the world would come off victorious. But there is a day to follow for mankind, not only the great day of eternity, but a day of bright prospects on earth. The prophetic word tells us that the time of antichrist is to be suddenly interrupted and put an end to, by the coming of the

Lord, by His manifestation in a visible and extraordinary manner, to found, by a fresh exercise of His power, a new era. He will "consume antichrist *with the spirit of His mouth*, and destroy him with the brightness of His coming" (2 Thess. ii. 8), "and establish the millennial kingdom" (Rev. xx. 4). We must, however, remark that the definition of time has here also only a *symbolical* meaning (a thousand years are with the Lord as one day, and one day as a thousand years). Many fantastic notions have indeed been combined with this prophecy, and the mode of its fulfilment must for the most part remain in very undefined outline; but the substance of the expectation here held out is, and will be, the universal supremacy of Christianity upon earth. Even before the final consummation in the kingdom of glory, the Church is to experience an earthly consummation, a sabbatic period, which, as a time of rest, looks back to the conflicts and tribulations of past times, and at the same time as a preparation for the sabbath to the future glory. This period will exhibit the results, the ripened fruit of all past labour for the kingdom of God, and will at the same time serve as a pledge and prelude of the heavenly kingdom; for the powers of the heavenly world will then be beheld and tasted as they have never before been in this world. "Satan will be bound" (Rev. xx. 2 sq.), *i.e.* antichristian principles will be banished from public life and kept in their impotence, and Christianity alone will rule in public life and its institutions. The kingdom and lordship of the world have now become God's, belong to Him and to Christ (Rev. xi. 15). Now will be found in a true and full sense an alliance of nations, and, according to hints given us in Scripture, the converted nation of Israel will be at its head, Christendom will be one flock under one Shepherd (Christ), and the ideals of humanity, a Christian family and a Christian State, Christian art and Christian science, will be fully realized. This *golden age* will be a period of earthly *consummation*, but at the same time a period of restoration and revival. Justice will then be done to truths long laid aside and suppressed, to efforts which were checked and forgotten, and what was lost through negligence in the preceding development will now be recovered. Labour upon earth will then find its conclusion in its oneness with peace upon earth.   That prophetic word, " on earth peace," in the praises of the heavenly hosts at Bethlehem, will then find its perfect fulfilment.

It is only when we look forward to such a time that we can say, that this *earthly life* will one day attain its relative independence and importance.   This earthly life is not always to continue a life under crosses and trials, in a vale of sorrow ; but, like life in each of God's worlds, to develope a special excellence by means of the gifts of nature as well as those of grace.   This special beauty and excellence of earthly life will reach its most perfect manifestation in the golden age, which will be truly a time of refreshing (Acts iii. 20).   The men to whom it will be granted to dwell on the earth in those days will live a life in the *fulness* of both nature and grace, as far as such a life is possible under *earthly* conditions.   " A lover of earth,"—a poetic expression, applicable not only in a bad, but also in a good sense,—one who delights to behold the glory of God in these earthly forms and fashions, and to see it as comprised within the limits here prescribed, and bringing forth by their means just this wondrously copious play of colour ; one who rejoices to live in this human community, in these dwellings and tents, temporary as they are,—such an one must long and yearn after a time like that described, because without it human nature could never fully and thoroughly live out its life on earth, could not experience, beside its fulness of sorrows, that fulness of joy and happiness of which it is capable.   In this golden age the most perfect delight in the present life will be united with a waiting and longing for the life to come, the powers of which are already so vividly felt.

This kingdom, however, is only one of *earthly happiness* in a Christian sense, and nothing more.   Its limitation is that it does not remain, that it is not " a kingdom which cannot be moved."   Sin still exists, though its power is nonsuited, restricted and repressed.   Death, too, is there, and with it also the transitoriness and vanity to which the creature is subject (Rom. viii. 20).   They, however, are not without some support in Scripture who think that the power of death will be also restrained and repressed, that diseases will be far fewer, and of a milder character, that men will live far longer than now, as they did in the times of the patriarchs, that the inhabitants of the earth will then breathe a purer atmosphere, that even in the animal and vegetable worlds the noxious and destructive powers will be kept in check, and that all nature, becoming more receptive of the invisible influence of celestial and beneficent powers, will present to view rather a state of peace than one of destructive conflict (Isa. xi. 6 sqq., lxv. 20 sqq.). In this great period of transition, communications between heaven and earth are also conceivable, appearances from the other world, visible manifestations of Christ to believers, as in the forty days following His resurrection (comp. the author's *Dogmatics*, p. 452, Clark's translation). We cannot, however, in the present connection enter farther into these transcendental conditions, but must rather turn our attention to the moral world and life. We only add, that Satan is bound not by any human power, not by culture and civilisation,—an expectation which denotes the worst kind of Chiliasm,—but by an approach, a coming of the Lord to effect by miraculous agency, not only in the realm of nature, but in actual human life, a purification of the social atmosphere, by means of which all the good which was restrained under antichrist is set free to develope itself. But just because the devil is only *bound*, there is but a relative and not an absolute difference between this state of things and the present. Scripture tells us, and the transitory nature of happiness involves it, that there is an evening to this earthly kingdom, that Satan is again loosed (Rev. xx. 7), and that a great apostasy again takes place.

Not till then does the last, visible coming (the glorious return) of the Lord ensue, and with it the last judgment, the new heavens and the new earth, the eternal kingdom of blessedness and glory. This kingdom remains in *the power of an endless life* (Heb. vii. 16), while life during the millennial kingdom is terminable. Not till then will the day which has no evening dawn. It belongs not to ethics but to dogmatics to treat more particularly of the *general* resurrection to take place at Christ's last coming, of the *first* resurrection connected with the millennial kingdom, and of the state of souls in the realm of the dead.

WAITING FOR THE DAY OF THE LORD.

§ 160.

To wait for the day of the Lord means to expect the last
advent or appearing of Christ for the consummation of the
kingdom of God, and includes the expectation of those
catastrophes, events and periods by means of which He will
at His own time introduce that consummation. The Church
has from the beginning been directed to keep this object in
view, and to watch as those who wait by night for their
Lord's return. The night during which the Church is to watch
is this whole era. The return of the Lord, together with the
judgment and full redemption, is to be present to the mind
as a thing imminent, but accompanied by the consciousness
that the crisis may possibly be still remote, whether because
of certain works of the Lord, which He will perform during
the present era, or because He will still exercise long-suffering
towards the world, and so grant it a longer respite or space
for repentance (2 Pet. iii. 9). These two aspects of waiting
for the day of the Lord are brought to view with typical
significance in the apostolic Church. It has often been said,
that the apostles were in error in expecting the coming of
the Lord during their own lifetime. Such an assertion
arises from a misconception of the prophetic mode of view
and the prophetic manner of expression, according to which
the remote draws near and appears as present, and from a
one-sided apprehension of single passages, wrested from their
connection with the whole. The apostles indeed say expressly
that much must happen before the Lord appears for the final
consummation of all things, that antichrist must first come,
also that the preaching of the gospel in the whole world and
the conversion of Israel must first take place. Besides, we
cannot suppose that they entirely forget their Lord's parable
of the kingdom of heaven being like leaven, which is to
penetrate the whole mass. Undoubtedly they imagined that
all this would happen in a far shorter time than was really
necessary. But this limitation of their historical and temporal circle of vision is in perfect harmony with the Lord's
saying (Matt. xxiv. 36), according to which that day and

hour is known only to the Father in heaven. It is, moreover, quite unessential to their religious view of the world, which combines the two moments here necessary, and which are to accompany the Church throughout this whole era.

There are then two extremes which must always be opposed in waiting for the day of the Lord. The one is to conceive of this day as removed to a distance enveloped in impenetrable obscurity. The transition from such a conception to unbelief is easy, and one which appeared even in the days of the apostles, when scoffers said: "Where is the promise of His coming? for since the fathers fell asleep, all things continue as they were from the foundation of the world" (2 Pet. iii. 4). And even if the promise is embraced as an article of faith, but not regarded as casting light on or having reference to the present, the result will be a worldly security, a false peace, contented with this world and its ever reiterated course. This false security appears not alone in the merely worldly-minded, who, as in the days of Noah and Lot, only build and plant, and are engrossed in earthly concerns; it is found not alone in those who have neither eyes nor hearts for the signs of the times and the perils of the Church, and many of whom will, in the times of antichrist, receive the mark of the beast, be full of enthusiasm for the progress of civilisation, and raise it to the very heavens. This false security will also be found in the "slumbering virgins," who are at all times numerous, viz. believers, who, although they began their course with lamps brightly burning, have in a spiritual sense fallen asleep. To all these will the day of the Lord come like a thief in the night, and they will be as much terrified as surprised when at midnight the cry is made, when those great revolutions occur, in the presence of which they will feel that they have suddenly lost their bearings, and are utterly helpless before those things which are coming upon the world. It may here be not out of place to remember, that in a purely personal respect there is something which might no less destroy this false security than the thought of the last judgment, viz. the thought of death, which must throughout his whole lifetime be hovering before every man, as near and inevitable, though its appointed day and hour are always uncertain even in old age. But in the expectation of the last day, the question is not so much the relation in which the individual stands, as that in which the world and the Church stand to the Lord. And in this respect the Christian view of the world will become faded and ineffective, if the day of the Lord is removed to a dim and remote distance. It will then be more and more forgotten, that the object set not only before individuals, but before the Church, God's kingdom on earth, is not a mundane, but a super-mundane one, viz. the kingdom of heavenly glory, that even the future golden age upon earth will be but transitory, and also that the way which leads to this period of earthly happiness is through crosses and tribulations. Through such negligence concerning her future, the Church will be brought to a one-sided optimistic view of secular affairs, will herself fall into worldly conformity and repose. That holy desire which finds its expression in the sigh: " Come, Lord Jesus " (Rev. xxii. 20), will be more and more stifled, and that frame of mind developed in which the unfaithful servant says: " My Lord delayeth His coming," and proceeds to act accordingly by beating his fellow-servants, and eating and drinking with the drunken (Matt. xxiv. 48 sq.), a state of things reminding us of so many occurrences not only in the Papacy, but also in false state-churchmanship.

It is the other extreme when men imagine the day of the Lord so near, as even to think they can calculate the day and hour, in opposition to the express declaration of Christ Himself, that " of that day and hour knoweth no man " (Matt. xxv. 13 ; Acts i. 7); and when in their thoughtlessness they pass over middle terms, events of which Scripture says decidedly that they must occur before the Lord comes. As the opposite to the above-named worldly security, and easy contentment with this world, there is in their case a morbid desire for and grasping at anything new, while here too false security sets in, though from an opposite quarter, viz. from a false confidence in an imagined knowledge, a supposed infallible perception of the signs of the times. A false pessimist view of the condition of the world is formed, which is regarded as so radically corrupt that the Lord must of necessity descend, rain down fire from heaven, and put an end to the whole. With this pessimism is combined, as a rule, a false optimism, the gaze of hope being not so much directed to the eternal kingdom of glory, as the heart, mind and aspirations set upon the millennial kingdom, and surrendered to imaginations, more or less carnal, of a state of earthly enjoyment, in which the saints are to rule over and exercise vengeance upon the ungodly. This is the *Chiliasm* which is rejected in the Confession of Augsburg (Art. 17). With these impatient and really worldly aspirations, the fact is overlooked that the Lord is long-suffering (2 Pet. iii. 9), and that those, too, who entertain them stand in need of His patience and forbearance for their own purification. Duties are also neglected, because interest is withdrawn from the affairs of the world around, and all co-operation in the tasks of a community, regarded as doomed to destruction, refused, as so much labour lost. The consequence of such a view is an idle expecting and waiting, without any energetic exertion. Its adherents are like a man who, without any certain and urgent reasons, expects every day to die next morning, and therefore enters into no more worldly enterprises, lets all his uncompleted work alone, because it is no longer of any use to try and finish it, and confines himself entirely to what concerns his final preparation; while all his calculations may be overthrown by the fact that the Lord may have decided concerning him, that he shall live some years longer, shall be responsible for the use he makes of this present year, and shall one day give an account of it.

To *Irvingism* we are indisputably indebted for having contributed to the revival of eschatological notions, and of the great hope of the Church in our times. But it cannot be absolved from the reproach of having a too pessimist view of the state of the world, and regarding *a priori* the Lord's advent as too imminent. And when it teaches that the "rapture of the saints," of true believers, *i.e.* of *its* adherents, their disappearance from the stage of this world without death intervening, will take place before the appearance of antichrist, and that only weak and imperfect Christians will have to go through the times of antichrist, and that for punishment as well as for purification, we are constrained to ask whether this desire to be received up into glory, without needing first to tread the way of the cross and of the last tribulation, may not be an erroneous anticipation, whether this is not to regard from a too optimist view-point the preparedness and ripeness of " the saints " for this supernatural departure. A being caught up to meet the Lord is indeed, according to 2 Thess. iv. 17, to take place ; but in whatever period we place it, we cannot, at all events consistently with the law universally established in the development of the kingdom of God, help accepting it as a fact, that such glory cannot appear till after a time of tribulation. "We must through much tribulation enter the kingdom of God " (Acts xix. 22). " If we suffer with Him, we shall also reign with Him " (2 Tim. ii. 12).[1]

§ 161.

The ethic view-point to be at all times and under all circumstances adhered to, in waiting for the last day, is, to wait for the Lord in the belief that He will come quickly, but not to think that this "quickly" can be measured by our clocks ; never to suffer the holy longing for the redemption of the Church, its freedom from the bondage of corruption, to be extinguished in our hearts, to watch and pray against the great temptations which have come or are yet to come upon us, but so to wait for the Lord that when He comes He may find us *working* in the duties of our calling, in just the *tasks of the present moment*. The chief concern of our times is to expect that coming of antichrist, which so many signs already announce, and which will be inseparable from a closer union of Christians with each other, a more intensive gathering to secret communion with the Lord in the hour of darkness. We must, however, by no means so wait for antichrist as ourselves to hasten his coming, by withdrawing from the duties of Christian association ; but must, on the contrary, devote all our energies to the strengthening of those conservative upholding and withholding forces of the age, which serve to delay his coming. And at all times we should lay to heart those words of Christ, the meaning of which extends not to teachers only, but to Christians in general, to each in that state of life to which he has been called : " Let your loins be girded," hold yourselves in readiness to start on a journey,

---

[1] Luthardt, *Die Lehre von den letzten Dingen*, p. 54. L. Gude, *Die Bedeutung des Irvingianismus in unserer Zeit* (Danish).

" and your lights burning " (Luke xii. 35); and : " Who then is a faithful and wise servant, whom his Lord hath made ruler over His household, to give them meat in due season ? Blessed is that servant, whom his Lord when He cometh shall find so *doing*."

INDEX OF SUBJECTS.

INDEX OF NAMES.

AGRICOLA, J., an antinomist, i. 439.
Antigone, family affection, ii. 22 ; lamentation over premature death, ii. 372.
Apocalypse, i. 164, iii. 355.
Aristotle, eudaimonism, i. 152 ; his pessimism, i. 183 ; on natural and ethic virtues, ii. 7 ; on the habit of virtue, ii. 41 ; description of virtue, ii. 64 ; on slavery, iii. 131.
Arnauld, A., on frequent communion, ii. 196.
Athenians, the, desirous of new things, ii. 93.
Auberlen, C. A., iii. 354, note.
Augsburg, Confession and Apology of, on the *ordinationes Dei*, iii. 298 ; on the Anabaptists, iii. 396 ; on the Church in the special sense of the word, i. 445 ; on the use of the sacraments (N.B. Art. 13), ii. 193; on the remembrance of the saints, ii. 264 ; on intercession for the dead, ii. 270.
Augustine, on the mass of corruption, i. 127 ; on self-knowledge, i. 291 ; a contemplative and practical character, i. 342 ; desire for God, i. 364 ; *Coge intrare*, i. 445.
Augustinianism, i. 113.

BAADER, Franz, on nature in God, i. 68 ; Christian theism, i. 221 ; on the humiliation of Christ, i. 261, note ; on power and authority, i. 352 ; on existence freed from time, i. 427 ; on Thorwaldsen's statue of Schiller, ii. 61 ; on the kingdom of darkness, ii. 129, note ; on dissection, ii. 274 ; on the oppression of the law, ii. 340; his journals, ii. 410 ; on policy, i. 183 ; on the representation of the fourth class, iii. 241 ; on evolution and revolution, iii. 230; on the Holy Alliance, iii. 239.
Babel, the tower of, iii. 95.

Bach's passion music of St. Matthew, iii. 245.
Baggesen, on Sanderson, the blind optician, i. 84, note ; on friendship, iii. 73 ; a national poet, iii. 248.
Baruch, the scribe of the prophet Jeremiah, ii. 336.
Beccaria, on capital punishment, iii. 179.
Bengel, Alb., on eschatological theologian, i. 39.
Bernhard, St., on contemplation and business, ii. 305.
Böhme, Jas., on nature in God, i. 68.
Bossuet, J., on Fénélon's disinterested love to God, i. 321 ; his *Politique tirée de la Sainte Ecriture*, iii. 100 ; an advocate of absolutism, iii. 188.
Brandis, A., ii. 64, note.
Brethren, the United, their one-sided love of the Lord, i. 310.
Brorson, H. A., on the grace of God in Christ, i. 329.
Bruyère, La, ii. 68.
Buridan's ass, i. 118.
Byron, Lord, on tedium, i. 162 ; his pessimism, i. 178 ; on the unhappiness of emancipation, i. 239 ; read by English workmen, iii. 147.

CAIAPHAS, i. 384.
Calderon, P., iii. 245.
Calixtus, G., i. 36.
Calvin, J., and Christian joy, ii. 387.
Carlyle, Thomas, on operatives in English cotton factories, iii. 147.
Carpocrates, the Gnostic, i. 386, ii. 111.
Cassandra, i. 367.
Chantal, Mme., i. 327.
Christ, the ethic Mediator with God, i. 23 ; our Example and Saviour, i. 242 ; unique in history, i. 242 ; a lawgiver, i. 381, 383 ; the heavenly Samaritan, ii. 202 ; the enemy of all falsehoods of necessity, ii. 226 ; His meekness in suffering, ii. 258 ; His poverty, ii. 364 ; His celibacy, iii.

INDEX OF TEXTS.

OLD TESTAMENT.

NEW TESTAMENT.

PUBLICATIONS OF
T. & T. CLARK,
38 GEORGE STREET, EDINBURGH.

Abbott (T. K., B.D., D.Lit.)—EPHESIANS AND COLOSSIANS. (*International Critical Commentary.*) Post 8vo, 10s. 6d.

Adams (Prof. John. B.Sc.)—PRIMER ON TEACHING, with special reference to Sunday School Work. 6d.

Adamson (Rev. R. M., M.A.)—THE CHRISTIAN DOCTRINE OF LORD'S SUPPER. Imperial 16mo (8 × 6), 4s. 6d. net.

Adamson (T., D.D.)—THE SPIRIT OF POWER. 2nd Ed., fcap. 8vo, 1s.

Ahlfeld (Dr.), etc.—THE VOICE FROM THE CROSS. Cr. 8vo, price 5s.

Aitken (Rev. James, M.A.)—THE BOOK OF JOB. With Introduction and Notes. Crown 8vo, 1s. 6d.

Alcock (Deborah)—THE SEVEN CHURCHES OF ASIA. 1s.

Alexander (Prof. W. Lindsay)—BIBLICAL THEOLOGY. Two vols. 8vo, 21s.

Allen (Prof. A. V. G., D.D.)—CHRISTIAN INSTITUTIONS. (*International Theological Library.*) Post 8vo, 12s.

Ancient Faith in Modern Light, The. 8vo, 10s. 6d.

Andrews (S. J.)—THE LIFE OF OUR LORD. Large post 8vo, 9s.

Ante-Nicene Christian Library—A COLLECTION OF ALL THE WORKS OF THE FATHERS OF THE CHRISTIAN CHURCH PRIOR TO THE COUNCIL OF NICÆA. Twenty-four vols. 8vo, Subscription price, £6, 6s. Selection of Four Volumes at Subscription price of 21s. *Additional Volume, containing MSS. discovered since the completion of the Series,* 12s. 6d. net.

Augustine's Works—Edited by MARCUS DODS, D.D. Fifteen vols. 8vo, Subscription price, £3, 19s. net. Selection of Four Volumes at Subscription price of 21s.

Balfour (R. G., D.D.)—CENTRAL TRUTHS AND SIDE ISSUES. 3s. 6d.

Ball (W. E., LL.D.)—ST. PAUL AND THE ROMAN LAW. Post 8vo, 4s. 6d.

Ballard (Frank, M.A., B.Sc.)—THE MIRACLES OF UNBELIEF. Sixth Edition. Post 8vo, 2s. 6d. net.

Bannerman (Prof.)—THE CHURCH OF CHRIST. Two vols. 8vo, 21s.

Bannerman (D. D., D.D.)—THE DOCTRINE OF THE CHURCH. 8vo, 12s.

Bartlet (Prof. J. Vernon, M.A.)—THE APOSTOLIC AGE: ITS LIFE, DOCTRINE, WORSHIP, AND POLITY. (*Eras of Church History.*) Crown 8vo, 6s.

Baumgarten (Professor)—APOSTOLIC HISTORY. Three vols. 8vo, 18s. net.

Bayne (P., LL.D.)—THE FREE CHURCH OF SCOTLAND. Post 8vo, 3s. 6d.

Beck (Dr.)—OUTLINES OF BIBLICAL PSYCHOLOGY. Crown 8vo, 4s.

—— PASTORAL THEOLOGY OF THE NEW TESTAMENT. Crown 8vo, 6s.

Bengel—GNOMON OF THE NEW TESTAMENT. With Original Notes, Explanatory and Illustrative. Five vols. 8vo, Subscription price, 31s. 6d. *Cheaper Edition, the five volumes bound in three,* 24s.

Besser's CHRIST THE LIFE OF THE WORLD. Price 6s.

Beveridge (Rev. John, B.D.)—THE COVENANTERS. (*New Bible Class Primer.*) Paper covers, 6d.; cloth covers, 8d.

Beveridge (Rev. W., M.A.)—A SHORT HISTORY OF THE WESTMINSTER ASSEMBLY. Crown 8vo, 2s. 6d. net.

Beyschlag (W., D.D.)—NEW TESTAMENT THEOLOGY. Two vols. demy 8vo, Second Edition, 18s. net.

Bible Class Handbooks. Crown 8vo. Forty-seven Volumes, 1s. 3d. to 3s. each. Edited by Prof. MARCUS DODS, D.D., and ALEX. WHYTE, D.D. *Detailed List free on application.*

*** Detailed Catalogue free on application.*

Bible Class Primers. Forty-four now issued in the Series. Edited by Princ. S. D. F. SALMOND, D.D. Paper covers, 6d. each ; free by post, 7d. In cloth, 8d. ; free by post, 9d. *Detailed List free on application.*

Bible Dictionary. Edited by JAS. HASTINGS, D.D. *Special Prospectus on application.* In Five Volumes, imperial 8vo, price per Volume, in cloth, 28s. ; in half-morocco, 34s. Sets can also be had in various styles of leather bindings.

Bigg (Prof. C., D.D.)—ST. PETER AND ST. JUDE. (*International Critical Commentary.*) Post 8vo, 10s. 6d.

Blaikie (Prof. W. G., D.D.)—THE PREACHERS OF SCOTLAND FROM THE 6TH TO THE 19TH CENTURY. Post 8vo, 7s. 6d.

Blake (Buchanan, B.D.)—HOW TO READ THE PROPHETS. Part I.—The Pre-Exilian Minor Prophets (with Joel). Second Edition, 4s. Part II.—Isaiah (ch. i.-xxxix.). Third Edition, 2s. 6d. Part III.—Jeremiah, 4s. Part IV.—Ezekiel, 4s. Part V.—Isaiah (ch. xl.-lxvi.), and the Post-Exilian Prophets. *The Series being now complete, Messrs. Clark offer the Set of Five Volumes for 15s.*

———— JOSEPH AND MOSES : FOUNDERS OF ISRAEL. Crown 8vo, 4s.

Bleek's INTRODUCTION TO THE NEW TESTAMENT. 2 vols. 8vo, 12s. net.

Briggs (Prof. C. A., D.D.)—GENERAL INTRODUCTION TO THE STUDY OF HOLY SCRIPTURE (*Replacing the Author's* 'Biblical Study,' *entirely re-written and greatly enlarged*). 8vo, 12s. net.

———— THE MESSIAH OF THE APOSTLES. Post 8vo, 7s. 6d.

———— THE MESSIAH OF THE GOSPELS. Post 8vo, 6s. 6d.

———— THE BIBLE, THE CHURCH, AND THE REASON. Post 8vo, 6s. 6d.

Brockelmann (C.)—LEXICON SYRIACUM. With a Preface by Professor T. NÖLDEKE. Crown 4to, 30s. net.

Brown (Prof. W. Adams)—THE ESSENCE OF CHRISTIANITY. Post 8vo, 6s. net.

Bruce (Prof. A. B., D.D.)—THE TRAINING OF THE TWELVE ; exhibiting the Twelve Disciples under Discipline for the Apostleship. 6th Ed., 10s. 6d.

———— THE HUMILIATION OF CHRIST. 5th Edition, 8vo, 10s. 6d.

———— THE KINGDOM OF GOD ; or, Christ's Teaching according to the Synoptical Gospels. Post 8vo, 7s. 6d.

———— APOLOGETICS ; OR, CHRISTIANITY DEFENSIVELY STATED. (*International Theological Library.*) Third Edition, post 8vo, 10s. 6d.

———— ST. PAUL'S CONCEPTION OF CHRISTIANITY. Post 8vo, 7s. 6d.

———— THE EPISTLE TO THE HEBREWS : The First Apology for Christianity. Second Edition, post 8vo, 7s. 6d.

Bruce (Rev. R., D.D., Hon. Canon of Durham Cathedral.)—APOSTOLIC ORDER AND UNITY. Crown 8vo, 2s. 6d. net.

Bruce (W. S., D.D.)—THE ETHICS OF THE OLD TESTAMENT. Cr. 8vo, 4s.

———— THE FORMATION OF CHRISTIAN CHARACTER. Crown 8vo, 5s.

Buhl (Prof. F.)—CANON AND TEXT OF THE OLD TESTAMENT. 8vo, 7s. 6d.

Bungener (Felix)—ROME AND THE COUNCIL IN 19TH CENTURY. Cr. 8vo, 5s.

Burton (Prof. E.)—SYNTAX OF THE MOODS AND TENSES IN NEW TESTAMENT GREEK. Post 8vo, 5s. 6d. net.

Caldecott and H. R. Mackintosh (Profs.)—SELECTIONS FROM THE LITERATURE OF THEISM. 7s. 6d. net.

Calvin's INSTITUTES OF CHRISTIAN RELIGION. (Translation.) 2 vols. 8vo, 14s.

———— COMMENTARIES. Forty-five Vols. *Price on application.*

Calvini Institutio Christianæ Religionis. Curavit A. THOLUCK. Two vols. 8vo, Subscription price. 14s.

Candlish (Prof. J. S., D.D.)—THE KINGDOM OF GOD, BIBLICALLY AND HISTORICALLY CONSIDERED. 8vo, 10s. 6d.

———— THE CHRISTIAN SALVATION. Lectures on the Work of Christ. 8vo, 7s. 6d.

Caspari (C. E.)—INTRODUCTION TO THE LIFE OF CHRIST. 8vo, 7s. 6d.

Caspers (A.)—THE FOOTSTEPS OF CHRIST. Crown 8vo, 7s. 6d.

Cassel (Prof.)—COMMENTARY ON ESTHER. 8vo, 6s. net.

Cave (Principal A., D.D.)—THE SCRIPTURAL DOCTRINE OF SACRIFICE AND ATONEMENT. Second Edition, 8vo, 10s. 6d.

—————— AN INTRODUCTION TO THEOLOGY. Second Edition, 8vo, 12s.

Chapman (Principal C., LL.D.)—PRE-ORGANIC EVOLUTION AND THE BIBLICAL IDEA OF GOD. Crown 8vo, 6s.

Christlieb (Prof. T., D.D.)—MODERN DOUBT AND CHRISTIAN BELIEF. 8vo, 6s. net.

—————— HOMILETIC: Lectures on Preaching. 7s. 6d.

Clark (Professor W. R., LL.D., D.C.L.)—THE ANGLICAN REFORMATION. (*Eras of Church History.*) 6s.

—————— THE PARACLETE. The Person and Work of the Holy Spirit. Crown 8vo, 3s. 6d.

—————— PASCAL AND THE PORT ROYALISTS. Crown 8vo, 3s.

—————— WITNESSES TO CHRIST. A Contribution to Christian Apologetics. Crown 8vo, 4s.

Clarke (Professor W. N., D.D.)—AN OUTLINE OF CHRISTIAN THEOLOGY. Thirteenth Edition, post 8vo, 7s. 6d.

—————— THE USE OF THE SCRIPTURES IN THEOLOGY. Post 8vo, 4s.

—————— WHAT SHALL WE THINK OF CHRISTIANITY? Cr. 8vo, 2s. 6d.

—————— CAN I BELIEVE IN GOD THE FATHER? Crown 8vo, 3s.

Concordance to the Greek Testament—MOULTON (W. F., D.D.) and GEDEN (A. S., M.A.). Second Edition, crown 4to, 26s. net.

Cooper and Maclean.—THE TESTAMENT OF OUR LORD. With Introduction and Notes by Prof. COOPER, D.D., and Bishop MACLEAN. 8vo, 9s.

Crawford (J. H., M.A.)—THE BROTHERHOOD OF MANKIND. Post 8vo, 5s.

Cremer (Professor)—BIBLICO-THEOLOGICAL LEXICON OF NEW TESTAMENT GREEK. Third Edition, with Supplement, demy 4to, 38s.

Crippen (Rev. T. G.)—A POPULAR INTRODUCTION TO THE HISTORY OF CHRISTIAN DOCTRINE. 8vo, 9s.

Cunningham (Principal)—HISTORICAL THEOLOGY. Two vols. 8vo, 21s.

Curtiss (Dr. S. I.)—THE LEVITICAL PRIESTS. Crown 8vo, 5s.

—————— FRANZ DELITZSCH: A Memorial Tribute. *Portrait.* Cr. 8vo, 3s.

Dahle (Bishop)—LIFE AFTER DEATH. Demy 8vo, 10s. 6d.

Dalman (Prof. G.)—THE WORDS OF JESUS. Demy 8vo, 7s. 6d. net.

Davidson (Prof. A.B., D.D., LL.D.)—AN INTRODUCTORY HEBREW GRAMMAR. With Progressive Exercises in Reading and Writing. 17th Edition, 8vo, 7s. 6d.

—————— A SYNTAX OF THE HEBREW LANGUAGE. 3rd Ed., 8vo, 7s. 6d.

—————— OLD TESTAMENT PROPHECY. Edited by Prof. J. A. PATERSON, D.D. Demy 8vo, 10s. 6d. net.

—————— THE THEOLOGY OF THE OLD TESTAMENT. (*International Theological Library.*) Edited by Principal SALMOND, D.D. 12s.

—————— THE CALLED OF GOD. With Biographical Introduction by A. TAYLOR INNES, M.A., Advocate, and Portraits. Post 8vo, Second Edition, 6s.

—————— WAITING UPON GOD. A Further and Final Selection of Sermons. Post 8vo, 6s.

—————— THE EPISTLE TO THE HEBREWS. Crown 8vo, 2s. 6d.

Davidson, Dr. Samuel. Autobiography and Diary. Edited by his DAUGHTER. 8vo, 7s. 6d.

Davies (Principal D. C.)—THE ATONEMENT AND INTERCESSION OF CHRIST. Crown 8vo, 4s.

Deane (Wm., M.A.)—PSEUDEPIGRAPHA : The Books which influenced our Lord and the Apostles. Post 8vo, 7s. 6d.

Deissmann (Dr. G. A.)—BIBLE STUDIES. Second Edition, 8vo, 9s.

Delitzsch (Prof.)—SYSTEM OF BIBLICAL PSYCHOLOGY, 8vo, 6s. net; NEW COMMENTARY ON GENESIS, 2 vols. 8vo, 12s. net; PSALMS, 3 vols., 18s. net; PROVERBS, 2 vols., 12s. net; SONG OF SOLOMON AND ECCLESIASTES, 6s. net; ISAIAH, Fourth Edition, rewritten, 2 vols., 12s. net; HEBREWS, 2 vols., 12s. net.

*** Any Four Volumes may be had at original Subscription price of 21s. net.

Deussen (Prof. P.)—THE PHILOSOPHY OF THE UPANISHADS. The Religion and Philosophy of India. 8vo.

Dictionary of the Bible, A. (*See page 2.*)

Dods (Prof. Marcus)—THE BIBLE: ITS ORIGIN AND NATURE. Crown 8vo, 4s. 6d. net.

Dods (Marcus, M.A.)—FORERUNNERS OF DANTE. Crown 8vo, 4s. net.

Doedes—MANUAL OF NEW TESTAMENT HERMENEUTICS. Cr. 8vo, 3s.

Döllinger (Dr.)—HIPPOLYTUS AND CALLISTUS. 8vo, 6s. net.

——— DECLARATIONS AND LETTERS ON THE VATICAN DECREES, 1869-1887. Authorised Translation. Crown 8vo, 3s. 6d.

Dorner (Professor)—HISTORY OF THE DEVELOPMENT OF THE DOCTRINE OF THE PERSON OF CHRIST. Five vols. Subscription price, 26s. 3d. net.

——— SYSTEM OF CHRISTIAN DOCTRINE. Subscription price, 21s. net.

——— SYSTEM OF CHRISTIAN ETHICS. 8vo, 14s.

Driver (Prof. S. R., D.D.)—AN INTRODUCTION TO THE LITERATURE OF THE OLD TESTAMENT. (*International Theological Library.*) 7th Edition, post 8vo, 12s.

——— DEUTERONOMY : A Critical and Exegetical Commentary. (*International Critical Commentary.*) Third Edition, post 8vo, 12s.

Drummond (R. J., D.D.)—THE RELATION OF THE APOSTOLIC TEACHING TO THE TEACHING OF CHRIST. Second Edition, 8vo, 10s. 6d.

Du Bose (Prof. W. P., D.D.)—THE ECUMENICAL COUNCILS. (*Eras of Church History.*) 6s.

Duff (Prof. David, D.D.)—THE EARLY CHURCH. 8vo, 12s.

Dyke (Paul Van)—THE AGE OF THE RENASCENCE. With an Introduction by HENRY VAN DYKE. (*Eras of Church History.*) 6s.

Eadie (Professor)—COMMENTARIES ON ST. PAUL'S EPISTLES TO THE EPHESIANS, PHILIPPIANS, COLOSSIANS. New and Revised Editions, Edited by Rev. WM. YOUNG, M.A. Three vols. 8vo, 10s. 6d. each ; *or set, 18s. net.*

Ebrard (Dr. J. H. A.)—THE GOSPEL HISTORY. 8vo, 6s. net.

——— APOLOGETICS. Three vols. 8vo, 18s. net.

——— COMMENTARY ON THE EPISTLES OF ST. JOHN. 8vo, 6s. net.

Edgar (R. M'C., D.D.)—THE GOSPEL OF A RISEN SAVIOUR. 7s. 6d.

Elliott—ON THE INSPIRATION OF THE HOLY SCRIPTURES. 8vo, 6s.

Eras of the Christian Church—*Now complete in Ten Volumes*—

DU BOSE (Prof. W. P., D.D.)—The Ecumenical Councils. 6s.
WATERMAN (L., D.D.)—The Post-Apostolic Age. 6s.
DYKE (PAUL VAN)—The Age of the Renascence. 6s.
LOCKE (CLINTON, D.D.)—The Age of the Great Western Schism. 6s.
LUDLOW (J. M., D.D.)—The Age of the Crusades. 6s.
VINCENT (Prof. M. R., D.D.)—The Age of Hildebrand. 6s.
CLARK (Prof. W. R., LL.D., D.C.L.)—The Anglican Reformation. 6s.
WELLS (Prof. C. L.)—The Age of Charlemagne. 6s.
BARTLET (Prof. J. VERNON, M.A.)—The Apostolic Age. 6s.
WALKER (Prof. W., Ph.D., D.D.)—The Protestant Reformation. 6s.

Ernesti—BIBLICAL INTERPRETATION OF NEW TESTAMENT. Two vols., 8s.

Ewald (Heinrich)—HEBREW SYNTAX. 8vo, 8s. 6d.

Ewald (Heinrich)—REVELATION : Its Nature and Record. 8vo, 6s. net.
——— OLD AND NEW TESTAMENT THEOLOGY. 8vo, 6s. net.
Expository Times. Edited by JAMES HASTINGS, D.D. Monthly, 6d.
Fairbairn (Prin.)—THE REVELATION OF LAW IN SCRIPTURE, 8vo, 10s. 6d.
——— EZEKIEL AND THE BOOK OF HIS PROPHECY. Fourth Edition
8vo, 10s. 6d.
——— PROPHECY. Second Edition, 8vo, 10s. 6d.
——— PASTORAL THEOLOGY. Crown 8vo, 6s.
Fairweather (Rev. W., M.A.)—ORIGEN AND GREEK PATRISTIC
THEOLOGY. 3s.
Falconer (J. W., B.D.)—FROM APOSTLE TO PRIEST. A Study of
Early Church Organisation. Crown 8vo, 4s. 6d.
Ferries (Rev. George, D.D.)—THE GROWTH OF CHRISTIAN FAITH.
8vo, 7s. 6d. net.
Fisher (Prof. G. P., D.D., LL.D.)—HISTORY OF CHRISTIAN DOCTRINE.
(*International Theological Library.*) Second Edition, post 8vo, 12s.
Forbes (J. T., M.A.)—SOCRATES. (*In the Series of the World's
Epoch-Makers.*) Crown 8vo, 3s.
Foreign Theological Library—Four Volumes for One Guinea. *Detailed List on application.*
Forrest (D. W., D.D.)—THE CHRIST OF HISTORY AND OF EX-
PERIENCE. Fourth Edition, post 8vo, 6s.
Frank (Prof. F. H.)—SYSTEM OF CHRISTIAN CERTAINTY. 8vo, 6s. net.
Funcke (Otto)—THE WORLD OF FAITH AND THE EVERYDAY WORLD,
as displayed in the Footsteps of Abraham. Post 8vo, 7s. 6d.
Garvie (Prof. A. E., D.D.)—THE RITSCHLIAN THEOLOGY. 2nd Ed., 8vo, 9s.
Gebhardt (H.)—THE DOCTRINE OF THE APOCALYPSE. 8vo, 6s. net.
Geere (H. Valentine)—BY NILE AND EUPHRATES. A Record of
Discovery and Adventure. Demy 8vo, price 8s. 6d. net.
Gerlach—COMMENTARY ON THE PENTATEUCH. 8vo, 6s. net.
Gieseler (Dr. J. C. L.)—ECCLESIASTICAL HISTORY. Four vols. 8vo, 21s.
Given (Rev. Prof. J. J.)—THE TRUTH OF SCRIPTURE IN CONNECTION
WITH REVELATION, INSPIRATION, AND THE CANON. 8vo, 6s.
Gladden (Washington, D.D., LL.D.) THE CHRISTIAN PASTOR AND
THE WORKING CHURCH. (*International Theol. Library.*) Post 8vo, 10s. 6d.
Glasgow (Prof.) — APOCALYPSE TRANSLATED AND EXPOUNDED.
8vo, 10s. 6d.
Gloag (Paton J., D.D.)—THE MESSIANIC PROPHECIES. Cr. 8vo, 7s. 6d.
——— INTRODUCTION TO THE CATHOLIC EPISTLES. 8vo, 10s. 6d.
——— INTRODUCTION TO THE SYNOPTIC GOSPELS. 8vo, 7s. 6d.
——— EXEGETICAL STUDIES. Crown 8vo, 5s.
——— THE PRIMEVAL WORLD. Crown 8vo, 3s.
Godet (Prof. F.)—AN INTRODUCTION TO THE NEW TESTAMENT—
I. THE EPISTLES OF ST. PAUL. 8vo, 12s. 6d. net.
II. THE GOSPEL COLLECTION, AND ST. MATTHEW'S GOSPEL. 8vo, 6s. net.
——— COMMENTARY ON ST. LUKE'S GOSPEL. 2 vols. 8vo, 12s. net.
——— COMMENTARY ON ST. JOHN'S GOSPEL. 3 vols. 8vo, 18s. net.
——— COMMENTARY ON EPISTLE TO THE ROMANS. 2 vols. 8vo, 12s. net.
——— COMMENTARY ON 1ST EPISTLE TO CORINTHIANS. 2 vols. 8vo,
12s. net.
。 Any Four Volumes at the original Subscription price of 21s. net.
——— DEFENCE OF THE CHRISTIAN FAITH. Crown 8vo, 4s.
Goebel (Siegfried)—THE PARABLES OF JESUS. 8vo, 6s. net.

Gotthold's Emblems; or, INVISIBLE THINGS UNDERSTOOD BY THINGS THAT ARE MADE. Crown 8vo, 5s.

Gould (Prof. E. P., D.D.)—ST. MARK. (*International Critical Commentary.*) Post 8vo, 10s. 6d.

Gray (Prof. G. Buchanan, D.D.)—NUMBERS. (*International Critical Commentary.*) Post 8vo, 12s.

Grimm's GREEK-ENGLISH LEXICON OF THE NEW TESTAMENT. Translated, Revised, and Enlarged by JOSEPH H. THAYER, D.D. Demy 4to, 36s.

Guyot (Arnold, LL.D.)—CREATION; or, The Biblical Cosmogony in the Light of Modern Science. With Illustrations. Crown 8vo, 5s. 6d.

Hagenbach (Dr. K. R.)—HISTORY OF DOCTRINES. 3 vols. 8vo, 18s. net.

———— HISTORY OF THE REFORMATION. 2 vols. 8vo, 12s. net.

Halcombe (Rev. J. J., M.A.)—WHAT THINK WE OF THE GOSPELS? 3s. 6d.

Hall (Newman, D.D.)—DIVINE BROTHERHOOD. 3rd Ed., cr. 8vo, 4s.

Hamilton (T., D.D.)—BEYOND THE STARS; or, Heaven, its Inhabitants, Occupations, and Life. Third Edition, crown 8vo, 3s. 6d.

Harless (Dr. C. A.)—SYSTEM OF CHRISTIAN ETHICS. 8vo, 6s. net.

Harper (Pres. W. R., Ph.D.)—AMOS AND HOSEA. (*International Critical Commentary.*) Post 8vo, 12s.

Harris (S., D.D.)—GOD THE CREATOR AND LORD OF ALL. Two vols. post 8vo, 16s.

Hastie (The late Prof.)—THEOLOGY OF THE REFORMED CHURCH IN ITS FUNDAMENTAL PRINCIPLES (*Croall Lectures*). Crown 8vo, 4s. 6d. net.

———— OUTLINES OF PASTORAL THEOLOGY. For Young Ministers and Students. 1s. 6d. net.

Haupt (Erich)—THE FIRST EPISTLE OF ST. JOHN. 8vo, 6s. net.

Hävernick (H. A. Ch.)—INTRODUCTION TO OLD TESTAMENT. 6s. net.

Heard (Rev. J. B., M.A.)—THE TRIPARTITE NATURE OF MAN. Cr. 8vo, 6s.

———— OLD AND NEW THEOLOGY. A Constructive Critique. Cr. 8vo, 6s.

———— ALEXANDRIAN AND CARTHAGINIAN THEOLOGY CONTRASTED. The Hulsean Lectures, 1892-93. Crown 8vo, 6s.

Hefele (Bishop)—A HISTORY OF THE COUNCILS OF THE CHURCH. Vol. I., to A.D. 325. Vol. II., A.D. 326 to 429. Vol. III., A.D. 431 to the close of the Council of Chalcedon, 451. Vol. IV., A.D. 451 to 680. Vol. V., A.D. 626 to 787. 8vo, 12s. each.

Henderson (Rev. H. F., M.A.)—THE RELIGIOUS CONTROVERSIES OF SCOTLAND. Post 8vo, 4s. 6d. net.

Hengstenberg (Professor)—COMMENTARY ON PSALMS, 3 vols. 8vo, 18s. net; ECCLESIASTES, ETC., 8vo, 6s. net; EZEKIEL, 8vo, 6s. net; THE GENUINENESS OF DANIEL, ETC., 8vo, 6s. net; HISTORY OF THE KINGDOM OF GOD, 2 vols. 8vo, 12s. net; CHRISTOLOGY OF THE OLD TESTAMENT, 4 vols., 21s. net; ST. JOHN'S GOSPEL, 2 vols. 8vo, 21s.

*** Any Four Volumes at the original Subscription price of 21s. net.

Herkless (Prof. J., D.D.)—FRANCIS AND DOMINIC. Crown 8vo, 3s.

Herzog—ENCYCLOPÆDIA OF LIVING DIVINES, ETC., OF ALL DENOMINATIONS IN EUROPE AND AMERICA. (*Supplement to Herzog's Encyclopædia.*) Imp. 8vo, 8s.

Hill (Rev. J. Hamlyn, D.D.)—ST. EPHRAEM THE SYRIAN. 8vo, 7s. 6d.

Hilprecht (Prof. H. V.)—EXPLORATIONS IN BIBLE LANDS. Large 8vo, 12s. 6d. net.

Hodgson (Principal J. M., M.A., D.Sc., D.D.)—THEOLOGIA PECTORIS: Outlines of Religious Faith and Doctrine. Crown 8vo, 3s. 6d.

Holborn (Alfred, M.A.)—THE PENTATEUCH IN THE LIGHT OF TO-DAY. A Simple Introduction to the Pentateuch on the Lines of the Higher Criticism. Second Edition, crown 8vo, 2s. net.

Hudson (Prof. W. H.)—ROUSSEAU, AND NATURALISM IN LIFE AND THOUGHT. Crown 8vo, 3s.

Inge (W. R., D.D.)—FAITH AND KNOWLEDGE. Post 8vo, 4s. 6d. net.

Innes (A. D., M.A.)—CRANMER AND THE ENGLISH REFORMATION. Crown 8vo, 3s.

Innes (A. Taylor)—THE TRIAL OF JESUS CHRIST. In its Legal Aspect. Second Edition, post 8vo, 2s. 6d.

International Critical Commentary.
> GRAY (Prof. G. BUCHANAN, D.D.)—Numbers. 12s.
> DRIVER (Prof. S. R., D.D.)—Deuteronomy. 12s.
> MOORE (Prof. G. F., D.D.)—Judges. 12s.
> SMITH (Prof. H. P., D.D.)—Samuel. 12s.
> TOY (Prof. C. H., D.D.)—Proverbs. 12s.
> HARPER (Pres. W. R.)—Amos and Hosea. 12s.
> GOULD (Prof. E. P., D.D.)—St. Mark. 10s. 6d.
> PLUMMER (ALFRED, D.D.)—St. Luke. 12s.
> SANDAY (Prof. W., D.D.) and HEADLAM (Prin. A. C., D.D.)—Romans. 12s.
> ABBOTT (Prof. T. K., B.D., D.Lit.)—Ephesians and Colossians. 10s. 6d.
> VINCENT (Prof. M. R., D.D.)—Philippians and Philemon. 8s. 6d.
> BIGG (Prof. C., D.D.)—St. Peter and St. Jude. 10s. 6d.
> *For List of future Volumes see* p. 15.

International Theological Library.
> DAVIDSON (Prof. A. B.)—Theology of the Old Testament. 12s.
> DRIVER (Prof. S. R., D.D.)—An Introduction to the Literature of the Old Testament. 12s.
> SMITH (Prof. H. P.)—Old Testament History. 12s.
> SMYTH (NEWMAN, D.D.)—Christian Ethics. 10s. 6d.
> BRUCE (Prof. A. B., D.D.)—Apologetics. 10s. 6d.
> FISHER (Prof. G. P., D.D., LL.D.)—History of Christian Doctrine. 12s.
> ALLEN (Prof. A. V. G., D.D.)—Christian Institutions. 12s.
> McGIFFERT (Prof. A. C., Ph.D.)—The Apostolic Age. 12s.
> GLADDEN (WASHINGTON, D.D.)—The Christian Pastor. 10s. 6d.
> STEVENS (Prof. G. B., D.D.)—The Theology of the New Testament. 12s.
> —— The Christian Doctrine of Salvation. 12s.
> RAINY (Prin. R.)—The Ancient Catholic Church. 12s.
> *For List of future Volumes see* p. 14.

Iverach (Princ. James, D.D.)—DESCARTES, SPINOZA, AND THE NEW PHILOSOPHY. Crown 8vo, 3s.

Janet (Paul)—FINAL CAUSES. Second Edition, demy 8vo, 12s.

—— THE THEORY OF MORALS. Demy 8vo, 10s. 6d.

Johns (C. H. W., M.A.)—THE OLDEST CODE OF LAWS IN THE WORLD. The Code of Laws promulgated by Hammurabi, King of Babylon, B.C. 2285–2242. Crown 8vo, 1s. 6d. net.

—— BABYLONIAN AND ASSYRIAN LAWS, CONTRACTS, AND LETTERS. Demy 8vo, 12s. net.

Johnstone (P. De Lacy, M.A.)—MUHAMMAD AND HIS POWER. 3s.

Johnstone (Prof. R., D.D.)—COMMENTARY ON 1ST PETER. 8vo, 10s. 6d.

Jones (E. E. C.)—ELEMENTS OF LOGIC. 8vo, 7s. 6d.

Jordan (Rev. Louis H., B.D.)—COMPARATIVE RELIGION: Its Genesis and Growth. Introduction by Principal FAIRBAIRN, D.D. 8vo, 12s. net.

Kaftan (Prof. J., D.D.)—THE TRUTH OF THE CHRISTIAN RELIGION. *Authorised Translation.* 2 vols. 8vo, 16s. net.

Kant—THE METAPHYSIC OF ETHICS. Crown 8vo, 6s.

—— PHILOSOPHY OF LAW. Trans. by W. HASTIE, D.D. Cr. 8vo, 5s.

—— PRINCIPLES OF POLITICS, ETC. Crown 8vo, 2s. 6d.

Kennedy (James, D.D.)—THE NOTE-LINE IN THE HEBREW SCRIPTURES. 4s. 6d. net.

Keil (Prof.)—PENTATEUCH, 3 vols. 8vo, 18s. net; JOSHUA, JUDGES, AND RUTH, 8vo, 6s. net; SAMUEL, 8vo, 6s. net; KINGS, 8vo, 6s. net; CHRONICLES, 8vo, 6s. net; EZRA, NEHEMIAH, ESTHER, 8vo, 6s. net; JEREMIAH, 2 vols. 8vo, 12s. net; EZEKIEL, 2 vols. 8vo, 12s. net; DANIEL, 8vo, 6s. net; MINOR PROPHETS, 2 vols. 8vo, 12s. net; INTRODUCTION TO THE CANONICAL SCRIPTURES OF THE OLD TESTAMENT, 2 vols. 8vo, 12s. net; HANDBOOK OF BIBLICAL ARCHÆOLOGY, 2 vols. 8vo, 12s. net.
  *** Any Four Volumes at the original Subscription price of 21s. net.

Keymer (Rev. N., M.A.)—NOTES ON GENESIS. Crown 8vo, 1s. 6d.

Kidd (James, D.D.)—MORALITY AND RELIGION. 8vo, 10s. 6d.

Killen (Prof.)—THE FRAMEWORK OF THE CHURCH. 8vo, 9s.

———— THE OLD CATHOLIC CHURCH. 8vo, 9s.

———— THE IGNATIAN EPISTLES ENTIRELY SPURIOUS. Cr. 8vo, 2s. 6d.

Kilpatrick (Prof. T. B., D.D.)—CHRISTIAN CHARACTER. 2s. 6d.

König (Dr. Ed.)—THE EXILES' BOOK OF CONSOLATION (Deutero-Isaiah). Crown 8vo, 3s. 6d.

König (Dr. F. E.)—THE RELIGIOUS HISTORY OF ISRAEL. Cr. 8vo, 3s. 6d.

Krause (F. C. F.)—THE IDEAL OF HUMANITY. Crown 8vo, 3s.

Krummacher (Dr. F. W.)—THE SUFFERING SAVIOUR. Cr. 8vo, 6s.

———— DAVID, THE KING OF ISRAEL. Second Edition, cr. 8vo, 6s.

———— AUTOBIOGRAPHY. Crown 8vo, 6s.

Kurtz (Prof.)—HANDBOOK OF CHURCH HISTORY (from 1517). 8vo, 7s. 6d.

———— HISTORY OF THE OLD COVENANT. Three vols. 8vo, 18s. net.

Ladd (Prof. G. T.)—THE DOCTRINE OF SACRED SCRIPTURE. Two vols. 8vo, 1600 pp., 24s.

Laidlaw (Prof. J., D.D.)—THE BIBLE DOCTRINE OF MAN. Post 8vo, 7s. 6d.

Lambert (Rev. J. C., B.D.)—THE SACRAMENTS IN THE NEW TESTAMENT. Demy 8vo, price 10s. 6d.

Lane (Laura M.)—LIFE OF ALEXANDER VINET. Crown 8vo, 7s. 6d.

Lange (J. P., D.D.)—THE LIFE OF OUR LORD JESUS CHRIST. Edited by MARCUS DODS, D.D. 2nd Edition, in 4 vols. 8vo, price 28s. net.

———— COMMENTARIES ON THE OLD AND NEW TESTAMENTS. Edited by PHILIP SCHAFF, D.D. OLD TESTAMENT, 14 vols.; NEW TESTAMENT, 10 vols.; APOCRYPHA, 1 vol. Subscription price, net, 15s. each.

———— ST. MATTHEW AND ST. MARK, 3 vols. 8vo, 18s. net; ST. LUKE, 2 vols. 8vo, 12s. net; ST. JOHN, 2 vols. 8vo, 12s. net.
  *** Any Four Volumes at the original Subscription price of 21s. net.

Le Camus (E., Bishop of La Rochelle)—THE CHILDREN OF NAZARETH. Fcap. 4to. 4s.

Lechler (Prof. G. V., D.D.)—THE APOSTOLIC AND POST-APOSTOLIC TIMES. Their Diversity and Unity in Life and Doctrine. 2 vols. cr. 8vo, 16s.

Lehmann (Pastor)—SCENES FROM THE LIFE OF JESUS. Cr. 8vo, 3s. 6d.

Lewis (Tayler, LL.D.)—THE SIX DAYS OF CREATION. Cr. 8vo, 7s. 6d.

Lidgett (Rev. J. Scott)—THE FATHERHOOD OF GOD IN CHRISTIAN TRUTH AND LIFE. 8vo, 8s. net.

Lilley (J. P., D.D.)—THE LORD'S SUPPER: Its Origin, Nature, and Use. Crown 8vo, 5s.

———— THE PASTORAL EPISTLES. 2s. 6d.

———— PRINCIPLES OF PROTESTANTISM. 2s. 6d.

Lillie (Arthur)—BUDDHA AND BUDDHISM. Crown 8vo, 3s.

Lindsay (Prin. T. M., D.D.)—LUTHER AND THE GERMAN REFORMATION. Crown 8vo, 3s.

Lisco (F. G.)—PARABLES OF JESUS EXPLAINED. Fcap. 8vo, 5s. .

Locke (Clinton, D.D.)—THE AGE OF THE GREAT WESTERN SCHISM. (*Eras of Church History.*) 6s.

Lotze (Hermann)—MICROCOSMUS : An Essay concerning Man and his relation to the World. Cheaper Edition, 2 vols. 8vo (1450 pp.), 24s.

Ludlow (J. M., D.D.)—THE AGE OF THE CRUSADES. (*Eras of Church History.*) 6s.

Luthardt, Kahnis, and Brückner—THE CHURCH. Crown 8vo, 5s.

Luthardt (Prof.)—ST. JOHN THE AUTHOR OF THE FOURTH GOSPEL. 7s. 6d.

—————— COMMENTARY ON ST. JOHN'S GOSPEL. 3 vols. 8vo, 18s. net.

————— HISTORY OF CHRISTIAN ETHICS. 8vo, 6s. net.

————— APOLOGETIC LECTURES ON THE FUNDAMENTAL (7 *Ed.*), SAVING (5 *Ed.*), MORAL TRUTHS OF CHRISTIANITY (4 *Ed.*). 3 vols. cr. 8vo, 6s. each.

Macdonald—INTRODUCTION TO PENTATEUCH. Two vols. 8vo, 12s. net.

————— CREATION AND THE FALL. 8vo, 6s. net.

Macgregor (Rev. Jas., D.D.) — THE APOLOGY OF THE CHRISTIAN RELIGION. 8vo, 10s. 6d.

————— THE REVELATION AND THE RECORD : Essays on Matters of Previous Question in the Proof of Christianity. 8vo, 7s. 6d.

————— STUDIES IN THE HISTORY OF NEW TESTAMENT APOLOGETICS. 8vo, 7s. 6d.

Macgregor (Rev. G. H. C., M.A.)—SO GREAT SALVATION. Cr. 32mo, 1s.

Macpherson (Rev. John, M.A.)—COMMENTARY ON THE EPISTLE TO THE EPHESIANS. 8vo, 10s. 6d.

————— CHRISTIAN DOGMATICS. Post 8vo, 9s.

McCosh (James), Life of. 8vo, 9s.

McGiffert (Prof. A. C., Ph.D.)—HISTORY OF CHRISTIANITY IN THE APOSTOLIC AGE. (*International Theological Library.*) Post 8vo, 12s.

————— THE APOSTLES' CREED. Post 8vo, 4s. net.

M'Hardy (G., D.D.)—SAVONAROLA. Crown 8vo, 3s.

M'Intosh (Rev. Hugh, M.A.)—IS CHRIST INFALLIBLE AND THE BIBLE TRUE ? Third Edition, post 8vo, 6s. net.

Mackintosh (Prof. R., D.D.)—HEGEL AND HEGELIANISM. Crown 8vo, 3s.

M'Realsham (E. D.)—ROMANS DISSECTED. A Critical Analysis of the Epistle to the Romans. Crown 8vo, 2s.

Mair (A., D.D.)—STUDIES IN THE CHRISTIAN EVIDENCES. Third Edition, Revised and Enlarged, crown 8vo, 6s.

Martensen (Bishop)—CHRISTIAN DOGMATICS. 8vo, 6s. net.

————— CHRISTIAN ETHICS. (GENERAL — INDIVIDUAL — SOCIAL.) Three vols. 8vo, 6s. net each.

Matheson (Geo., D.D.)—GROWTH OF THE SPIRIT OF CHRISTIANITY, from the First Century to the Dawn of the Lutheran Era. Two vols. 8vo, 21s.

Meyer (Dr.) — CRITICAL AND EXEGETICAL COMMENTARIES ON THE NEW TESTAMENT. Twenty vols. 8vo. *Subscription price, £5, 5s. net ; selection of Four Volumes at Subscription price of 21s. ; Non-Subscription price, 10s. 6d. each volume.*

ST. MATTHEW, 2 vols. ; MARK AND LUKE, 2 vols. ; ST. JOHN, 2 vols. ; ACTS, 2 vols. ; ROMANS, 2 vols. ; CORINTHIANS, 2 vols. ; GALATIANS, one vol. ; EPHESIANS AND PHILEMON, one vol. ; PHILIPPIANS AND COLOSSIANS, one vol. ; THESSALONIANS (*Dr. Lünemann*), one vol. ; THE PASTORAL EPISTLES (*Dr. Huther*), one vol. ; HEBREWS (*Dr. Lünemann*), one vol. ; ST. JAMES AND ST. JOHN'S EPISTLES (*Huther*), one vol. ; PETER AND JUDE (*Dr. Huther*), one vol.

Michie (Charles, M.A.)—BIBLE WORDS AND PHRASES. 18mo, 1s.

Milligan (George, D.D.)—THE THEOLOGY OF THE EPISTLE TO THE HEBREWS. Post 8vo, 6s.

Milligan (Prof. W., D.D.)—THE RESURRECTION OF THE DEAD. Second Edition, crown 8vo, 4s. 6d.

Milligan (Prof. W., D.D.) and Moulton (W. F., D.D.) — COMMENTARY ON THE GOSPEL OF ST. JOHN. Imp. 8vo, 9s.

Moffatt (James, D.D.)—THE HISTORICAL NEW TESTAMENT. Second Edition, demy 8vo, 16s.

Moore (Prof. G. F., D.D.)—JUDGES. (*International Critical Commentary.*) Second Edition, post 8vo, 12s.

Morgan (J., D.D.)—SCRIPTURE TESTIMONY TO THE HOLY SPIRIT. 7s. 6d.

——— EXPOSITION OF THE FIRST EPISTLE OF JOHN. 8vo, 7s. 6d.

Moulton (James H., D.Litt.)—A GRAMMAR OF NEW TESTAMENT GREEK. Part I. The Prolegomena. Part II. (*In the Press.*)

Moulton (W. F., D.D.) and Geden (A. S., M.A.)—A CONCORDANCE TO THE GREEK TESTAMENT. Crown 4to, 26s. net, and 31s. 6d. net.

Muir (Sir W.)—MOHAMMEDAN CONTROVERSY, ETC. 8vo, 7s. 6d.

——— INDIAN MUTINY. Two vols. 36s. net.

Muirhead (Dr. Lewis A.)—THE TIMES OF CHRIST. New Edition. With Map. 2s.

Müller (Dr. Julius)—THE CHRISTIAN DOCTRINE OF SIN. 2 vols., 12s. net.

Murphy (Professor)—COMMENTARY ON THE PSALMS. 8vo, 6s. net.

——— A CRITICAL AND EXEGETICAL COMMENTARY ON EXODUS. 9s.

Naville (Ernest)—THE PROBLEM OF EVIL. Crown 8vo, 4s. 6d.

——— THE CHRIST. Translated by Rev. T. J. DESPRÉS. Cr. 8vo, 4s. 6d.

——— MODERN PHYSICS. Crown 8vo, 5s.

Neander (Dr.)—CHURCH HISTORY. Eight vols. 8vo, £2, 2s. net.

Nicoll (W. Robertson, M.A., LL.D.)—THE INCARNATE SAVIOUR. Cheap Edition, price 3s. 6d.

Novalis—HYMNS AND THOUGHTS ON RELIGION. Crown 8vo, 4s.

Oehler (Prof.)—THEOLOGY OF THE OLD TESTAMENT. 2 vols., 12s. net.

Olshausen (Dr. H.)—BIBLICAL COMMENTARY ON THE GOSPELS AND ACTS. Four vols., 21s. net. Crown 8vo Edition, 4 vols., 24s.

——— ROMANS, one vol. 8vo, 6s. net; CORINTHIANS, one vol. 8vo, 6s. net; PHILIPPIANS, TITUS, AND FIRST TIMOTHY, one vol. 8vo, 6s. net.

Oosterzee (Dr. Van)—THE YEAR OF SALVATION. Two vols., 6s. each.

——— MOSES: A Biblical Study. Crown 8vo, 6s.

Orelli (Dr. C. von)—OLD TESTAMENT PROPHECY; COMMENTARY ON ISAIAH; JEREMIAH; THE TWELVE MINOR PROPHETS. 4 vols. Subscription price, 21s. net; separate vols., 6s. net, each.

Orr (Prof. James, D.D.)—DAVID HUME. Crown 8vo, 3s.

Owen (Dr. John)—WORKS. *Best and only Complete Edition.* Edited by Rev. Dr. GOOLD. Twenty-four vols. 8vo, Subscription price, £4, 4s.
The 'Hebrews' may be had separately, in seven vols., £1, 5s. net.

Palestine, Map of. Edited by J. G. BARTHOLOMEW, F.R.G.S., and Prof. G. A. SMITH, M.D., D.D. With complete Index. Scale—4 Miles to an Inch. In cloth, 10s. 6d.; mounted on rollers, varnished, 15s.

Patrick (Rev. Principal W., D.D.)—JAMES THE BROTHER OF OUR LORD. Post 8vo.

Philippi (F. A.)—COMMENTARY ON THE ROMANS. Two vols. 8vo, 12s. net.

Piper—LIVES OF LEADERS OF CHURCH UNIVERSAL. Two vols. 8vo, 21s.

Popular Commentary on the New Testament. Edited by PHILIP SCHAFF, D.D. With Illustrations and Maps. Vol. I.—THE SYNOPTICAL GOSPELS. Vol. II.—ST. JOHN'S GOSPEL, AND THE ACTS OF THE APOSTLES. Vol. III.—ROMANS TO PHILEMON. Vol. IV.—HEBREWS TO REVELATION. In four vols. imperial 8vo, 12s. 6d. each.

Plummer (Alfred, D.D.)—ST. LUKE. (*International Critical Commentary.*) Fourth Edition, post 8vo, 12s.

——— ENGLISH CHURCH HISTORY, 1509-1575. Crown 8vo, 3s. net.

——— ENGLISH CHURCH HISTORY, 1575-1649. Crown 8vo, 3s. net.

Pressensé (Edward de)—THE REDEEMER: Discourses. Crown 8vo, 6s.

Profeit (Rev. W., M.A.)—THE CREATION OF MATTER ; or, Material Elements, Evolution, and Creation. Crown 8vo, 2s. net.

Punjer (Bernhard)—HISTORY OF THE CHRISTIAN PHILOSOPHY OF RELIGION FROM THE REFORMATION TO KANT. 8vo, 16s.

Purves (Rev. Dr. D.)—THE LIFE EVERLASTING. Crown 8vo, 4s. net.

Rabiger (Prof.)—ENCYCLOPÆDIA OF THEOLOGY. Two vols. 8vo, 12s. net.

Rainy (Principal) — DELIVERY AND DEVELOPMENT OF CHRISTIAN DOCTRINE. 8vo, 10s. 6d.

———— THE ANCIENT CATHOLIC CHURCH. (*International Theological Library.*) Post 8vo, 12s.

Rashdall (Rev. H., D.C.L.)—CHRISTUS IN ECCLESIA. Post 8vo, 4s. 6d. net.

Reusch (Prof.)—NATURE AND THE BIBLE : Lectures on the Mosaic History of Creation in relation to Natural Science. Two vols. 8vo, 21s.

Reuss (Professor)—HISTORY OF THE SACRED SCRIPTURES OF THE NEW TESTAMENT. 640 pp. 8vo, 15s.

Riehm (Dr. E.)—MESSIANIC PROPHECY. New Edition. Post 8vo, 7s. 6d.

Ritchie (Prof. D. G., M.A.)—PLATO. Crown 8vo, 3s.

Ritschl (Albrecht, D.D.)—THE CHRISTIAN DOCTRINE OF JUSTIFICATION AND RECONCILIATION. Second Edition, 8vo, 14s.

Ritter (Carl)—COMPARATIVE GEOGRAPHY OF PALESTINE. 4 vols. 8vo, 21s.

Robinson (Rev. S., D.D.)—DISCOURSES ON REDEMPTION. 8vo, 7s. 6d.

Robinson (E., D.D.)—GREEK AND ENG. LEXICON OF THE N. TEST. 8vo, 9s.

Rooke (T. G., B.A.)—INSPIRATION, and other Lectures. 8vo, 7s. 6d.

Ross (C.)—OUR FATHER'S KINGDOM. Crown 8vo, 2s. 6d.

Ross (D. M., D.D.)—THE TEACHING OF JESUS. (*Bible-Class Handbooks.*) 2s.

Rothe (Prof.)—SERMONS FOR THE CHRISTIAN YEAR. Cr. 8vo, 4s. 6d.

Saisset—MANUAL OF MODERN PANTHEISM. Two vols. 8vo, 10s. 6d.

Salmond (Princ. S. D. F., D.D.)—THE CHRISTIAN DOCTRINE OF IMMORTALITY. Fifth Edition, post 8vo, 9s.

Sanday (Prof. W., D.D.) and Headlam (Principal A. C., D.D.)—ROMANS. (*International Critical Commentary.*) Third Edition, post 8vo, 12s.

Sanday (Prof. W.)—OUTLINES OF THE LIFE OF CHRIST. Post 8vo, 5s. net.

Sartorius (Dr. E.)—DOCTRINE OF DIVINE LOVE. 8vo, 6s. net.

Sayce (Prof. A. H., LL.D.)—THE RELIGIONS OF ANCIENT EGYPT AND BABYLONIA. Post 8vo, 8s. net.

Schaff (Professor)—HISTORY OF THE CHRISTIAN CHURCH. (New Edition, thoroughly Revised and Enlarged.) Six 'Divisions,' in 2 vols. each, extra 8vo.

    1. APOSTOLIC CHRISTIANITY, A.D. 1-100, 2 vols. 21s. 2. ANTE-NICENE, A.D. 100-325, 2 vols., 21s. 3. NICENE AND POST-NICENE, A.D. 325-600, 2 vols., 21s. 4. MEDIÆVAL, A.D. 590-1073, 2 vols., 21s. (*Completion of this Period*, 1073-1517, *in preparation*). 5. THE SWISS REFORMATION, 2 vols., extra demy 8vo, 21s. 6. THE GERMAN REFORMATION, 2 vols., extra demy 8vo, 21s.

Schleiermacher's CHRISTMAS EVE. Crown 8vo, 2s.

Schubert (Prof. H. Von., D.D.)—THE GOSPEL OF ST. PETER. Synoptical Tables. With Translation and Critical Apparatus. 8vo, 1s. 6d. net.

Schultz (Hermann)—OLD TESTAMENT THEOLOGY. Two vols. 18s. net.

Schürer (Prof.)—HISTORY OF THE JEWISH PEOPLE. Five vols. Subscription price, 26s. 3d. net.

    . Index. In separate Volume. 2s. 6d. net.

Schwartzkopff (Dr. P.)—THE PROPHECIES OF JESUS CHRIST. Cr. 8vo, 5s.

Scott (Jas., M.A., D.D.)—PRINCIPLES OF NEW TESTAMENT QUOTATION ESTABLISHED AND APPLIED TO BIBLICAL CRITICISM. Cr. 8vo, 2nd Edit., 4s.

Sell (K., D.D.)—THE CHURCH IN THE MIRROR OF HISTORY. Cr. 8vo, 3s. 6d.

Shaw (R. D., D.D.)—THE PAULINE EPISTLES: Introductory and Expository Studies. 8vo, 8s. net.

Shedd—SERMONS TO THE SPIRITUAL MAN. 8vo, 7s. 6d.

—— DOGMATIC THEOLOGY. Three vols. ex. 8vo, 37s. 6d.

Sime (James, M.A.)—WILLIAM HERSCHEL AND HIS WORK. Cr. 8vo, 3s.

Simon (Prof.)—RECONCILIATION BY INCARNATION. Post 8vo, 7s. 6d.

Skene-Bickell—THE LORD'S SUPPER & THE PASSOVER RITUAL. 8vo, 5s.

Smeaton (Oliphant, M.A.)—THE MEDICI AND THE ITALIAN RENAISSANCE. 3s.

Smith (Prof. H. P., D.D.)—I. AND II. SAMUEL. (*International Critical Commentary.*) Post 8vo, 12s.

—— OLD TESTAMENT HISTORY. (*International Theological Library.*) 12s.

Smith (Professor Thos., D.D.)—MEDIÆVAL MISSIONS. Cr. 8vo, 4s. 6d.

—— EUCLID: HIS LIFE AND SYSTEM. Crown 8vo, 3s.

Smyth (John, M.A., D.Ph.)—TRUTH AND REALITY. Crown 8vo, 4s.

Smyth (Newman, D.D.)—CHRISTIAN ETHICS. (*International Theological Library.*) Third Edition, post 8vo, 10s. 6d.

Snell (F. J., M.A.)—WESLEY AND METHODISM. Crown 8vo, 3s.

Somerville (Rev. D., D.D.)—ST. PAUL'S CONCEPTION OF CHRIST. 9s.

Stählin (Leonh.)—KANT, LOTZE, AND RITSCHL. 8vo, 9s.

Stalker (Prof. Jas., D.D.)—LIFE OF CHRIST. Large Type Edition, crown 8vo, 3s. 6d.

—— LIFE OF ST. PAUL. Large Type Edition, crown 8vo, 3s. 6d.

Stanton (V. H., D.D.)—THE JEWISH AND THE CHRISTIAN MESSIAH. A Study in the Earliest History of Christianity. 8vo, 10s. 6d.

Stead (F. H.)—THE KINGDOM OF GOD. 1s. 6d.

Steinmeyer (Dr. F. L.)—THE MIRACLES OF OUR LORD. 8vo, 7s. 6d.

—— THE PASSION AND RESURRECTION OF OUR LORD. 8vo, 6s. net.

Stevens (Prof. G. B., D.D.)—THE THEOLOGY OF THE NEW TESTAMENT. (*International Theological Library.*) Post 8vo, 12s.

—— THE CHRISTIAN DOCTRINE OF SALVATION. (*International Theological Library.*) Post 8vo, 12s.

Stevenson (Mrs.)—THE SYMBOLIC PARABLES. Crown 8vo, 3s. 6d.

Steward (Rev. G.)—MEDIATORIAL SOVEREIGNTY. Two vols. 8vo, 21s.

—— THE ARGUMENT OF THE EPISTLE TO THE HEBREWS. 8vo, 10s. 6d.

Stier (Dr. Rudolph)—ON THE WORDS OF THE LORD JESUS. Eight vols. 8vo, Subscription price of £2, 2s. Separate volumes, price 6s. net.

—— THE WORDS OF THE RISEN SAVIOUR, AND COMMENTARY ON THE EPISTLE OF ST. JAMES. 8vo, 6s. net.

—— THE WORDS OF THE APOSTLES EXPOUNDED. 8vo, 6s. net.

Stirling (Dr. J. Hutchison)—PHILOSOPHY AND THEOLOGY. Post 8vo, 9s.

—— DARWINIANISM: Workmen and Work. Post 8vo, 10s. 6d.

—— WHAT *IS* THOUGHT? 8vo, 10s. 6d.

Strachan (Rev. J., M.A.), HEBREW IDEALS; from the Story of the Patriarchs. Part I. Crown 8vo, 2s. Part II. (*In the Press.*)

Tholuck (Prof.)—THE EPISTLE TO THE ROMANS. Two vols. fcap. 8vo, 8s.

Thomson (J. E. H., D.D.)—BOOKS WHICH INFLUENCED OUR LORD AND HIS APOSTLES. 8vo, 10s. 6d.

Thomson (Rev. E. A.)—MEMORIALS OF A MINISTRY. Crown 8vo, 5s.

Tophel (Pastor G.)—THE WORK OF THE HOLY SPIRIT. Cr. 8vo, 2s. 6d.

Toy (Prof. C. H., D.D.)—PROVERBS. (*International Critical Commentary.*) Post 8vo, 12s.

Troup (Rev. G. Elmslie, M.A.)—WORDS TO YOUNG CHRISTIANS: Being Addresses to Young Communicants. On antique laid paper, chaste binding, fcap. 8vo, 4s. 6d.

Uhlhorn (G.)—CHRISTIAN CHARITY IN THE ANCIENT CHURCH. Cr. 8vo, 6s.

Ullmann (Dr. Carl)—THE SINLESSNESS OF JESUS. Crown 8vo, 5s.

Urwick (W., M.A.)—THE SERVANT OF JEHOVAH: A Commentary upon Isaiah lii. 13-liii. 12; with Dissertations upon Isaiah xl.-lxvi. 8vo, 3s.

Vinet (Life and Writings of). By L. M. LANE. Crown 8vo, 7s. 6d.

Vincent (Prof. M. R., D.D.)—THE AGE OF HILDEBRAND. (*Eras of Church History.*) 6s.

—————— PHILIPPIANS AND PHILEMON. (*International Critical Commentary.*) Second Edition, post 8vo, 8s. 6d.

Walker (James, of Carnwath)—ESSAYS, PAPERS, AND SERMONS. Post 8vo, 6s.

Walker (J., D.D.)—THEOLOGY AND THEOLOGIANS OF SCOTLAND. New Edition, crown 8vo, 3s. 6d.

Walker (Prof. W., D.D.)—THE PROTESTANT REFORMATION. (*Eras of Church History.*) 6s.

Walker (Rev. W. L.)—THE SPIRIT AND THE INCARNATION. 2nd Ed., 8vo, 9s.

—————— THE CROSS AND THE KINGDOM. 8vo, 9s.

Warfield (B. B., D.D.)—THE RIGHT OF SYSTEMATIC THEOLOGY. Crown 8vo, 2s.

Waterman (L., D.D.)—THE POST-APOSTOLIC AGE. (*Eras of Church History.*) 6s.

Watt (W. A., M.A., D.Ph.)—THE THEORY OF CONTRACT IN ITS SOCIAL LIGHT. 8vo, 3s.

—————— A STUDY OF SOCIAL MORALITY. Post 8vo, 6s.

Watts (Professor)—THE NEWER CRITICISM AND THE ANALOGY OF THE FAITH. Third Edition, crown 8vo, 5s.

—————— THE REIGN OF CAUSALITY: A Vindication of the Scientific Principle of Telic Causal Efficiency. Crown 8vo, 6s.

—————— THE NEW APOLOGETIC. Crown 8vo, 6s.

Weir (J. F., M.A.)—THE WAY: THE NATURE AND MEANS OF REVELATION. Ex. crown 8vo, 6s. 6d.

Weiss (Prof.)—BIBLICAL THEOLOGY OF NEW TESTAMENT. 2 vols., 12s. net.

—————— LIFE OF CHRIST. Three vols. 8vo, 18s. net.

Welch (Rev. A. C., B.D.)—ANSELM AND HIS WORK. 3s.

Wells (Prof. C. L.)—THE AGE OF CHARLEMAGNE. (*Eras of the Christian Church.*) 6s.

Wendt (H. H., D.D.)—THE TEACHING OF JESUS. Two vols. 8vo, 21s.

—————— THE GOSPEL ACCORDING TO ST. JOHN. 8vo, 7s. 6d.

Wenley (R. M.)—CONTEMPORARY THEOLOGY AND THEISM. Cr. 8vo, 4s. 6d.

White (Rev. M.)—SYMBOLICAL NUMBERS OF SCRIPTURE. Cr. 8vo, 4s.

Williams (E. F., D.D.)—CHRISTIAN LIFE IN GERMANY. Crown 8vo, 5s.

Winer (Dr. G. B.)—A TREATISE ON THE GRAMMAR OF NEW TESTAMENT GREEK, regarded as the Basis of New Testament Exegesis. Third Edition, edited by W. F. MOULTON, D.D. Ninth English Edition, 8vo, 15s.

Witherow (Prof. T., D.D.)—THE FORM OF THE CHRISTIAN TEMPLE. 8vo, 10/6.

Woods (F. H., B.D.)—THE HOPE OF ISRAEL. Crown 8vo, 3s. 6d.

Workman (Prof. G. C.)—THE TEXT OF JEREMIAH; or, A Critical Investigation of the Greek and Hebrew, etc. Post 8vo, 9s.

Wright (C. H., D.D.)—BIBLICAL ESSAYS. Crown 8vo, 5s.

Zahn (Prof. Theodor)—BREAD AND SALT FROM THE WORD OF GOD. Sermons. Post 8vo, 4s. 6d. net.

THE INTERNATIONAL THEOLOGICAL LIBRARY.

This Library is designed to cover the whole field of Christian Theology. Each volume is to be complete in itself, while, at the same time, it will form part of a carefully planned whole. It is intended to form a Series of Text-Books for Students of Theology. The Authors will be scholars of recognised reputation in the several branches of study assigned to them. They will be associated with each other and with the Editors in the effort to provide a series of volumes which may adequately represent the present condition of investigation.

TWELVE VOLUMES OF THE SERIES ARE NOW READY, VIZ. :—

An Introduction to the Literature of the Old Testament. S. R. DRIVER, D.D., D.Litt., Regius Professor of Hebrew, and Canon of Christ Church, Oxford. [*Seventh Edition.* 12s.

Christian Ethics. NEWMAN SMYTH, D.D., Pastor of the First Congregational Church, New Haven, Conn. [*Third Edition.* 10s. 6d.

Apologetics. The late A. B. BRUCE, D.D., Professor of New Testament Exegesis, Free Church College, Glasgow. [*Third Edition.* 10s. 6d.

History of Christian Doctrine. G. P. FISHER, D.D., LL.D., Professor of Ecclesiastical History, Yale University. *Second Edition.* [12s.

A History of Christianity in the Apostolic Age. ARTHUR CUSHMAN McGIFFERT, Ph.D., D.D., Professor of Church History, Union Theological Seminary, New York. [12s.

Christian Institutions. A. V. G. ALLEN, D.D., Professor of Ecclesiastical History, Episcopal Theological School, Cambridge, Mass. [12s.

The Christian Pastor. WASHINGTON GLADDEN, D.D., LL.D., Pastor of Congregational Church, Columbus, Ohio. [10s. 6d.

The Theology of the New Testament. GEORGE B. STEVENS, D.D., LL.D., Professor of Systematic Theology in Yale University, U.S.A. [12s.

The Ancient Catholic Church. ROBERT RAINY, D.D., Principal of the New College, Edinburgh. [12s.

Old Testament History. H. P. SMITH, D.D., Professor of Biblical History, Amherst College, U.S.A. [12s.

The Theology of the Old Testament. The late A. B. DAVIDSON, D.D., LL.D. Edited by the late Principal SALMOND, D.D. [12s.

Doctrine of Salvation. GEORGE B. STEVENS, D.D., LL.D., Professor of Systematic Theology, Yale University. [12s.

VOLUMES IN PREPARATION :—

The Reformation. T. M. LINDSAY, D.D., Principal of the United Free College, Glasgow.

The Literature of the New Testament. JAMES MOFFATT, D.D., United Free Church, Dundonald, Scotland.

Contemporary History of the Old Testament. FRANCIS BROWN, D.D., D.Lit., Professor of Hebrew, Union Theological Seminary, New York.

The Early Latin Church. CHARLES BIGG, D.D., Regius Professor of Church History, and Canon of Christ Church, Oxford.

Canon and Text of the New Testament. CASPAR RENÉ GREGORY, D.D., LL.D., Professor in the University of Leipzig.

Contemporary History of the New Testament. FRANK C. PORTER, Ph.D., Yale University, New Haven, Conn.

Philosophy of Religion. ROBERT FLINT, D.D., LL.D., Emeritus Professor of Divinity, University of Edinburgh.

Later Latin Church. E. W. WATSON, M.A., Professor of Church History, King's College, London.

The Christian Preacher. W. T. DAVISON, D.D., Professor of Systematic Theology, Richmond, Surrey.

The Greek and Oriental Churches. W. F. ADENEY, D.D., Principal of Lancashire College, Manchester.

Biblical Archæology. G. BUCHANAN GRAY, D.D., Professor of Hebrew, Mansfield College, Oxford.

The History of Religions. GEORGE F. MOORE, D.D., LL.D., Professor in Harvard University.

Doctrine of God. WILLIAM N. CLARKE, D.D., Professor of Systematic Theology, Hamilton Theological Seminary, N.Y.

Doctrine of Christ. H. R. MACKINTOSH, D.Phil., Professor of Systematic Theology, The New College, Edinburgh.

Doctrine of Man. WILLIAM P. PATERSON, D.D., Professor of Divinity, University of Edinburgh.

Canon and Text of the Old Testament. F. C. BURKITT, M.A., University Lecturer on Palæography, Trinity College, Cambridge.

The Life of Christ. WILLIAM SANDAY, D.D., LL.D., Lady Margaret Professor of Divinity, and Canon of Christ Church, Oxford.

Christian Symbolics. C. A. BRIGGS, D.D., D.Lit., Professor of Theological Encyclopædia, Union Seminary, New York.

Rabbinical Literature. S. SCHECHTER, M.A., President of the Jewish Theological Seminary, N.Y.

THE INTERNATIONAL CRITICAL COMMENTARY.

TWELVE VOLUMES NOW READY, viz. :—

Numbers (Dr. Gray), **Deuteronomy** (Dr. Driver), **Judges** (Dr. Moore), **I. and II. Samuel** (Dr. H. P. Smith), **Proverbs** (Dr. Toy), **Amos and Hosea** (Dr. Harper), **S. Mark** (Dr. Gould), **S. Luke** (Dr. Plummer), **Romans** (Dr. Sanday), **Ephesians and Colossians** (Dr. Abbott), **Philippians and Philemon** (Dr. Vincent), **S. Peter and S. Jude** (Dr. Bigg).

The following other Volumes are in course of preparation :—

THE OLD TESTAMENT.

Genesis. JOHN SKINNER, D.D., Professor of Hebrew and Old Testament Exegesis, Westminster College, Cambridge.

Exodus. A. R. S. KENNEDY, D.D., Professor of Hebrew, University of Edinburgh.

Leviticus. J. F. STENNING, M.A., Fellow of Wadham College, Oxford ; and the late H. A. White, M.A., Fellow of New College, Oxford.

Joshua. GEORGE ADAM SMITH, D.D., LL.D., Professor of Hebrew, United Free Church College, Glasgow.

Ruth. C. P. FAGNANI, D.D., Associate Professor of Hebrew, Union Theological Seminary, New York.

Kings. FRANCIS BROWN, D.D., Litt.D., LL.D., Professor of Hebrew and Cognate Languages, Union Theological Seminary, New York.

Chronicles. EDWARD L. CURTIS, D.D., Professor of Hebrew, Yale University, New Haven, Conn.

Ezra and Nehemiah. L. W. BATTEN, D.D., late Professor of Hebrew, P. E. Divinity School, Philadelphia.

Esther. L. B. PATON, Ph.D., Professor of Hebrew, Hartford Theological Seminary.

Psalms. CHARLES A. BRIGGS, D.D., Professor of Theological Encylopædics and Symbolics, Union Theological Seminary, New York.

Ecclesiastes. G. A. BARTON, Ph.D., Professor of Biblical Literature, Bryn Mauer College, Pa., U.S.A.

Song of Songs and Lamentations. C. A. BRIGGS, D.D., Union Theological Seminary, New York.

Isaiah. S. R. DRIVER, D.D., and G. BUCHANAN GRAY, D.D., Oxford.

Jeremiah. A. F. KIRKPATRICK, D.D., Lady Margaret Professor of Divinity, and Master of Selwyn College, Cambridge.

Ezekiel. G. A. COOKE, M.A., Fellow of Magdalen College, and C. F. BURNEY, Litt.D., Fellow and Lecturer in Hebrew, St. John's College, Oxford.

Daniel. JOHN P. PETERS, D.D., late Professor of Hebrew, P. E. Divinity School, Philadelphia, now Rector of St. Michael's Church, New York.

Minor Prophets. W. R. HARPER, LL.D., President of the University of Chicago.

[Amos and Hosea ready, 12s.

THE NEW TESTAMENT.

Synopsis of the Four Gospels. W. SANDAY, D.D., LL.D., Lady Margaret Professor of Divinity, and Canon of Christ Church, Oxford ; and W. C. ALLEN, M.A., Exeter College, Oxford.

Matthew. WILLOUGHBY C. ALLEN, M.A., Chaplain, Fellow, and Lecturer in Theology and Hebrew, Exeter College, Oxford.

Luke. ALFRED PLUMMER, D.D., late Master of University College, Durham.

[Ready, 12s.

Acts. C. H. TURNER, M.A., Fellow of Magdalen College, Oxford ; and H. N. BATE, M.A., late Fellow and Dean of Divinity in Magdalen College, Oxford, now Vicar of St. Stephen's, Hampstead, and Examining Chaplain to the Bishop of London.

Corinthians. The Right Rev. ARCH. ROBERTSON, D.D., Lord Bishop of Exeter ; and R. J. KNOWLING, D.D., Professor of Theology, Durham.

Galatians. ERNEST D. BURTON, A.B., Professor of New Testament Literature, University of Chicago.

Thessalonians. JAMES E. FRAME, M.A., Professor of Biblical Theology Union, Theological Seminary, New York.

The Pastoral Epistles. WALTER LOCK, D.D., Dean Ireland's Professor of Exegesis, Oxford.

Hebrews. A. NAIRNE, M.A., Professor of Hebrew, King's College, London.

James. JAMES H. ROPES, D.D., Bussey Professor of New Testament Criticism in Harvard University.

The Johannine Epistles. A. E. BROOKE, Fellow of, and Divinity Lecturer in King's College, Cambridge.

Revelation. ROBERT H. CHARLES, D.D., Professor of Biblical Greek in the University of Dublin.

Other engagements will be announced shortly.

The World's Epoch-Makers.

EDITED BY OLIPHANT SMEATON, M.A.

NEW SERIES. IN NEAT CROWN 8vo VOLUMES. PRICE 3s. EACH.

'An excellent series of biographical studies.'—*Athenæum.*

'We advise our readers to keep a watch on this most able series. It promises to be a distinct success. The volumes before us are the most satisfactory books of the sort we have ever read.'—*Methodist Times.*

The following Volumes have now been issued:—

Buddha and Buddhism. By ARTHUR LILLIE.

Luther and the German Reformation. By Principal T. M. LINDSAY, D.D.

Wesley and Methodism. By F. J. SNELL, M.A.

Cranmer and the English Reformation. By A. D. INNES, M.A.

William Herschel and his Work. By JAMES SIME, M.A.

Francis and Dominic. By Professor J. HERKLESS, D.D.

Savonarola. By G. M'HARDY, D.D.

Anselm and his Work. By Rev. A. C. WELCH, B.D.

Origen and Greek Patristic Theology. By Rev. W. FAIRWEATHER, M.A.

Muhammad and his Power. By P. DE LACY JOHNSTONE, M.A. (Oxon.).

The Medici and the Italian Renaissance. By OLIPHANT SMEATON, M.A., Edinburgh.

Plato. By Professor D. G. RITCHIE, M.A., LL.D., University of St. Andrews.

Pascal and the Port Royalists. By Professor W. CLARK, LL.D., D.C.L., Trinity College, Toronto.

Euclid. By Emeritus Professor THOMAS SMITH, D.D., LL.D.

Hegel and Hegelianism. By Professor R. MACKINTOSH, D.D., Lancashire Independent College, Manchester.

Hume and his Influence on Philosophy and Theology. By Professor J. ORR, D.D., Glasgow.

Rousseau and Naturalism in Life and Thought. By Professor W. H. HUDSON, M.A.

Descartes, Spinoza, and the New Philosophy. By Principal J. IVERACH, D.D., Aberdeen.

Socrates. By Rev. J. T. FORBES, M.A., Glasgow.

The following have also been arranged for:—

Marcus Aurelius and the Later Stoics. By F. W. BUSSELL, D.D., Vice-Principal of Brasenose College, Oxford. [*In the Press.*

Augustine and Latin Patristic Theology. By Professor B. B. WARFIELD, D.D., Princeton.

Scotus Erigena and his Epoch. By Professor R. LATTA, Ph.D., D.Sc., University of Aberdeen.

Wyclif and the Lollards. By Rev. J. C. CARRICK, B.D.

The Two Bacons and Experimental Science. By Rev. W. J. COUPER, M.A.

Lessing and the New Humanism. By Rev. A. P. DAVIDSON, M.A.

Kant and his Philosophical Revolution. By Professor R. M. WENLEY, D.Sc., Ph.D., University of Michigan.

Schleiermacher and the Rejuvenescence of Theology. By Professor A. MARTIN, D.D., New College, Edinburgh.

Newman and his Influence. By C. SAROLEA, Ph.D., Litt. Doc., University of Edinburgh.